SINGLE-CASE
INTERVENTION
RESEARCH

School Psychology Book Series

SINGLE-CASE INTERVENTION RESEARCH

Methodological and Statistical Advances

Edited by **Thomas R. Kratochwill** and **Joel R. Levin**

American Psychological Association • Washington, DC

Published by
American Psychological Association
750 First Street, NE
Washington, DC 20002
www.apa.org

To order
APA Order Department
P.O. Box 92984
Washington, DC 20090-2984
Tel: (800) 374-2721; Direct: (202) 336-5510
Fax: (202) 336-5502; TDD/TTY: (202) 336-6123
Online: www.apa.org/pubs/books
E-mail: order@apa.org

In the U.K., Europe, Africa, and the Middle East, copies may be ordered from
American Psychological Association
3 Henrietta Street
Covent Garden, London
WC2E 8LU England

Typeset in New Century Schoolbook by Circle Graphics, Inc., Columbia, MD

Printer: United Book Press, Baltimore, MD
Cover Designer: Mercury Publishing Service, Inc., Rockville, MD

The opinions and statements published are the responsibility of the authors, and such opinions and statements do not necessarily represent the policies of the American Psychological Association.

Library of Congress Cataloging-in-Publication Data
Single-case intervention research : methodological and statistical advances / edited by Thomas R. Kratochwill and Joel R. Levin.
    p. cm.
  Includes bibliographical references and index.
  ISBN-13: 978-1-4338-1751-9 (alk. paper)
  ISBN-10: 1-4338-1751-9 (alk. paper)
  1. Single subject research. I. Kratochwill, Thomas R. II. Levin, Joel R.
  BF76.6.S56S555 2014
  150.72'3—dc23

                                                                          2013047658

British Library Cataloguing-in-Publication Data
A CIP record is available from the British Library.

Printed in the United States of America
First Edition

http://dx.doi.org/10.1037/14376-000

Dedicated to the loving memory of our fathers, Rudy and Norman

Contents

Contributors

Jonathan G. Boyajian, BA, Department of Psychological Sciences, University of California at Merced

Jacquelyn A. Buckley, PhD, Institute of Education Sciences, National Center for Special Education Research, Washington, DC

Matthew K. Burns, PhD, Department of Educational Psychology, University of Minnesota, Minneapolis

John L. Davis, MA, Department of Educational Psychology, Texas A&M University, College Station

Anya S. Evmenova, PhD, College of Education and Human Development, George Mason University, Fairfax, VA

John M. Ferron, PhD, Department of Educational Measurement and Research, University of South Florida, Tampa

Randy G. Floyd, PhD, Department of Psychology, The University of Memphis, Memphis, TN

Boris S. Gafurov, PhD, Division of Special Education and Disability Research, George Mason University, Fairfax, VA

Larry V. Hedges, PhD, Department of Statistics, Northwestern University, Evanston, IL

Robert H. Horner, PhD, Department of Special Education and Clinical Sciences, University of Oregon, Eugene

Ann P. Kaiser, PhD, Department of Special Education, Peabody College of Vanderbilt University, Nashville, TN

Randy W. Kamphaus, PhD, College of Education, Georgia State University, Atlanta

Thomas R. Kratochwill, PhD, School Psychology Program, University of Wisconsin–Madison

Joel R. Levin, PhD, College of Education, University of Arizona, Tucson

Joan E. McLaughlin, PhD, Institute of Education Sciences, National Center for Special Education Research, Washington, DC

Samuel L. Odom, PhD, Frank Porter Graham Child Development Institute, University of North Carolina at Chapel Hill

Richard I. Parker, PhD, Department of Educational Psychology, Texas A&M University, College Station

James E. Pustejovsky, PhD, Department of Educational Psychology, The University of Texas at Austin

David M. Rindskopf, PhD, Department of Educational Psychology, The Graduate Center, City University of New York, New York

William R. Shadish, PhD, Department of Psychological Sciences, University of California at Merced

Susan M. Sheridan, PhD, Nebraska Center for Research on Children, Youth, Families, and Schools, University of Nebraska–Lincoln

Deborah L. Speece, PhD, School of Education, Virginia Commonwealth University, Richmond

Kristynn J. Sullivan, BS, Department of Psychological Sciences, University of California at Merced

Christopher M. Swoboda, PhD, Department of Educational Studies, University of Cincinnati, Cincinnati, OH

Kimberly J. Vannest, PhD, Department of Educational Psychology, Texas A&M University, College Station

Series Foreword

Outside of their homes, children spend more time in schools than in any other settings. From tragedies such as Sandy Hook and Columbine to more hopeful developments such as the movement toward improved mental health, physical health, and academic achievement, there is an ongoing need for high-quality writing that explains how children, families, and communities associated with schools worldwide can be supported through the application of sound psychological research, theory, and practice.

Thus, for the past several years the American Psychological Association (APA) Books Program and APA Division 16 (School Psychology) have partnered to produce the School Psychology Book Series. The mission of this series is to increase the visibility of psychological science, practice, and policy for those who work with children and adolescents in schools and communities. The result has been a strong collection of scholarly work that appeals not only to psychologists but also to individuals from all fields who have reason to seek and use what psychology has to offer in schools.

Many individuals have made significant contributions to the School Psychology Book Series. First, we would like to acknowledge the dedication of past series editors: Sandra L. Christensen, Jan Hughes, R. Steve McCallum, David McIntosh, LeAdelle Phelps, Susan Sheridan, and Christopher H. Skinner. Second, we would like to acknowledge the outstanding editorial vision of the scholars who have edited or authored books for the series. The work of these scholars has significantly advanced psychological science and practice for children and adolescents worldwide.

We welcome your comments about this volume and other topics you would like to see explored in this series. To share your thoughts, please visit the Division 16 website at www.apadivisions.org/division-16.

Linda A. Reddy, PhD
Series Editor

Acknowledgments

We appreciate and admire the contributing authors' commitment of time and work to this volume and to the single-case design literature. We also thank our support staff, Karen O'Connell and Dolores Fries, for their assistance on various aspects of this project. Finally, we are grateful to Dr. Linda Reddy for her support of our book within the American Psychological Association book series.

SINGLE-CASE INTERVENTION RESEARCH

Introduction: An Overview of Single-Case Intervention Research

Thomas R. Kratochwill and Joel R. Levin

Single-case intervention research has a rich tradition of providing evidence about the efficacy of interventions applied both to solving a diverse range of human problems and to enriching the knowledge base established in many fields of science (Kratochwill, 1978; Kratochwill & Levin, 1992, 2010). In the social sciences the randomized controlled trial (RCT) experiment has, in recent years, dominated to the point that it has been acknowledged as the "gold standard" for the evidence-based practice movement (Shavelson & Towne, 2002). Single-case intervention designs have also been featured as an important methodology in this movement in that major task forces of the American Psychological Association (APA) recommend single-case designs alongside RCTs in their evidence standards. For example, the APA Divisions 12/53 (Clinical and Clinical Child, respectively) Task Force on Evidence-Based Interventions (Weisz & Hawley, 2000) and the APA Division 16 (School Psychology) Task Force on Evidence-Based Interventions (Kratochwill & Stoiber, 2002) developed research-coding criteria for reviewing single-case intervention research. In education, the National Reading Panel (2000) included single-case designs in their review of reading interventions; and more recently the Institute of Education Sciences (IES) developed standards for review of single-case intervention designs to be incorporated by the What Works Clearinghouse (WWC)—see Kratochwill et al. (2010, 2013). Other professional groups and scholars have also featured appraisal criteria for review of single-case design research (J. D. Smith, 2012; Wendt & Miller, 2012). In short, single-case intervention designs are currently playing a major role in developing the research knowledge base in diverse scientific fields. The present volume endeavors to elaborate on and expand this role.

Over the past decade advances in single-case intervention research, which have included exciting new developments in research design, visual and statistical analysis, and methods for summarizing single-case intervention research in literature reviews, have been remarkable. Readers of this volume will learn that in comparison with a generation ago (Kratochwill & Levin, 1992), single-

http://dx.doi.org/10.1037/14376-001
Single-Case Intervention Research: Methodological and Statistical Advances, by T. R. Kratochwill and J. R. Levin

case design methodology and data-analysis strategies have grown in sophistication and will continue to play an even more central role in applied and clinical research in psychology, education, and related fields than in past decades. It is our hope that this volume will provide a compendium of information and tools for researchers adopting single-case design in their investigations, as well as for those individuals involved in the review of intervention research to advance evidence-based practices.

Development of the current volume represents several passages in our own professional career history. We were exposed to single-case design in the early 1970s where we gained a deep appreciation of the contributions of this methodology to science and to what is now called the evidence-based practice movement. Concern over the application of traditional parametric statistics to single-case data initially prompted us to publish a commentary (Kratochwill et al., 1974). Our enduring interest in single-case research design and analysis was crystallized in an edited volume by the first author (Kratochwill, 1978) and a contributed chapter on randomization tests by the second author (Levin, Marascuilo, & Hubert, 1978), in which a variety of optional design and data-analysis strategies were presented. Many of these developments—and in particular, the statistical analysis of single-case data—were highly controversial at the time in that various statistical critiques and recommendations ran counter to researchers' philosophical allegiances within the experimental and applied behavior analysis fields. (As an aside, many such allegiances remain steadfast to this day.) Nevertheless, these developments were extended further in our collaborative work and resulted in editing an updated volume devoted to single-case design and analysis (Kratochwill & Levin, 1992). In that book we introduced readers to a variety of emerging single-case quantitative data-analytic strategies and effect-size measures for single-case research investigations.

Following the 1992 edited volume, we continued our quest to improve the state of single-case design and data analysis. To further extend that work we received an IES statistics and methodology grant that focused on innovations in single-case research methodology and data analysis (Kratochwill & Levin, R324U0600001; 2006–2010). One of the outcomes of that project was a conference held at the University of Wisconsin–Madison in the fall of 2010, in which most of the distinguished contributors to the present book were in attendance. At the conference participants were asked to provide their perspectives on the most recent advances in the topical areas that are represented in the current volume. The current volume blends a long line of work that has featured single-case design methodology and data analysis in psychology, education, and related applied and clinical fields.

Single-case research design had its origins within quasi-experimental investigations in the tradition of Campbell and Stanley (1963) and in the experimental and applied behavior analysis fields (Sidman, 1960). The major developments in single-case design occurred in the field of applied behavior analysis primarily because this methodology was generally the only method used by investigators to advance theory and practice (Kennedy, 2005). Nevertheless, the applications of single-case methodology have continued with contributions across a variety of professional fields, moving beyond their quasi-experimental and behavior analysis origins (see Chapter 3, this volume for more detailed information on the history of single-case design). Of special note is the diversity of disciplines in which single-case designs are being implemented including, for example, applied behavior analysis (e.g., Bailey, 1977; Johnson & Pennypacker, 1980, 2009), clinical psychology (e.g., Barlow & Hersen, 1985; Barlow, Nock, & Hersen, 2009; Kazdin, 2011), social work (e.g., DiNoia & Tripodi, 2008; Fischer, 1978), education and special education (e.g., Gast, 2010; Kennedy, 2005; Tawney & Gast, 1984), communicative disorders (e.g., McReynolds & Kearns, 1983), sport and exercise psychology (Barker, McCarthy, Jones, & Moran, 2011), and medicine and the health sciences (e.g., Janosky, 2009; Morgan & Morgan, 2008; Ottenbacher, 1986). We anticipate that in the future many of these authors will revise their texts to represent the most recent developments in single-case design and data analysis.

Developments in Single-Case Methodology

In 1992, the influence of single-case methodology as a major source of scientific information in various fields was increasing. As researchers in these areas adopted single-case designs, some developed a number of methodological and statistical applications that have been refined over the past few decades. These areas include advances in case-study methodology, research design components, and appraisal standards used to summarize single-case research investigations. Below we highlight and summarize some of these advances.

"Case-study" research has been associated with a variety of methodological approaches, and that terminology has been confused (or used interchangeably) with "single-case" research. Traditional case-study methodology has been relegated to a rather low level of scientific knowledge, which most single-case intervention researchers would regard as appropriately so because (a) case studies typically involve solely a narrative description of the research process with (b) no experimental manipulation of the independent variable and no replication components. Absent the latter and other methodological features (including the adoption of some form of randomization), findings and conclusions based on case-study research cannot be regarded as "scientifically credible" (Levin, 1994). That is, most case studies represent, at most, "demonstrations" that do not allow an investigator to rule out critical threats to internal validity and, therefore, such studies do not qualify as "true experiments" or even "quasi-experiments" that are capable of documenting the influence of an intervention on desired outcomes (Levin & Kratochwill, 2013; Shadish, Cook, & Campbell, 2002).

Nevertheless, not all case studies share the same limitations and when certain elements of single-case design and corresponding internal validity considerations are added to this methodology, one can improve the inferences that can be drawn from the data. Several authors have discussed methodological additions that allow one to draw improved inferences from these types of studies (e.g., Kazdin, 1981, 1982, 2011; Kazdin, Kratochwill, & VandenBos, 1986; Kratochwill, 1985). Although we will not repeat the specifics of methods to improve (and elevate) case-study investigation here, Figure 1 provides a list of dimensions that can be considered to improve case-study investigations by

Characteristics	Low Inference	High Inference
Type of data	Subjective data	Objective data
Assessment occasions	Single point or pretest posttest measurement	Repeated measurement across all phases
Planned vs. ex post facto	Ex post facto treatment	Planned treatment
Projections of performance	Acute problem	Chronic problem
Effect size	Small	Large
Effect impact	Delayed	Immediate
Number of participants	$N = 1$	$N > 1$
Heterogeneity of participants	Homogeneous	Heterogeneous
Treatment operationally specified/standardized	Non-standardized treatment	Standardized treatment
Integrity of treatment	No monitoring	Repeated monitoring
Impact of treatment	Impact on single measure	Impact on multiple measures
Generalization and follow-up assessment	No formal assessment	Formal assessment

Figure 1.   Dimensions of case study investigations. From *Research Methods in Clinical Psychology* (p. 62), by A. S. Bellack and M. Hersen (Eds.), 1984, New York, NY: Pergamon. Copyright 1984 by Pergamon. Adapted with permission.

adopting elements of single-case design and considering various dimensions of causal inference.

Case-study investigations may also play an important role in the advancement of evidence-based practices in research, especially with respect to adopting and implementing interventions in practice settings. As part of the first author's work with the APA Task Force on Evidence-Based Practice for Children and Adolescents (2008), recommendations were made for enhancing an "ecological" approach to the adoption and implementation of evidence-based practices through a *practice-based research* framework (Kratochwill et al., 2012). Practice-based evidence research "involves practitioners contributing to the knowledge base by collaborating with researchers and sharing information with the research community during the course of providing academic and mental health interventions in typical practice settings" (Kratochwill et al., 2012, p. 220). We proposed five criteria to improve the obtainment of acceptable evidence, including (a) conducting systematic reviews of the research literature to identify evidence-based prevention and interventions in practice, (b) adhering to intervention integrity during implementation, (c) adopting standards for assistance in drawing valid inferences from interventions, (d) using credible assessments to measure intervention outcomes, and (e) using formal data-analysis procedures to evaluate intervention outcomes. In this framework, case-study investigations (with various methodological upgrades) can assist researchers in understanding how interventions are delivered and how they are successful or unsuccessful in typical practice, thereby contributing to understanding the current gap in the evidence-based practice movement. Whether this framework and the proposed role that case-study research might take in the movement are viable remains to be observed in the scientific literature. We now turn to elements of methodology and data analysis that strengthen a single-case research approach in scientific pursuits.

Replication, Randomization, and Data Analysis

Advances have occurred for both the methodology and data analyses (both visual and statistical) associated with single-case intervention studies. Historically, traditional single-case research designs have relied on *replication* opportunities for the intervention to demonstrate an effect (not to be confused with replication of the study's operations with new participants and settings) to establish the credibility of the intervention (Barlow et al., 2009; Kazdin, 2011). Accordingly, the three major design types, including ABAB, multiple-baseline, and alternating treatments designs, all incorporate a within-study replication component (see Chapter 1, this volume; Horner et al., 2005)—and for ABAB and alternating treatments designs, more than one replication component when two or more cases are included in the study. Replication in the experiment can allow the researcher to eliminate many threats to internal validity and a replication feature has been adopted in the WWC pilot single-case design standards (see Kratochwill et al., 2010, 2013).

To increase the credibility of single-case intervention research a researcher also has the option to incorporate some type of randomization into the study's design. The randomization component can be added to replication for improving the experiment and further reducing threats to internal validity (Kratochwill & Levin, 2010). In our 2010 *Psychological Methods* article we described how the three major design types can be structured to include randomization; and in the present chapters by Kratochwill and Levin (Chapter 2), Ferron and Levin (Chapter 5), and Levin, Evmenova, and Gafurov (Chapter 6), applications of randomization in the three classes of single-case designs are extended. Our hope is that researchers will increasingly adopt randomization in their use of single-case research designs to improve their studies' scientific credibility.

One important value-added feature of adopting randomization in the design of a single-case experiment is that the researcher opens the door to a variety of data-analysis strategies that extend beyond the tradition of graphical–visual analysis (see Chapters 3 and 4 for a discussion of visual-analysis techniques that are currently available). Statistical options for randomized designs involve permutation and randomization tests, and these tests can complement the more traditional visual-analysis methods to increase a single-case experiment's statistical conclusion validity. The reader is referred to Chapter 5 for an overview of the types of randomization and associated statistical tests that can be incorporated into single-case designs.

Methods for Synthesizing the Single-Case Intervention Research Literature

As single-case investigators have conducted research in various applied and clinical areas, there has been great interest in synthesizing the body of work to create evidence-based interventions and practices (Horner & Kratochwill, 2012). With the increasing emphasis on meta-analysis for research synthesis (e.g., Ahn, Ames, & Myers, 2012), it has been quite predictable that researchers would try to find ways to develop single-case design effect-size measures to quantify bodies of information. In fact, increasing use of previously conducted research syntheses within a focused content domain has stimulated the development of new guidelines for these activities (Cooper & Koenka, 2012), and because of such efforts single-case researchers now have a number of conceptual and methodological standards to guide their synthesis work. These standards, alternatively referred to as *guidelines*, have been developed by a number of professional organizations and authors interested primarily in providing guidance to individuals reviewing the literature in a particular content domain (J. D. Smith, 2012; Wendt & Miller, 2012). The development of these standards has also provided researchers who are designing their own intervention studies with a protocol that is capable of meeting or exceeding the proposed standards.

Wendt and Miller (2012) identified seven "quality appraisal tools" and compared these standards with the single-case research criteria advanced by Horner et al. (2005). Wendt and Miller's (2012) analysis included the Evaluative Method (Reichow, Volkmar, & Cicchetti, 2008) and the V. Smith, Jelen, and Patterson (2010) scales that were created to review research on autism spectrum disorders; the Certainty Framework (Simeonsson & Bailey, 1991); Evidence in Augmentative and Alternative Communication (EVIDAAC), a tool that includes the Single-Subject Scale (Schlosser, 2011) and the Comparative Single-Subject Experimental Design Rating Scale (CSSEDARS; Schlosser, Sigafoos, & Belfiore, 2009);[1] the Logan Scale (Logan, Hickman, Harris, & Heriza, 2008); the Single-Case Experimental Design Scale (Tate et al., 2008); and the WWC Single-Case Design Pilot Standards (Kratochwill et al., 2010, 2013).

Table 1 presents the Wendt and Miller (2012) appraisal tools for evaluating a number of comparison dimensions. The authors concluded that the Evaluation Method, the Certainly Framework, the WWC Single-Case Design Pilot Standards, and the EVIDAAC scales were most appropriate for critical appraisal of single-case designs. They also cautioned users of the various tools to consider

---

[1]The Certainty Framework and the EVIDAAC were created for augmentative and alternative communication disorder research.

the purpose and context of the review being conducted when an appraisal tool is selected.

J. D. Smith (2012) reviewed research design and various methodological characteristics of single-case designs in peer-reviewed journals, primarily from the psychological literature (over the years 2000–2010). On the basis of his review, six standards for appraisal of the literature (some of which overlap with the Wendt and Miller, 2012, review) were presented, including (a) the WWC Single-Case Design Pilot Standards (Kratochwill et al., 2010, 2013); (b) the APA Division 12 Task Force on Psychological Interventions, with contributions from the Division 12 Task Force on Promotion and Dissemination of Psychological Procedures, and the APA (Division 12) Task Force for Psychological Intervention Guidelines (reported by Chambless & Hollon, 1998; Chambless & Ollendick, 2001); (c) the APA Division 16 Task Force on Evidence-Based Interventions in School Psychology (Kratochwill et al., 2003; Kratochwill & Stoiber, 2002); (d) the National Reading Panel (NRP; National Institute of Child Health and Human Development, 2000); (e) the Single-Case Experimental Design Scale (Tate et al., 2008); and (f) the reporting guidelines for Ecological Momentary Assessment presented by Stone and Shiffman (2002).

Table 2 from J. D. Smith (2012) presents the single-case research design standards and guidelines, Table 3 presents the single-case measurement and assessment standards and guidelines, and Table 4 presents the single-case data-analysis standards and guidelines used by the respective professional groups or authors. J. D. Smith reported that of 409 single-case design studies, the majority was in accordance with the various standards presented in the tables. Visual analysis was the most common data-analysis method, but various statistical tests appeared to be on the increase over the assessment period.

Both J. D. Smith (2012) and Wendt and Miller (2012) featured the WWC Single-Case Design Pilot Standards in their review of single-case design appraisal tools. Because several of the present volume's authors were involved in the development of these appraisal guidelines, we focus on them in various chapters here (in particular, in Chapters 1, 2, and 3). The WWC Single-Case Design Pilot Standards can be viewed and downloaded from the IES website (http://ies.ed.gov/ncee/wwc/documentsum.aspx?sid=229).

Overview of the Chapters

Following the current introductory chapter, Chapter 1, by Robert H. Horner and Samuel L. Odom, provides an overview of the basic rationale and components of single-case design. The authors present the importance of developing a "logic model" in conceptualizing, conducting, and analyzing single-case design experiments. In so doing, they present the case for beginning the research process with selection of dependent variable(s) for the investigation. Readers will find an overview of the three major classes of single-case design, namely ABAB, alternating treatment, and multiple-baseline designs. The authors then consider each of these design classes, along with examples of their application, in relation to satisfying the WWC pilot standards and the important role played by replication.

Table 1. Current Quality Appraisal Tools for Single-Subject Experimental Designs (SSEDs)

Characteristics / Properties	Tool (maximum quality score)						
	Certainty Framework (no max. score)	Evaluation Method (max. = 12)	EVIDAAC Scales (max. = 10 or 19)	Logan et al. Scale (max. = 14)	SCED Scale (max. = 10)	V. Smith et al. Scale (max. = 15)	WWC Standards (no max. score)
Composition of tool	Ranks certainty of evidence as "conclusive" (highest), "preponderant," "suggestive," or "inconclusive" (lowest), based on research design, inter-observer agreement of dependent variable, and treatment integrity	12-item rating scale divided into primary and secondary indicators; strength of research ranked "strong," "adequate," or "weak" based on number and level of indicators achieved	One treatment scale: 10 items; two or more treatments scale: 19 items; higher score = higher quality	14 questions containing 16 items; studies are rated "strong" (11–14 points), "moderate" (7–10 points), or "weak" (less than 7 points)	11-item rating scale; item 1 assesses clinical history information; items 2–11 allow calculation of quality score; higher score = higher quality	15-item rating scale; higher score = higher quality	*Design Standards* rank internal validity as "Meets Standards", "Meets Standards with Reservations", and "Does not Meet Standards"; *Evidence of Effect Standards* rate effects strength as (1) "Strong Evidence," (2) "Moderate Evidence," or (3) "No Evidence"
Content validity established	No	Yes	No	No	Yes	No	No
Inter-rater reliability provided	No	Yes, including expert and novice raters	No	Yes, including the four authors of the scale	Yes, including expert and novice raters	No	No

Note. EVIDAAC = evidence in augmentative and alternative communication; SCED = single-case experimental design; WWC = What Works Clearinghouse. An extended version of this table containing further details on the various tools is available from the first author on request. From "Quality Appraisal of Single-Subject Experimental Designs: An Overview and Comparison of Different Appraisal Tools," by O. Wendt and B. Miller, 2012, *Education and Treatment of Children, 35*, pp. 240–241. Copyright 2012 by West Virginia University Press. Reprinted with permission.

In Chapter 2, APA has graciously permitted the reproduction (with selected updates) of our 2010 *Psychological Methods* article (Kratochwill & Levin, 2010) on the methodological advantages of incorporating some form of randomization into single-case designs. Building on prior work on what randomization can add to the internal validity of single-case design experiments, we review the three design classes (ABAB, multiple-baseline, and alternating treatment designs) while discussing and illustrating various options for including randomization in the design structure. We argue that even the most basic designs (e.g., AB designs) can be improved from an internal validity standpoint when randomization is a component of the planned experiment. The chapter sets the stage for subsequent chapters' exposition of the logic and value of randomization statistical tests in single-case intervention studies.

Chapter 3 by Thomas R. Kratochwill, Joel R. Levin, Robert H. Horner, and Christopher M. Swoboda provides a comprehensive overview of visual analysis as applied in single-case design. The authors begin by tracing the history and rationale for visual analysis, emphasizing its early roots in applied behavior analysis. An increasing body of research on various aspects of visual analysis has challenged researchers' exclusive reliance on graphed data to draw conclusions about the effect of an intervention. Although recent work is promising for the continued use of visual analysis, Kratochwill et al. suggest not just that more research is needed, but rather that the priority is for research that takes into account the real context of visual analysis as it is applied in single-case investigations (i.e., single-case designs that incorporate various forms of replication in the design structure, as occurs in ABAB designs). The authors argue that a key to good visual analysis is high-quality training in this methodology and they conclude by reviewing recent protocols that they have developed for that purpose.

To complement visual analysis, researchers have at their disposal a number of nonoverlap effect-size measures in single-case design research. In Chapter 4 Richard I. Parker, Kimberly J. Vannest, and John L. Davis describe various nonoverlap indices, including (a) the extended celeration line (b) the percent of nonoverlapping data, (c) the percent of Phase B data exceeding the Phase A median, (d) the percent of all nonoverlapping data, (e) the robust improvement rate difference, (f) nonoverlap of all pairs, (g) the percent of data exceeding the median trend, and (h) the hybrid nonoverlap-plus-trend index, TauU. The authors discuss the pros and cons of each method, demonstrate calculation of the indices from a hypothetical data set, and provide interpretation guidelines. Especially helpful to the reader is Parker et al.'s comparison of the indices across seven criteria: visual analysis, hand calculation, simple meaning, small study, minimum statistics, trend analysis, and precision-power of the measure. The reader will find the overview helpful in selection and implementation of a non-overlap method for single-case outcome data.

In Chapter 5, John M. Ferron and Joel R. Levin provide an overview of permutation and randomization statistical tests as applied to single-case intervention research. They make an important distinction between the two types of tests, with permutation tests comparing the obtained test statistic to an empirical distribution formed by all possible permutations of the data, and randomization tests requiring randomization in the design structure and the data permutations restricted to those that align with the randomization scheme.

Table 2. Research Design Standards and Guidelines

	What Works Clearinghouse	APA Division 12 Task Force on Psychological Interventions
1. Experimental manipulation (independent variable; IV)	The independent variable (i.e., the intervention) must be systematically manipulated as determined by the researcher	Need a well-defined and replicable intervention for a specific disorder, problem behavior, or condition
2. Research designs General guidelines	At least 3 attempts to demonstrate an intervention effect at 3 different points in time or with 3 different phase repetitions	Many research designs are acceptable beyond those mentioned
Reversal (e.g., ABAB)	Minimum of 4 A and B phases	(Mentioned as acceptable. See analysis table for specific guidelines.)
Multiple-baseline/ combined series	At least 3 baseline conditions	At least 3 different, successive subjects
Alternating treatment	At least 3 alternating treatments compared with a baseline condition or two alternating treatments compared to each other	N/A
Simultaneous treatment	Same as for alternating treatment designs	N/A
Changing/shifting criterion	At least 3 different criteria	N/A
Mixed designs	N/A	N/A
Quasi-experimental	N/A	N/A
3. Baseline (see also Measurement and Assessment Standards)	Minimum of 3 data points	Minimum of 3 data points
4. Randomization specifications	N/A	N/A

Note. From "Single-Case Experimental Designs: A Systematic Review of Published Research and Recommendations for Researchers and Reviewers," by J. D. Smith, 2012, *Psychological Methods*, *17*, p. 517. Copyright 2012 by the American Psychological Association.

APA Division 16 Task Force on Evidence-Based Interventions in School Psychology	National Reading Panel	The Single-Case Experimental Design Scale (Tate et al., 2008)	Ecological Momentary Assessment (Stone & Shiffman, 2002)
Specified intervention according to the Institute of Medicine's (1994) classification system	Specified intervention	Scale was designed to assess the quality of interventions; thus, an intervention is required	Manipulation in EMA is concerned with the sampling procedure of the study (see Measurement and Assessment table for more information)
The stage of the intervention program must be specified		The design allows for the examination of cause and effect to demonstrate efficacy	EMA is almost entirely concerned with measurement of variables of interest; thus, the design of he study is determined solely by the research question(s)
Mentioned as acceptable	N/A	Mentioned as acceptable	N/A
Both within and between subjects Considered the strongest because replication occurs across individuals	Single-subject or aggregated subjects	Mentioned as acceptable	N/A
Mentioned as acceptable	N/A	Mentioned as acceptable	N/A
Mentioned as acceptable	N/A	Mentioned as acceptable	N/A
N/A	N/A	N/A	N/A
Mentioned as acceptable	N/A	N/A	N/A
N/A	Mentioned as acceptable		N/A
Minimum of 3, although more observations are preferred	No minimum specified	No minimum ("sufficient sampling of behavior occurred pretreatment")	N/A
Yes	Yes	N/A	N/A

Table 3. Measurement and Assessment Standards and Guidelines

	What Works Clearinghouse	APA Division 12 Task Force on Psychological Interventions	APA Division 16 Task Force on Evidence-Based Interventions in School Psychology
1. Dependent variable (DV)			
Selection of DV	N/A	≥ 3 clinically important behaviors that are relatively independent	Outcome measures that produce reliable scores (validity of measure reported)
Assessor(s)/ reporter(s)	More than one (self-report not acceptable)	N/A	Multi-source (not always applicable)
Inter-rater reliability	On at least 20% of the data in each phase and in each condition; must meet minimal established thresholds	N/A	N/A
Method(s) of measurement/ assessment	N/A	N/A	Multi-method (e.g., at least 2 assessment methods to evaluate primary outcomes; not always applicable)
Interval of assessment	Must be measured repeatedly over time (no minimum specified) within and across different conditions and levels of the IV	N/A	N/A
Other guidelines			
2. Baseline measurement (see also Research Design Standards)	Minimum of 3 data points across multiple phases of a reversal or multiple baseline design; 5 data points in each phase for highest rating 1 or 2 data points can be sufficient in alternating treatment designs	Minimum of 3 data points (in order to establish a linear trend)	1. Minimum of 3 data points (more is preferred) 2. Stability (limited variability) 3. Absence of overlap between baseline and other phases 4. Level (severe enough to warrant intervention) 5. Absence of trends
3. Compliance and missing data guidelines	N/A	N/A	N/A

Note. From "Single-Case Experimental Designs: A Systematic Review of Published Research and Recommendations for Researchers and Reviewers," by J. D. Smith, 2012, *Psychological Methods*, *17*, p. 520. Copyright 2012 by the American Psychological Association.

National Reading Panel	The Single-Case Experimental Design Scale (Tate et al., 2008)	Ecological Momentary Assessment (Stone & Shiffman, 2002)
Standardized or investigator-constructed outcomes measures (report reliability)	Measure behaviors that are the target of the intervention	Determined by research question(s)
N/A	Independent (implied minimum of 2)	Determined by research question(s)
N/A	Inter-rater reliability is reported	N/A
Quantitative or qualitative measure	N/A	Description of prompting, recording, participant-initiated entries, data acquisition interface (e.g., diary)
List time points when dependent measures were assessed	Sampling of the targeted behavior (i.e., DV) occurs during the treatment period	Density and schedule are reported and consistent with addressing research question(s)
		Define "immediate and timely response"
	Raw data record provided (represent the variability of the target behavior)	
No minimum specified	No minimum (sufficient sampling of behavior [i.e., DV] occurred pretreatment)	N/A
N/A	N/A	Rationale for compliance decisions, rates reported, missing data criteria and actions

Table 4. Analysis Standards and Guidelines

	What Works Clearinghouse	APA Division 12 Task Force on Psychological Interventions
1. Visual analysis	4 step, 6 variable procedure (based on Parsonson & Baer, 1978)	Acceptable (no specific guidelines or procedures offered)
2. Statistical analysis procedures	Estimating effect sizes: nonparametric and parametric approaches, multilevel modeling, and regression (recommended)	Preferred when the number of data points warrants statistical procedures (no specific guidelines or procedures offered)
3. Demonstrating an effect (applies only to standards for single-case intervention research)	1. Documented consistency of level, trend, and variability within each phase 2. Documented immediacy of the effect, the proportion of overlap, the consistency of the data across phases 3. Identify for whom the intervention is and is not effective, if available 4. Examine external factors and anomalies	ABAB—stable baseline established during first A period, data must show improvement during the first B period, reversal or leveling of improvement during the second A period, and resumed improvement in the second B period (no other guidelines offered)
4. Replication/combining studies to determine efficaciousness of an intervention (applies only to standards for single-case intervention research)	1. Minimum of 5 studies 2. The studies must be conducted by at least 3 different research teams at 3 different geographical locations 3. The combined number of experiments (i.e., single-case design examples) across the studies totals at least 20	1. 3 replications of ≥ 3 subjects each 2. Replications conducted by ≥ 2 independent research groups

Note. From "Single-Case Experimental Designs: A Systematic Review of Published Research and Recommendations for Researchers and Reviewers," by J. D. Smith, 2012, *Psychological Methods, 17*, pp. 525–526. Copyright 2012 by the American Psychological Association.

APA Division 16 Task Force on Evidence-Based Interventions in School Psychology	National Reading Panel	The Single-Case Experimental Design Scale (Tate et al., 2008)	Ecological Momentary Assessment (Stone & Shiffman, 2002)
1. Change in level 2. Minimal score overlap 3. Change in trend 4. Adequate length (≥3) 5. Stable data (Franklin, Gorman, Beasley, & Allison, 1997; Parsonson & Baer, 1992)	N/A	Not acceptable ("use statistical analyses or describe effect sizes" p. 389)	N/A
Rely on the guidelines presented by Wilkinson and the Task Force on Statistical Inference of the APA Board of Scientific Affairs (1999)	Type not specified—report value of the effect size, type of summary statistic, and number of people providing the effect size information	Specific statistical methods are not specified, only their presence or absence is of interest in completing the scale	1. Aggregated or disaggregated approach 2. Model used in analyses 3. Details of procedures (e.g., autocorrelation approach, random effect levels)
1. 0.05 alpha levels 2. Nonsignificant or negative outcomes noted 3. Type of effect size, type of data on which effect size is based, effect size statistic 4. Clinical/educational significance (e.g., social comparison) 5. Follow-up of original study participants and multiple intervals with same outcome measures	N/A	N/A	N/A
1. Same intervention (treatment protocol and duration) 2. Same target problem and sample 3. Independent evaluation	N/A	Replication occurs across subjects, therapists, or settings	N/A

The randomization options in single-case design research include (a) *phase-order randomization*, where the order in which the within-case phases of the design is randomized; (b) *intervention randomization*, where the different interventions are randomly assigned either to individual cases or to members within case pairs; (c) *intervention start-point randomization*, where the intervention start point is randomly selected from a range of start points; and (d) *case randomization*, where cases are randomly assigned to different staggered replications. The authors present the conceptual logic and procedural applications of randomization and permutation tests within the context of examples from various single-case designs and they illustrate novel approaches that combine randomization statistical tests with visual analysis for evaluating single-case outcomes based on "response-guided" intervention designs.

Although there have been a number of computer program applications for various single-case statistical analyses (e.g., time-series, hierarchical linear modeling, randomization), few are specifically linked to the types of randomization noted above in Chapter 5. Building on the types of randomization in design presented in Chapters 2 and 5, Joel R. Levin, Anya S. Evmenova, and Boris S. Gafurov provide details in Chapter 6 about their recently developed single-case data-analysis ExPRT (Excel Package of Randomization Tests) microcomputer programs for (a) generating and displaying complete randomization distributions, (b) conducting randomization statistical tests on single-case intervention data, and (c) providing outcome summaries in both graphical and numerical formats (i.e., effect sizes). The authors include illustrations of the program applications for several types of single-case design (i.e., AB, ABA, ABAB, and multiple-baseline designs), while presenting ExPRT input and output for actual data applications.

Chapter 7 by David M. Rindskopf and John M. Ferron provides an overview of multilevel models for analyzing single-case design data, a special application when the researcher selects multiple cases for investigation. In such circumstances, the researcher has the option to conduct a "single-level analysis" for each case in the study. However, with multilevel models the researcher can examine all cases simultaneously, thereby allowing for a wider range of research questions to be addressed as, for example: (a) how large the treatment effect is for each case, (b) how the treatment effect changes over time for cases, (c) what the average treatment effect is across cases, (d) how that average treatment effect changes over the period of the investigation, (e) the degree to which the treatment effect varies across cases, and (f) if the variation is explained by case characteristics. In this regard, the authors advance the position that even though multilevel modeling applications require more stringent assumptions in comparison to other alternative single-case statistical approaches, they still may represent an attractive, more versatile data-analysis option.

Chapter 8 by William R. Shadish, Larry V. Hedges, James E. Pustejovsky, David M. Rindskopf, Jonathan G. Boyajian, and Kristynn J. Sullivan presents a comprehensive overview of their recent efforts to develop analogs of "group design" d effect-size measures for single-case ABAB . . . AB intervention designs. Such efforts, based on a hierarchical linear model framework, also include Bayesian approaches to the same and similar models, hierarchical generalized linear models that model outcomes as binomial or Poisson rather than the usual assumptions of normality, and semi-parametric generalized additive models that allow for diagnosis of trend and linearity. Throughout the chapter, the authors provide illustrations of each of these analyses using a common example, and they show how the different analyses provide different insights into the data. They conclude the chapter with a discussion of the skepticism and potential criticisms that have been expressed by various researchers about such analyses, along with reasons why the field of single-case intervention research is increasingly likely to develop and use such analyses despite the criticisms.

In recent years IES has invested in single-case design methodology in several ways. Because IES is the only federal organization to fund work on single-case design in a comprehensive manner, we invited IES officers Jacquelyn A. Buckley, Deborah L. Speece, and Joan E. McLaughlin to provide an overview of IES support for single-case design methodology in various domains of the organization. In Chapter 9 they describe IES's legislative mission as related to evidence-based education including the agency's perspective on research methodologies for education research agendas that include randomized controlled trials, quasi-experiments, and single-case designs. Important in this context is that single-case design is considered an acceptable research methodology for several goal domains. In this area Buckley and her colleagues provide several examples of how single-case design studies have been funded within IES. Single-case design methodology has also been supported in other initiatives including the development of the WWC pilot standards, funding single-case design methodology and statistics research and training grants, and the sponsorship of a single-case design training institute (for 3 years as of this date).

For the final section of this book, we asked researchers and journal editors to share their perspectives on single-case research in psychology and education. Chapters 12 through 14 include five "reactions from the field" sections consisting of contributions from (a) researchers who have used single-case intervention designs in their programs of research and (b) school psychology journal editors who have published single-case intervention research in their respective journals.

In Chapter 10, Susan M. Sheridan provides an overview of her successful research program on conjoint behavioral consultation. Conjoint behavioral consultation represents a problem-solving model that involves parents and teachers in an indirect mediator-based process for delivering interventions to a child/client. Sheridan's research program began with single-case research designs and then transitioned to randomized controlled trial investigations. Sheridan provides examples of her own work with both research methodologies.

In Chapter 11, Ann P. Kaiser describes her own comprehensive program of research in which she has adopted both single-case and conventional group designs to develop an effective early communication intervention called Enhanced Milieu Teaching (EMT). EMT is a naturalistic language intervention that promotes functional use of new language forms in the context of interactions with care providers (e.g., teachers, parents). Kaiser discusses advantages and limitations of the application of single-case designs in her line of research and, like Sheridan, she offers ways in which single-case research might be used to inform the design of RCTs.

The final three chapters were written by editors whose journals publish single-case design research in the field of school psychology. Chapter 12 presents the views of Randy G. Floyd, editor of the *Journal of School Psychology*, on both the perceived contributions of single-case design and his future perspectives on publishing single-case design research in the journal. Chapter 13 includes a contribution from Randy W. Kamphaus, editor of *School Psychology Quarterly*. Kamphaus discusses several issues that single-case design researchers should consider when publishing in the journal and in other fields. In Chapter 14, Matthew K. Burns, editor of the *School Psychology Review*, offers his views on publishing single-case intervention research and on several developments described in earlier chapters, along with their implications for future research appearing in the journal.

To reiterate, we are very excited to bring recent developments in single-case intervention methodology and data analysis to the attention of applied and clinical scientific researchers. Our ultimate hope, of course, is that we have offered such researchers new insights and critical tools for advancing science with respect to evidence-based practices in psychology and education.

References

Ahn, S., Ames, A. J., & Myers, N. D. (2012). A review of meta-analyses in education: Methodological strengths and weaknesses. *Review of Educational Research, 82,* 436–476.

American Psychological Association Task Force on Evidence-Based Practice for Children and Adolescents. (2008). *Disseminating evidence-based practice for children and adolescents: A systems approach to enhancing care.* Washington, DC: American Psychological Association.

Bailey, J. S. (1977). *A handbook of research methods in applied behavior analysis.* Gainesville: University of Florida.

Barker, J., McCarthy, P., Jones, M., & Moran, A. (2011). *Single-case research methods in sport and exercise psychology.* New York, NY: Routledge.

Barlow, D. H., & Hersen, M. (1985). *Single case experimental designs: Strategies for studying behavior change* (2nd ed.). New York, NY: Pergamon.

Barlow, D. H., Nock, M. K., & Hersen, M. (2009). *Single-case experimental designs: Strategies for studying behavior change* (3rd ed.). Boston, MA: Allyn & Bacon.

Bellack, A. S., & Hersen, M. (Eds.). (1984). *Research methods in clinical psychology.* New York, NY: Pergamon.

Campbell, D. T., & Stanley, J. C. (1963). *Experimental and quasi-experimental designs for research.* Chicago, IL: Rand McNally.

Chambless, D. L., & Hollon, S. D. (1998). Defining empirically supported therapies. *Journal of Consulting and Clinical Psychology, 66,* 7–18. doi:10.1037/0022-006X.66.1.7

Chambless, D. L., & Ollendick, T. H. (2001). Empirically supported psychological interventions: Controversies and evidence. *Annual Review of Psychology, 52,* 685–716. doi:10.1146/annurev.psych.52.1.685

Cooper, H., & Koenka, A. C. (2012). The overview of reviews: Unique challenges and opportunities when research syntheses are the principal elements of new integrative scholarship. *American Psychologist, 67,* 446–462. doi:10.1037/a0027119

DiNoia, J., & Tripodi, T. (2008). *Single-case design for clinical social workers.* Washington, DC: NASW press.

Fischer, J. (1978). *Effective casework practice: An eclectic approach.* New York, NY: McGraw-Hill.

Franklin, R. D., Gorman, B. S., Beasley, T. M., & Allison, D. B. (1997). Graphical display and visual analysis. In R. D. Franklin, D. B. Allison, & B. S. Gorman (Eds.), *Design and analysis of single-case research* (pp. 119–158). Mahwah, NJ: Erlbaum.

Gast, D. L. (2010). *Single subject research methodology in behavioral sciences.* New York, NY: Routledge.

Horner, R. H., Carr, E. G., Halle, J., McGee, G., Odom, S., & Wolery, M. (2005). The use of single-subject research to identify evidence-based practice in special education. *Exceptional Children, 71,* 165–179.

Horner, R. H. & Kratochwill, T. R. (2012). Synthesizing single-case research to identify evidence-based practices: Some brief reflections. *Journal of Behavioral Education.* Advance online publication. doi:10.1007/s10864-012-9152-2

Institute of Medicine. (1994). *Reducing risks for mental health disorders: Frontier for prevention intervention research.* Washington, DC: National Academy Press.

Janosky, J. E. (2009). *Single subject designs in biomedicine.* New York, NY: Springer. doi:10.1007/978-90-481-2444-2

Johnson, J. M., & Pennypacker, H. S. (1980). *Strategies and tactics of human behavioral research.* Hillsdale, NJ: Erlbaum.

Johnson, J. M., & Pennypacker, H. S. (2009). *Strategies and tactics of behavioral research* (3rd ed.). New York, NY: Routledge.

Kazdin, A. (2011). *Single-case research designs: Methods for clinical and applied settings* (2nd ed.). New York, NY: Oxford University Press.

Kazdin, A. E. (1981). Drawing valid inferences from case studies. *Journal of Consulting and Clinical Psychology, 49,* 183–192. doi:10.1037/0022-006X.49.2.183

Kazdin, A. E. (1982). *Single-case research designs: Methods for clinical and applied settings.* New York, NY: Oxford Press.

Kazdin, A. E., Kratochwill, T. R., & VandenBos, G. (1986). Beyond clinical trials: Generalizing from research to practice. *Professional Psychology: Research and Practice, 3,* 391–398.

Kennedy, C. H. (2005). *Single-case designs for educational research.* Boston, MA: Allyn & Bacon.

Kratochwill, T. R. (Ed.). (1978). *Single subject research: Strategies for evaluating change.* New York, NY: Academic Press.

Kratochwill, T. R. (1985). Case study research in school psychology. *School Psychology Review, 14,* 204–215.

Kratochwill, T. R., Alden, K., Demuth, D., Dawson, D., Panicucci, C., Arntson, P., . . . Levin, J. (1974). A further consideration in the application of an analysis-of-variance model for the intrasubject replication design. *Journal of Applied Behavior Analysis, 7,* 629–633. doi:10.1901/jaba.1974.7-629

Kratochwill, T. R., & Levin, J. R. (Eds.). (1992). *Single-case research design and analysis: New directions for psychology and education.* Hillsdale, NJ: Erlbaum.

Kratochwill, T. R., & Levin, J. R. (2010). Enhancing the scientific credibility of single-case intervention research: Randomization to the rescue. *Psychological Methods, 15,* 124–144. doi:10.1037/a0017736

Kratochwill, T. R., Hoagwood, K. E., Kazak, A. E., Weisz, J., Vargas, L. A., & Banez, G. A. (2012). Practice-based evidence for children and adolescents: Advancing the research agenda in schools. *School Psychology Review, 41,* 215–220.

Kratochwill, T. R., Hitchcock, J., Horner, R. H., Levin, J. R., Odom, S. L., Rindskopf, D. M., & Shadish, W. R. (2010). *Single-case designs technical documentation.* Retrieved from http://ies.ed.gov/ncee/wwc/pdf/wwc_scd.pdf

Kratochwill, T. R., Hitchcock, J. H., Horner, R. H., Levin, J. R., Odom, S. L., Rindskopf, D. M., & Shadish, W. (2013). Single-case intervention research design standards. *Remedial and Special Education, 34,* 26–38. doi:10.1177/0741932512452794

Kratochwill, T. R., & Stoiber, K. C. (2000). Empirically supported interventions in school psychology: Conceptual and practice issues—Part II. *School Psychology Quarterly, 15,* 233–253.

Kratochwill, T. R., & Stoiber, K. C. (2002). Evidence-based interventions in school psychology: Conceptual foundations of the Procedural and Coding Manual of Division 16 and the Society for the Study of School Psychology Task Force. *School Psychology Quarterly, 17,* 341–389. doi:10.1521/scpq.17.4.341.20872

Kratochwill, T. R., Stoiber, K. C., Christensen, S., Durlack, J., Levin, J. R., Talley, R., ... Waas, G. A. (2003). *Task Force on Evidence Based Interventions in School Psychology.* Retrieved from http://www.indiana.edu/~ebi/EBI-Manual.pdf

Levin, J. R. (1994). Crafting educational intervention research that's both credible and creditable. *Educational Psychology Review, 6,* 231–243. doi:10.1007/BF02213185

Levin, J. R., & Kratochwill, T. R. (2013). Educational/psychological intervention research circa 2012. In B. Weiner (Series Ed.) & W. M. Reynolds & G. E. Miller (Volume Eds.), *Handbook of psychology: Vol. 7. Educational psychology* (2nd ed., pp. 465–492). New York, NY: Wiley.

Levin, J. R., Marascuilo, L. A., & Hubert, L. J. (1978). *N* = nonparametric randomization tests. In T. R. Kratochwill (Ed.), *Single subject research: Strategies for evaluating change* (pp. 167–196). New York, NY: Academic Press. doi:10.1016/B978-0-12-425850-1.50010-7

Logan, L. R., Hickman, R. R., Harris, S. R., & Heriza, C. B. (2008). Single-subject research design: Recommendations for levels of evidence and quality rating. *Development Medicine & Child Neurology, 50,* 99–103.555

McReynolds, L. V., & Kearns, K. P. (1983). *Single-subject experimental designs in communicative disorders.* Baltimore, MD: University Park Press.

Morgan, D. L., & Morgan, R. K. (2008). *Single-case research methods for the behavioral and health sciences.* Thousand Oaks, CA: Sage.

National Institute of Child Health and Human Development. (2000). *Report of the National Reading Panel. Teaching children to read: An evidence-based assessment of the scientific research literature on reading and its implications for reading instruction* (NIH Publication No. 00-4769). Washington, DC: U.S. Government Printing Office.

National Reading Panel. (2000). *Report of the National Reading Panel: Teaching children to read: An evidence-based assessment of the scientific research literature on reading and its implications for reading instruction.* Jessup, MD: National Institute for Literacy.

Ottenbacher, K. J. (1986). *Evaluating clinical change: Strategies for occupational and physical therapists.* Baltimore, MD: Williams & Wilkins.

Parsonson, B. S., & Baer, D. M. (1978). The analysis and presentation of graphic data. In T. Kratochwill (Ed.), *Single subject research* (pp. 101–166). New York, NY: Academic Press.

Reichow, B., Volkmar, F. R., & Cicchetti, D. V. (2008). Development of the evaluative method for evaluating and determining evidence-based practices in autism. *Journal of Autism and Developmental Disorders, 38,* 1311–1319. doi:10.1007/s10803-007-0517-7

Schlosser, R. W. (2011). *EVIDAAC Single-Subject Scale.* Retrieved from http://www.evidaac.com/ratings/Single_Sub_Scale.pdf

Schlosser, R. W., Sigafoos, J., & Belfiore, P. (2009). *EVIDAAC Comparative Single-Subject Experimental Design Scale (CSSEDARS).* Retrieved from http://www.evidaac.com/ratings/CSSEDARS.pdf

Shadish, W. R., Cook, T. D., & Campbell, D. T. (2002). *Experimental and quasi-experimental designs for generalized causal inference.* Boston, MA: Houghton Mifflin.

Shavelson, R. J., & Towne, L. (Eds.). (2002). *Scientific research in education.* Washington, DC: National Research Council, National Academy Press.

Sidman, M. (1960). *Tactics of scientific research.* New York, NY: Basic Books.

Simeonsson, R., & Bailey, D. (1991). Evaluating programme impact: Levels of certainty. In D. Mitchell & R. Brown (Eds.), *Early intervention studies for young children with special needs* (pp. 280–296). London, England: Chapman & Hall.

Smith, J. D. (2012). Single-case experimental designs: A systematic review of published research and recommendations for researchers and reviewers. *Psychological Methods, 17,* 510–550. doi:10.1037/a0029312

Smith, V., Jelen, M., & Patterson, S. (2010). Video modeling to improve play skills in a child with autism: A procedure to examine single-subject experimental research. *Evidence-Based Practice Briefs, 4,* 1–11.

Stone, A. A., & Shiffman, S. (2002). Capturing momentary, self-report data: A proposal for reporting guidelines. *Annals of Behavioral Medicine, 24,* 236–243. doi:10.1207/S15324796ABM2403_09

Tate, R. L., McDonald, S., Perdices, M., Togher, L., Schultz, R., & Savage, S. (2008). Rating the methodological quality of single-subject designs and n-of-1 trials: Introducing the single-case experimental design (SCED) scale. *Neuropsychological Rehabilitation*, *18*, 385–401. doi:10.1080/09602010802009201

Tawney, J. W., & Gast, D. L. (1984). *Single subject research in special education*. Columbus, OH: Merrill.

Weisz, J. R., & Hawley, K. M. (2000*). Procedural and coding manual for identification of beneficial treatments*. Washington, DC: American Psychological Association, Society for Clinical Psychology Division 12 Committee on Science and Practice.

Wendt, O., & Miller, B. (2012). Quality appraisal of single-subject experimental designs: An overview and comparison of different appraisal tools. *Education & Treatment of Children*, *35*, 235–268. doi:10.1353/etc.2012.0010

Wilkinson, L., & the Task Force on Statistical Inference of the APA Board of Scientific Affairs. (1999). Statistical methods in psychology journals: Guidelines and explanations. *American Psychologist, 54*, 594–604.

Part I ————————————————

Methodologies and Analyses

1

Constructing Single-Case Research Designs: Logic and Options

Robert H. Horner and Samuel L. Odom

Research is the process of asking questions systematically, and research designs are the vehicle for adding precision to that process. An effective intervention research design documents that improvement has occurred (e.g., students acquire reading skills; problem behavior decreases; social interaction increases) and that this improvement occurred only when an intervention was implemented (e.g., reading performance improved only after introduction of systematic instruction; problem behavior decreased only after implementation of a function-based behavior support plan; social interactions by young children with autism improved only after peers were taught how to initiate and sustain social contact). The purpose of this chapter is to review how single-case research designs contribute to this process. We emphasize experimental single-case designs (i.e., as opposed to case studies) and begin with the often overlooked need to define the conceptual model, research question(s), and measures before selecting a design. Our goal is to provide the reader with (a) the logic for developing single-case research designs, (b) a summary of traditional design options, and (c) the framework for building new designs that match new research questions.

Basic Logic

The fundamental and compelling logic of single-case research designs is the repeated measurement of the individual participant or case[1] throughout the study. Single-case designs allow individual participants to serve as their own

---

[1]In single-case design studies, most often an individual, such as a child, adolescent, parent, teacher, is the unit of interpretation of "case." However, in some studies, a classroom of children, students in an entire school, or a whole community might be the case or participant in the study. In this chapter, when we refer to *participant*, we are referring to the case, which may include more than one individual (see, e.g., Chapter 2, this volume).

http://dx.doi.org/10.1037/14376-002
Single-Case Intervention Research: Methodological and Statistical Advances, by T. R. Kratochwill and J. R. Levin

"control" while documenting socially important change. Rather than assessing the average or mean level of performance (experimental group compared with control group) and comparing change in group performance at a small number of points (e.g., pretreatment and, later, posttreatment), the single-case design logic dictates measurement of each participant's performance repeatedly before, during, and after intervention. The goal is to depict the process of change as well as the end level of change. To build credibility in the finding, (a) everything about the context except the independent variable is held constant over the course of the study, and (b) the design requires repeated demonstration that manipulation of the independent variable is associated with predicted change in the dependent variable. Planning of single-case research design studies, however, should always begin by articulating the dependent variable or variables that give the study social relevance, the logic model that defines the conceptual foundation for the research, and the research questions that guide formal selection of the research design.

Begin With the Dependent Variable

When building a single-case research design, it is useful to begin with the dependent variable. A program of research starts by defining and describing what you want to influence. Defining the dependent variable(s) with precision sets up (a) construction of the logic model that guides selection of the independent variable(s), (b) construction of the research question(s), (c) selection of specific measurement tools and procedures, and (d) definition of research design requirements. Too often researchers begin either with the intervention (the independent variable) or the design they wish to employ (reversal–withdrawal design). This sequence can easily lead to selection of a design that inadequately fits the full research agenda by failing to control all relevant variables or focusing on only a portion of the research question. A research design should be selected to fit the conceptual model, dependent variable, and research questions of the study. As such, it is important to have clarity about these elements before selecting the design.

Consider, for example, that a research team was interested in the role of typically developing peers on the social interaction patterns of young children with disabilities. The team might start with social interactions as the dependent variable, defining this variable with precision, and building a conceptual model that organizes the range of variables most influential on development and use of social interaction skills. From this model the research team would be well-positioned to select measures of the dependent variable, identify the independent variables that would be the focus of their study, build precise research questions, and then select an appropriate research design. Our major message is that selecting a research design begins by defining the logic and foundation variables that will drive the design.

Use a Conceptual Model to Guide Selection of a Research Design

In an intervention-research context, a conceptual model, or "theory of change," defines assumptions about what is being targeted, what change is expected, and why change is expected. Specifically a conceptual model results in articulation of the (a) social goals guiding the research (e.g., the dependent variable), (b) factors that affect that goal or variable (e.g., what may be manipulated to achieve change), (c) presumed mechanisms responsible for that change, and (d) speed with which change is expected. Building a conceptual model sets up key decisions related to selecting a research design.

Measurement of the Dependent Variable

Defining the dependent variable with precision guides decisions related to selection of the metric for measuring the dependent variable, selection of the schedule of measurement, and decisions about how measurement will occur. Single-case designs are built to document change over time, and decisions about how the dependent variables will be measured are paramount. In single-case designs the dependent variable often is assessed numerous times (e.g., 20, 30, 40 times). The conceptual model will help guide selection of a measure that is both logically linked to the research question (e.g., focused on the targeted outcome) and likely to be sensitive to change over the time frame of the study. For example, a study focused on disruptive behavior in the classroom may build from a logic model predicting that disruptive behaviors are more likely if they are followed by escape from difficult tasks. This logic model may suggest a dependent measure of the frequency of disruptive behavior per 10-minute session coupled with a count of the number (or proportion) of disruptive behaviors followed by reduction in task demands. The logic model can affect the selection of measures.

Measurement of the Independent Variable

Defining the conceptual model also influences decisions about which factors will be selected for independent variable manipulation, which interactions are expected, which factors need to be held constant across the study, and what should be measured to document independent variable treatment integrity. A study focused on the effects of peer tutoring on the acquisition of literacy skills by young children might build from a conceptual model suggesting that peers are able to provide more opportunities for literacy responses, with faster and more frequent feedback. The conceptual model would guide identification of the core features of the independent variable (e.g., peer tutoring), and if impact on literacy was predicted to occur only if several core features were present (e.g., elevated frequency of response options plus more immediate feedback), then each of the features would be expected to be assessed in the measurement of the independent variable.

Research Design Features

The conceptual model specifies not only the dependent and independent variables, but (a) the presumed mechanisms responsible for change (e.g., positive

reinforcement, increased opportunity, decreased level of anxiety), (b) the anticipated speed and abruptness of change, and (c) the likelihood that the change
would reverse if the independent variable was withdrawn. These features dictate
what a research design will need to allow, and be prepared to document.

Consider, for example, the conceptual model for oral reading fluency provided in Figure 1.1. Note that the model emerged from the "right" to the
"left" (e.g., the model was built by starting with the dependent variable), and
that many different conceptual models are possible for the same dependent

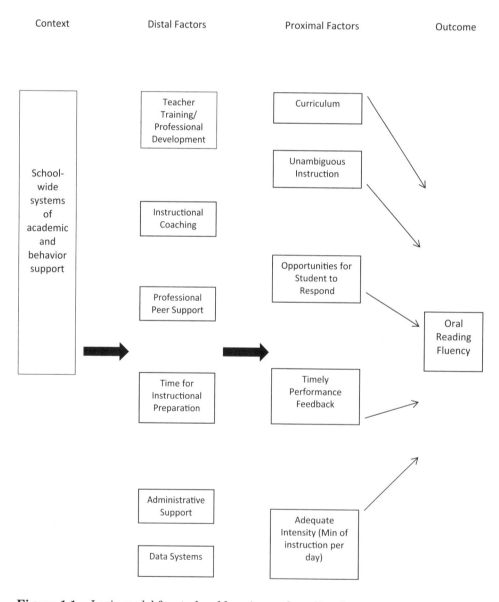

Figure 1.1.   Logic model for study addressing oral reading fluency.

variable based on researcher assumptions and level of focus. The example in Figure 1.1 assumes that each of the five proximal factors independently affects student oral reading fluency. The arrows indicate a direct effect, and in a well-defined conceptual model the mechanism associated with each arrow is identified. For example, unambiguous instruction influences oral reading fluency because it involves providing the student with a range of teaching examples that establish strong stimulus control by isolating relevant stimulus features, recruiting correct responses from students, and providing rewarding feedback. Distal factors are viewed in the conceptual model as combining to influence the presence of the proximal factors, and the larger contextual variables are typically viewed as influencing access to, or effectiveness of, the distal factors.

The conceptual model in Figure 1.1 would predict that oral reading fluency will improve gradually rather than precipitously, and that once improved, oral reading fluency will not be subject to rapid reversal. The conceptual model further identifies distal factors (teacher training), and context conditions (school-wide systems) that may affect the likelihood that proximal factors are available to a student. The goal of the conceptual model is to lay out a complete picture of the array of variables that the current theory or research literature suggests would affect the outcome variable. Scholars and advocates will embrace or disagree with some part of nearly every conceptual model, but the key message is that when researchers (or research teams) launch a program of study, decisions related to their conceptual model should be clearly defined, and used to guide selection of the research designs they propose.

A research design guided by the conceptual model in Figure 1.1 will be expected to (a) measure oral reading fluency repeatedly, (b) assume that change in oral reading fluency would occur gradually, thereby taking significant time (e.g., 2 weeks) between measures, and (c) use a design that does not require reversal of effects. Further, the selection of the independent variable (e.g., opportunities to respond) will be drawn from the list of proximal variables. Systematic manipulation of the selected independent variable will occur (and fidelity of this manipulation will be measured). In addition, any non-selected distal, or proximal variables listed in the model will need to be held constant across the study as the selected independent variable is manipulated.

Researchers building single-case designs are encouraged to share the conceptual model that guides their research. Studies driven by a well-conceived conceptual model (a) have clearly defined dependent variables that are measured with precision; (b) have clearly defined independent variables that are measured with precision; (c) hold constant over time all relevant non-manipulated variables in the conceptual model; (d) select a design that fits the expected magnitude, speed, and reversibility of the dependent variable; and (e) use assumptions about the mechanisms affecting the dependent variable to adapt the study if initially expected effects are not observed.

Our basic recommendation is to take time early in the development of a research program to define the dependent variable, articulate the guiding conceptual model, and build the precise research questions that are needed to select a research design. Research designs should fit the research question.

Selecting a Single-Case Design

Single-case research designs are organized to (a) document a pattern of responding that is in need of change, (b) demonstrate "basic effects" through change in the dependent variable when (and only when) the independent variable is manipulated, and (c) demonstrate experimental control via documentation of at least three basic effects each occurring at a different point in time. Different single-case designs achieve these outcomes in different ways, and those differences will be the focus of the following sections. It is appropriate to affirm that a set of basic quality indicators is consistent across designs (Horner et al., 2005; Kratochwill et al., 2013). All single-case designs are expected to repeatedly measure the dependent variable with reliability and validity, operationally define the setting and participants, and operationally define and measure the fidelity with which the independent variable is implemented. The distinguishing features of different single-case case designs, however, are *how* they achieve the three core outcomes of (a) documenting a pattern of responding in need of change, (b) demonstrating a basic effect, and (c) documenting experimental control.

Documenting a Pattern of Responding in Need of Change

Most single-case designs include a "baseline." The purpose of the baseline is to document a formal pattern of responding when all elements of the conceptual model are held constant. The baseline pattern of responding is expected to document a "problem." Said differently, the observed pattern of responding deviates from a preferred pattern of responding (i.e., problem behavior is too high, desirable behavior is too low). The baseline pattern of responding should also provide demonstration of a consistent level (i.e., mean score for data within a phase), trend (e.g., slope of the best-fitting straight line for data within a phase), and variability (i.e., range of scores about the best-fitting straight line) that are sufficient for predicting future responding if no change in controlling variables were to occur. Kratochwill et al. (2013) recommended a minimum of five data points in baseline to document a pattern, but they recognized that more data points may be needed if high variability, outliers, or trend is observed in the data. Figure 1.2 provides three baselines intended to frame this message. In each case, the dependent variable is frequency of tantrums per day. Figure 1.2a demonstrates five data points that have a stable level with minimal variability and trend. These data document a clear problem in the level of tantrums per day, and the pattern is sufficiently consistent to allow confident prediction about future responding if no changes are made. The data in Figure 1.2a would constitute a useful baseline.

The data in Figure 1.2b also document a predictable pattern, but the level of responding is so low that these data do not document a pattern in need of change, and as such provide a poor baseline for assessing an intervention targeted to improve tantrums. The data in Figure 1.2c have a stable level and trend, but the high variability makes it much less clear what would be expected in the next sessions. The higher variability in Figure 1.2c requires

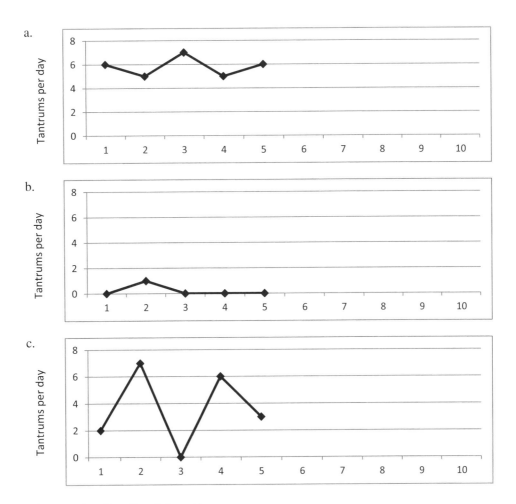

Figure 1.2.   Baseline data patterns.

that additional baseline data points be gathered before confidence in the baseline pattern could be achieved.

Documenting a pattern in need of change in single-case research requires
measuring the dependent variables under conditions where the core elements of
the conceptual model are held constant, a pattern of responding is documented
through consistency across multiple measures, and the observed pattern demonstrates the need for the proposed intervention (i.e., that there is a problem).

Documenting a "Basic Effect"

A basic effect is demonstrated by comparing the data from temporally adjacent
phases in a single-case design and concluding that the pattern of data from
one phase is not predicted by the data from the preceding phase. This comparison is done by first assessing the pattern of the data within each phase. The

within-phase "pattern" is a description of all data within a phase in terms of (a) level for the data points, (b) trend, and (c) variability (also taking into consideration data points that are unusual or "outliers" in the data set). In addition, when comparing the data from the two phases, the researcher should give additional consideration to (a) immediacy of observed effects and (b) overlap of data from one phase to the other. Immediacy of effect is typically assessed by comparing the last three data points from one phase with the first three data points of the next. The question to ask is "How quickly is change demonstrated in level, trend, and/or variability?" Overlap typically focuses on the proportion of data points in the second phase that are within the range of data points from the preceding phase. The less the amount of overlap, and the more immediate the observed change, the more compelling the demonstration of a "basic effect."

Consider the data in Figure 1.3. The level, trend, and variability in baseline data are compared to the same features for intervention data. The observed differences are further assessed in terms of the immediacy of change and degree of data overlap. The data in both phases are sufficient to document a clear pattern, and the pattern of data from the Intervention phase is not predicted from the data in the baseline phase. Taken together, Figure 1.3a data constitute a "basic effect." This decision contrasts with comparison of the data in Figure 1.3b, where because the Intervention data replicate the baseline data, no basic effect is demonstrated.

Documenting Experimental Control

The fundamental question addressed by single-case research designs is whether there is a functional relation between implementation of the independent variable and change in the dependent variable. A functional relation, also called experimental control, has been demonstrated when the study documents basic effects within a design that controls for the possibility that these effects could be due to any variables other than the manipulated independent variable. Research texts refer to "internal validity" as the reliability of basic effects when potentially confounding variables (i.e., threats to internal validity) are controlled (Campbell & Stanley, 1966; Gast, 2010; Kratochwill, 1978). Within single-case designs, internal validity is achieved, and a functional relation demonstrated, through repeated documentation of basic effects while holding the potentially confounding variables (such as those in the logic model) constant. Both the magnitude of basic effects and the replication of these basic effects influence the decision about whether experimental control has been demonstrated. Although many rubrics for determining experimental control exist, Kratochwill and his colleagues (Kratochwill et al., 2010, 2012) endorsed the emerging standard that experimental control has been demonstrated within a single-case design when the full set of data from a study (e.g., all data in all phases) document at least three demonstrations of a basic effect, with each of these basic effects occurring at a different point in time.

Experimental control should be viewed on a continuum, not as something that is either present or absent. Assuming that all potentially confounding variables are controlled, the strength of experimental control is affected by

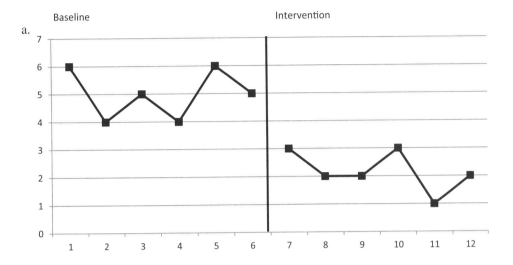

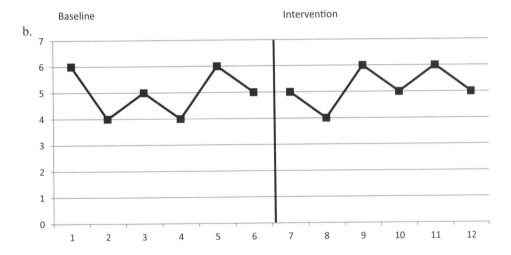

Figure 1.3. Basic effects in single case designs.

the magnitude of the basic effects (e.g., size of the effect), the number and spacing of the basic effects (e.g., the basic effects occur at three different points in time), and the absence of additional demonstrations of noneffects (i.e., effects occur only at three predicted points in time but not at any other points). It is reasonable to argue that a study may document experimental control, but "with reservation" because of such issues as unexplained outliers, one participant in a multiple-baseline design (to be described) not responding to the intervention, or variability producing elevated overlap with respect to some of the basic effects.

The emerging standard proposed for documenting experimental control is controversial in part because it is more demanding than has traditionally been used in some research communities. For example, single-case research designs that compare one baseline phase (A) with one intervention phase (B) allow documentation of one basic effect, but would not meet the criterion of three demonstrations of a basic effect, each at a different point in time. The AB design is a useful clinical tool, and a helpful evaluation design, but it is not a design with sufficient replication to allow demonstration of experimental control. Similarly, an ABA design allows two demonstrations of a basic effect (viz., AB and BA), but does not meet the minimal standard of replication needed to demonstrate experimental control. Finally, the multiple-baseline design (to be described) with only two replicated series would allow for two demonstrations of the basic effect, and may provide useful clinical information, but would not meet the standard for documenting experimental control.

Varieties of Single-Case Designs

In subsequent sections, we outline how different single-case research designs achieve the three features of (a) documenting a baseline pattern of responding in need of change, (b) allowing documentation of basic effects, and (c) allowing the opportunity to demonstrate experimental control. In most cases, single-case designs address research questions related to treatment or intervention efficacy. There are also designs that compare the efficacy of one or more treatment–intervention approach.

ABAB Designs

The ABAB design bears many labels. Baer, Wolf, and Risley (1968), for example, described the ABAB as a *reversal* design, and Leitenberg (1973) referred to it as a *withdrawal* design. We propose here that the ABAB design, unlike the AB or ABA designs, is a true experimental design. Each condition (A or B) is defined with operational precision. The reader of a research report should be able to replicate the core features of an "A" condition or a "B" condition with special attention to the status of those variables identified in the conceptual model to be held constant across the conditions. The features of the ABAB design allow demonstration of experimental control.

First, each phase of the design includes sufficient data points to allow demonstration of predictable pattern of responding. As noted previously, Kratochwill et al. (2010) recommended at least five data points per phase, but the central concern is that the pattern of data in *each* phase is convincing. For example, a study may address the number of positive social interactions with peers in which a child with autism engages, documenting a low level of performance in baseline.

Second, the initial basic effect (AB) is demonstrated when change in the dependent variable is documented during the B condition, while all core features of the A condition are held constant, and only the independent variable is actively manipulated (e.g., the researcher determines when and how the independent variable will be changed). The B condition not only represents introduction of the independent variable (e.g., behavior support, teaching procedure, social interaction intervention), but sustained implementation of all other features of the A condition. If there is a substantive, and reliable, change in the dependent variable, this constitutes one "basic effect" and begins to establish the claim for a functional relation between introduction of the independent variable and desired change in the dependent variable. For example, a teacher may begin to use a peer-mediated intervention to promote social interaction and the amount of social interactions increase.

Third, the basic effect is demonstrated within an ABAB design when the independent variable is withdrawn, and the core features of the initial A condition are replicated. (This BA comparison constitutes the second direct manipulation of the independent variable with a predicted impact on the dependent variable.) It is important to note that here again the goal during this BA comparison is to hold all features of the context constant except the removal of the independent variable. If the dependent variable returns to the prior pattern observed in the first A phase, this outcome adds confidence to the likelihood of a functional relation between introduction of the independent variable and change in the dependent variable. Following the example from above, the peer-mediated intervention is withdrawn resulting in a decrease in social interaction.

Documenting this "return to baseline" is of tremendous importance. It is not just the second demonstration of a basic effect, but a challenging test of the research hypothesis defined in the conceptual model. If the initial (AB) effect was due to maturation, or weather, or some other uncontrolled event, then we would not expect a return to baseline levels of performance. However, if the initial AB effect was functionally related only to introduction of the independent variable, then removal of that variable may be expected to result in return to prior A-condition performance. Note that this assumes that the measure of the dependent variable is susceptible and ethically reasonable to being reversed. Some dependent variables, such as reading skills or physical maturation would not be susceptible to reversal. Other dependent variables such as self-injury or social skills for young children may be possible to reverse, but ethically unreasonable. A central decision when considering use of an ABAB design is the feasibility and ethical acceptability of the BA reversal.

Fourth, the final basic effect in an ABAB design is assessed in the AB comparison by reimplementing the B condition. This second introduction of the intervention provides not only the third manipulation of the independent variable (e.g., introduced, removed, reintroduced) but the opportunity to replicate the direct clinical effect under consideration (e.g., the AB comparison). Again, using the previous example, the peer-mediated intervention is reimplemented, and the child's number of interactions increase.

Taken together, the four phases of an $A_1B_1A_2B_2$ design document responding across time with the possibility of asserting the following: (a) The A_1 phase demonstrates a compelling pattern of undesirable responding under well-defined conditions, (b) the introduction of the B_1 phase allows comparison of responding in A_1 to responding in B_1 where all core features of the A_1 condition remained constant except the manipulation of the independent variable, (c) reversal to the original A_1 condition in the A_2 phase allows an opportunity to assess whether those changes in the dependent variable that were observed during B_1 maintain, or revert to initial A_1 levels, and (d) the final introduction of B_1 conditions in the B_2 phase allows both replication of the A-B clinical effect and documentation of the third basic effect (at a third point in time) in which manipulation of the independent variable is associated with predictable change in the dependent variable.

A study that meets this pattern of replicated effects is deemed to have documented experimental control. A central feature of the design is that it not only provides an opportunity to assess whether the intervention in the B conditions produces an effect (e.g., AB), but it exposes the process to disproof by limiting the likelihood that any other variables are likely to be responsible for the observed changes in the dependent variable. The data are unlikely to demonstrate the required ABAB pattern if some variable other than the independent variable was responsible for change in the dependent variable. The convincing power of the design lies in demonstrating socially important change in the dependent variable via (a) repeated measurement, (b) active manipulation of the independent variable, and (c) meticulous constancy in all other features of the context throughout the phases of the study.

A hypothetical study depicted in Figure 1.4 may provide further elaboration of the intricacies of this design. The study is focused on improving the social behavior of children with disabilities in instructional settings. The primary dependent variable is disruptive hitting, kicking, spitting, throwing, and screaming. The dependent measure is a simple count of disruptive behavior events during 10 min of instruction. The logic model predicts that if (a) the behavioral function of disruptive behavior is identified, (b) socially appropriate communication strategies for achieving this function are taught, and (c) disruptive behavior is not followed by access to this behavioral function, the child will be more likely to use the socially appropriate behaviors and less likely to use the disruptive behaviors. This paradigm has been labeled *functional communication training* (Durand & Carr, 1985). As a piece of a proposed program of research, the staff posed the question, "Is there a functional relation between use of functional communication training and decrease in the frequency of disruptive behavior during instruction?" The researchers selected an ABAB design with the A-phase containing all the core features of a regular instructional session, and all the typical consequences that the staff delivers for disruptive behavior. The B-phase involved teaching the socially appropriate alternative skill, making sure the behavioral function (i.e., adult attention) followed appropriate social communication by the child and limiting access to the behavioral function when disruptive behavior occurred.

Consider the data in Figure 1.4a. The Baseline (A_1) phase documents high and consistent levels of disruptive behavior with clear predictability, and clear demonstration of a problem in need of a solution. The A_1 B_1 comparison provides demonstration of the first "basic effect." The data in FCT (B_1) document an immediate and dramatic change in the frequency of disruptive behavior, and this change is in the direction predicted by the logic model.

With the reintroduction of the Baseline (A_2) phase, the research team returned to the A conditions in which disruptive behavior led to access to adult attention. Note that during the A_2 phase, conditions were as similar to the A_1 as possible. Disruptive behavior in the A_2 returned to a pattern very similar to the

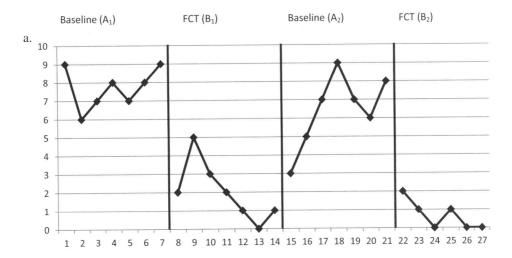

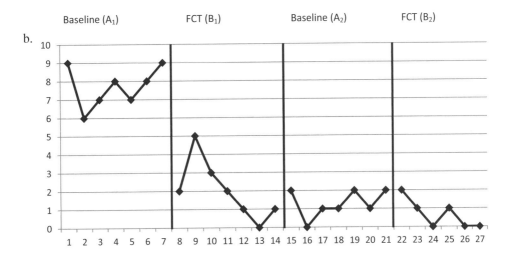

Figure 1.4. Reversal designs. Frequency of disruptions in 10 minute instructional periods.

A_1 phase. Re-introduction of the intervention in the B_2 phase was associated with immediate and dramatic return to near-zero levels of disruptive behavior. Taken together, the data in Figure 1.4a provide a strong demonstration of experimental control using an ABAB design.

The data in Figure 1.4b, however, provide a useful contrast. Note that the hypothetical data in Figure 1.4b are identical to the data in Figure 1.4a with the exception of the A_2 phase. These data indicate that following initial introduction of the intervention in B_1 there was a dramatic change in the level of disruptive behavior, but this basic effect was not followed by a reversal in the response pattern when the intervention was removed during the A_2 phase.

The data in Figure 1.4b demonstrate that change occurred in the frequency of disruptive behavior, and the change was clinically desirable. Taken together, however, the data in Figure 1.4b demonstrate only one basic effect, and they do not provide sufficient replication to document experimental control–functional relation.

The ABAB single-case design has a long and distinguished history in the fields of applied behavior analysis, psychology, and education. When used within a coherent logic model, and with a reversible dependent measure, the design has the ability to demonstrate strong functional relations.

Multiple-Baseline Designs

The multiple-baseline design (MBL) is among the more creative and substantive contributions from applied behavior analysis to the single-case design approach. The MBL addresses the thorny problem of how to study a dependent variable when it is not feasible, ethical, or desirable to reverse the initial effect. The MBL grew from the simple AB design in which repeated measurement of a variable in baseline was used to document a basic effect following introduction of the intervention (independent variable) in the B condition. The oft-cited problem with AB designs is not their ability to document change, but their lack of control for competing explanations for that change. Experimental research designs are constructed to allow both demonstration of change, and the inference that it is unlikely that anything other than the independent variable was responsible for the observed change in the dependent variable. Multiple-baseline designs achieve this dual goal by (a) ensuring that manipulation of the independent variable is "active" rather than "passive," (b) incorporating replication of at least three basic effects, and (c) staggering onset of the independent variable across at least three different points in time (lengths of baseline).

The researcher actively manipulates the independent variable by selecting when and how the independent variable is introduced. As an example, a study examining the effects of teacher reinforcement on student performance would be judged to "actively" manipulate the independent variable by selecting in advance how much reinforcement a teacher would provide to a student in a class. Passive manipulation would involve simply monitoring how much reinforcement typically occurs, and this passive approach would not allow sufficient control to meet the criteria of an experimental single-case design.

The staggered onset of the independent variable is the most signature feature of the MBL design. The staggered onset feature is achieved by first defining at least three "data series." A *data series* is a set of repeated measurements (e.g., the rate of social initiations for a child each day). Defining three data series could be achieved by measuring the dependent variable across each of three or more students. The data for each student would establish a data series. Three or more data series could also, however, be created by monitoring the behavior of *one student* in three or more different routines (e.g., snack, morning circle, science time, play time). Also, a data series could be applied to different behaviors measured for a single participant (e.g., focusing on faces, turn taking, joint attention). These are called MBL designs across participants, settings, or behaviors, respectively.

The researcher should start data collection at the same time for all data series in a MBL study. The initial goal is to define three or more baselines, each of which documents a clear pattern of responding, and each of which documents a "problem" level of responding (e.g., high levels of disruptive behavior, low numbers of social interactions with peers). The first series (see Figure 1.5), for example, would typically include five or more baseline (A_1) data points prior

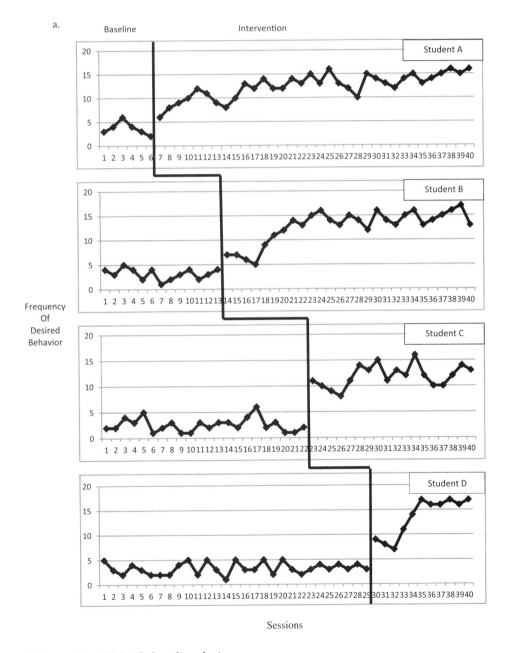

Figure 1.5.   Multiple baseline designs.

(continued on next page)

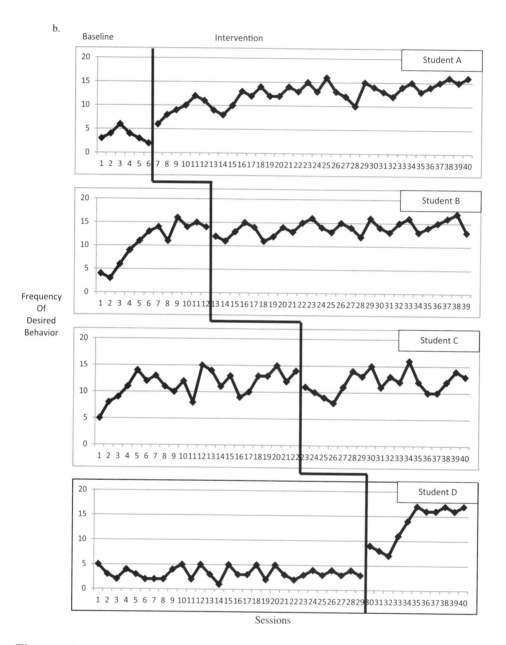

Figure 1.5. Multiple baseline designs *(Continued)*.

to introduction of the intervention. Data collection in all series would then continue until the data in the first series demonstrated change in pattern (e.g., level, trend, variability). Only after there was a documented effect in the first series would the intervention be introduced in the second series. Once again the study would continue until there was documented change in the second series before the intervention was introduced in the third series. This process would continue until the intervention was introduced in all series. Providing three staggered points in time when the independent variable is manipulated (e.g., intervention is introduced) provides control for the likelihood that change in the dependent variable is due to some other (uncontrolled) events in the setting, or that simply familiarity with the measurement process resulted in change (e.g., getting used to observers being present; building practice on the reading test protocol).

Figures 1.5a and 1.5b offer guidance on the MBL designs. Both figures represent an MBL design across students with "Frequency of some desired behavior" as the dependent variable, and "Intervention" as the independent variable. Figure 1.5a displays four baselines that are low, stable, and similar. It is important to mention that an MBL design with only three series potentially provides the minimum number of intervention effects (i.e., changes between A and B phases) necessary to demonstrate experimental control–functional relations. We, however, recommend designing MBL studies with at least four series in recognition that one series may encounter problems (e.g., a participant moves to a different city and must withdraw from the study) and yet the overall design could still be successfully implemented. Additional series in the MBL design can also be guided by certain statistical tests that increase the statistical power of the analysis (see Chapter 2, this volume).

In Figure 1.5a, following introduction of the intervention, there is an immediate increase in level and trend with an elevated level sustained through the intervention phase. In each series, when the intervention was introduced in one series (for one student) there was change in the frequency of desired behavior before the intervention was introduced in the next series. Analysis of the data for each student demonstrates a basic effect when baseline data are compared to intervention data. The four students offer four demonstrations of a basic effect each at a different point in time. Taken together, the data in Figure 1.5a document a strong functional relation.

The data in Figure 1.5b have many similar features, and the results from Student A and Student D are the same as the data in Figure 1.5a. The difference is in the data for Students B and C. In each case, those students demonstrated improved performance before the point of intervention. The data for Students B and C do not demonstrate basic effects, and the data do not control for the likelihood that some uncontrolled events in the setting may have been responsible for the improved level of performance. The data in Figure 1.5b document clinical improvement (high levels of desired behavior) for all four students, but the data do not demonstrate a functional relation between implementation of the intervention and improved behavior. As with the ABAB design, the MBL design relies on replication of basic effects to demonstrate experimental control. Again, the minimal standard for documenting an experimental effect is three demonstrations of basic effects, each at a different point in time. This standard is met and exceeded by the data in Figure 1.5a, but it is not achieved by the data in Figure 1.5b.

Alternating Treatments Designs

Researchers have used the ABAB and MBL designs primarily to address research questions about efficacy of an intervention or treatment approach in comparison to a control (i.e., no intervention) condition. In the alternating treatment design (ATD),[2] researchers address questions primarily related to the relative strength of two or more interventions or treatment approaches (Gast, 2010; Kazdin, 2011). For example, researchers might use an ATD to compare student "on-task" behavior under high and low rates of opportunity to respond. Such treatment comparisons are accomplished by rapidly alternating the implementation of treatments in a systematic, or even a random (see Chapter 2, this volume), manner. An ATD with the A condition representing Treatment A and the B condition representing Treatment B could be designed with systematically alternating ABABABAB conditions, with one outcome observation per condition. The designs are appropriate for intervention comparisons in which the interventions may have *independent* effects on the dependent variable; that is, the effect of the first intervention on the participant will not affect the participant's performance when she or he is exposed to the second intervention. When intervention effects are not independent, a condition called *multiple-treatment interference* or *multiple-treatment interaction* occurs (Kennedy, 2005), and so the ATD would not be appropriate. For example, in comparing the effect of two spelling interventions on a participant's performance on a common set of spelling words, the individual may learn to spell better from one intervention and will continue to spell better in the other intervention. In contrast, a study of a student's on-task behavior may be different under two instructional conditions, such as an independent work system approach and a group contingency approach, without participation in the one approach affecting the students on-task behavior when the second approach occurs (i.e., the student did not learn to be more on-task).

Like ABAB and some MBL designs, ATDs operate within a single participant, although they often are replicated directly with several other participants. They may begin with a baseline condition, in which a researcher documents performance of the participant in a typical context that will serve as the contrast to the alternating intervention conditions that follow. Depending on the research question, ATDs sometimes may not include baselines, but begin immediately with the comparison of different treatment conditions. In another variation of ATDs, a baseline condition is included as one of the alternating conditions to be evaluated.

The primary feature of ATDs is the alternating implementation of treatment conditions. The treatment sessions or conditions may be implemented on the same day or they may be alternated each day or session of the study. The sequencing of the implementation of the intervention is a key feature of this design because the order of the treatment must be systematically (or randomly) alternated to make sure that an "order effect" does not occur. That is, if Treatment 2 always followed Treatment 1, the researcher could not rule out the possibility that the effects for one Treatment (e.g., Treatment 2) are affected by just having been exposed to the prior Treatment (e.g., Treatment 1). The order of treatments may be altered in the same way across the study. For example, if two treatments were being examined on subsequent days, the daily order might be reversed every two days. Similarly, the order of treatments might be

---

[2]In some studies, ATDs are also called *simultaneous treatment designs* (Kazdin, 2011).

determined by random assignment for each 2-day block of treatments, or the treatment on a specific day may be randomly selected from the two possibilities (i.e., on a single day, the treatment to be delivered is randomly selected—see, e.g., Chapter 2, this volume).

The performance of a participant on the same dependent variable is assessed in each treatment condition and charted regularly (typically each day). The functional relation between the independent and dependent measure is demonstrated by the magnitude and consistency of a "separation" between the data points in the different conditions (i.e., the lack of overlap among data points in different conditions). Most contemporary criteria for ATDs recommend that there should be at least four data points of comparison among the treatment conditions (although three data points per condition is considered acceptable with reservation) and little overlap in data for treatment conditions (Kratochwill et al., 2010). In some multiple-treatment ATDs, the researcher plans a final phase of the study in which the treatment with the strongest effects is implemented and the other treatment conditions are discontinued to further rule out the possibility of multiple-treatment interference.

A hypothetical example of an alternating treatment design is presented in Figure 1.6, where a researcher may want to investigate the effects of peer-mediated versus adult-prompted social initiations on the rate of social interactions with typical peers for children with autism spectrum disorders (ASDs). During a baseline condition, children with ASD and typically developing children were enrolled in integrated playgroups, and frequency of social initiations to peers by the child with ASD was recorded. After a stable baseline was established, the researcher implemented the peer-mediated and teacher-prompted conditions in play sessions, and the order of the implementation of the two days was randomly determined (with no more than one repetition of a condition allowed). After 5 days, the frequency of social initiations in the teacher-prompted condition was substantially greater than in the peer-mediated condition. To rule

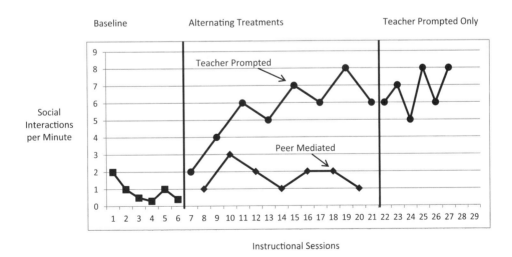

Figure 1.6. Hypothetical example of an Alternating Treatments Design.

out the possibility of multiple-treatment interaction, the researcher discontinued the peer-mediated intervention in the final phase of the study and implemented the teacher-prompted condition. The consistency of the separation seen during the second phase of the study demonstrated the functional relationship necessary to establish experimental control.

Data from ATDs may be displayed in different ways, although the research question remains the same: "Is there a comparative difference in the dependent variable when given treatment A versus treatment B?" When data are shown as different "elements" on the same graph, this type of display has been called *multi-element*, and researchers have even called these *multi-element designs*, although we define them synonymously with ATDs. A different way of displaying the data is for each implementation of a treatment condition to be characterized as a phase, with only one data point per phase.

In Figure 1.7, a hypothetical researcher is comparing the frequency of disruptive behavior under three conditions: "Attention" following occurrence of disruption, "Escape" from task demands following occurrence of disruption, and "Play" with a preferred task where disruptive behavior was ignored. The two graphs are displaying the same data, Figure 1.7a displays the data in a multi-element format, and Figure 1.7b displays the same data with each data point functioning as a unique phase. The results from both graphs indicate that disruptive behavior was much more likely to occur when followed by attention (e.g., in the Attention condition), and there was no difference between the Play and Escape conditions.

Combined Single-Case Designs

Basic single-case designs (ABAB, MBD, and ATD) can be combined to allow multiple questions within a single design or to adapt a design in midstudy if unanticipated patterns arise. A major advantage of single-case designs is their flexibility and the capacity to incorporate multiple design features in combined designs (Kazdin, 2011; Kennedy, 2005). For example, it is possible to incorporate an ABAB design within a MBL design, or to embed an ATD within an ABAB design, if the research questions dictate. An example of a combined design focusing on multiple research questions was provided in a study of peer-mediated intervention by Odom, Hoyson, Jamieson, and Strain (1985), as illustrated in Figure 1.8. The authors initially employed an MBL design across settings to first address the research question, "Is there a functional relation between peer social initiations and increases in the social interactions of children with ASD?" In addition, however, the authors used a withdrawal-of-treatment reversal design to assess a second research question, which was, "Is there a functional relation between teacher prompts and the occurrence of peer's initiations to the children with ASD?" By combining the MBL and ABAB features into a single analysis the authors were able to examine their conceptual model more effectively. They demonstrated that teacher prompts increased the likelihood of peer-mediated social initiations and that these initiations were functionally related to an increase in the overall rate of social interaction for young children with ASD. The combined design demonstrated not only that peer social initiations

a.

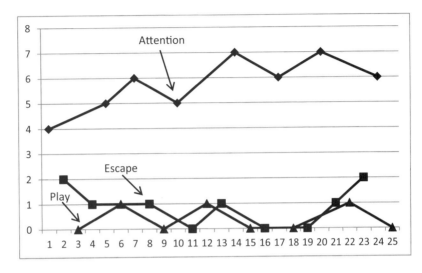

Sessions

b.

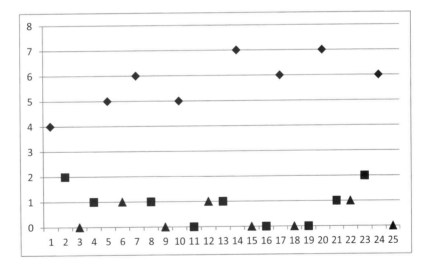

Sessions

Figure 1.7.   (a) Hypothetical example of ATD in a multi-element format used within a functional analysis: frequency of disruptive behavior during 5 minute instructional sessions. (b) Hypothetical example of ATD with each data point as an independent phase used within a functional analysis: frequency of disruptive behavior during 5 minute instructional sessions.

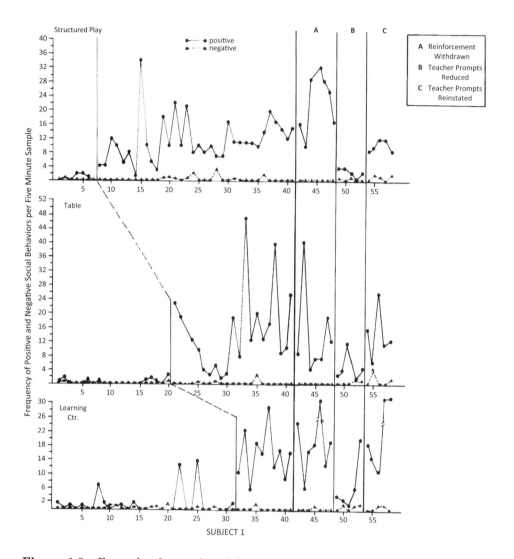

Figure 1.8. Example of a combined design. From "Increasing Handicapped Pre-schoolers' Peer Social Interactions: Cross-Setting and Component Analysis," by S. L. Odom, M. Hoyson, B. Jamieson, and P. S. Strain, 1985, *Journal of Applied Behavior Analysis, 18*, p. 12. doi:10.1901/jaba.1985.18-3. Copyright 1985 by Wiley. Reprinted with permission.

were associated with improved social interactions by children with ASD but that teacher prompting of peer social initiations was an essential component of the intervention.

Combined designs are not, however, always predetermined. Consider, for example, the data in Figure 1.9 from a hypothetical study examining the functional relation between functional communication training (FCT; Durand & Carr, 1985) and problem behavior. In this study, a multiple-baseline design across participants was proposed to assess the effect of introducing FCT on problem behavior. All four participants demonstrated high, consistent levels

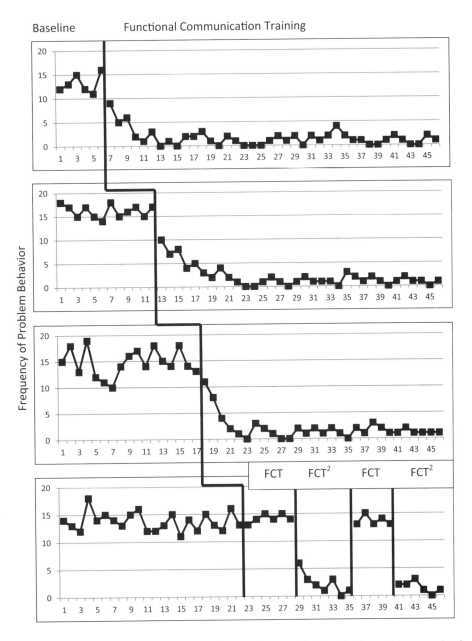

Figure 1.9. Hypothetical example of a single-case design that combines multiple baseline and reversal-design features.

of problem behavior during baseline. For the first three participants (Able, Bob, and Carl), the introduction of FCT was associated with an immediate and substantive reduction in the level of problem behavior. For the fourth participant (Dwayne), however, introduction of FCT was not associated with changes in problem behavior. The research team reassessed Dwayne's problem behavior and concluded that his problem behavior was maintained by a different behavioral function than was initially assumed. The team used this new information to design a different form of FCT (FCT²) and then applied an ABAB design with Dwayne to document the effect of the modified intervention. Taken together, the data from Figure 1.9 demonstrate that FCT was functionally related to reduction in problem behavior, but if the initial functional behavioral assessment is flawed, then FCT will not be effective. In this example, the ability to combine single-case design elements allowed for a more precise analysis of the basic conceptual model proposed by the researchers.

A hallmark of single-case research designs is their flexibility to address the nuances in complex conceptual models. This process often is accomplished by combining basic single-case designs (ABAB, MBL, ATD) so that a single investigation may address multiple questions, multiple parts of a complex question, or better understand unanticipated data patterns that arise during a study.

Summary

Single-case research designs offer an important option for documenting experimental control in applied and clinical research. The basic logic guiding single-case designs mirrors that of traditional group designs: (a) Document a controlled baseline, (b) systematically compare the baseline with an intervention, and (c) provide replication-and-design stipulations to control for threats to internal validity. The mechanism by which single-case designs achieve these features, however, is different from traditional group designs. The controlled baseline is not defined by assessing a group of individuals once or a small number of times, but by collecting a larger series of measures on one or more participants. The "pattern" of responding during baseline is defined by the consistency across multiple baseline scores.

The comparison of baseline and intervention conditions also occurs within single-case designs, but the single-case design allows each individual participant to serve as his/her own control. The same participant is monitored multiple times in both baseline and intervention conditions. The comparison of baseline and intervention patterns allows the documentation of a "basic effect." This basic effect is then replicated to allow for three demonstrations of a basic effect, each occurring at a different point in time. It is this replication of basic effects that allows for the control of threats to internal validity, which is needed to document experimental control.

The most commonly used single-case designs incorporate ABAB, MBL, or ATD forms. Our goal here, however, is not just to provide the logic for these basic designs but to encourage the individual and combined use of current designs to better address new and more complex research questions. There are new single-case designs to be developed and new ways to use or adapt existing designs. Research teams that master the logic of single-case research start with a carefully defined dependent variable, articulate the conceptual model that guides their science, and use that model to select specific dependent measures and independent variables will more likely formulate precise research questions that make it possible to match single-case design features to the key issues under analysis.

References

Baer, D. M., Wolf, M. M., & Risley, T. R. (1968). Some current dimensions for applied behavior analysis. *Journal of Applied Behavior Analysis, 1*, 91–97. doi:10.1901/jaba.1968.1-91

Campbell, D. T., & Stanley, J. C. (1966). *Experimental and quasi-experimental designs for research.* Chicago, IL: Rand McNally.

Durand, V. M., & Carr, E. G. (1985). Self-injurious behavior: Motivating conditions and guidelines for treatment. *School Psychology Review, 14*, 171–176.

Gast, D. L. (2010). *Single subject research methodology in behavioral sciences.* New York, NY: Routledge.

Horner, R. H., Carr, E. G., Halle, J., McGee, G., Odom, S., & Wollery, M. (2005). The use of single subject research to identify evidence-based practice in special education. *Exceptional Children, 71*, 165–179.

Kazdin, A. E. (2011). *Single-case research designs: Methods for clinical and applied settings* (2nd ed.). New York, NY: Oxford University Press.

Kennedy, C. H. (2005). *Single-case designs for educational research.* Boston, MA: Allyn & Bacon.

Kratochwill, T. R. (Ed.). (1978). *Single subject research: Strategies for evaluating change.* New York, NY: Academic Press.

Kratochwill, T. R., Hitchcock, J., Horner, R. H., Levin, J. R., Odom, S. L., Rindskopf, D. M., & Shadish, W. R. (2010). Single case designs technical documentation. In *What Works Clearinghouse: Procedures and standards handbook* (Version 2.0). Retrieved from http://ies.ed.gov.ncee.wwc.pdf.wwc_procedures_v2_standards_handbook.pdf

Kratochwill, T. R., Hitchcock, J. H., Horner, R. H., Levin, J. R., Odom, S. L., Rindskopf, D. M., & Shadish, W. R. (2013). Single-case intervention research design standards. *Remedial and Special Education, 34,* 26–38.

Kratochwill, T. R., Hoagwood, K. E., Kazak, A. E., Weisz, J. R., Hood, K., Vargas, L. A., & Banez, G. A. (2012). Practice-based evidence for children and adolescents: Advancing the research agenda in schools. *School Psychology Review, 41*, 215–220.

Leitenberg, H. (1973). The use of single-case methodology in psychotherapy research. *Journal of Abnormal Psychology, 82*, 87–101. doi:10.1037/h0034966

Odom, S. L., Hoyson, M., Jamieson, B., & Strain, P. S. (1985). Increasing handicapped preschoolers' peer social interactions: Cross-setting and component analysis. *Journal of Applied Behavior Analysis, 18*, 3–16. doi:10.1901/jaba.1985.18-3

2

Enhancing the Scientific Credibility of Single-Case Intervention Research: Randomization to the Rescue

Thomas R. Kratochwill and Joel R. Levin

Traditionally, a premium has been placed on the use of randomized experimental design methodology—and synonymously in selected contexts, randomized controlled trials (RCTs)—for evaluating the efficacy of psychological and educational interventions. Indeed, the term "gold standard" has often been applied to intervention research that adheres to the principle of randomization when imputing causal connections between interventions and outcomes (e.g., Mosteller & Boruch, 2002; Reyna, 2005; Shadish, Cook, & Campbell, 2002; Shavelson & Towne, 2002; Slavin, 2002). RCTs are typically experiments that minimize (although not necessarily eliminate) major internal-validity threats to drawing scientifically valid inferences from the data (Shadish et al., 2002). Multiple-participant experimental designs (referred to here as *group designs*) have played the primary role in the development of what are contemporaneously referred to as "scientifically credible" (e.g., Levin, 1994) and "evidence-based" (e.g., Hayes, Barlow, & Nelson-Gray, 1999) interventions. In such research, random assignment of participants (or analogous "units," discussed in a following section) to the different intervention (or intervention and control) conditions is the typical method for helping to assuage internal invalidity concerns.

Single-case (formerly, until about the mid-1980s, *single-subject*) research designs have also been used to establish an empirical basis for evidence-based interventions and techniques in a variety of disciplines. In recent years there has been renewed interest in the role that single-case designs can play

The preparation of this chapter was facilitated by Institute of Education Sciences (IES) Grant No. R324U060001 to Thomas R. Kratochwill and Joel R. Levin. We are grateful to Jacquelyne Buckley of IES for her support and to Cathlin Foy for her assistance in constructing the figures. The chapter is an adapted (essentially condensed and updated) version of a 2010 journal article of the same title by Thomas R. Kratochwill and Joel R. Levin, published in *Psychological Methods*, Volume 15, pages 122–144.

http://dx.doi.org/10.1037/14376-003
Single-Case Intervention Research: Methodological and Statistical Advances, by T. R. Kratochwill and J. R. Levin

in establishing the scientific basis for various educational and psychological interventions (Horner et al., 2005; Horner & Spaulding, 2010; Kratochwill, 2007; Smith, in press; Wendt & Miller, 2012). Single-case designs have been adopted in several areas of scientific research, with the most prominent publication outlet being the *Journal of Applied Behavior Analysis* that initiated publication in 1968. Numerous journals now publish single-case design studies in such fields as psychology (i.e., clinical psychology, counseling psychology, school psychology), social work, speech and language fields, and special education. In 2008, the increasing role that single-case design plays in education research was emphasized through the establishment of a Single-Case Design Panel sponsored by the Institute of Education Sciences. The specific charge to that panel was to develop multiple-dimension coding standards for single-case designs with the ultimate goals of (a) summarizing single-case studies in select substantive areas and (b) reporting results of literature reviews in the What Works Clearinghouse (WWC). The WWC's *Single-Case Design Technical Documentation Version 1.0* is available at their website (http://ies.ed.gov/ncee/wwc/pdf/wwc_scd.pdf; see also Hitchcock et al., in press; Kratochwill et al., 2013). In development of the single-case design standards, intervention replication was adopted as the design standard for all single-case designs used in conducting reviews for the WWC (see Introduction and Chapter 1, this volume). A number of appraisal tools have been developed in psychology, education, and speech, language, and hearing sciences (see Smith, in press; Wendt & Miller, 2012, for an overview of various tools).

Despite many areas of application, traditional single-case designs have typically not met the criteria for an RCT and thus, relative to conventional group designs, they have not been included in the WWC literature reviews that establish a research domain's evidence. In fact, a perusal of journals that publish single-case designs exclusively (e.g., *Journal of Applied Behavior Analysis*) or frequently (e.g., *School Psychology Review*) demonstrates that randomization, the aforementioned hallmark of scientifically credible intervention research, is not applied in the basic formation of the designs. Adding randomization to the structure of single-case designs can augment this type of research in at least two important respects.

First, randomization can strengthen the internal validity of these designs. As was just noted and as is discussed in the following section, single-case designs depend on some form of replication to argue against internal validity threats. Although replication represents a strong design option, randomization represents a higher level of methodological soundness in such applications. In this chapter we introduce different randomization schemes and variations for single-case intervention researchers to consider. Second, including a randomization scheme in the design allows the researcher to apply various statistical tests based on randomization models, which can improve the statistical-conclusion validity of the research (for several randomization-test possibilities, see Chapter 5, this volume; Borckardt et al., 2008; Edgington & Onghena, 2007; Koehler & Levin, 1998; Levin, Ferron, & Kratochwill, 2012; Levin & Wampold, 1999; Wampold & Worsham, 1986).

The purpose of this chapter is (a) to review the various types of single-case research designs that can be used in intervention research and (b) to provide scientifically credible extensions of these designs—in particular, extensions incorporating randomized experimental schemes that allow investigators to draw more valid inferences from their research. Common data-analysis strategies associated with these design variations include visual/graphical analysis (see Chapter 3, this volume) and statistical analysis (see Chapter 5, this volume).

Basic Single-Case Design Structures for Establishing Experimental Control

Like conventional group intervention designs, traditional single-case intervention designs are structured to take into account a study's major threats to internal validity. However, unlike the most scientifically credible group intervention designs, traditional single-case researchers typically have not used randomization to reduce or eliminate internal-validity threats. As an alternative, single-case designs address internal validity concerns through some type of *replication* during the course of the experiment. The replication criterion advanced by Horner et al. (2005) represents a fundamental characteristic of single-case designs: "In most cases experimental control is demonstrated when the design documents three demonstrations of the experimental effect at three different points in time with a single participant (within-subject replication), or across different participants (inter-subject replication)" (p. 168). As these authors noted, an experimental effect is demonstrated when the predicted changes in various outcome measures covary with the manipulated variable after taking into account the baseline (preintervention) series' trend, level, and variability. However, it must be noted that there is no empirical basis for the "three demonstrations" recommendation; rather, it represents a conceptual norm among published research and textbooks that recommend methodological standards for single-case intervention designs (Kratochwill et al., 2013).

The methodology for establishing experimental control that relies on replication generally falls into three major design "types," as originally discussed by Hayes (1981).[1] The design types, reproduced in Table 2.1, are the basic building blocks for the construction of single-case designs. In this chapter, we expand on these building blocks by adapting various randomization tactics that will strengthen a single-case researcher's case for drawing valid inferences from the study. We first review each of the design types. Then, within each design type, we provide suggestions for (and illustrations of) the incorporation of randomization into the basic design structure. Each design type is accompanied by an example from the published literature, along with a description of how some form of randomization could have been built into the original experiment. Our purpose in so doing is to illustrate how to transform traditional single-case intervention designs into more scientifically credible *randomized* single-case intervention designs.

---

[1]We adopt Hayes's (1981) design-type designations as an organizational framework here, even though there are fuzzy distinctions among them in contemporary single-case applications.

Table 2.1. Major Types of Single-Case Designs and Associated Characteristics

Design type	Representative example	Characteristics
Within series	Simple phase change [e.g., AB; ABA; ABAB; BCBC] Couples phase change [e.g., interaction element: B(B+C)B; C(B+C)C]	In these designs, estimates of level, trend, and variability within a data series are assessed under similar conditions; the manipulated variable is introduced and concomitant changes in the outcome measure(s) are assessed in the level, trend, and variability between phases of the series.
Between series	Alternating intervention design	In these designs, estimates of level, trend, and variability in a data series are assessed in measures within specific conditions and across time. Changes/differences in the outcome measure(s) are assessed by comparing the series associated with different conditions.
Combined series	Multiple baseline (e.g., across subjects, across behaviors, across situations)	In these designs, comparisons are made both between and within a data series. Repetitions (replications) of a single simple phase change are scheduled, each with a new series and in which both the length and timing of the phase change differ across repetitions.

Note. "A" represents a baseline series; "B" and "C" represent two different intervention series. From "Single-Case Experimental Designs and Empirical Clinical Practice," by S. C. Hayes, 1981, *Journal of Consulting and Clinical Psychology*, *49*, p. 208. Copyright 1981 by the American Psychological Association.

Within-Series Single-Case Designs

In within-series designs, participant performance is measured within each condition of the investigation and compared between or among conditions. Although not "acceptable" by the WWC Standards (Kratochwill et al., 2013), the most fundamental within-series intervention design is the two-conditions AB design, where the A condition is a baseline or preintervention series/phase and the B condition is an intervention series/phase. This design is sometimes called the *basic time-series design* or an *interrupted (or two-phase) time-series design* and is truly quasi-experimental in that (a) no type of randomization is used and (b) no replication of the baseline and intervention phases is scheduled in the design (Shadish et al., 2002). However, as we note later, even in this most basic within-series design consisting of only one experimental unit receiving one baseline and one intervention series of observations or measures, the researcher can structure the study so that it includes a randomization component—thereby enhancing the design's scientific credibility.

The most common form of the within-series design that meets the replication criterion advanced by Horner et al. (2005) is the ABAB design, which includes four alternating baseline and intervention phases (or four alternating intervention phases, BCBC), and hence there is an opportunity to produce a within-subject replication of the intervention effect. Specifically, in this four-phase design, intervention effects are assessed during the first B phase and then again during the second B or replication phase. Figure 2.1 illustrates the ABAB design with hypothetical data. The four-phase ABAB design was initially proposed (and is now universally accepted) as a more scientifically and clinically convincing single-case design relative to both the historically earlier implemented basic AB and single-reversal (or "return-to-baseline") ABA designs (see Hersen & Barlow, 1976). In addition to satisfying Horner et al.'s (2005) within-subject replication criterion, the ABAB design has numerous methodological merits. Moreover, the design's external validity can be further enhanced by the inclusion of more than one case (i.e., a replicated ABAB design, discussed later in this chapter), thereby providing an opportunity to produce a between-subjects replication. The four-phase ABAB design currently represents the minimum within-series standard for single-case intervention researchers seeking to publish their work in top-tier academic journals (see Hayes et al., 1999; Horner et al., 2005; Kratochwill et al., 2013).

As was noted earlier, the just-discussed alternating-phase design can also be applied to two different interventions, B and C. For example, the researcher might compare Intervention B with Intervention C at several different time points or sessions in an alternating replicated series (i.e., BCBC . . . BC). The designation of the phase labels as B and C is somewhat arbitrary for, as was noted earlier, the "baseline" phase might actually consist of some known intervention that is already operating in the context of the experiment. The important issue in comparing two intervention conditions is whether the manipulated

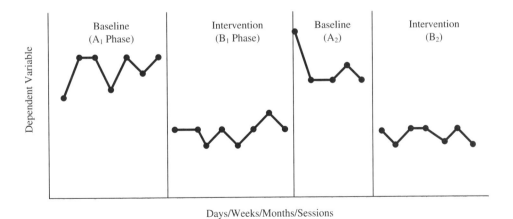

Figure 2.1.   Hypothetical data for an ABAB design with one experimental unit.

variable (Intervention B vs. Intervention C) is strong enough to produce clear, predicted, and different intervention effects, given the absence of a baseline condition. Some regard this test as a higher criterion of evidence for evidence-based interventions (Kazdin, 2004).

The within-series ABAB . . . AB design (or its ABCABC . . . ABC extension) is typically designated as a *simple phase-change* design structure. However, it is also possible for the researcher to structure more *complex phase-change* strategies in this class of within-series designs. In all cases, the designs in this domain operate under the same logic; more complex phase-change structures allow the investigator to examine the effects of multiple interventions and/or interventions compared with each other. In this way the researcher can manipulate various combinations of interventions that are tested against each of their individual components, as the following example illustrates.

Consider an alternating two-conditions within-series design where a researcher compares one intervention, designated here as B, with an intervention "package" that consists of three components (here, B+C+D). The researcher examines (through a within-series replication) the intervention package across phases of the study using the same basic design logic [i.e., B B+C+D B B+C+D . . . B B+C+D] as that for the ABAB . . . AB design. The conditions compared in the experiment can encompass more components, depending on the nature of the intervention "package" under investigation (e.g., B+C+D+E+F+G vs. any of the individual components). Note that this design variation includes the same replication criterion when extended to multiple within-phase intervention components as when it is applied with only one intervention component within a phase.

The within-series design is actually a very common strategy in psychology and education research and has been used numerous times with different participant populations and in different contexts, especially in applications of applied behavior analysis techniques and procedures. However, these within-series design structures have some potential shortcomings. A major issue is that they require a withdrawal of the intervention as part of the replication requirement (designated here as the B phase in an ABAB design). However, for a variety of reasons, withdrawal of the intervention may not result in the outcome measures returning to baseline levels. Depending on how this non-return to baseline is manifested in terms of the series' level and trend, it may be more difficult to draw inferences about the magnitude and extent of the intervention effect, or even to determine whether any intervention effect occurred. To deal with this issue, the within-series design typically is not generally recommended under conditions where participants would be expected to acquire certain skills or where learning new behaviors would likely result in their not returning to baseline levels of performance. In other words, the design has some features that the researcher should be cognizant of and take into account when considering this option. Of even greater concern perhaps, a within-series design might not be appropriate under conditions where withdrawal of the intervention is unethical or would provide physical or psychological discomfort for the participants in the investigation.

Another type of within-series design, mentioned only in passing here, is the *changing criterion design* (CCD)—a within-series variation that is seldom used outside of its applied behavior analysis origins. In its most straight-forward application, this design attempts to rule out threats to the study's internal validity by providing opportunities for the outcome measure to covary with changing criteria that are scheduled in a series of predetermined steps or "sub-phases" within the study (Hall & Fox, 1977; Hartmann & Hall, 1976). The most basic form of the CCD begins with a baseline (A) phase, followed by a series of intervention (B) phases, with the intervention implemented continuously over time as changing criterion levels for "improved" outcome-measure performance are specified. Repeated replications of these stepwise changes and corresponding changes in the outcome measure argue for the credibility of the intervention effect across time.

Between-Series Single-Case Designs

Between-series designs are structured to provide a comparison of two or more conditions (e.g., a baseline and intervention or two intervention series) in a more rapid fashion than is possible in conventional within-series designs. Two applications are the *alternating intervention design* (AID) and the *simultaneous intervention design* (SID). The AID is the most frequently used design option and allows researchers to expose a participant to different interventions administered in close proximity for equal periods of time (Barlow & Hayes, 1979; Hayes et al., 1999). Specifically, in the design the researcher might establish a baseline and then alternate between two intervention series for a brief time. For example, one intervention could be administered in a morning session and a second intervention in an afternoon session, over several days. The interventions are alternated systematically, by counterbalancing, or as we will suggest below for its true experimental counterpart, by randomly assigning the two conditions to the study's different sessions. With the AID, the researcher can compare two or more conditions or interventions relatively quickly. This strategy avoids some of the major disadvantages of other multiple-intervention within-series designs, where (as was discussed earlier) intervention withdrawal for an extended period of time is often necessary before a second intervention can be introduced. Figure 2.2 illustrates a two-intervention AID with hypothetical data.

The SID, a unique application in the between-series domain, involves presenting interventions to the units simultaneously (Kazdin & Hartmann, 1977). For example, a researcher may present two rewards to a participant simultaneously with the option for the participant to select the more preferred reward. The simultaneous presentations are repeated over a designated time period and arranged in either counterbalanced or random order. The simultaneous presentation of interventions in the design structure, however, does not ensure that the participant is exposed to all interventions for equal time amounts or durations. Instead, the design guarantees that the different interventions are simultaneously and equally "available" in each session, with the participant able to select the particular intervention to which she or he prefers to be exposed. Thus, it is possible that the SID could provide a researcher with information on client responsiveness to interventions where differential preferences are likely to exist. Like the AID, the SID is not restricted to two conditions

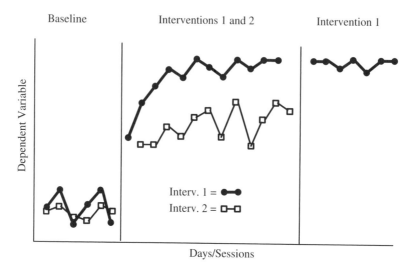

Figure 2.2. Hypothetical example of an alternating intervention design. During the baseline phase a series of alternating "Intervention 1" and "Intervention 2" baseline assessments is made (e.g., during a morning and afternoon session over six successive days). During the intervention phase, the two interventions are administered in an alternating fashion (e.g., in 12 morning and 12 afternoon sessions) over several days, with the data plotted by intervention type. In the final phase, the more effective intervention (Intervention 1) is implemented.

or interventions and so a researcher can make available several interventions and compare a participant's "preferences" for the different interventions. However, the conditions and implementation of such a multiple-intervention study can become quite complex and therefore, for practical reasons, single-case research based on the SID and AID typically includes only two interventions. Illustrative applications of these designs are found in numerous places in the literature and are discussed in several sources (see Hayes et al., 1999; Kazdin, 2011).

Combined-Series Single-Case Designs

With combined-series designs the researcher makes both within- and between-series comparisons to draw valid inferences from the data. The most common design in this domain is called the *multiple-baseline design* (MBD) and includes a simple within-phase element while replicating the intervention across participants (or other units), settings, or behaviors (or more generally, other outcome measures). The internal validity of the design is strengthened through a staggering or sequential introduction of the interventions across time, with desired changes in the outcome measure occurring repeatedly and selectively with the successive intervention introductions (see Levin, 1992, for additional discussion of the favorable internal-validity characteristics associated with this design). The MBD is typically structured so that at least four replications are scheduled within the experiment, although applications of the design can range from two to several (i.e., more than four) replications, depending on the research questions, circumstances of the experiment, and practical and logistical issues. As will be mentioned later, the extent to which the intervention's effect is similar across replications helps to establish different aspects of the external validity (generalizability) of the intervention. Numerous examples of the design have been published in the literature and are discussed in greater detail in several sources (e.g., Hayes et al., 1999). Figure 2.3 illustrates the MBD across participants with hypothetical data.

Incorporating Randomization Into Single-Case Intervention Designs

In this section of the chapter, we present a case for incorporating randomization into single-case intervention designs, thereby strengthening the causal conclusions that can be drawn from them. We first provide an overview of the importance of randomization, describe the various types of randomization that can be considered for single-case designs, and then discuss specific randomization strategies that can be accommodated by the within-, between-, and combined-series designs that were presented previously. Examples from the published single-case research design literature are presented to illustrate how some form of randomization can be built into these designs.

A Stage Model of Educational/Psychological Intervention Research: Applications to Single-Case Designs

In a recent chapter in the *Handbook of Psychology*, Levin and Kratochwill (2013) offered a number of suggestions directed at improving the "awful reputation" of educational research (Kaestle, 1993). Specifically, they recommended that intervention researchers should design and conduct research that fulfills the following:

> (1) makes explicit different research "stages," each of which is associated with its own assumptions, purposes, methodologies, and standards of evidence;
> (2) concerns itself with research credibility through high standards of internal validity;
> (3) concerns itself with research creditability through high standards of external validity and educational/societal importance; and most significantly
> (4) includes a critical stage that has heretofore been missing in the vast majority of intervention research, namely, a randomized "classroom trials" link (modeled after the "clinical trials" stage of medical research) between the initial development and limited testing of the intervention and the prescription and implementation of it. (pp. 477–478)

In our conceptual framework (originally developed by Levin & O'Donnell, 1999, and presented here as Figure 2.4), the *randomized classroom trials stage* refers to a broad range of educational and psychological randomized experiments,

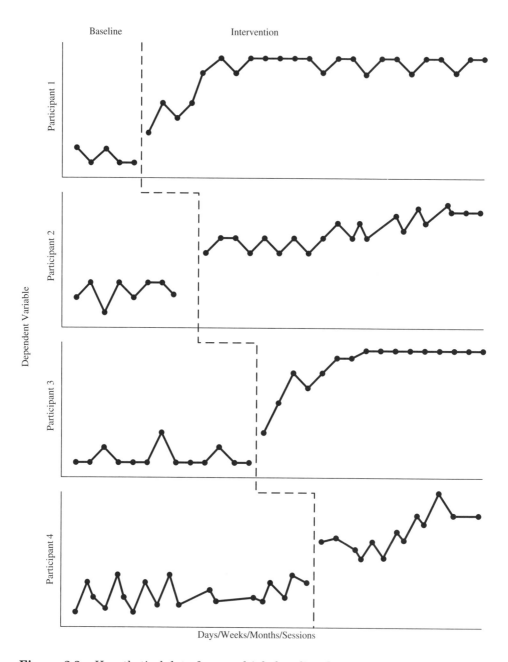

Figure 2.3. Hypothetical data for a multiple-baseline design across units, in which the intervention is introduced to four units at different points in time. Note the repeated and selective increase in outcome-measure performance, in temporal correspondence with the intervention's introduction.

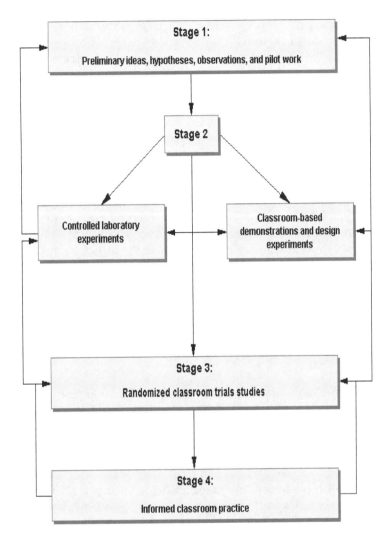

Figure 2.4. A stage model of educational intervention research. From "What to Do About Educational Research's Credibility Gaps?" By J. R. Levin and A. M. O'Donnell, 1999, *Issues in Education: Contributions from Educational Psychology*, 5, p. 205. Copyright 1999 by Information Age Publishing. Reprinted with permission.

ranging from those with the experimental units comprised of individual partic-ipants to those consisting of one or more classrooms, schools, or communities. Hereafter we refer to this stage as the *randomized trials* stage of credible inter-vention research. We argue that the scientific credibility of traditional single-case designs would be greatly enhanced by including a randomized-trial component in the evaluation of experimental interventions or programs.

As was noted earlier, the methodological and analytic units are important desiderata in our case for extending randomization to single-case designs. The researcher must first determine the units upon which random assignment to the study's conditions or levels are based, where the methodological units could refer to a single participant in a behavior-modification study, dyads or small groups of students in a tutoring context, classrooms and schools in a study examining alternative classroom management strategies, or school districts where various institutional or systemic changes are being evaluated. Alternatively, and as will be seen in our discussion of specific designs, randomization might also be represented by the within- and between-series sequences in which the study's intervention conditions are implemented, as well as by the assignment of units to different "intervention start points" within the time series. Following a determination of the desired methodological units and the conduct of the experiment, the researcher must then adopt a statistical strategy for which the methodological and analytic units are congruent. In the present context, by "congruent" we mean that studies in which interventions are assigned randomly and administered independently to individuals are analyzed by statistical methods that treat individuals as the units of analysis, whereas studies involving the assignment of interventions and administration of them to intact groups are analyzed by statistical methods that take the group structure (or *cluster*) into account. The issue of specific "units-appropriate" (Levin, 2005, p. 13) single-case statistical strategies is discussed in more detail in Chapter 5, this volume.

Considerations in Incorporating Randomization Into Single-Case Designs

Incorporating randomization into single-case designs requires a more flexible type of thinking about experimental randomization, in that—in contrast to traditional group designs—with single-case designs there frequently are not multiple independent units to be randomly assigned to the study's intervention conditions (but see subsequent discussion). Specifically, and as was just noted, what *can* be randomly assigned (instead of units to intervention conditions) are the within-series sequencing of A and B phases, the specific time points at which each A and B phase commences, or both in multiple-unit replication designs (see Chapter 5, this volume; Dugard, File, & Todman, 2012; Edgington, 1975, 1992; Edgington & Onghena, 2007; Koehler & Levin, 1998; Levin & Wampold, 1999; Max & Onghena, 1999; Onghena & Edgington, 2005). As in Chapter 5 of this volume, we refer to the former randomization scheme as *phase randomization* and to the latter as *start-point randomization*. With these two schemes at hand, a single-case intervention researcher is able to incorporate randomization into a design structure that does not, on the surface, possess the internal validity criteria of a true experiment (e.g., such as in an AB design). In addition, in single-case intervention-comparison experiments where more than one independent unit/case is available, random assignment of cases to intervention conditions (*case randomization*) can be combined with the two other randomization schemes just described. We revisit each of these randomization schemes and associated issues throughout the chapter.

A presentation by Reichardt (2006) on "size-of-effect factors" in intervention research further clarifies how randomization can be applied in single-case designs. He noted that an intervention effect is a function of four factors, consisting of recipient, setting, time, and outcome measures. The application of the earlier discussed MBD nicely illustrates how the effect of an intervention can vary according to these four factors.

The *recipient* refers to the entities or units (typically, but not necessarily, participants) that receive the intervention and to which the outcome measures are administered. In addition to an intervention effect being attributed to the intervention per se, it is also a function of the participants inasmuch as the effect can be moderated by the study's recipients/units. In our earlier discussed MBD across participants, the researcher hopes that the effect of the intervention (and its magnitude) will be replicated in each series, and therefore can be thought to generalize across recipients/units. The extent to which the intervention effect is similar across recipients helps to enhance the *population* external validity of the intervention (Bracht & Glass, 1968).

As Reichardt (2006) detailed, the *setting* refers to the environment or situational context in which the intervention is initially implemented and subsequently assessed with respect to the various outcome measures of the study. The setting can refer to both physical characteristics of the research investigation and functional characteristics that occur in the context of the intervention. In the application of the MBD where the intervention is implemented across settings, the intervention may have unique effects on the recipients and/or units, depending on the setting in which it is applied (e.g., home, school, community). The extent to which intervention effects are similar in the study's different settings helps to increase the intervention's *ecological* external validity (Bracht & Glass, 1968). Alternatively, the extent to which the effects differ across settings can represent a desirable *discriminant* validity aspect of the intervention (Campbell & Fiske, 1959; Levin, 1992).

The *time* dimension refers to

> the chronological times at which both [an intervention] is implemented and an outcome [measure] is assessed, which thereby specifies the lag between these two times. The size of [an intervention] effect can differ both for different times in history and for different time lags. (Reichardt, 2006, p. 2)

Again, a key internal-validity requirement of the MBD is the intervention's demonstration of a *selective* effect, namely the demonstration of an effect only when the intervention is applied to a recipient/unit at its personally targeted time period or start point. In the MBD across participants, the extent to which the intervention effect is similar for participants with differently staggered intervention start points helps to establish the intervention's ecological and *referent generality* external validity (Snow, 1974).

Finally, the size of an intervention effect is typically assessed across a number of pre-selected *outcome measures*. The size of the effect may be similar or different from one outcome measure to the next, depending on the measure's sensitivity, reliability, and *construct validity* (Cronbach & Meehl, 1955), as well as other factors. In the MBD application across behaviors (or more generally, across different outcome measures), either similar or different effects of the intervention can result. The extent to which an intervention produces similar effects across outcome measures helps to establish the referent generality external validity and *convergent validity* (Cronbach & Meehl, 1955) of the intervention. Conversely, the extent to which an intervention effect differs across outcome measures in prespecified ways can represent a positive discriminant validity credibility feature of the intervention (Levin, 1992).

Reichardt (2006) labeled these four categories the "size-of-effect factors" and advanced the *principle of parallelism*, which states that "if a methodological option exists for any one of the four size-of-effect factors of the recipient, setting, time, and outcome variable, a parallel option exists for each of the other three factors as well" (p. 2). An important consideration based on Reichardt's work is that in an ideal comparison an unambiguous determination of the intervention effect requires that everything other than the intervention remains the same at a given point in time. However, from a practical standpoint the four study factors that Reichardt has specified (recipient, setting, time, and outcome measure) will typically vary with the intervention. Nevertheless, as Reichardt argued, it is possible—and desirable—to take these factors into account when interpreting size-of-effect outcome comparisons.

In particular, the *prominent* size-of-effect factor in the four types of comparison has a relationship to randomization and each can vary either randomly or nonrandomly with the intervention conditions. That is, "if the prominent size-of-effect factor varies randomly with the [intervention] conditions, the comparison is called a *randomized experiment*. If the prominent size-of-effect factor varies nonrandomly with the [intervention], the comparison is called a *nonrandomized experiment*" (Reichardt, 2006, p. 4). Reichardt further distinguished between two types of nonrandomized experiment: "those based on an explicit quantitative ordering and those not based on an explicit quantitative ordering" (Reichardt, 2006, p. 4). The 12 possible combinations of prominent size-of-effect factors (recipients, times, settings, outcome variables) and type of experiment and assignment to intervention conditions (random, nonrandom explicit quantitative ordering, nonrandom no explicit quantitative ordering) are presented in Table 2.2. There it can be observed that if the intervention conditions are assigned randomly to either recipients, times, settings, or outcome measures, then these comparisons represent a randomized experiment (referred to in the first column of Table 2.2). However, as Reichardt noted, varying an intervention randomly across a particular prominent size-of-effect factor will not necessarily guarantee that the intervention varies randomly across the other size-of-effect factors. For example, recipients may be randomly assigned to intervention conditions, but if there are nonrandom conditions-related differences on any of the other factors (times, settings, or outcome variables) the scientific integrity of the experiment will be compromised.

Table 2.2 (from Reichardt, 2006) also includes interrupted time-series designs in the "nonrandom explicit quantitative ordering" column. Reichardt (2006) indicated that when time is a prominent size-of-effect factor, a time-series design is composed of days (or sessions) prior to and following some structured aspects of the design (e.g., an intervention). It is worth pointing out, however, that Reichardt's characterization of a "time-series design" is its most "basic" operationalization, namely, an interrupted time-series design (or what we have called here the AB design), with the intervention effect manifested as a break, discontinuity, or "interruption" in the pre- and postintervention regression lines at the point of intervention. Although Reichardt was correct in noting that interrupted time-series intervention designs—with their

Table 2.2. A Typology of Comparisons

Prominent size-of-effect factor	Random	Nonrandom	
		Explicit quantitative ordering	No explicit quantitative ordering
Recipients	Randomized recipient design	Regression-discontinuity design	Nonequivalent recipient design
Times	Randomized time design	Interrupted time-series design	Nonequivalent time design
Settings	Randomized setting design	Discontinuity across settings design	Nonequivalent setting design
Outcome variables	Randomized outcome variable design	Discontinuity across outcome variables design	Nonequivalent variable design

Note. From "The Principle of Parallelism in the Design of Studies to Estimate Treatment Effects," by C. S. Reichardt, 2006, *Psychological Methods, 11*, p. 5. Copyright 2006 by the American Psychological Association.

nonrandomized time comparisons based on an explicit quantitative ordering— are most frequently implemented in the clinical and applied literature (e.g., behavior analysis research), we illustrate in the remainder of this chapter how randomization variations (in consideration of the four effect-size factors) can be incorporated into such designs to transform them into more scientifically credible randomized experiments.

Specifically, we show how single-case interrupted time-series designs can be structured to satisfy one or more of the randomized experimental design criteria outlined in the first column of Table 2.2. In particular, and as is illustrated in the next section, both recipients/units and times can be structured randomly to allow a randomized trial to be conducted with the three classes of single-case design (within-, between-, and combined-series). Other features of the design (i.e., settings and outcome measures) can and should remain constant so as not to compromise the internal validity of the study. For example, for the combined-series MBD across settings or behaviors to be regarded as a randomized experiment, the order–sequence in which the settings/behaviors are examined would need to be randomly determined.

Illustrations of Randomized Single-Case Intervention Designs

In this section of the chapter we illustrate how randomization can be implemented in single-case intervention designs with reference to the three design classes reviewed earlier: within-, between-, and combined-series design elements. We present a number of randomization schemes (many of which were also described by Edgington, 1992, and Edgington & Onghena, 2007), followed by design-option variations and extensions within each of those schemes. For each design option, once again consideration must be given to the methodological units on which randomization is based within the experiment (e.g., individuals, small groups, classrooms, schools), as well as to the other size-of-effect factors noted by Reichardt (2006). As was just mentioned, we will demonstrate that it is possible to structure single-case intervention designs in a way that satisfies the randomized experimental design criteria outlined in the first column of Table 2.2. In particular, any of the four size-of-effect factors can accommodate some appropriate type of randomization.

A few preliminary remarks are in order. First, we intend the following single-case intervention design randomization strategies to be representative, and not exhaustive, of those that could be implemented. Second, in the variations for which we provide randomization illustrations, we consider the possibility of applying some form of either *simple* or *blocked randomization*. Compared with nonrandomized single-case designs, both randomized variations are generally more scientifically credible. The blocked variations are even more methodologically sound and have the potential to provide statistical power advantages (Levin, Ferron, & Gafurov, 2014; Levin et al., 2012; Levin & Wampold, 1999), analogous to those associated with randomized block designs relative to completely randomized designs in the traditional experimental design literature (e.g., Keppel & Wickens, 2004; Kirk, 1995; Levin, 1997; Maxwell & Delaney, 2004). Third, several units-appropriate single-case statistical analysis strategies (see Chapter 5, this volume; Levin et al., 2012) have been developed on a design-by-design basis. Finally, the number of units–cases in the design is represented by N, the number of within-conditions interventions (either intervention and control/baseline or alternative interventions) by c, the number of between-series intervention conditions (where applicable) by k, the number of time periods or sessions by t, and the number of potential intervention start points (where applicable) by s.

Within-Series Randomized Phase Designs

RANDOMIZED ABAB . . . AB DESIGN. It will be remembered that a common single-case within-series design possesses an ABAB . . . AB design structure (see Figure 2.1). Incorporation of randomization into this design is relatively straightforward but requires that the series' condition replications (represented in this design by sessions or time periods) are determined on a random basis (Edgington, 1992; Levin, Marascuilo, & Hubert, 1978; Onghena, 1992). This is analogous to the process of randomly assigning treatment-administration orders to participants in conventional group designs. The *randomized phase* within-series design illustrates an a priori randomized sequence in the ABAB . . . AB design with a single case. For a simple phase-randomization scheme, the A and B conditions (assumed in the following examples to be equally represented) are randomly assigned to the t time periods, with the consequence that there is no restriction in the number of A or B time periods that can follow one another consecutively. For a blocked phase-randomization scheme, successive time periods are considered in blocks of two, with one A and one B session randomly assigned to each pair of time periods. This assignment procedure guarantees that conditions of the same type (A or B) cannot appear in more than two consecutive time periods. A hypothetical randomized single-unit ABAB . . . AB design is presented in Exhibit 2.1.

Exhibit 2.1.   Randomized ABAB . . . AB Design

Simple Randomization
ABBBABABAA

Blocked Randomization
ABABBAABBA

Note. $N = 1$ case, $c = 2$ within-series conditions, and $t = 10$ time periods.

The incorporation of randomization into within-series designs is relatively straightforward but adds some complexities to the research process. Depending on the experimental question and other practical realities of applied research, the following considerations need to be addressed. First, most behavioral and instructional intervention implementations require that an initial baseline–no intervention A phase precedes the first intervention B phase (see also the following AID discussion). Second, the randomization scheme and corresponding statistical analysis that are applied by the researcher must be adapted to satisfy that requirement. The randomized ABAB . . . AB design and its variations could be modified accordingly so that it commences with one or more A (baseline/warm-up/adaptation) phases, if that is deemed desirable or necessary by the researcher. In such cases, the experiment proper (i.e., the actual experimental sequence of randomized A and B phases) would follow an initial sequence of one or more mandatory A phases, with the stipulation that the researcher's interpretation of the results (and the statistical analysis of the data, when applicable) be modified to suit the experiment proper.[2]

As a published example of a traditional single-case ABAB intervention design with a true baseline condition, Thompson, Cotnoir-Bichelman, McKerchar, Tate, and Dancho (2007, Experiment 2) conducted a study in which two infants were taught to replace their typical crying and whining "demands" with simple infant-initiated signs, using delayed prompting and reinforcement techniques. Replication of the effects occurred within the ABAB sequence, thereby meeting the criterion proposed by Horner et al. (2005). In accord with our immediately preceding discussion, the authors could have incorporated randomization into their design. Assuming that the researchers elected to include (a) an initial A phase (baseline, consisting of reinforcers provided whenever crying or whining occurred) before the signing intervention (B) was introduced and (b) two adjacent A and B phases, then the following randomized ABAB . . . AB design could have been constructed. First, require that one or more initial A periods be administered, represented here by A′. Then, randomly assign As and Bs until two

---

[2]With these design modifications and stipulations in mind, the present form of randomization will likely prove to be more practicable in four-phase ABAB intervention designs when the A and B phases consist of two different intervention conditions than when they consist of a baseline and intervention condition, respectively (but see Chapter 5, this volume). At the same time, the possibility of applying our previously noted second form of randomization for the ABAB design—namely, start-point randomization—has been incorporated into other within-series designs and will comprise a major topic discussed later in the chapter.

adjacent A and B phases are produced. With a simple randomization scheme, the sequence might turn out to be something like A′BBABAAAB; whereas for a blocked randomization scheme, it might be A′BAABABAB. Either randomization scheme would likely have worked well in this experiment because the effect of the intervention (sign training) was relatively rapid and short returns to baselines were achieved, thereby allowing more phase replications to occur. Other randomization possibilities could have been added to Thompson et al.'s (2007) research in that the authors had two infants available for each of the study's two experiments. In particular, and as is discussed in the later "replicated randomized ABAB . . . AB design" section, in each experiment the two infants could have been assigned *different* random A and B phase sequences (see also Footnote 2).

RANDOMIZED ABCABC . . . ABC DESIGN. The use of randomization in the single-unit AB . . . AB design can be extended to the inclusion of three or more within-series conditions, such as when two interventions are compared with each other and with a baseline condition. In such cases, randomization could be applied to the three conditions in either a simple or blocked fashion. With the latter, the three conditions (A, B, and C) are randomized in blocks of three, which guarantees that a unit will be assigned no more than two consecutive time periods of the same intervention condition. This example is illustrated in Exhibit 2.2.

As a published example of a multiple-intervention design, Manuel, Sunseri, Olson, and Scolari (2007) conducted a study in which they developed interventions to increase students' selection of reusable dinnerware in a university cafeteria. Some 75 observation sessions were conducted, with an average of 251 students observed per session. The study consisted of nine phases, with A = baseline and various intervention components involving B = increased counter space and signs promoting reusable tableware, C = environmental impact posters, D = employee prompting of cafeteria patrons to reuse dinnerware, and E = experimenter prompting with motivational signs. In particular, the authors implemented an ABA B+C AB B+D B+D+E B design to evaluate intervention effects with respect to two outcome measures (i.e., students' selection of reusable cups and reusable plates). Technically, the design did not adhere to the replication standards stated earlier. Nevertheless, our focus here is on the notion that the researchers could have incorporated a randomized order of intervention introduction into their design, insofar as the internal validity of the design would be strengthened by comparing the several within-series intervention conditions in an unbiased fashion (i.e., in a time-series sequence that

Exhibit 2.2. Randomized ABCABC . . . ABC Design

Simple Randomization
ACABBBCCBCAACBA

Blocked Randomization
ACBCBAABCBACBAC

Note. $N = 1$ case, $c = 3$ within-series conditions, and $t = 15$ time periods.

Exhibit 2.3.   Replicated Randomized ABAB . . . AB Design

Within-Unit Simple Randomization
Case 1: ABBBABABAA
Case 2: BBBAAAABAB
Case 3: ABABABAABB
Case 4: AABBBBAAAB

Within-Unit Blocked Randomization
Case 1: ABBABABAAB
Case 2: BABABAABAB
Case 3: BAABABBAAB
Case 4: ABABBAABBA

Note. $N = 4$ cases, $c = 2$ within-series conditions, and $t = 10$ time periods.

is random, rather than one that is researcher determined). Moreover, because the study was conducted with a large number of students, the researchers might have been able to develop a replicated randomized intervention design (as discussed in the next section), in either its simple or blocked form, thereby increasing the internal validity of their experiment. As an aside, it is interesting to note that the authors invoked single-case methodology and terminology in presenting their results graphically, while at the same time calculating and reporting conventional effect sizes based on the outcome means and standard deviations (i.e., Cohen ds).

REPLICATED RANDOMIZED ABAB . . . AB DESIGN. Another option with within-series designs is to apply randomization in a multiple-case study. In that situation, there is the same within-series randomization structure as was just illustrated except that more than one case participates in the study (as was true for the two infants in each of the earlier discussed Thompson et al., 2007, experiments). In their study, each infant could have been assigned randomly to his/her own within-series sequence of the design, either in a simple (unrestricted) or blocked (restricted) fashion. This replicated randomized within-series design could, for example, be structured as shown in Exhibit 2.3. The design could encompass additional intervention conditions, cases, or time periods, depending on the number of cases available, the resources of the researcher, and research-specific logistical issues, among other factors. Generally speaking, the more replications that are included in the design (represented by either the number of cases or the number of time periods), the more statistical power the researcher will have in the statistical analysis.[3]

---

[3]Greater statistical power with additional cases or time periods will be achieved as long as the intervention effect size is assumed to remain constant across both of those factors (i.e., there is no interaction involving the intervention and either cases or time periods). In the special class of single-case designs that we later present here, for which the intervention start point is randomly determined for each case, increased statistical power is also associated with a greater number of potential intervention start points (Lall & Levin, 2004).

Note that in these randomized ABAB . . . AB designs, the sequence in which conditions (A and B) are administered is randomized in either a simple or blocked fashion, in contrast to the systematically alternating administration of conditions in traditional ABAB . . . AB designs (see Levin et al., 2012). Potential confounding of the intervention with Reichardt's (2006) time, settings, or outcome measures size-of-effect factors prevent the latter (traditional ABAB . . . AB designs) but not the former (randomized ABAB . . . AB designs) from being regarded as a randomized experiment. Similar comments apply to Reichardt's (2006) traditional within-subjects letter-pronunciation example, where for the two-condition experiment to be considered a scientifically valid "randomized" experiment, the specific letters would need to be presented in a random order (ideally, individually randomized on a unit-by-unit basis as well) to avoid a confounding with either time or outcome measures.

RANDOMIZED DESIGNS WITH A WITHIN-SERIES FACTORIAL STRUCTURE. Factorial within-series intervention designs can be constructed to answer research questions about both the separate and joint effects of different intervention types or interventions combined with other factors. As a published example of a single-case factorial design, Twardosz, Cataldo, and Risley (1974, Experiment 3) used three successive within-series designs (consisting of 19, 14, and 13 days, respectively) to investigate how two specific combinations of illumination (A_1 = light, A_2 = dark) and sound (B_1 = quiet, B_2 = noise) affected the sleeping patterns of 13 preschool children. In particular, the researchers were most interested in comparing a light, noisy combination with a dark, quiet combination, as shown in Exhibit 2.4.

Twardosz et al. (1974) provided a rationale for investigating the two particular illumination-sound combinations that they did. If, instead their interest had been in examining both the separate and joint contributions of illumination and sound, they could have adopted a randomized single-series 2×2 factorial design (Edgington, 1992). Suppose, for example, that 12 time periods are included. With a simple randomization scheme, an unrestricted sequence of an illumination condition (A_1 = light or A_2 = dark) combined with a sound conditions (B_1 = quiet or B_2 = noise) is allowed. In contrast, with a blocked randomization scheme, each possible combination of the A and B levels can be represented in four consecutive time periods, and so with 12 time periods each AB combination would be represented three times. The design is illustrated in Exhibit 2.5.

CONSIDERATIONS IN WITHIN-SERIES RANDOMIZED PHASE DESIGNS. Adoption of within-series designs presents two domains of challenges to researchers, namely (a) those associated with use of randomization in systematically struc-

Exhibit 2.4. Twardosz et al.'s (1974) Illumination/Sound Study 3

	Day		
	1 19	20 33	34 46
Child 1–13	A_1B_2	A_2B_1	A_1B_2

Note. Based on $N = 13$ preschool children observed over $t = 46$ days.

Exhibit 2.5.   Randomized 2×2 Factorial Design

Simple Randomization
$A_1B_2\ A_2B_2\ A_2B_2\ A_1B_1\ A_1B_2\ A_1B_1\ A_2B_1\ A_1B_2\ A_2B_2\ A_2B_1\ A_2B_1\ A_1B_1$

Blocked Randomization
$A_2B_1\ A_2B_2\ A_1B_1\ A_1B_2\ A_1B_1\ A_2B_1\ A_2B_2\ A_1B_2\ A_1B_2\ A_2B_1\ A_2B_2\ A_1B_1$

Note. $N = 1$ Case, $c_1 = 2$ within-series levels of A (illumination), $c_2 = 2$ within-series of B (noise), and $t = 12$ time periods.

tured designs and (b) those associated with a within-series replication specification (i.e., the replication criterion of Horner et al., 2005). The former issue was discussed previously in relation to intervention experiments that do and do not readily permit for randomized A (baseline) and B (intervention) phases and, in particular, with respect to the common requirement that such experiments generally must begin with a baseline phase. The latter issue is one that is well known in the research literature (e.g., Kazdin, 1982; Kratochwill, 1978) and requires use of outcome measures that "reverse" or "return to baseline" levels when the intervention is withdrawn during the return to baseline phase. For this reason the researcher must pre-select a design where exposure to the intervention is not likely to cause such dramatic changes in behavior or acquisition of knowledge or skills that return to baseline phase levels would be difficult or unlikely. Also, there may be ethical considerations that must be addressed when an intervention is withdrawn especially in cases where participants and/or staff are at risk of injury or harm.

As was noted earlier, in behavior-change research contexts, the unit's partial or complete return to the baseline level (following changes attributable to the intervention) strengthens the credibility of imputing a causal connection between intervention and outcome. However, should such returns to baseline not occur, researchers may be limited in the number of within-series replications that they can schedule. That is, although the logic of the design depends on replication, there may be limited numbers of these replications obtained for an appropriate and sufficiently powerful statistical test to be conducted. Another potential problem is that the amount of time required to conduct the ideal intervention experiment may be excessive, given the desired number of replications that need to be included. Therefore, randomized within-series designs may work best when phases consist of short sessions consisting of the unit responding in a relatively rapid fashion to the intervention (as was the case in the Thompson et al., 2007, experiment and as could be structured in the next design type to be presented).

Between-Series Randomized Phase Designs

RANDOMIZED ALTERNATING INTERVENTION DESIGNS. The earlier discussed AID is the most frequently adopted design in the between-series domain and will be the focus of our discussion here. In that design, the researcher begins with a baseline period to establish the performance level with which

Exhibit 2.6.   Randomized Alternating Intervention Design

	Day						
	1	2	3	4	5	6	7
Simple Randomization							
Morning	A′	A	B	B	A	B	B
Afternoon	B	A	A	A	B	A	
Blocked Randomization							
Morning	A′	B	A	A	B	B	A
Afternoon	A	B	B	A	A	B	

Note. In the randomized versions of this design, the random sequencing of six A and six B time
periods occurs following the required initial A′ time period. $N = 1$ case, $c = 2$ within-series
conditions, and $t = 13$ time periods (7 morning and 6 afternoon).

the intervention condition(s) will be compared (see Figure 2.2). It will be
remembered that the AID involves a more rapid alternation of the phases
relative to the within-series applications discussed above. With the incorporation of randomization into this design, the researcher basically follows
the same procedures that were outlined for the randomized within-series
ABAB . . . AB design, with one important difference: If A truly represents
a "baseline" or "control" condition, then the time series must begin with an
A phase (here, A′). That is, following an initially mandated baseline/control
(A′) phase, the researcher then randomly assigns time periods of the design
to compare the intervention (B) phase with A′.[4]

For example, consider an intervention-versus-baseline comparison in a
randomized AID design with a single case measured over 13 time periods
(7 days consisting of seven morning and six afternoon sessions). In this experiment, a blocked randomization of the intervention could be applied either to
just one dimension of the design (logically, time of day on a day-to-day basis) to
produce a *partially counterbalanced* design or to both dimensions (across and
within days) to produce a *completely counterbalanced* design. The latter double-blocking approach requires an even number of days excluding the initial A′
baseline session, and adopting that approach (as is illustrated in Exhibit 2.6)
would control for Reichardt's (2006) setting and outcome measure size-of-effect
factor biases and would impart a "scientifically credible" status to the design.

Similar to the previously discussed randomized within-series applications
that are extended to more than two-condition comparisons, the randomized
AID (or SID) can be applied when the researcher wishes to compare three
within-series conditions (either a baseline and two intervention conditions or
three intervention conditions). In this case, randomization would be applied
to the three conditions of the experiment (here, breakfast, lunch, and dinner
sessions). With a double-blocking procedure, a multiple of 6 days (excluding

---

[4]The same comments apply to the earlier discussed SID, for which the randomization rationale and
procedures follow those presented here.

Exhibit 2.7. Randomized Alternating Intervention Design

	Day						
	1	2	3	4	5	6	7
Simple Randomization							
Breakfast	A′	B	C	B	A	C	B
Lunch	C	A	C	B	A	A	
Dinner	C	A	B	B	C	A	
Blocked Randomization							
Breakfast	A′	C	A	B	A	B	C
Lunch	B	C	A	B	C	A	
Dinner	A	B	C	C	A	B	

Note. In the randomized versions of this design, the random sequencing of six A, six B, and six C time periods occurs following the required initial A′ time period. $N = 1$ case, $c = 3$ within-series conditions, and t = time periods (7 breakfast, 6 lunch, and 6 dinner).

the initial A′ baseline day) is required to produce a completely counterbalanced design, as is illustrated in Exhibit 2.7. Note that two interventions can be compared relatively quickly within the structure of this design, which may circumvent our previously discussed concerns about extended replications in the within-series applications.

REPLICATED RANDOMIZED ALTERNATING INTERVENTION DESIGN. It is also possible to extend the randomized AID (and SID) to replications across cases, as was earlier illustrated with the randomized within-series designs. With this extension, the double-blocked randomization process (illustrated here) would be conducted on a case-by-case basis and would require an even number of days (excluding the initial A′ baseline day) to be completely counterbalanced. The extension of the randomized AID across cases is illustrated in Exhibit 2.8 with $N = 3$ cases and a comparison of a baseline and intervention condition over 7 days, consisting of 7 morning and 6 afternoon sessions.

As a published example of a replicated AID, Fisher, Kodak, and Moore (2007) compared three methods of teaching discriminations to two children with autism: trial and error (a control condition), least-to-most prompting, and identity matching, The trial-and-error method basically involved presenting the participant with a sample stimulus (a picture of someone) and asked him/her to point to the named person, with no feedback provided for correct and incorrect responses. In the least-to-most condition, correct responding resulted in access to a reward whereas incorrect responding led to a modeled prompt with the correct picture. The identity matching condition included the least-to-most condition procedures but added a task in which the experimenter held a picture that was identical to the correct comparison stimulus and then named the stimulus. In a 34-session AID format, the researchers compared the percent of correct spoken-word-to-picture relations by children in the three intervention conditions. A visual–graphical analysis revealed that the identity-matching condition was superior to the two other conditions for

Exhibit 2.8. Randomized Alternating Intervention Design

	1	2	3	Day 4	5	6	7
Within-Unit Simple Randomization							
Case *1*							
Morning	A′	B	B	B	A	A	B
Afternoon	B	A	B	A	A	A	
Case *2*							
Morning	A′	A	B	B	B	A	B
Afternoon	B	A	A	A	B	A	
Case *3*							
Morning	A′	A	A	B	B	B	A
Afternoon	A	B	A	B	B	A	
Within-Unit Blocked Randomization							
Case *1*							
Morning	A′	B	A	A	B	B	A
Afternoon	A	B	B	A	A	B	
Case *2*							
Morning	A′	A	A	B	A	B	B
Afternoon	B	B	A	B	A	A	
Case *3*							
Morning	A′	B	B	A	B	A	A
Afternoon	A	A	B	A	B	B	

Note. In the randomized versions of this design, the random sequencing of six A and six B time periods occurs following the required initial A′ time period. $N = 3$ cases, $c = 2$ within-series conditions, and $t = 11$ time periods (7 morning, 6 afternoon).

both children. Although the authors did not describe their intervention-order assignment method in the Method section, an examination of the time-series graph reveals that (a) for the first child, what appears to be a partially block-randomized order was employed (namely, 3 of the 6 possible block-randomized orders were systematically selected and randomized throughout), and (b) for the second child, either a haphazard or simple randomized order of the interventions was adopted, resulting in 12 trial-and-error, 10 least-to-most, and 12 identity-matching administrations over the study's 34 sessions.

CONSIDERATIONS IN BETWEEN-SERIES RANDOMIZED PHASE DESIGNS. In the AID and SID there are certain considerations that are an important part of the design and that randomization may not address. One such consideration is the design's potential for unwanted "carryover effects" from one intervention condition to the other. That is, an intervention introduced in one session may "carry over" to a control or alternative intervention in the next session, thereby making it likely that an experimental effect will be underestimated, or in some cases, even detected. Randomizing the order of intervention conditions will not necessarily eliminate this problem. Carryover effects might be assumed to be more prevalent in the AID and SID between-series designs (relative to many within-series ABAB . . . AB-type applications) in that with the former the different intervention conditions generally are administered in closer proximity and with more rapid switches from one intervention to the next. The foregoing statement need not apply to all between- and within-series applications. Within-series experiments also become increasingly complex to design and administer with three or more intervention conditions—as might be appreciated to some extent from our AID example with three different intervention conditions implemented at three different times of day over 6 days.

Combined-Series Randomized Phase Designs

RANDOMIZED MULTIPLE-BASELINE DESIGN (ACROSS UNITS, SETTINGS, OR BEHAVIORS). The domain of combined-series single-case intervention designs comprises three design types. These consist of variations of the MBD and include replication across either participants (or other case types), settings, or behaviors (or outcome measures). As in Figure 2.3, here we focus on an MBD application across participants–units, although the design can be similarly applied to multiple settings or multiple behaviors (but see our cautionary comments below). This MBD across cases is the strongest application of the design (and arguably the strongest of all single-case designs discussed in this paper) from an internal-validity perspective, as was indicated in our earlier discussion. The design requires replication across selected cases, with repetition of the intervention sequentially introduced across phases of the design.

The most straightforward application of randomization in the MBD across cases involves randomly assigning each case to the design's staggered intervention start points (see, e.g., Revusky, 1967, and later Wampold & Worsham, 1986, who proposed the randomized MBD and associated statistical analyses). That is, each case begins its exposure to the sequential introduction of the intervention in a random order. Interestingly, traditional applications of the MBD make no mention of assigning the case replicates randomly to the staggered sequences. Yet, doing so strengthens the design's internal validity and, with the Revusky and Wampold-Worsham analyses, its statistical-conclusion validity as well. Exhibit 2.9 illustrates the design for five cases and 10 time periods, with the intervention start point randomly assigned to cases, beginning at Time

Exhibit 2.9. Randomized Multiple-Baseline Design

Case 3: AAABBBBBBB
Case 5: AAAABBBBBB
Case 2: AAAAABBBBB
Case 4: AAAAAABBBB
Case 1: AAAAAAABBB

Note. $N = 5$ randomized cases, $c = 2$ within-series conditions, $t = 10$ time periods, and a staggered intervention introduction of one time period.

Exhibit 2.10.   Randomized Multiple-Baseline Design

Setting/Behavior 2: AAABBBBBBBBBB
Setting/Behavior 1: AAAAABBBBBBBB
Setting/Behavior 4: AAAAAAABBBBBB
Setting/Behavior 3: AAAAAAAAABBBB

Note. $N = 4$ randomized settings/behaviors, $c = 2$ within-series conditions, $t = 13$ time periods, and a staggered intervention introduction of two time periods.

Period 4 with a staggered introduction of the intervention occurring one time period after each preceding one.

As was just indicated, the incorporation of randomization into the MBD across settings or behaviors (or other measures) is also straightforward and involves randomly assigning the settings/behaviors to the predetermined staggered intervention start points. This procedure is illustrated in Exhibit 2.10 for four settings–behaviors and 13 time periods, with the intervention start point randomly assigned to settings/behaviors, beginning at Time Period 4 with a stagger of two time periods thereafter. As a published example of an MBD, Reeve, Reeve, Townsend, and Poulson (2007) introduced a multicomponent package to four children with autism, to determine whether the children could acquire appropriate responses for helping adults on a variety of different tasks (e.g., locating objects, putting items away, carrying objects). Following a baseline phase in which the children exhibited no correct helping responses, the intervention was implemented in sequential MBD fashion to each of the four children. In this example, the children could have been randomly assigned to the four staggered intervention start points—and, in fact, they may have been, although the authors did not specify the nature of their assignment process.

CONSIDERATIONS IN COMBINED-SERIES RANDOMIZED PHASE DESIGNS. Application of randomization to combined series designs is straightforward with respect to assignment of cases to intervention start points. Randomization applied to the "across cases" version of this design class looks much like a traditional group experiment in which participants (or other units) are assigned randomly to experimental conditions. In fact, the design can be structured analogously to a traditional group experiment with random assignment of participants to conditions (as was indicated for the Reeve et al., 2007, study). In this regard, the randomized MBD across cases represents the strongest inference design in the class of combined-series designs, and perhaps even in the entire class of single-case designs. The application of the randomized MBD across settings or behaviors within a single case is not as strong as the randomized MBD across cases, namely because the latter application provides multiple sources of intervention-efficacy evidence that are independent whereas the former applications do not. Given this independence issue, the randomized MBD across cases results in an experiment that, relative to its across-settings and across-measures counterparts, is both more scientifically credible and has greater population external validity because it includes a more solid replication component (see Levin, 1992).

Randomized Start-Point Designs

In addition to the preceding randomized phase designs that were just discussed, single-case intervention researchers can incorporate a different form of randomization into their experiments, namely one in which they randomly determine the specific time points at which the various phases of the time series begin. This novel form of randomization similarly enhances a single-case intervention study's scientific credibility. In this section, we discuss several design variations that capitalize on a randomized intervention start-point scheme.

AB DESIGN. As we noted earlier in this chapter, the most basic form of the within-series design is the AB design in which the A phase is a baseline or pretest series and the B is the intervention phase. In this interrupted time-series design, the researcher can structure the study so that the point of intervention, or *intervention start point*, is determined on a random basis (Edgington, 1975, 1992; Chapter 5, this volume). In Edgington's inventive incorporation of randomization into an interrupted time-series design, the researcher initially specifies the total number of A and B time periods from which data are to be collected (e.g., 20). Then, based on the researcher's specification of the minimum number of A (baseline/control) and intervention (B) time periods that she or he considers to be "acceptable" for the study (e.g., 4 and 3, respectively), a "range of potential intervention start points" is determined. Given the present two specifications, this range would be between Time Periods 5 and 17 inclusive, resulting in 13 potential intervention start points. A single (actual) intervention start point is then randomly selected from the 13 start points available. The design, with the actual randomly selected intervention start point being Time Period 9, can be illustrated as in Exhibit 2.11.

Edgington's (1975) randomized intervention start-point approach not only serves to bestow a "true experiment" status on the traditional AB (interrupted time-series) design, but as Edgington demonstrated, it also lends itself directly to an appropriate statistical analysis of the resulting outcomes (e.g., Edgington, 1992; Edgington & Onghena, 2007; Levin & Wampold, 1999). Moreover, in single-case intervention experiments containing more than just one A and one B phase (i.e., ABAB . . . AB designs), the logic of Edgington's basic approach can be extended in a straightforward fashion to encompass multiple randomized phase start points (Edgington & Onghena, 2007; see also Chapter 5, this volume).

Exhibit 2.11. AB Design

									Time Period										
1	2	3	4	5	6	7	8	9	10	11	12	13	14	15	16	17	18	19	20
A	A	A	A	A	A	A	A	B*	B	B	B	B	B	B	B	B	B	B	B

Note. $N = 1$ case, $c = 2$ within-series conditions, $t = 20$ time periods, and $s = 13$ potential intervention start points (between time periods 5 and 17 inclusive).
*Randomly selected intervention start point.

SPECIAL CONSIDERATION OF THE RANDOMIZED FOUR-PHASE ABAB DESIGN. In an earlier section we discussed a randomization scheme for the four-phase ABAB design, namely randomizing the order in which the four phases are administered (e.g., BAAB) in what we termed a "randomized phase design." Although that approach is methodologically appropriate and practically defensible in situations where the A and B phases represent two alternative intervention conditions (including a "standard" [B] and a "new" [C] method or technique), we noted that in situations where the A phases consist of a true baseline condition it would be difficult to justify not beginning the experiment with a baseline (A) phase. The rationale is analogous to that for a conventional pretest–intervention–posttest design (i.e., Campbell & Stanley's, 1966, original O_1XO_2 design), where a pretest assessment (O_1) logically precedes a postintervention assessment (O_2). For related discussions, see Edgington and Onghena (2007) and Chapter 5, this volume.

In addition, clinical–behavioral single-case researchers generally demand that in the ABAB design (represented here as $A_1B_1A_2B_2$), following a demonstration of an "initial intervention" effect (A_1B_1), both a "return-to-baseline" effect (B_1A_2) and a "replicated intervention" effect (A_2B_2). For researchers wishing to assess these three effects, not adhering to the universally applied ABAB sequence would be a source of consternation. As an example, if the sequence BBAA were to result from a random selection process, none of the desired effects could be assessed and then not in a "pure" uncontaminated fashion. That is, even though a return to baseline (BA) is nested within this sequence, the "return" is not really a return because there is no initial baseline phase. In addition, that effect would be subject to the influence of other extraneous variables, intervention carryover being a major one, along with the usual time-tied confounders such as Campbell and Stanley's (1966) "maturation" (e.g., practice and fatigue). Note that we are applying the term *pure* strictly in relation to the present single-case time-series experimental context. That is, although we recognize that other unwanted variables—intervention novelty, as a primary one—can seriously contaminate effect assessment in a conventional pretest-posttest design, the multiple-observations feature of a time-series experiment would help to mitigate such concerns here (e.g., Shadish et al., 2002).

A visual, and more complete, representation of the interpretative challenges associated with a randomized phase-sequence scheme for the four-phase ABAB design with a true baseline condition is presented in Table 2.3. There it may be seen that the three sequences that commence with an intervention phase (B) rather than a baseline phase (i.e., the three final phase-sequence possibilities in Table 2.3) do not permit a "pure" assessment of any of the three desired effects.

With the preceding rationale and concerns, then, it would appear that a fixed ABAB administration sequence is the "order of the day" and that any permutation of that sequence through randomization would be eschewed by many single-case researchers. For that reason, a multiple (here, three-part) randomized phase start-point model approach, as an extension of that discussed for the AB design, could be considered (see Edgington & Onghena, 2007). With this approach, before the $A_1B_1A_2B_2$ experiment begins the researcher randomly determines (a) the initial intervention start point from a set of acceptable start

Table 2.3. All Phase-Sequence Possibilities for the Four-Phase ABAB Design

Phase sequence	Randomization scheme	Initial intervention effect?	Return-to-baseline effect?	Replicated intervention effect?
ABAB	1,2	Y	Y	Y
ABBA	1,2	Y	Y	N
AABB	1	Y	N	N
BABA	1,2	N	N	N
BAAB	1,2	N	N	N
BBAA	1	N	N	N

Note. Effect assessments are based on a four-phase ABAB design with a true baseline condition. With a simple phase-sequence randomization scheme (1), all six phase sequences are possible; whereas with a blocked phase-sequence randomization scheme (2), only four phase sequences are possible. Also included are the effects that can and cannot be "purely" assessed with each sequence.

points (i.e., the A_1 to B_1 phase-transition point), (b) the return-to-baseline start point from a similarly acceptable set (the B_1 to A_2 phase-transition point), and (c) the replicated intervention start point from an acceptable set (the A_2 to B_2 phase-transition point). This three-part randomized phase start-point approach meshes well methodologically with the Edgington (1975) original randomized phase start-point model while at the same time responding to the "fixed intervention order" concern of many single-case researchers. Finally, as was true for the AB design, this ABAB randomized phase start-point approach also lends itself to an appropriate statistical analysis.[5]

REPLICATED AB DESIGN. The replicated AB design with randomized phase start points, and its associated analysis, were initially proposed by Marascuilo and Busk (1988) as an extension of Edgington's (1975) AB randomization model for a single experimental case. In this extension, each case's intervention start point is determined separately and on a random basis from the predesignated set of permissible start points. This design bears a resemblance to the previously discussed randomized MBD across cases (and see below). Note, however, that in contrast to that design with its systematically staggered introduction of the intervention, in this replicated AB application it would be possible for the intervention to be introduced in a less staggered (or even in an overlapping) fashion, which would weaken the internal and discriminant validity characteristics of the experiment. The design is illustrated in Table 2.4.

---

[5]Edgington and Onghena's (2007) randomization test for the ABAB . . . AB-type designs compares the mean of the combined A phases with that of the combined B phases. That tests a different statistical hypothesis than those targeting the three individual effects that we have specified here as typically being of concern in clinical/behavioral single-case applications (viz., initial intervention effect, return-to-baseline effect, and replicated intervention effect).

Table 2.4. Replicated AB Design

	Time period																			
	1	2	3	4	5	6	7	8	9	10	11	12	13	14	15	16	17	18	19	20
Case 1	A	A	A	A	A	A	A	A	B*	B	B	B	B	B	B	B	B	B	B	B
Case 2	A	A	A	A	A	A	A	A	A	A	A	A	A	B*	B	B	B	B	B	B
Case 3	A	A	A	A	A	B*	B	B	B	B	B	B	B	B	B	B	B	B	B	B

Note. $N = 3$ cases, $c = 2$ within-series conditions, $t = 20$ time periods, and $s = 13$ potential intervention start points (between time periods 5 and 17 inclusive).
*Randomly selected intervention start point for each case.

MULTIPLE-BASELINE DESIGN. A more systematically structured version of the Marascuilo and Busk (1988) replicated AB design with separately randomized phase start points for each experimental case is Koehler and Levin's (1998) "regulated randomization" MBD. That design allows for more start-point possibilities than the previously discussed MBD, while at the same time maintaining the systematically staggered intervention introduction that is not incorporated into the Marascuilo–Busk approach. In particular, and as we have been discussing for the Edgington class of designs, a second randomization component is added to that of the earlier discussed randomized MBD by preexperimentally designating one or more potential intervention start points for each case, with each actual start point determined on a random basis. With this second randomization component, both the Marascuilo–Busk and Koehler–Levin procedures may be regarded as between-units generalizations/replications of the randomized intervention start-point model. This design is illustrated in a 15-time-period example of Table 2.5, where researcher and research exigencies led to three a priori designated potential intervention start points for Cases 1 and 3 and two potential intervention start points for Cases 2 and 4.[6] Actual research examples of this design's application, and its associated randomization statistical analysis, are provided by Koehler and Levin (1998) and McKie (1998).

COMPARATIVE AB DESIGN. Extending the just-discussed randomized intervention start-point models, Levin and Wampold (1999) developed the comparative AB design and its associated analysis to accommodate a scientifically credible comparison of two different between-series interventions (or of an intervention and control condition) in a single-case AB design. For example, with one case randomly assigned to Intervention X (B) and another case to Intervention Y (C), the design allows for a direct between-case comparison of the A-B and A-C changes produced by the two interventions, akin to the interaction of a between-subjects factor (e.g., treatment) and a within-subjects factor (e.g., time), as with a split-plot arrangement in the conventional experimental design literature (see Maxwell & Delaney, 2004). Levin and Wampold proposed

---

[6]Although not illustrated here, this design also allows for any unit to be randomly assigned a single pre-designated intervention start point (Koehler & Levin, 1998).

Table 2.5. Multiple-Baseline Design

	1	2	3	4	5	6	7	8	9	10	11	12	13	14	15
							Time period								
Case 1	A	A	A	**B**	**B**	**B**	B	B	B	B	B	B	B	B	B
Case 3	A	A	A	A	A	**B**	**B**	**B**	B	B	B	B	B	B	B
Case 2	A	A	A	A	A	A	A	A	A	**B**	**B**	B	B	B	B
Case 4	A	A	A	A	A	A	A	A	A	A	A	**B**	**B**	B	B

Note. For each case the intervention start point is one of the randomly predetermined bolded **B**s. $N = 4$ randomized cases, $c = 2$ within-series conditions, and $t = 15$ time periods, $s_i = 3, 3, 2$, and 2 potential intervention start points for units 1, 3, 2, and 4, respectively, and a staggered intervention introduction of at least one time period.

two different intervention start-point randomization approaches, the independent intervention start-point and the simultaneous intervention start-point models (corresponding to our present simple and blocked randomization approaches, respectively). As we have previously discussed here for other AB-type designs, the latter (simultaneous intervention start-point) model has the methodological advantage of controlling for potential time/measures confounding. The two models are illustrated in Table 2.6.

Levin and Wampold (1999) developed two different statistical tests to accompany these models, one called the test of the "general intervention effect" and the other the test of the "comparative intervention effect." The former test assesses the within-series A-to-B change averaged across the two experimental cases (equivalent to an intervention "main effect") and which amounts to the same randomization test proposed by Marascuilo and Busk (1988). As was just noted, the latter test (which is associated with the comparative AB design discussed in this and the next section) compares the A-to-B changes in the two intervention conditions, X and Y.[7]

REPLICATED COMPARATIVE AB DESIGN. The replicated version of the just-discussed comparative AB design with randomized intervention start points, and its associated analysis, were initially proposed by Levin and Wampold (1999) and are illustrated in Table 2.7. In addition, the simultaneous intervention model has recently been extended to allow for blocked random assignment of cases (with a corresponding randomization statistical test) to more than two intervention conditions (Levin, Lall, & Kratochwill, 2011). Cases may be blocked either arbitrarily (e.g., in order of their enlistment in the experiment) or on the basis of a relevant pre-experimental variable (e.g., a variable related to the outcome being measured in the experiment). Compared with a simple randomization scheme, greater experimental control is gained with these two blocking variations (Levin et al., 2011; Levin & Wampold, 1999).

---

[7]Lall and Levin (2004) discussed a caveat associated with the statistical test of Levin and Wampold's independent start-point model's comparative intervention effect—which is not an issue in the simultaneous start-point model.

Table 2.6.   Comparative AB Design

Independent Start-Point Model

								Time period													
	1	2	3	4	5	6	7	8	9	10	11	12	13	14	15	16	17	18	19	20
Intervention X																				
Case 1	A	A	A	A	A	A	A	A	B*	B	B	B	B	B	B	B	B	B	B	B
Intervention Y																				
Case 2	A	A	A	A	A	B*	B	B	B	B	B	B	B	B	B	B	B	B	B	B

Simultaneous Start-Point Model

								Time period													
	1	2	3	4	5	6	7	8	9	10	11	12	13	14	15	16	17	18	19	20
Case 1x	A	A	A	A	A	A	A	A	A	A	A	B†	B	B	B	B	B	B	B	B
Case 1y	A	A	A	A	A	A	A	A	A	A	A	B†	B	B	B	B	B	B	B	B

Note. $N = 2$ cases representing $k = 2$ different between-series conditions (Intervention X and Intervention Y), $c = 2$ within-series conditions, $t = 20$ time periods, and $s = 13$ potential intervention start points (between time periods 5 and 17 inclusive).
*Randomly selected intervention start point for each case.
†Randomly selected intervention start point for the case pair.

Table 2.7.   Replicated Comparative AB Design

Independent Start-Point Model

								Time period													
	1	2	3	4	5	6	7	8	9	10	11	12	13	14	15	16	17	18	19	20
Intervention X																				
Case 1	A	A	A	A	A	A	A	A	B*	B	B	B	B	B	B	B	B	B	B	B
Case 2	A	A	A	A	A	B*	B	B	B	B	B	B	B	B	B	B	B	B	B	B
Intervention Y																				
Case 3	A	A	A	A	A	A	A	A	A	A	A	B*	B	B	B	B	B	B	B	B
Case 4	A	A	A	A	A	B	B*	B	B	B	B	B	B	B	B	B	B	B	B	B

Simultaneous Start-Point Model

								Time period													
	1	2	3	4	5	6	7	8	9	10	11	12	13	14	15	16	17	18	19	20
Case 1x	A	A	A	A	A	A	A	A	A	A	A	B†	B	B	B	B	B	B	B	B
Case 1y	A	A	A	A	A	A	A	A	A	A	A	B†	B	B	B	B	B	B	B	B
Case 2x	A	A	A	A	A	A	A	A	B†	B	B	B	B	B	B	B	B	B	B	B
Case 2y	A	A	A	A	A	A	A	A	B†	B	B	B	B	B	B	B	B	B	B	B

Note. $N = 4$ cases representing different $k = 2$ between-series conditions, $c = 2$ within-series conditions, $t = 20$ time periods, and $s = 13$ potential intervention start points (between time periods 5 and 17 inclusive).
*Randomly selected intervention start point for each case.
†Randomly selected intervention start point for each case pair.

Concluding Remarks and Limitations of Randomized Single-Case Intervention Designs

In this chapter we have discussed how various interrupted time-series investigations (as represented here by single-case intervention designs) can be transformed from Reichardt's (2006) nonrandomized experiments to randomized experiments by incorporating randomization into the design structure. Each of the designs requires various practical, logistical, and conceptual trade-offs, depending on what type of randomization scheme is implemented in the design. Generally speaking, the simple randomization schemes presented here strengthen the internal validity characteristics of single-case designs relative to traditional nonrandomized single-case designs, whereas the blocked randomization schemes greatly strengthen those internal validity characteristics. Thus, on an internal-validity continuum, Reichardt's nonrandomized time-series experiments would anchor the weak side and the present block-randomized time-series experiments (including block-randomized on multiple factors where applicable) would anchor the strong side.

In addition, the type of randomization scheme implemented dictates the kinds of units-appropriate statistical analyses that should be conducted. Even in the absence of a suitable statistical test, a single-case intervention design's inclusion of appropriate forms of randomization enhances the experiment's scientific credibility (as reflected by internal-validity considerations). Randomization therefore represents a highly recommended component of single-case and related time-series designs, designs in which randomization is not considered as a part of the traditional modus operandi (see also Levin & Kratochwill, 2013).

There are however, limitations associated with the use of randomization in single-case intervention designs. First, a randomized phase-order scheme does not guarantee that a given number of A versus B comparisons will occur within a fixed number of time periods. For example, in the traditional four-phase ABAB design, there is a guaranteed initial intervention versus baseline (B vs. A) comparison followed by a guaranteed second intervention versus baseline comparison. Thus, the design satisfies the replication standard prescribed by Horner et al. (2005) and meets the design specifications of the WWC Single-Case Design Standards within a four time-period experiment. With both the simple and blocked phase-sequence randomization schemes, on the other hand, more (and perhaps many more) time periods might need to be built into the experiment to produce two adjacent AB phases for an initial and a replication comparison. With reference to the 10-time-period ABAB . . . AB design of Exhibit 2.1, for instance, there are five adjacent B versus A comparison opportunities in the traditional nonrandomized design, but only three in the two randomized design variations that happened to be produced for the Exhibit 2.1 sequence. For the two randomized phase-order variations, therefore, the cost of the research would necessarily increase in that additional time, measurement, and other resources might be required to conduct the experiment. At the same, it is possible for single-case researchers to overcome these concerns by adopting a different type of randomization scheme, namely, the randomized intervention start-point model that has been discussed here (see also Edgington & Onghena, 2007).

Second, one of the features of traditional single-case designs that is often regarded as central to their use is the flexibility accorded to the researcher concerning when to change phases, which includes (among other aspects) extending measurement until some degree of outcome stability has occurred (Hayes et al., 1999). That is, some traditional single-case intervention studies may be likened to "design research" in the learning sciences field, where the design unfolds as candidate interventions are auditioned and data are forthcoming (see Levin & Kratochwill, 2013). Randomization may eliminate some of this phase-determination flexibility in that it is an a priori design consideration/specification. Although one cannot endorse a design-research format when conducting scientifically credible intervention experiments (see our previous discussion of Levin O'Donnell's, 1999, stage model in Figure 2.2), we recognize that this feature might be advantageous in applied and clinical single-case research situations, often for the same reasons that it might not be possible or convenient to implement randomized group studies in those settings.

Third, randomized designs may limit the kinds of statistical analysis that are applied to the data, thereby possibly reducing the statistical conclusion validity of the study. The most direct and straightforward application of statistical tests to the specific designs we have featured in this article fall into the category of nonparametric randomization (or permutation) tests (e.g., Edgington & Onghena, 2007; Levin & Wampold, 1999; Chapter 5, this volume). However, because such tests require a certain sufficient number of phases to have adequate statistical power for detecting intervention effects, it is possible that single-case researchers will put these design-and-analysis concerns ahead of substantive, clinical, and practical ones—a case of the "tail wagging the dog."

Despite the potential issues and limitations in the design of randomized single-case experiments, we have offered researchers several options that can increase the validity of this class of design and thereby enhance the scientific credibility of intervention-research findings in applied and clinical fields. Ultimately, what these randomized single-case intervention designs have to offer will become evident in both the greater scientific credibility of research findings and the integrative summaries of our knowledge base for evidence-based interventions across areas of research in psychology and related fields.

References

Barlow, D. H., & Hayes, S. C. (1979). Alternating treatments design: One strategy for comparing the effects of two treatments in a single subject. *Journal of Applied Behavior Analysis, 12,* 199–210. doi:10.1901/jaba.1979.12-199

Borckardt, J. J., Nash, M. R., Murphy, M. D., Moore, M., Shaw, D., & O'Neil, P. (2008). Clinical practice as natural laboratory for psychotherapy research: A guide to case-based time-series analysis. *American Psychologist, 63,* 77–95. doi:10.1037/0003-066X.63.2.77

Bracht, G. H., & Glass, G. V. (1968). The external validity of experiments. *American Educational Research Journal, 5,* 437–474. doi:10.3102/00028312005004437

Campbell, D. T., & Fiske, D. W. (1959). Convergent and discriminant validation by the multitrait-multimethod matrix. *Psychological Bulletin, 56,* 81–105. doi:10.1037/h0046016

Campbell, D. T., & Stanley, J. C. (1966). *Experimental and quasi-experimental designs for research.* Chicago, IL: Rand McNally.

Cronbach, L. J., & Meehl, P. E. (1955). Construct validity in psychological tests. *Psychological Bulletin, 52*, 281–302. doi:10.1037/h0040957

Dugard, P., File, P., & Todman, J. (2012). *Single-case and small-n experimental designs: A practical guide to randomization tests* (2nd ed.). New York, NY: Routledge.

Edgington, E. S. (1975). Randomization tests for one-subject operant experiments. *Journal of Psychology: Interdisciplinary and Applied, 90*, 57–68. doi:10.1080/00223980.1975.9923926

Edgington, E. S. (1992). Nonparametric tests for single-case experiments. In T. R. Kratochwill & J. R. Levin (Eds.), *Single-case research design and analysis* (pp. 133–157). Hillsdale, NJ: Erlbaum.

Edgington, E. S., & Onghena, P. (2007). *Randomization tests* (4th ed.). Boca Raton, FL: Chapman & Hall/CRC.

Fisher, W. W., Kodak, T., & Moore, J. W. (2007). Embedding an identity-matching task within a prompting hierarchy to facilitate acquisition of conditional discriminations in children with autism. *Journal of Applied Behavior Analysis, 40*, 489–499. doi:10.1901/jaba.2007.40-489

Hall, R. V., & Fox, R. G. (1977). Changing-criterion designs: An alternate applied behavior analysis procedure. In C. C. Etzel, J. M. LeBlanc, & D. M. Baer (Eds.), *New developments in behavioral research: Theory, method, and application* (pp. 151–166). Hillsdale, NJ: Lawrence Erlbaum Associates.

Hartmann, D. P., & Hall, R. V. (1976). A discussion of the changing criterion design. *Journal of Applied Behavior Analysis, 9*, 527–532. doi:10.1901/jaba.1976.9-527

Hayes, S. C. (1981). Single-case experimental designs and empirical clinical practice. *Journal of Consulting and Clinical Psychology, 49*, 193–211. doi:10.1037/0022-006X.49.2.193

Hayes, S. C., Barlow, D. H., & Nelson-Gray, R. O. (1999). *The scientist practitioner: Research and accountability in the age of managed care* (2nd ed.). Needham Heights, MA: Allyn & Bacon.

Hersen, M., & Barlow, D. H. (1976). *Single-case experimental designs: Strategies for studying behavior change*. New York, NY: Pergamon.

Hitchcock, J. H., Horner, R. H., Kratochwill, T. R., Levin, J. R., Odom, S. L., Rindskopf, D. M., & Shadish, W. R. (in press). The What Works Clearinghouse "Single-Case Design Pilot Standards": Who will guard the guards? *Remedial and Special Education.*

Horner, R., & Spaulding, S. (2010). Single-case research designs. In N. J. Salkind (Ed.), *Encyclopedia of research design* (pp. 1386–1394). Thousand Oaks, CA: Sage. doi:10.4135/9781412961288.n424

Horner, R. H., Carr, E. G., Halle, J., McGee, G., Odom, S., & Wolery, M. (2005). The use of single-subject research to identify evidence-based practice in special education. *Exceptional Children, 71*, 165–179.

Kaestle, C. F. (1993). The awful reputation of education research. *Educational Researcher, 22*, 23–31.

Kazdin, A. E. (1982). *Single-case research designs: Methods for clinical and applied settings*. New York, NY: Oxford University Press.

Kazdin, A. E. (2004). Evidence-based treatments: Challenges and priorities for practice and research. *Child and Adolescent Psychiatric Clinics of North America, 13*, 923–940.

Kazdin, A. E. (2011). *Single-case research designs: Methods for clinical and applied settings* (2nd ed.). New York, NY: Oxford University Press.

Kazdin, A. E., & Hartmann, D. P. (1977). The simultaneous-treatment design. *Behavior Therapy, 8*, 682–693. doi:10.1016/S0005-7894(77)80200-1

Keppel, G., & Wickens, T. D. (2004). *Design and analysis: A researcher's handbook* (4th ed.). Upper Saddle River, NJ: Pearson Prentice Hall.

Kirk, R. E. (1995). *Experimental design: Procedures for the behavioral sciences* (3rd ed.). Pacific Grove, CA: Brooks/Cole.

Koehler, M. J., & Levin, J. R. (1998). Regulated randomization: A potentially sharper analytical tool for the multiple-baseline design. *Psychological Methods, 3*, 206–217. doi:10.1037/1082-989X.3.2.206

Kratochwill, T. R. (Ed.). (1978). *Single subject research: Strategies for evaluating change*. New York, NY: Academic Press.

Kratochwill, T. R. (2007). Preparing psychologists for evidenced-based school practice: Lessons learned and challenges ahead. *American Psychologist, 62*, 829–843. doi:10.1037/0003-066X.62.8.829

Kratochwill, T. R., Hitchcock, J. H., Horner, R. H., Levin, J. R., Odom, S. L., Rindskopf, D. M., & Shadish, W. R. (2013). Single-case intervention research design standards. *Remedial and Special Education, 34*, 26–38. doi:10.1177/0741932512452794

Lall, V. F., & Levin, J. R. (2004). An empirical investigation of the statistical properties of generalized single-case randomization tests. *Journal of School Psychology, 42*, 359–383.

Levin, J. R. (1992). Single-case research design and analysis: Comments and concerns. In T. R. Kratochwill & J. R. Levin (Eds.), *Single-case research design and analysis: New directions for psychology and education* (pp. 213–224). Hillsdale, NJ: Erlbaum.

Levin, J. R. (1994). Crafting educational intervention research that's both credible and creditable. *Educational Psychology Review, 6*, 231–243. doi:10.1007/BF02213185

Levin, J. R. (1997). Overcoming feelings of powerlessness in "aging" researchers: A primer on statistical power in analysis of variance designs. *Psychology and Aging, 12*, 84–106. doi:10.1037/0882-7974.12.1.84

Levin, J. R. (2005). Randomized classroom trials on trial. In G. D. Phye, D. H. Robinson, & J. R. Levin (Eds.), *Empirical methods for evaluating educational interventions* (pp. 3–27). San Diego, CA: Elsevier. doi:10.1016/B978-012554257-9/50002-4

Levin, J. R., Ferron, J. M., & Gafurov, B. S. (2014). Improved randomization tests for a class of single-case intervention designs. Unpublished manuscript, University of Arizona, Tucson.

Levin, J. R., Ferron, J. M., & Kratochwill, T. R. (2012). Nonparametric statistical tests for single-case systematic and randomized ABAB . . . AB and alternating treatment intervention designs: New developments, new directions. *Journal of School Psychology, 50*, 599–624. doi:10.1016/j.jsp.2012.05.001

Levin, J. R., & Kratochwill, T. R. (2013). Educational/psychological intervention research circa 2012. In I. B. Weiner (Series Ed.) & W. M. Reynolds & G. E. Miller (Volume Eds.), *Handbook of psychology* (2nd edition): *Vol. 7. Educational psychology* (pp. 465–492). New York, NY: Wiley.

Levin, J. R., Lall, V. F., & Kratochwill, T. R. (2011). Extensions of a versatile randomization test for assessing single-case intervention effects. *Journal of School Psychology, 49*, 55–79.

Levin, J. R., Marascuilo, L. A., & Hubert, L. J. (1978). *N* = nonparametric randomization tests. In T. R. Kratochwill (Ed.), *Single subject research: Strategies for evaluating change* (pp. 167–196). New York, NY: Academic Press.

Levin, J. R., & O'Donnell, A. M. (1999). What to do about educational research's credibility gaps? *Issues in Education: Contributions From Educational Psychology, 5*, 177–229. doi:10.1016/S1080-9724(00)00025-2

Levin, J. R., & Wampold, B. E. (1999). Generalized single-case randomization tests: Flexible analyses for a variety of situations. *School Psychology Quarterly, 14*, 59–93. doi:10.1037/h0088998

Manuel, J. C., Sunseri, M. A., Olson, R., & Scolari, M. (2007). A diagnostic approach to increase reusable dinnerware selection in a cafeteria. *Journal of Applied Behavior Analysis, 40*, 301–310. doi:10.1901/jaba.2007.143-05

Marascuilo, L. A., & Busk, P. L. (1988). Combining statistics for multiple-baseline AB and replicated ABAB designs across subjects. *Behavioral Assessment, 10*, 1–28.

Max, L., & Onghena, P. (1999). Some issues in the statistical analysis of completely randomized and repeated measures designs for speech, language, and hearing research. *Journal of Speech, Language, and Hearing Research, 42*, 261–270.

Maxwell, S. E., & Delaney, H. D. (2004). *Designing experiments and analyzing data: A model comparison perspective* (2nd ed.). Mahwah, NJ: Erlbaum.

McKie, A. (1998). *Effectiveness of a neoprene hand splint on grasp in young children with cerebral palsy.* Unpublished masters thesis, University of Wisconsin, Madison, WI.

Mosteller, F., & Boruch, R. (Eds.). (2002). *Evidence matters: Randomized trials in education research.* Washington, DC: Brookings Institute.

Onghena, P. (1992). Randomization tests for extensions and variation of ABAB single-case experimental designs: A rejoinder. *Behavioral Assessment, 14*, 153–171.

Onghena, P., & Edgington, E. S. (2005). Customization of pain treatments: Single-case design and analysis. *The Clinical Journal of Pain, 21*, 56–68. doi:10.1097/00002508-200501000-00007

Reeve, S. A., Reeve, K. F., Townsend, D. B., & Poulson, C. L. (2007). Establishing a generalized repertoire of helping behavior in children with autism. *Journal of Applied Behavior Analysis, 40*, 123–136. doi:10.1901/jaba.2007.11-05

Reichardt, C. S. (2006). The principle of parallelism in the design of studies to estimate treatment effects. *Psychological Methods, 11*(1), 1–18. doi:10.1037/1082-989X.11.1.1

Revusky, S. H. (1967). Some statistical treatments compatible with individual organism methodology. *Journal of the Experimental Analysis of Behavior, 10*, 319–330.

Reyna, V. F. (2005). The *No Child Left Behind Act*, scientific research and federal education policy: A view from Washington, DC. In G. D. Phye, D. H. Robinson, & J. R. Levin (Eds.), *Empirical methods for evaluating educational interventions* (pp. 29–52). San Diego, CA: Elsevier Academic Press. doi:10.1016/B978-012554257-9/50003-6

Shadish, W. R., Cook, T. D., & Campbell, D. T. (2002). *Experimental and quasi-experimental designs for generalized causal inference.* Boston, MA: Houghton Mifflin.

Shavelson, R. J., & Towne, L. (2002). *Scientific research in education.* Washington, DC: National Academy Press.

Slavin, R. E. (2002). Evidence-based education policies: Transforming educational research and practice. *Educational Researcher, 31*(7), 15–21. doi:10.3102/0013189X031007015

Smith, J. D. (in press). Single-case experimental designs: A systematic review of published research and recommendations for researchers and reviewers. *Psychological Methods,*

Snow, R. E. (1974). Representative and quasi-representative designs for research on teaching. *Review of Educational Research, 44,* 265–291.

Thompson, R. H., Cotnoir-Bichelman, N. M., McKerchar, P. M., Tate, T. L., & Dancho, K. A. (2007). Enhancing early communication through infant sign training. *Journal of Applied Behavior Analysis, 40,* 15–23. doi:10.1901/jaba.2007.23-06

Twardosz, S., Cataldo, M. F., & Risley, T. R. (1974). Open environment design for infant and toddler day care. *Journal of Applied Behavior Analysis, 7,* 529–546. doi:10.1901/jaba.1974.7-529

Wampold, B. E., & Worsham, N. L. (1986). Randomization tests for multiple-baseline designs. *Behavioral Assessment, 8,* 135–143.

Wendt, O., & Miller, B. (2012). Quality appraisal of single-subject experimental designs: An overview and comparison of different appraisal tools. *Education & Treatment of Children, 35,* 235–268. doi:10.1353/etc.2012.0010

3

Visual Analysis of Single-Case Intervention Research: Conceptual and Methodological Issues

Thomas R. Kratochwill, Joel R. Levin, Robert H. Horner, and Christopher M. Swoboda

In any science, assumptions surrounding the basic methods to establish knowledge must be critically analyzed from time to time. This scrutiny can create useful dialogues that may advance the methods of science and, hence, understanding of various phenomena. Within a class of quantitative research designs, single-case experiments have a long and rich tradition of providing evidence about interventions applied both to solving a diverse range of human problems and to enriching the knowledge base established in many fields of science (Kazdin, 2011; Chapter 2, this volume). In particular, recent reviews of various clinical and applied psychology and education journals reveal that single-case designs are used with regularity (Hammond & Gast, 2010; Shadish & Sullivan, 2011). Hammond and Gast (2010) reviewed eight journals in special education between 1983 and 2007. Of 1,936 articles they reviewed, 456 of them (about 24%) used at least one single-case design in a total of 556 designs. Shadish and Sullivan (2011) reported 809 single-case designs in 113 studies in 21 journals during 2008. In addition, single-case research has often been included in meta-analyses of intervention outcomes (e.g., Carr et al., 1999; Horner, Sugai, & Anderson, 2010).

In the social sciences, randomized controlled trials (RCTs) have dominated to the point that they are now acknowledged as the "gold standard" for evidence-based practice (Gersten et al., 2005; Shavelson & Towne, 2002). Even in this arena however, single-case designs are now also being featured as an important methodology. The major task forces of the American Psychological Association

The authors express sincere appreciation to Jim Halle for his thoughtful comments on an earlier version of this chapter. We also express our thanks to Kurt Brown in the Wisconsin Center for Education Research (WCER) for his edits on an earlier version of this chapter. Any opinions, findings, or conclusions expressed in this chapter are those of the authors and do not necessarily reflect the views of funding agencies, WCER, or cooperating institutions.

http://dx.doi.org/10.1037/14376-004
Single-Case Intervention Research: Methodological and Statistical Advances, by T. R. Kratochwill and J. R. Levin

(APA) incorporated single-case designs alongside randomized controlled trials in their evidence standards. For example, the APA Division 12/53 Task Force on Evidence-Based Interventions (Weisz & Hawley, 2001) and the APA Division 16 Task Force on Evidence-Based Interventions (Kratochwill & Shernoff, 2003; Kratochwill & Stoiber, 2002) developed design criteria for review of single-case intervention research. Rating criteria (e.g., the Single-Case Experimental Design Scale) that allow for a rating of the methodological quality of single-case designs have been developed in the field of neuropsychological rehabilitation (see Tate et al., 2008) and a variety of scales and rating criteria have been featured for appraisal of single-case design research in such fields as speech, language, and the hearing sciences (Smith, 2012; Wendt & Miller, 2012).

In medicine single-case designs are typically called "N-of-1 trials" and have been applied in a variety of studies on medical conditions such as asthma, arthritis, fibromyalgia, surgery, and attention deficit hyperactivity disorder (Gabler, Duan, Vohra, & Kravitz, 2011). Standards in medicine are developing based on the Consolidated Standards of Reporting Trials (CONSORT) (see Moher et al., 2010), the extension of CONSORT to CENT (the CONSORT Extension of reporting guidelines for N-of-1 Trials) and these developments have led to the creation of the SCRIBE (Single-Case Reporting guideline In Behavioral Interventions) to be available in 2014 (Robyn Tate, personal communication, August 2013).

In education, the National Reading Panel (2000) included single-case designs in its review of reading interventions, the Council for Exceptional Children proposed a set of quality standards for single-case designs (Horner et al., 2005), and subsequently, the U.S. Department of Education's Institute of Education Sciences developed standards for review of single-case intervention designs to be incorporated by the What Works Clearinghouse (see Kratochwill et al., 2010). As the frequency and value of single-case designs become more prominent, it is appropriate to revisit the design and interpretation logic that adds experimental rigor to single-case designs (see Chapter 1, this volume). Central to this discussion is the role of visual analysis and the supplemental value of statistical analysis as means of evaluating outcomes within single-case methods.

The purposes of this chapter are to (a) review the traditional applications of and arguments for visual analysis in single-case intervention research, (b) review research on visual analysis, and (c) recommend options for supplementing visual analysis of data with recently proposed formal statistical procedures.

The Tradition of Visual Analysis in Single-Case Designs

Visual analysis refers to the examination of graphed data to assess the level of functional relation between the manipulation of an independent variable and a change in a dependent variable (Parsonson & Baer, 1978). The process begins by plotting the data on a graph, with various sequentially introduced conditions, interventions, or phases of the study (the independent variable) represented on the horizontal axis and response measures (the dependent variable) represented on the vertical axis. The data are plotted across phases in a variety of single-case design types, including what Hayes (1981) has referred to as *within series* (e.g., the ABAB "reversal" design), *between series* (e.g., the alternating treatment design), and *combined series* (e.g., the multiple-baseline design)—see, for example, Kazdin (1982, 2011) and Chapters 1 and 2, this volume. Visual analysis then continues by examining features of the data within and between phases (e.g., level [mean], trend [slope], variability, overlap, immediacy of effect) to assess the extent to which data in adjacent phases document change in data patterns, and the extent to which data across the full set of phases document sufficient size and replication of the desired effect to constitute a demonstration of experimental control. The vast majority of published single-case intervention research has incorporated visual analysis as the primary method of outcome evaluation (Busk & Marascuilo, 1992; Fahmie & Hanley, 2008; Kratochwill & Brody, 1978). Among the many methodology texts that have discussed single-case designs over the past 50 years, the majority have featured visual analysis as the major method to examine experimental outcomes.[1]

There are at least three reasons for the near-exclusive reliance of behavioral scientists on visual analysis in their single-case intervention research: (a) the longstanding traditions associated with the theoretical paradigms of experimental and applied behavior analysis, including the professional journals in that field (e.g., the *Journal of Applied Behavior Analysis* [*JABA*], the *Journal of Experimental Analysis of Behavior*); (b) the inability of inferential statistical procedures to take into account the multiplicity and complexity of factors considered by visual analysts when deciding whether interventions are causally related to outcomes; and (c) the application of single-case designs to evaluate clinical practice, where emphasis on change in the behavior of individuals has been the focus. Each of these forces that have driven the popularity of visual analysis will be discussed in turn.

Applied Behavior Analysis

Authors of single-case research design texts in the field of experimental and applied behavior analysis have typically emphasized visual analysis of data (e.g., Bailey & Burch, 2002; Fahmie & Hanley, 2008; Johnston & Pennypacker, 1980, 1993, 2009; Poling, Methot, & LeSage, 1995). Although the origins of graphs for examining and understanding scientific data are diverse (see Tufte, 1983; Wainer & Thissen, 1993), it was the development of the experimental analysis of behavior that launched a new tradition of displaying data in graphs to understand the behavior of organisms in the social sciences.[2] In

---

[1]These texts include those devoted exclusively to single-case designs and those devoted to the broader class of "quasi-experimental" time-series designs (e.g., Campbell & Stanley, 1966).

[2]In domains outside of the experimental analysis of behavior, methodologists have used graphical displays to present data in single-case experiments. Two examples are noteworthy. First, in their classic text on experimental and quasi-experimental designs, Campbell and Stanley (1963) demonstrated quasi-experimental time-series and regression discontinuity design data in hypothetical graphical displays. Later, Cook and Campbell (1979) expanded on these graphical displays with both hypothetical- and real-data graphs depicting intervention outcomes in time-series designs. In the medical field, Chassan (1967, 1979) presented certain single-case outcomes with graphical displays but relied much more on tables and statistical summary information.

particular, B. F. Skinner (1953) and Sidman (1960) provided various graphical displays of single organisms by such methods as line graphs and cumulative record displays. Sidman referred to this method of data analysis as "criterion by inspection" and noted that

> one of the basic requirements for the success of "criterion-by-inspection" is that the experimental manipulations produce large behavioral changes. If the changes are of such magnitude as to be easily apparent by visual inspection, then such inspection automatically assumes greater validity as a stability criterion. A more quantitative criterion might show that the behavior in question is still undergoing development, and a more precise evaluation of the independent variable's effect might require a stricter behavioral specification. But the demonstration that a variable is effective does not require the attainment of a stringently defined stable state as long as the demonstrated change is large enough to override the baseline "noise." (Sidman, 1960, p. 268)

The emphasis on large changes has remained a prominent rationale for the primary reliance on visual analysis of data throughout the past 50 years and spawned a major debate over the application of data-analytic tools in single-case research (Kratochwill, 1978; Kratochwill & Levin, 1992). We examine the "large effects" argument in detail later in this chapter.

In the fields of experimental and applied behavior analysis, although the foundation of graphical displays has traditionally been the cumulative (or "moment to moment") individual data records (Ferster & Skinner, 1957), most of the graphs reported in *JABA* used some form of data aggregation to display intervention effects (Fahme & Hanley, 2008). Yet, no standards exist for processing the individual data records prior to displaying them in a graph. On a continuum ranging from displaying a single data point at the experimental condition level (i.e., plotting a condition mean) to displaying multiple data points to represent an individual's within-session performance, Fahmie and Hanley (2008) found that the majority of studies in *JABA* report data at the session level. The authors offered guidelines for future reports that emphasize within-session data displays when ethical, practical, and scientific factors are considered. Our perspective is that the analytic/inferential "grain size" should be guided by the research question under consideration (such as through the logic model developed by the researcher—see Chapter 1, this volume) and not by some arbitrary rule prescribing within- or across-session data display and interpretation.

Debate Surrounding Statistical Methods of Data Analysis

The practice of relying on visual analysis in single-case intervention research can be traced, in part, to the general dismissal of inferential statistical methods on the basis of their having been considered not applicable to single-case applied behavior-analysis data (see Kratochwill, 1978). Moreover, the outright rejection of conventional "group" designs was prominent in early writings in the field of the experimental analysis of behavior (e.g., Sidman, 1960; B. F.

Skinner, 1953) and was further emphasized in discussions of applied behavior analysis research (e.g., Baer, 1977; Johnston & Pennypacker, 1980, 1993; Michael, 1974; Parsonson & Baer, 1978).

Although single-case behavior-analysis researchers laid out clear rationales for their visual-analysis stance in early writings, a series of articles appearing in a 1974 issue of *JABA* set in motion a continuing debate over the use of inferential statistical methods in single-case designs. Previously, Gentile, Roden, and Klein (1972) proposed that the data from ABAB single-case designs be analyzed by standard analysis-of-variance (ANOVA) procedures. Several authors (Hartmann, 1974; Keselman & Leventhal, 1974; Kratochwill et al., 1974; Thoresen & Elashoff, 1974) responded to this suggestion, with most of the writers focusing on the problems related to applying standard ANOVA in single-case designs.[3] However, in a summary response to the *JABA* commentaries, Michael (1974) questioned the need for *any* inferential statistical method other than visual analysis of the data in applied behavior-analysis research. This perspective has generally been maintained over the years, with the continued and almost exclusive adoption of visual analysis for analyzing single-case data in that field.

The tradition of relying on visual analysis in single-case behavior-analysis research has also manifested itself in a rejection of group designs and their corresponding inferential statistical methods of analysis. As a potent example, Johnston and Pennypacker (1993) represented single-case designs as an approach to a "science of behavior" that emphasized visual analysis of data. Behavior analytic researchers have generally relied on standard metrics that are established independently of the research units being assessed (e.g., direct observational measurement of behavior in terms of such features as frequency, intensity, duration). Such measurement is typical in applied behavior-analysis single-case research in which multiple measures are collected over time.[4] Johnston and Pennypacker (1980; see also 1993, 2009) outlined the rationale for, and principles of, graphical display of single-case data based on the use of frequently repeated measures. In the tradition of early behavior-analytic writers, they noted that because experimental control is critical in single-case research, large and consistent effects will likely be produced and these effects can be examined visually. Johnson and Pennypacker (1980) added that "the

---

[3]A prevalent statistical concern was that in such designs a critical ANOVA assumption is violated: namely, that the errors associated with the outcome observations are mutually independent. Specifically, it was argued that in typical time-series investigations consisting of human-produced responses the outcome-observation errors are likely to be autocorrelated (discussed later in this chapter). Consequently, analyzing the individual observations by standard ANOVA methods could potentially produce statistically misleading conclusions about the presence/absence of an intervention effect.

[4]Johnson and Pennypacker emphasized direct nonarbitrary measures of behavior that had a meaningful outcome for the client (e.g., increase in a social skill or reduction of aggressive behavior). In their discussion of arbitrary metrics in intervention research, Blanton and Jaccard (2005) referenced many rating scales and checklists that are often only a proxy to the actual behavior of the client/patient. Akin to criterion-referenced measurement in the psychometric literature, the value of adopting nonarbitrary metrics is that they better correspond to "real-world" or meaningful outcomes for the client/patient.

potential of visual inspection for sensitive and stringent definition of stable responding . . . depends heavily on the training, experience and intellectual honesty of the researcher; at the same time, the inherent potential for abuse of visual inspection is considerable" (p. 240). It is important to note that even if single-case researchers wished to conduct statistical analyses to complement the visual analysis of data, there continue to be repeated problems related to (a) assumptions about the distribution of the outcome measures, (b) serial dependencies (autocorrelation, to be discussed shortly) typical of single-case time-series data, and (c) the fundamental inability of certain inferential statistical methods to address the specific intervention questions of interest in the research. On the basis of the view that current statistical methods applied to single-case research data analysis likely violate required distributional assumptions, Kennedy (2005) advanced a perspective that supports the status quo regarding visual analysis:

> The use of inferential statistics in single-case designs is largely an academic debate and not a practical issue for researchers looking for new analytical tools. If, in the future, inferential statistics can be developed that fit the design requirements of single-case research, then the issue will require renewed debate. Until that time arrives, however, single-case researchers will continue to use the visual analysis of data as a primary means of examining their data. (p. 192)

In short, there are no statistical methods currently available that incorporate the complete focal elements of visual analysis (e.g., level, trend, variability) that will be reviewed in this chapter (see Horner & Spaulding, 2010). As a result, single-case researchers are often faced with applying a data-analytic tool (statistical analysis) that (a) is less comprehensive than the focal elements of visual analysis and (b) typically does not provide raw data for readers of scientific reports to inspect and evaluate for themselves. In this regard, we recommend that statistical analysis is a complement to visual analysis of single-case data, which, in the latter case has some major and unique contributions to understanding outcomes of the experiment.

Empirical Clinical Practice

Visual analysis has been emphasized nearly exclusively when single-case designs are implemented to evaluate client–patient responsiveness to a treatment in applied and clinical settings. This is often called *empirical clinical practice* or *action research*, and a number of authors have adopted some form of single-case methodology, sometimes leading to compromises in the design (e.g., using a case-study design or a "weak" AB single-case intervention design), but nearly always with an emphasis on visual analysis rather than statistical analysis of the data (with a few exceptions noted later in this chapter). Although the approach has some of its origins in the behavior modification or behavior therapy field, the use of repeated assessment within a single-case design structure (sometimes labeled *time-series methodology*) was presented as a model that could be applied across diverse areas of therapy (Barlow & Hersen, 1984) and recently has resurfaced to help address concerns over negative results and negative effects in psycho-therapy research (Barlow, 2010; Barlow, Nock, & Hersen, 2009).

One of the earliest and most clearly articulated models of this approach was offered by Browning and Stover (1971), who introduced the use of single-case designs in what they called the *experimental-clinical method*, as applied to the evaluation of clients in residential treatment. Incorporating many early behavior modification treatment techniques, the authors outlined how, in the course of clinical practice, structured single-case designs (e.g., AB, ABC, BC, where A is a baseline phase and B and C are alternative-intervention phases) could furnish useful time-series data that could be shared with the scientific community to advance child treatment. In the same tradition, Barlow, Hayes, and Nelson (1984; repeated in the second edition Hayes, Barlow, & Nelson-Gray, 1999) argued for the use of single-case designs by practitioners:

> A major advance in our applied research efforts has been practitioners' increasing use of single-case experimental strategies in applied settings to determine the effectiveness of treatment or, on occasion, of active ingredi-ents within a treatment across a small series of patients. Nevertheless, the overwhelming majority of research activity involving single-case experi-mental designs to date continues to be carried out in applied research cen-ters rather than in the offices of practitioners. In part, this may be due to the unfamiliarity of this experimental approach and some of the perceived practical difficulties thought to conflict with the implementation of research of any kind in an applied setting. (pp. 71–72)

Hayes et al. (1999) developed detailed examples of how single-case designs could be implemented in practice, and their work has remained a significant prototype for subsequent efforts in this area.

Recommending the use of single-case design in practice is not limited to psychology and has been featured in a variety of disciplines, including physio-therapy (e.g., Riddoch & Lennon, 1991), social work (e.g., Bloom, Fischer, & Orme, 1999; DiNoia & Tripodi, 2007; Fischer, 1978; Jayaratne & Levy, 1973; Wodarski, 1981), and education (e.g., Brown-Chidsey & Steege, 2010; Riley-Tillman & Burns, 2009; C. H. Skinner, 2004; Vannest, Davis, & Parker, 2013). Over the past decade, the use of single-case designs to bridge science and practice has been emphasized in papers appearing in the *American Psychologist*. Morgan and Morgan (2001) stressed the importance of single-case designs to research and its relevance to the evaluation of practice, with both applications empha-sizing visual analysis of data. In an even stronger endorsement of the use of single-case designs, Borckardt et al. (2008) argued for both visual and statistical analysis of time-series intervention studies to advance psychological practice.

As recent examples, visual analysis of single-case data has been empha-sized in educational settings (e.g., Cipani, 2009) and in the new federal education initiative called "Response-to-Intervention," (RtI) wherein interventions are orga-nized in multiple tiers and monitored for effectiveness on a variety of academic and social–emotional outcome measures (e.g., Brown-Chidsey & Steege, 2010; Riley-Tillman & Burnes, 2009). Again, the focus of this RtI work is to implement visual analysis of single-case design outcomes in educational settings for evaluat-ing practice (even if not always with the potential for contributing to the scientific knowledge base). More recently Kratochwill et al. (2013) recommended strategies for developing practice-based evidence in which basic AB single-case designs were accompanied by visual and statistical analysis of outcome data.

Unresolved Issues in Visual Analysis of Single-Case Data

As single-case designs became more prevalent in research in the social sciences and education, an increasing number of issues were raised, many of which remain unresolved. In this section we review some of these major issues and identify research that has focused on this area, including (a) outcome criteria in visual analysis, (b) multiple criteria for making a decision from the visual display, (c) reliability of visual analysis, and (d) the effect of autocorrelation on the reliability and validity of visual analysis.

Applied Outcome Criteria and Visual Analysis

Generally, visual analysis is conducted to examine the existence of intervention effects based on an experimental criterion (e.g., Is the effect of the intervention evident when the visual analyst detects systematic patterns in the data, such as A [baseline] to B [intervention] changes in the series' level, trend, and variability?). Visual analysis of single-case data has also been linked to the concept of "social validity" or "social validation" (Wolf, 1978), which is used to determine whether the effects (or size of the effects) resulting from an intervention are of clinical importance (Kazdin, 1977, 2011). Social validation criteria are considered within the context of normative comparisons (involving comparison of the client's behavior or performance on targeted outcomes with that of peers behaving under the same conditions) and subjective evaluations (involving familiar others in a rating or judgment of the client's change in targeted outcomes). Thus, in certain single-case intervention research contexts, social validation can supplement an evaluation of the study's typical outcome measures. The presumption is that by incorporating outcomes that are socially valid, visual analysis becomes a more appropriate and more widely accepted data-analysis strategy because determining whether a client has met or surpassed clinical criteria should be readily detected. Despite the important conceptual underpinnings of social validation in visual analysis, there is a paucity of research to support its application to determine what it adds to the visual analysis process. What is needed is research that examines the relationship between experimental and social validation criteria. For example, experimental outcomes could be varied systematically, with judges asked to rate both dimensions of social validation with varying data series outcomes in the context of solving an applied problem in a single-case design that meets What Works Clearinghouse (WWC) Standards (i.e., ABAB, multiple-baseline, alternating treatment designs).

Decision Criteria in Visual Analysis

Any method of data analysis should yield consistent findings even when applied by different individuals. Visual analysis of outcome data has been the focus of much research over the years, but much of this work suffers from methodological limitations some of which we elucidate here. The reliability of visual analysis has been reviewed by several investigators (e.g., Brossart, Parker, Olson, & Mahadevan, 2006; Franklin, Gorman, Beasley, & Allison, 1997; Ottenbacher, 1993), and concerns have been noted. For example, the investigation by Ottenbacher (1993), in which 14 single-case studies (N = 789 participants) were reviewed, yielded information on three reliability dimensions of visual analysis. First, Ottenbacher found that interrater agreement was generally low (M = .58; Mdn = .58; SD = .12; range = .39–.84). Second, training generally did not increase agreement in that the outcomes were about the same for trained (.62) and untrained (.57) raters. Third, when trend lines were added to improve the interrater agreement of visual analysis (to be discussed in a later section), there was no substantial difference (with trend line = .64; without trend line = .59).

Similarly, Franklin et al. (1997) noted that researchers failed to demonstrate acceptable levels of interrater reliability in visual analysis and that most research has been based on simple AB designs, with no focus on alternating treatment designs, multiple-baseline designs, or other design variations. After reviewing some of the research on the reliability of visual analysis (e.g., De Prospero & Cohen, 1979; Harbst, Ottenbacher, & Harris, 1991; Ottenbacher, 1990; Park, Marascuilo, & Gaylord-Ross, 1990), Brossart et al. (2006) concluded that the reliability of visual judgments for AB effect assessments was generally low and unacceptable. They found that adding trend lines (see, e.g., De Prospero & Cohen, 1979; Greenspan & Fisch, 1992; Hojem & Ottenbacher, 1988; Skib, Deno, Marston, & Casey, 1989) did not improve reliability and "sometimes created dependencies, helped maintain inconsistent judgments, and led to overemphasis on trend to the neglect of other features" (p. 533).

More positive results regarding the reliability of visual analysis have been reported in subsequent research (e.g., Kahng, Chung, Gutshall, Pitts, Kao, & Girolami, 2010; Normand & Bailey, 2006). Normand and Bailey (2006) showed a 72% average agreement between individuals who were certified behavior analysts (five participants) and preestablished criteria presented by the authors. *Celeration* lines—lines representing the frequency of responding for a specific time divided by unit time (Kennedy, 2005)—did not improve the accuracy of visual judgments Nevertheless, similar to the findings of Ottenbacher (1993) and Brossart et al. (2006), trend lines did not improve the average interrater agreement (presence of trend line = .67 and absence of trend line = .78). Most recently Kahng et al. (2010) replicated and extended the research by De Prospero and Cohen (1979). Their participants, members of the board of editors and associate editors for the *Journal of Applied Behavior Analysis*, were asked to judge a series of 36 ABAB design graphs on a 100-point scale of "experimental control" in which they provided a dichotomous response to the control choice (yes or no for experimental control). The researchers found high levels of interrater reliability and agreement based on the intraclass correlation coefficient, Pearson correlation coefficient, and Cohen kappa measures. The researchers noted that the contrasting results with De Prospero and Cohen (1979) could be explained by several factors, including an increase in training of behavior analysts since the earlier study, different dependent variables in the two investigations (i.e., use of a rating of 0 to 100 in the earlier investigation), and various procedural differences between the two studies (e.g., instructions, participants).

These more positive studies, however, have a number of limitations. First, and as has been noted by previous researchers (e.g., Kahng et al., 2010), much of the research involves only judgments of AB phase differences and has not been extended to complete phase single-case research designs that meet WWC Standards (i.e., ABAB, alternating treatment, multiple-baseline). In this regard, the judgments called for by the rater are an analogue to the typical conditions that researchers would use in making decisions from graphic displays. Second, it is unclear how various patterns of data in the graphical display (e.g., trend, variability, score overlap) affect interrater judgments. Thus, one characteristic of the data may be especially problematic and account for the problem of unreliability (e.g., trend, outliers). Third, the components of training are not always clearly specified and so it is unknown what particular aspects of the data the judges have been instructed to attend to when making their assessments. These variations across studies may well contribute to the reported unreliability of visual analysis noted in the earlier studies. At this time, the question of reliability for visual analysis remains unresolved. Future research is needed. That research should use full research designs (not just A-B comparisons), with the reliability of observers' functional relation ratings from the data based on that full design assessed. It might be expected that under some conditions reliability will be high, and under others low, and a useful focus of future research would be to define those conditions.

Autocorrelation in Single-Case Data

In single-case intervention studies, the fact that repeated measurements are taken on the same case is of tremendous value in that multiple uncontrolled, idiosyncratic features of the case are held constant from one measure to the next. As a result, the researcher does not need a randomized control or comparison group to rule out various threats to the study's internal validity. At the same time, the potential methodological strengths associated with the repeated-measurement feature of single-case intervention research are accompanied by certain statistical-analysis challenges. In particular, because the multiple-outcome observations of a time-series experiment are produced by the same case (whether an individual, group, community, or some other entity) over time, those repeated observations are generally assumed to be *autocorrelated*, or *serially dependent* (e.g., Box & Jenkins, 1970; Glass, Willson, & Gottman, 1975; Shadish, Cook, & Campbell, 2002). That is, a given observation in the series is likely related to, or is a function of (in varying degrees), the preceding observation(s). Although it is possible that any particular time-series data set does not contain sequentially dependent observations, researchers and data analysts are obligated to proceed under an "autocorrelation" assumption, until this assumption is proven otherwise. Thus, as a general principle we would advocate calculating and reporting the autocorrelation in the series—even given the known variability associated with estimating population autocorrelations from their sample analogs (see, e.g., Marriott & Pope, 1954; Riviello & Beretvas, 2009; Shadish, Rindskopf, Hedges, & Sullivan, 2011).

Of what consequence to the visual analyst is acknowledging the existence of autocorrelation in time-series data (including single-case intervention experiments)?[5] As has been demonstrated in previous visual-analysis research (e.g., Fisch, 2001; Jones, Weinrott, & Vaught, 1978; Ottenbacher, 1993; Ximenes, Manolov, Solanas, & Quera, 2009), as more autocorrelation is introduced into the data series of a single-case time-series design, the accuracy/validity of visual analysts' judgments about the presence or absence of an intervention effect (based on formal statistical decision criteria) decreases. For that reason, exclusive reliance on visual analysis to assess the outcomes of single-case intervention experiments can be difficult—yet, as will be discussed in a following section, it is an exercise that has the potential to be improved through systematically informed training and practice.

Fisch (2001) found that trained behavior analysts were able to identify level shifts in AB-design time-series data with "modestly autocorrelated" data but trends were either not correctly identified or missed. Ximenes et al. (2009) conducted a Monte Carlo study to evaluate the accuracy of visual analysts' decisions (in terms of the magnitude of effect) for AB-design data with known parameters representing either zero or nonzero effects. Sixty 20-observation graphs were presented to 24 psychologists with expertise in visual analysis and to 33 undergraduate students, with instructions to judge the presence or absence of a treatment effect. The authors found that for both groups of participants (a) accuracy was generally low but (b) intrajudge consistency was higher for data patterns with nonexistent or small effects. Of relevance to the current discussion, (a) both groups misjudged nonzero treatment effects (i.e., produced Type I errors) in the presence of positive autocorrelation, and (b) with negative autocorrelation the task of detecting treatment effects became more difficult. Although the authors followed the recommendations of Brossart et al. (2006)—with the exception of providing a context for the data—the study included only AB designs for the visual judgment task.

To illustrate the foregoing autocorrelation discussion, consider the three hypothetical data patterns shown in Figure 3.1 that were produced by a single-case ABAB intervention design. As is detailed in the next section, the ABAB design represents a substantial improvement over the basic AB design when applying contemporary "standards" for documenting an intervention effect. However, to simplify the present discussion we focus primarily on the first A and first B phase of the three panels in Figure 3.1. It should be noted that in each of those panels, the A and B phase means are 2.5 and 3.5, respectively and, therefore the three panels produce identical mean intervention effects (an A-to-B average increase of 1.0 unit). The difference among the three panels is that the within-phase outcomes occur in different temporal orders, which in turn results in different degrees of "first order" autocorrelation in each series.

---

[5]In a recent review of single-case intervention research reported in 2008, Shadish and Sullivan (2011) found that the average autocorrelation was close to zero (mean = –0.04, with a range from –0.93 to 0.79). In addition, Shadish et al. (2011) have challenged the traditional methods of calculating the observed autocorrelation in single-case designs, arguing that estimates obtained in prior work may be biased because of the typically large amount of sampling error produced by studies with a small number of data points.

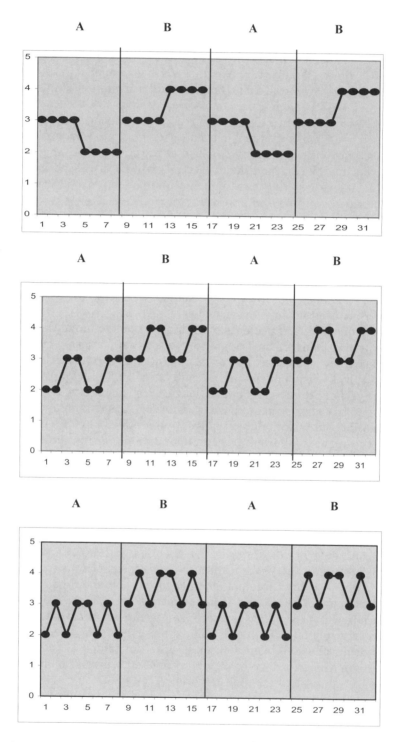

Figure 3.1. Hypothetical example of an ABAB intervention experiment with eight outcome observations per phase and three different degrees of autocorrelation (top panel, r = 0.75; middle panel, r = 0.167; bottom panel, r = –0.75).

Specifically, the autocorrelation for each phase's data in the top panel is +0.75, that for the middle panel data is +0.167 and that for the lower panel data is –0.75. With a larger autocorrelation (either positive or negative), a greater proportion of outcomes can be predicted from the immediately preceding outcome than is possible with a smaller autocorrelation. For example, with eight outcomes in both the first A and the first B phases of each panel, one can make a prediction about Outcomes 2–8 (for Phase A) and Outcomes 10–16 (for Phase B) being either "the same as" or "different from" the immediately preceding outcome. As may be determined from the top panel, where the autocorrelation is +0.75, of those seven predicted outcomes, six (or 86%) are correctly predicted to be "the same as" the immediately preceding outcome. Equivalently, for the bottom panel, where the autocorrelation is –0.75, six out of seven outcomes (again 86%) are correctly predicted to be "different from" the immediately preceding outcome. In contrast, for the middle panel, where the autocorrelation is +0.167, only four of the seven outcomes (57%) are correctly predicted to be "the same as" the immediately preceding outcome.

Of direct relevance to the present visual-analysis discussion is that even though the intervention effect of 1.0 unit is identical in the three panels, a formal statistical analysis would reveal that there is greater probabilistic evidence for an initial intervention effect (i.e., a greater A-to-B mean change) in the bottom panel (where the autocorrelation is –0.75) than there is in the middle panel (autocorrelation = +0.167), which in turn provides more convincing evidence than in the top panel (autocorrelation = +0.75). In fact, with an a priori Type I error probability of .05 designated to test for an initial intervention effect, one would conclude that the effect is statistically significant for both the bottom panel's series (where $p < .0001$) and the middle panel's series ($p < .01$) but not for the top panel's series ($p > .10$). In the absence of systematic training and practice, it is unlikely that a visual analyst would be able to arrive at the same conclusions. The bottom-line recommendation stemming from this example is that to make intervention-effect decisions that are consistent with those following from formal statistical analyses, visual analysts must be skilled in recognizing autocorrelated data in a graphical display (see also our subsequent section, "Training in Visual Analysis").

Single-Case Intervention Research Standards and Visual Analysis

As noted previously, certain professional groups, including divisions of the APA, have proposed standards for single-case intervention designs. In 2009 the WWC commissioned a panel to develop technical standards for such designs. One important outcome of this effort was the panel's decision to distinguish between *design* standards and *evidence* criteria (Kratochwill et al., 2010, 2013). This distinction is based on the assumption that a research study may satisfy an acceptable *design* standard (e.g., a specified number of replications are included in the design structure to establish validity) but may show no *evidence* of an intervention effect when the data are analyzed visually and/or statistically. Such a distinction has important implications for addressing the well-documented editorial bias against publishing studies that yield negative (i.e., statistically nonsignificant) results (see Greenwald, 1975; Sterling,

Rosenbaum, & Weinkam, 1995).[6] In particular, the panel adopted the position that a single-case intervention study with an acceptable design, but for which the intervention was unsuccessful, should be just as admissible to the content-area's database (professional journals included) as an acceptably designed study for which the intervention was successful. A compromise notion is that journals could be selective in publishing negative-results intervention studies by reporting only (a) investigations that contradict previous studies with positive findings (especially studies with weaker methodological characteristics) and (b) intervention-based practices that have widespread application and appeal, yet the empirical investigation under consideration demonstrates no positive support (James Halle, personal communication, September 19, 2012).

The design standards are summarized in Figure 3.2 and are now briefly discussed because they have a bearing on the application of visual analysis in single-case intervention research.

DESIGN STANDARDS. Single-case design standards focus on the methodology and operations of the research and are concerned with some of the same internal-validity "threats" that are associated with conventional experimental research (i.e., history, maturation, testing, regression toward the mean, etc.)—see, for example, Shadish et al. (2002). The internal validity of an individual single-case investigation is enhanced through various types of replication, including the ABAB design's repeated introduction and withdrawal of the intervention, the alternating treatment design's rapid alternation of different intervention conditions, and the multiple-baseline design's systematically staggered (i.e., replicated across units, behaviors, or settings) introduction of the intervention. In single-case designs, the critical features required for inferring causal connections between interventions and outcomes are (a) active manipulation of the independent variable (i.e., the intervention), (b) systematic measurement of the outcome variable(s) over time by more than one assessor (i.e., interobserver agreement must be established on each dependent variable), (c) at least three attempts to demonstrate an intervention effect at three different points in time or with three different phase repetitions (e.g., ABAB designs, multiple-baseline designs, and alternating treatment designs), and (d) a minimum of five data points within a phase (with certain exceptions noted in the Standards). Based on how the research study is evaluated on these four dimensions, the research design is classified as *meeting standards, meeting standards with reservations*, or *not meeting standards*.[7] Only when the study meets design standards (with or without reservations) should the assessor proceed to the evidence criteria stage (see Figure 3.2).

Sullivan and Shadish (2011) examined the WWC standards related to implementation of the intervention, acceptable levels of observer agreement–

---

[6]In addition, in most academic disciplines a literature bias—an overrepresentation of studies with statistically significant findings, along with inflated effect-size estimates—exists because of researchers' inclination not to write up and submit for publication their negative-results studies (e.g., Rosenthal, 1979).

[7]In the present version of the *Standards*, randomization in the design is not required but clearly can improve the internal validity of the research (for further discussion, see Chapter 2, this volume).

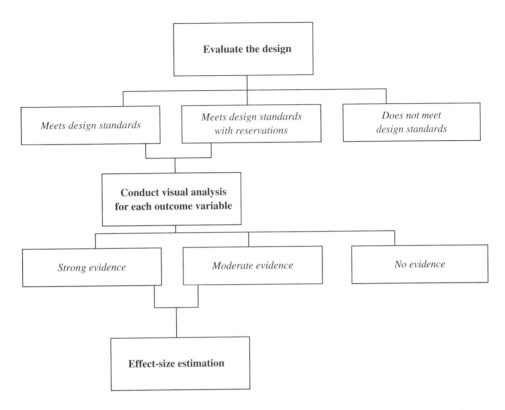

Figure 3.2. Procedure for applying single-case design standards: First evaluate the design and then, if applicable, evaluate the evidence. From "Single Case Designs Technical Documentation," (p. 13), by T. R. Kratochwill, J. Hitchcock, R. H. Horner, J. R. Levin, S. L. Odom, D. M. Rindskopf, and W. R. Shadish, 2010, U.S. Department of Education, Institute of Education Sciences, National Center for Education Evaluation and Regional Assistance, What Works Clearinghouse. In the public domain.

reliability, opportunities to demonstrate a treatment effect, and acceptable numbers of data points in a phase. Of the published single-case intervention studies in 21 journals for 2008, they found that nearly 45% of them met the strictest standards of design and 30% met the standards with some reservations. It therefore appears that about 75% of the single-case intervention research published in major journals for the particular year sampled would meet the WWC design standards.

EVIDENCE CRITERIA. The Single-Case Design Panel suggested that the evidence criteria be based primarily on visual analysis of the outcome data (see Figure 3.2) and noted that WWC reviewers of single-case intervention research should be trained in visual analysis, taking into account the factors reviewed by Horner and Spaulding (2010). In this process, visual analysis includes the combined evaluation of level, trend, variability, immediacy of effect, data overlap in adjacent phases, and consistency of data patterns in similar phases (see also Parsonson & Baer, 1978, 1992). These six factors are

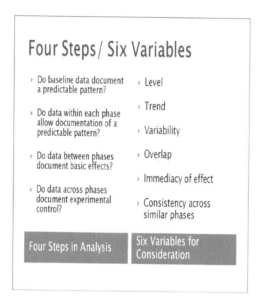

Figure 3.3. The four steps and six variables considered in visual analysis of single-case data.

considered in the four-step process depicted in Figure 3.3.[8] Depending on the nature of the intervention and the outcome measure, these factors can have quite different meaning and importance. For example, for various academic-skill outcome measures, one might anticipate gradual acquisition of the skill and therefore, an immediate effect might not be expected.

Once reviewers are trained to an acceptable level of reliability, they proceed to make an evidence determination based on published graphs in the original report, which in turn results in their declarations of *strong evidence, moderate evidence*, or *no evidence*. (More information on training individuals to conduct visual analysis is presented later in this chapter.) The evidence assessment is based on the graphic displays of the data and, therefore, such assessment cannot be conducted for single-case studies in which no graphical displays are provided—a rare occurrence in the single-case literature, but see DuPaul, Ervin, Hook, and McGoey (1998) for an example.

EXAMPLE APPLICATIONS OF THE STANDARDS. In a single-case investigation that meets WWC design and evidence standards, Schrandt, Townsend, and Poulson (2009) focused on teaching children empathy skills. Four children with autism were involved in a training program implemented sequentially in a multiple-baseline design across participants. The authors included four attempts to replicate the intervention (exceeding the WWC design standard of three attempts) and they met other design standards. The outcomes revealed

---

[8]An additional factor is considered for multiple-baseline designs: namely, there must be stability in the yet-to-be intervened series when an effect is demonstrated in the prior series.

clear changes for each child. The effects were particularly salient through visual analysis, as the children did not have the empathy skills during the baseline assessment but acquired the skills rapidly, coincident with the introduction of the intervention.

Another example of the design standards and evidence criteria can be illustrated in a study by Reichow, Barton, Sewell, Good, and Wolery (2010), who adopted an alternating treatment design to evaluate the effects of weighted vests on three children with autism and developmental disabilities. The hypothesis was that children with certain developmental disabilities would have fewer behavioral problems when wearing weighted vests because these better regulate and organize sensory input. In the Reichow et al. study, the researchers compared three different conditions: weighted vests, vests with no weights (included as a placebo condition), and no vests (to represent a baseline condition). The alternating treatment design included several replications to meet the design standard (these standards would be met "with reservations," which nonetheless allowed an assessor to proceed to the evidence-standard stage). The authors determined through visual inspection of the data that weighted vests had no effect relative to the baseline and placebo conditions (with which we concur), which led to the conclusion that there was "no evidence" to support the hypothesis that wearing weighted vests benefitted the children included in this study.

Methods to Improve Visual Analysis of Single-Case Data

Although historically there has been reliance on visual analysis of single-case data, in recent years a number of authors have made recommendations for improving the technique's reliability, validity, and ultimate acceptability. In this section we review several strategies proposed for such purposes, including (a) alternative forms of graphic display, (b) training in visual analysis, (c) standard protocols with component algorithms, (d) formal decision criteria, (e) randomization and masked assessment schemes, and (f) combining visual analysis and statistical analysis.

Alternative Forms of Graphical Display

One factor that can influence visual judgments of graphical display is the form in which the data are presented in the graph. Therefore, it is not surprising that some authors of single-case design texts have provided guidance on graph construction (e.g., Gast, 2010; Johnston & Pennypacker, 2009; Tawney & Gast, 1984), whereas others have provided guidelines for displaying such data components as variability and trend (e.g., Franklin et al. 1997). The *Journal of Applied Behavior Analysis* provides graph-preparation guidance to researchers submitting manuscripts for consideration by that journal. Recently, some authors have also developed software to facilitate presentation of single-case research outcomes in graphs. For example, Bulté and Onghena (2012) developed the "R Package" to present graphic display of single-case data and to transform graphical displays to raw data. Their program takes into account some visual analysis features discussed in the literature, including plotting the central location on the horizontal line, presenting variability (with range bars, range lines, and trended ranges), and displaying trends on the line graph (either by presenting linear trend or running medians). Currently there is no research on how the program affects visual analysis of single-case data. Gafurov and Levin's *ExPRT* (Excel® Package of Randomization Tests) statistical software, the focus of Chapter 6 in this volume, also includes graphical representations of the data produced by a variety of single-case designs.

A few empirical studies have compared alternative forms of graphical display (e.g., Knapp, 1983; Morales, Dominguez, & Jurado, 2001). Knapp (1983) asked undergraduate, graduate, and postgraduate individuals trained in behavior analysis to make judgments of AB graphs that varied on several dimensions. Cumulative, logarithmic, and frequency-polygon plots were mixed with three styles of presentation for the frequency polygon (separation of the AB phase by either a space or vertical line, or no separation). Although no judgment differences among the three different levels of the individuals trained in behavior analysis, differences were found among the graphic techniques and the mean levels of change. The author reported that most of the differences reflected problems in discriminating mean shifts in the data series. Knapp concluded that visual judgments of such shifts vary as a function of the graphical technique adopted by the researcher. Nevertheless, and as we noted above, issues of graphical display in the context of complete single-case research design studies (e.g., full ABAB or MBD, not just AB) must be taken into account for the field to move forward in this area.

Morales et al. (2001) exposed three judges (professors with a background in quantitative methods) to 3,000 graphs (1,000 line, 1,000 bar, and 1,000 Tukey box plots). Each of these graphs was presented within an AB design format, with a variety of effective and ineffective treatment outcomes represented in the data display. The authors found that each of the participants made more errors when the data were presented as line graphs or bar graphs than as box plots. In that most graphical displays in single-case research are presented as line graphs, this is an area of concern, deserving further research. Again, these findings require replication with complete single-case designs.

In summary, researchers have typically relied on traditional forms of data display (e.g., bar graphs, connected line graphs). Some journals such as the *Journal of Applied Behavior Analysis* have provided guidelines for data display to help standardize the process of reporting. Yet, relatively little research has been conducted with different forms of data display and their effects on visual-analysis outcomes. Priorities for research in this area include (a) additional studies that evaluate how different forms of data display influence visual judgments of outcomes and (b) studies that evaluate how different forms of data display are affected by formal training in visual analysis—a topic that has received recent attention and that we now consider.

Training in Visual Analysis

One proposed option to improve visual analysis of single-case outcomes is to provide visual analysts with formal training prior to having them make judgments of graphic displays. Although some researchers have sought to improve inter-judge reliability of visual analysis through training, some efforts have not been compelling (see James, Smith, & Milne, 1996; Ottenbacher, 1993). Others have argued that training individuals in visual analysis can both improve reliability of the process and reduce the incidence of Type 1 errors—namely, falsely concluding that an intervention effect occurred (Kennedy, 2005), which has been documented as one of the problems of visual analysis (James et al., 1996). For example, Wampold and Furlong (1981a, 1981b) exposed students to either visual-analysis training ($N = 14$) or multivariate statistical analysis ($N = 10$). Participants viewed 36 graphs and were asked to make a determination of statistically significant differences between the A and B phases. It was found that participants trained in visual analysis focused their attention on large phase differences but generally ignored variation, whereas participants trained in multivariate procedures paid more attention to variation. Nevertheless, both groups of participants improved their visual judgments only by a modest amount. Similarly, Harbst et al. (1991) found little improvement in participants' visual judgments following a training protocol. James et al. (1996) found that participants became more conservative following a training protocol with AB designs but experienced only limited improvement in their judgments of treatment effects.

Hagopian et al. (1997) reported three studies in which participants were exposed to functional analysis graphs, where "functional analysis" is a form of experimental assessment in which the functions of behavior (reasons for the behavior occurring) are identified and then empirically tested in single-case design formats. In the first study, three interns were exposed to graphs and demonstrated low interrater agreement in identifying the function of a problem behavior ($M = 45\%$). In the second study, 64 graphs were presented to two experts who then developed structured criteria for visual inspection of the data (e.g., checking for trends, counting data above and below a criterion). In the third study, these criteria were then presented to the three participants involved in the first study. Through application of the criteria, the authors demonstrated that the average interrater agreement increased to 81%. Although the authors improved the reliability of the visual-analysis process, the training materials were limited to functional-analysis applications in "multielement" single-case designs.

Several issues emerge in this area that have yet to be resolved and that represent a priority for single-case reliability-training research. First, one approach would be to compare novice participants before and after training with experts. Currently, however, there are no agreed-on criteria for what constitutes expertise in this domain. The possibilities include selecting editors and associate editors of journals that publish single-case research, researchers who have been involved in single-case design investigations, and individuals who have been trained previously to some acceptable level of reliability in visual analysis. Unfortunately, research has demonstrated that even so-called "experts" do not agree with one another in their judgments (e.g., Lieberman, Yoder, Reichow, & Wolery, 2010), as has been documented in other domains (e.g., McGuire et al., 1985). In addition, there is no consensus among experienced single-case intervention researchers about what constitutes a "convincing" intervention effect.

For example, should the major determinant of an intervention effect be based on visual- or statistical-analysis standards, or both?

Research on training in visual analysis also contains a number of methodological limitations, which have been recognized by Brossart et al. (2006) in offering the following recommendations for improving visual-analysis research: (a) Graphs should be fully contextualized, describing a particular client, target behavior(s), time frame, and data collection instrument; (b) judges should not be asked to predict the degree of statistical significance (i.e., a significance probability p-value) of a particular statistic but rather should be asked to judge graphs according to their own criteria of practical importance, effect, or impact; (c) judges should not be asked to make dichotomous yes–no decisions but rather to judge the extent or amount of intervention effectiveness; and (d) no single statistical test should be selected as "the valid criterion" but rather several optional statistical tests should be tentatively compared to the visual analyst's judgments.

These recommendations (with notable additions that we provide subsequently) can help advance work in the study of methods to improve visual analysis because most of the research in this area is not contextualized, does not involve judges using their own criteria in visual analysis, involves dichotomous judgments, and typically is based on only one statistical criterion. However, we would add that visual analysis needs to result in the researcher (a) determining if a data set documents experimental control (see WWC Single-Case Design Standards) and (b) evaluating the size of that effect. With respect to their fourth recommendation, Brossart et al. (2006) included five statistical techniques to validate visual-analysis judgments: (a) the binomial test on an extended phase A baseline (O. R. White & Haring, 1980), (b) the last treatment day procedure (D. M. White, Rusch, Kazdin, & Hartmann, 1989), (c) Gorsuch's trend effect-size procedure (Faith, Allison, & Gorman, 1996; Gorsuch, 1983), (d) Center's mean plus trend difference (Center, Skiba, & Casey, 1985–1986), and (e) Allison's mean plus trend difference (Allison & Gorman, 1993; Faith et al., 1996). They found that the Allison procedure (e) and D. M. White et al.'s last treatment day procedure (b) agreed most with visual judgments of intervention effects. Nevertheless, there was wide variation among the methods used, and the authors noted that no one statistical method should serve as the absolute criterion for comparing visual judgments.

Finally, we again emphasize that most research on visual analysis involves the use of basic AB designs (with the exception of the Kahng et al., 2010, study), which makes the artificial visual-analysis task only a distant cousin of actual visual analysis of research-based graphical displays. Swoboda, Kratochwill, Horner, and Levin (2012) developed a series of training materials that are applied to single-case designs (see subsequent discussion for more details). The graphs for each design type (ABAB, multiple baseline, and alternating treatment) represent the full design phases and therefore extend beyond the more traditional (and unacceptable) AB design format. Ongoing research with these graphs suggests that individuals exposed to the protocol can achieve high reliability across the three design classes. Nevertheless, research on visual analysis needs to focus on acceptable single-case designs rather than on decontextualized simple two-phase applications.

Standard Protocols With Component Algorithms

To improve the visual-analysis process, some writers have recommended formal application of a visual-analysis protocol that includes specific guidelines and component algorithms. For example, Tawney and Gast (1984) and Gast (2010) presented guidelines both within phases (i.e., phase length, estimate of trend, trend stability, data paths within trend, level stability and range, and level change) and between adjacent phases (number of variables changed, change in trend direction and effect, change in trend stability, change in level, and percentage of data overlap). Tawney and Gast noted that "with practice comes proficiency [in visual analysis]" (p. 186) and that such components could be standardized and built into visual-analysis training protocols.

Use of various methods to improve visual analysis requires numerous considerations. For example, visual analysis that accounts only for level and variability misses the added influence of time-dependent effects (e.g., trends) both within and between phases. Failing to account for trend can lead to erroneous inferences about intervention effects and can miss cyclicity in the data, which might be mistaken for an intervention effect if not disentangled. This problem is also much more serious in AB comparisons than in ABAB or multiple-baseline design formats. Here we discuss methods for considering both baseline trend and trend changes between the baseline and intervention phases.

One old method to assess baseline trend was to draw a free-hand linear trend line based on the plotted data. With this method researchers used their "best judgment" of approximately what the best-fitting straight line is for the baseline data. However, with options in current computer programs, a more precise method of generating a trend line is available. Specifically, superimposing a statistically based linear regression line over the baseline data is one way to overcome the limitations of a free-hand attempt. Most software and graphing programs will generate such a line automatically. By generating this regression line, the visual analyst will be able to take any baseline trend into account (either visually or statistically) when interpreting differences in level between the series of baseline and intervention outcome observations. At the same time, relying on a linear trend line is not recommended when there are outliers in the data, when only one or a few data points have undue influence ("leverage") on the resultant regression line, or when the trend is nonlinear.

A simpler, visual approach to compare the baseline and intervention phase levels in the presence of a baseline trend is the split middle (SM) method (Kazdin, 1982; Tawney & Gast, 1984; O. R. White, 1972). With this procedure one obtains a baseline trend line and compares the intervention-phase data with that trend line. To create an SM line, the baseline data series is split in half. A point is made in each half at the median time point and the median outcome measure for that half. A line is drawn to connect the two points to form the SM line. This line represents a trend line that is more robust to outliers because it relies on medians. An additional advantage of the SM line is that the median time can be shifted in either direction and new lines made to get a rough reliability estimate of the trend line. Two additional SM lines can also be calculated by selecting one time point below each baseline half median and one time point above to create a total of three lines. If the new SM lines are similar to the original SM line, it suggests some degree of reliability. If they are quite different, then the calculated SM line is highly dependent on that specific median value. Although a binomial statistical test can accompany the SM method, this option is not recommended because a standard binomial test is not appropriate for autocorrelated data (see Crosbie, 1993; Footnote 9 in this chapter). For limitations of the SM procedure, see Chapter 4, this volume.

As an alternative to the SM line for estimating the baseline trend line, the "resistant trend line" has been proposed (Franklin et al., 1997). The resistant trend line considers the data in three approximately equal-sized sections. If the section sizes cannot be made equal, one extra data point would be included in the middle section and two would be included in the two outside sections. The baseline regression line is constructed by calculating the slope between the median of the two outside sections: (right median outcome measure–left median outcome measure) / (right median time point–left median time point). The intercept is calculated using all three data sections. Much like the SM method, the trend can be constructed via graphed data without requiring calculations from the full raw data. Further, using a line like this prevents unreliable human judgments of trend. In comparison to the SM line, the resistant trend line is more sensitive to the data at the beginning and the end of the data series, with less attention paid to the middle section. With this method it is imperative that the data actually assume a linear trend.

In contrast, when it is concluded that the trend is nonlinear, the "running medians" (RM) method could be considered (Morley & Adams, 1991). The general idea of the RM method is to create a line for which each point is based on the median of all of the times around it. The number of time points considered in each median is specified by the "batch size." For example, if the batch size is set to 3, the line begins at the second time point and is the median of the first three outcome measures. The next point would be the median of the second, third, and fourth outcome measures. This process continues all the way to one less than the total number of time points and creates a series of points that are connected to produce a nonlinear RM3 line. The batch size can be set to 4, 5, or any number that makes sense according to the number of time points present.

In some research on visual analysis, judgments from the visual analyst have been compared to statistical "nonoverlap" methods to determine whether there is agreement between the two. Specifically, Wolery, Busick, Reichow, and Barton (2010) compared four methods of nonoverlap, including percentage of nonoverlapping data, pairwise data overlap squared, percentage of data exceeding the median, and percentage of data exceeding the median trend (see Chapter 4, this volume, for discussion of these methods). In the Wolery et al. study, visual analysts (consisting of the study's four authors) rendered judgments about whether or not a baseline-to-intervention-phase change occurred in 160 AB data sets from the *Journal of Applied Behavior Analysis*. The consensus judgments were then compared to the four aforementioned nonoverlap methods. The authors reported that each method was associated with high levels of visual-analysis disagreement, leading to the recommendation that such nonoverlap methods be abandoned in research syntheses of single-case effect sizes (see Chapter 8, this volume).

Formal Decision Criteria

An advancement of the SM technique, called the dual criterion (DC) method, was proposed by Fisher, Kelley, and Lomas (2003). The DC method calculates both a mean ("level") line and a trend line for the baseline phase, which is extended into the intervention phase. A binomial test is then conducted to assess whether (assuming the null hypothesis of no intervention effect) there are a sufficient number of data points above (or below) both lines in the treatment phase to conclude that an intervention effect has occurred. The DC method requires the intervention phase to "statistically beat" both the level and trend of the baseline phase to demonstrate a treatment effect. However, because Fisher et al.'s (2003) preliminary examination of the DC method found that it produced "unacceptably" high Type I error probabilities when autocorrelation was present in the series, those authors proposed the conservative dual criterion (CDC) method as an improvement. The CDC method is a modification of the DC method with a 0.25 standard deviation adjustment of both the trend and level lines in the direction of the intended intervention effect. The number of data points that exceeds both adjusted lines in the intended direction of the treatment outcome is presented as evidence for an effect compared with the number expected from the binomial formula.[9] The value of 0.25 standard deviations was determined empirically by Fisher et al. through trial and error from their data generation mechanism in an attempt to gain control of the Type I error probability while yielding respectable power.

Stewart, Carr, Brandt, and McHenry (2007) evaluated the CDC method in a single-case "withdrawal design embedded within a nonconcurrent multiple baseline design across participants" (p. 715) where, following a baseline phase, six university students were exposed to a traditional lecture on visual inspection, followed by instruction in the CDC method. According to the authors, the traditional lecture method did not improve visual inspection accuracy when students were exposed to AB graphs. The CDC method was effective in improving visual judgments when the level and trend lines were present on the graphs but not when they were removed. Thus, the maintenance of the effect of the CDC method on visual analysis accuracy (i.e., in the absence of superimposed level and trend lines) needs additional study in this training context. More important, because the two training conditions (lecture and CDC method) were introduced to the same six students in the same order (namely, lecture followed by the CDC method), it is not possible to disentangle the unique effects of the two training conditions. To do so would require a study either with the order of the two training conditions counterbalanced across participants or with participants randomly assigned to the two training conditions.

---

[9]As Swoboda, Kratochwill, and Levin (2010) have pointed out, however: "[J]ust as visual analysts do not take into account the autocorrelated nature of single-case data, neither does the binomial test applied by Fisher, Kodak, and Moore (2007) in their CDC [or DC] method. In addition, Fisher et al.'s binomial test is actually two tests in one (viz., a single test conducted in reference to both level and slope), and so the specific binomial probability incorporated into their test ($p = .5$) is not appropriate." As has been indicated by Swoboda et al. (2010, Footnote 1), work is currently underway to ameliorate the binomial-test problem.

The SM and CDC methods both represent attempts to improve the interrater reliability of the visual-analysis decision-making process. Nonetheless, the usefulness of such procedures can be challenged for a number of reasons. First, the decision about intervention effects is dependent upon application of a standard binomial statistical test, which, as has already been noted, is suspect in situations for which the data are autocorrelated (see Crosbie, 1993). Second, these methods have been proposed only for basic AB time-series intervention designs. As was mentioned earlier, Swoboda et al. (2010) have developed a training procedure that extends the CDC approach (albeit with the questionable binomial tests) to ABAB, multiple-baseline, and alternating treatment designs by repeating the decision-making process at each of the three phase transitions in ABAB designs (e.g., A to B, B to A withdrawal, and A to B replication) or with each different participant (or setting or behavior) in multiple-baseline designs. An additional concern is that the Swoboda et al. procedures have not been examined in a controlled training experiment and so it is not yet known whether these procedures actually improve the visual-analysis process. In that regard, evaluation of their training procedures would require some basis for comparison and would need to address the Brossart et al. (2006) recommendation to use multiple methods of analysis in comparative visual analysis studies.

Randomization and Masked Assessment Schemes

Limitations of visual analysis may extend to basic features of the single-case intervention research process. Todman and Dugard (2001) identified three issues that challenge the tradition of a sole reliance on visual analysis of data in a single-case intervention study: (a) experimental control, (b) response-guided experimentation, and (c) replication. These issues, which we consider next, may prompt researchers to consider supplements to visual analysis as an "intervention effect" evidence criterion.

EXPERIMENTAL CONTROL. Visual analysis may well be sufficient for conveying research outcomes to some audiences. The arguments favoring reliance on visual analysis in applied behavior analysis research have been advanced by Parsonson and Baer (1978, 1992) and include the emphasis on control of extraneous ("nuisance") variables while emphasizing large outcome-measure effects. When the researcher has nearly complete control of extraneous variables and the treatment produces large effects, there may be little need for statistical analysis of the experimental outcomes. Moreover, with the addition of randomization in design construction to control nuisance variables (Chapter 2, this volume), visual analysis may become increasingly acceptable for satisfying evidence criteria.

On the other hand, as science extends beyond the applied behavior analysis community, more scholars need to be aware of (and appreciate the scientific contribution of) single-case designs. In this process, single-case intervention researchers have new options to add data-analysis tools that enhance the validity of their interpretations of the data outcomes. Todman and Dugard (2001) noted that "it seems to us that there is no satisfactory justification for failing to use a random allocation procedure in single-case studies when variables are not under tight control or the expected effect is not large" (p. 25). This statement may appear radical to many researchers at this point in the history of single-case research endeavors. Nevertheless, we would encourage researchers to consider the benefits of randomization in single-case intervention research because without some appropriate form of randomization, it is difficult to control the many nuisance variables that are present in natural settings, such as school and communities (see also Chapter 2, this volume). That is, there is the possibility of bias being introduced into the interpretation of the findings, as Todman and Dugard (1999) illustrated in their hypothetical experiment in which the intervention start point was *response guided* rather than randomly determined—see the next section, which includes a more complete description of Todman and Dugard's study.

The goal of demonstrating large effects cannot always be achieved in applied and natural settings. When large effects are not evident, visual analysis may be more challenging in producing reliable effects across researchers, thereby opening the important issue of supplementing this method with other data-analysis procedures. The research process may begin by focusing on variables that have small or minimal effects not easily discerned by visual analysis. Later in the research process, these variables with small effects might be combined with other treatment procedures to produce larger effects. Nevertheless, the initial reliance on visual analysis only may obscure what could be important findings in developing new treatments (Kazdin, 2011).

RESPONSE-GUIDED EXPERIMENTATION. *Response-guided experimentation* refers to (a) the ongoing examination and analysis of data as they are collected during the flow of a single-case intervention study and then (b) use of those data to make timing decisions about the introduction or withdrawal of an intervention (e.g., Dugard, File, & Todman, 2012; Edgington, 1992; Ferron & Jones, 2006; Franklin et al., 1997; Chapter 5, this volume). This procedure can be illustrated in two design variations. First, in an ABAB design the researcher applies response-guided experimentation when the decision to move from the baseline to the intervention phase is determined on the basis of the baseline series' data pattern (i.e., the baseline series' trend and/or variability). An example of this process would be the researcher deciding not to introduce the intervention until it appears that the baseline series has stabilized. In a second design variation, with response-guided experimentation in a multiple-baseline design the researcher's decision about when to introduce the intervention to the second and subsequent replicates (cases, situations, or measures) is based on examination of the within- and between-series data.

Furthermore, if a study produces data that differ from what was expected, the new data points may be used to change the design. Consider, for example, a multiple-baseline design that does not result in initial change, thereby prompting the researcher to shift to a within-series design in which the original B condition has been modified to include additional treatment components (i.e., ABB'AB' design, where B' represents the new treatment). Response-guided experimentation has been the primary method of conducting single-case intervention research in the behavior-analysis and clinical and applied fields. Reliance on this procedure is premised on the major advantages that it is presumed to possess relative to alternative intervention-assignment schemes (Hayes et al., 1999)—namely, those in which the specific points of intervention, introduction, and withdrawal either are decided on before the experiment begins or are randomly determined (see Chapter 2, this volume). In this regard, Ferron and Jones (2006) conducted an informal survey of the use of response-guided experimentation in multiple-baseline designs. They reported that of 101 multiple-baseline studies between 1998 and 2001, in 31% the researchers were explicit in having adopted response-guided experimentation, and in another 51% the researchers appeared to have adopted response-guided experimentation. In only 4% of the studies were the points of intervention fixed, and in none of the studies did the points of intervention appear to have been randomly determined.

Several investigators have studied the response-guided process and its relationship to visual analysis (Austin & Mawhinney, 1999; Mawhinney & Austin, 1999; Vanselow, Thompson, & Karsina, 2011). In the Austin and Mawhinney (1999) study, for example, participants (two experts and two novices) were required to view and respond to published graphed data presented point by point (with the design phases removed from the display). Individuals in these studies were asked to comment on the characteristics of the data display, including, for example, stability, trend, and the point at which the treatment was introduced (as is typical in response-guided experimentation). The authors found that relative to novices, the experts took more of the data series into account, took more time to complete the protocol, and were somewhat more accurate in their identification of the point of intervention in the data series. To extend work in this area, Vanselow et al. (2011) presented published data to participants (expert behavior analysts, board-certified behavior analysts, and novices) point by point but also required them to report (a) whether they would continue the baseline series and (b) the rationale for their decision to continue or not to continue. In Study 1, under conditions of minimal information about the data set, the experts and board-certified behavior analysts generated baseline data of comparable lengths, which tended to differ from the lengths generated by the novices. When baseline variability was low, there was general agreement across participants, but this agreement decreased as the variability in the data increased. In Study 2, the authors provided specific information about the independent and dependent variables (e.g., the dependent variable was severe self-injury) and found that shorter baselines were generated than under conditions in which minimal information was provided.

Although the Vanselow et al. (2011) studies, along with the previously mentioned study by Kahng et al. (2010), show promise for the reliability of visual analysis under certain conditions, concerns have been raised about response-guided interventions. Despite its widespread use, response-guided experimentation has been challenged on both empirical and conceptual grounds. Todman and Dugard (1999) conducted a study to illustrate how response-guided experimentation can lead to inaccurate visual-analysis decisions. These investigators randomly generated 80 graphs of a 16-session AB intervention design that included a steady increase in outcomes between Sessions 1 and 16 (i.e., a linear trend across sessions) but no intervention effect. From the 80 generated graphs, 50 that produced a sequence of similar data points were selected. Two versions of each graph were constructed: one in which the point of intervention (i.e., the beginning of the B sessions) was indicated by a vertical line drawn following a series of several similar data points (response-guided); and one in which the point of intervention was assigned randomly somewhere between Sessions 5 and 12 inclusive (random). The 100 graphs were randomly ordered and presented to 12 students who were asked to place the graphs that they thought exhibited an intervention effect in one pile and those that did not in another. The mean percentage of graphs that were judged to exhibit an intervention effect was both statistically and substantially much higher with the response-guided intervention start-point graphs ($M = 66\%$) than with the randomly determined intervention start-point graphs ($M = 23\%$). The take-home message from this experiment is that visual analysts are far more likely to misattribute "significance" to randomly generated data when the intervention start point is response guided rather than randomly determined. Again, these results must be regarded as preliminary in that the study involved only a single AB phase-change design in the response-guided framework.

As alternatives to response-guided experimentation, intervention start points can be either randomly determined (as was just illustrated for the Todman & Dugard, 1999, study) or designated on a fixed or preexperimental basis. With these three start-point options, a critical tension exists for the single-case intervention researcher. On the one hand, in traditional implementations of clinical and applied interventions, a response-guided intervention start point is most preferred, a random intervention start point is least preferred, and a preexperimentally designated fixed start point falls somewhere between the two. On the other hand, from a scientific credibility (internal and statistical-conclusion validities) standpoint, the rank orderings would be exactly the opposite, with a random intervention start point being the most desirable (Dugard et al., 2012; Chapter 2, this volume), a response-guided intervention start point the least desirable, and a preexperimentally designated fixed start point somewhere between the two.

Regardless of which of these three start-point selection options is chosen, determining whether an A-to-B phase intervention effect exists may be difficult for visual analysts who have not had extensive experience or training. Reliable and valid visual analyses depend on the analyst's sensitivity to baseline series' variability, trend, autocorrelation (as was illustrated earlier in the context of Figure 3.1), and the potential for regression-toward-the-mean artifacts. Without such sensitivity, it is difficult to accurately conclude that apparent intervention effects are "real" rather than simply a product of the series' baseline-derived trend, cyclicity, or random fluctuations. In particular, a focal concern is that Type I error rates (falsely attributing random variation to an intervention effect) have been found to be even more unwieldy in response-guided designs than they are in nonresponse-guided designs (see, e.g., Allison, Franklin, & Heshka, 1992; Ferron, Foster-Johnson, & Kromrey, 2003; Ferron & Jones, 2006; Fisch, 2001; Fisher et al., 2003; Matyas & Greenwood, 1990; Stocks & Williams, 1995). Type I error rates are increased in response-guided designs because the researcher's flexibility–subjectivity in determining the intervention start point in such designs opens the door to the appearance of "intervention effects" that are in actuality due to chance (Ferron & Jones, 2006). In contrast, with the randomized start point approach, Type I error rates are adequately controlled (e.g., Edgington, 1975; Edgington & Onghena, 2007). Nevertheless, some authors (e.g., Kennedy, 2005) have argued that Type I error is not a serious problem in the visual analysis of single-case data because multiple individuals—researchers, reviewers, journal editors—are typically involved in the intervention-effect judgment process.

Visual Analysis and Statistical Analysis Combinations

A potential to "have one's cake and eat it too" in response-guided intervention is for researchers to incorporate some appropriate form of randomization into their designs—an approach that is also associated with an inferential statistical test (e.g., Edgington & Onghena, 2007; Ferron & Jones, 2006; Ferron & Ware, 1994; Koehler & Levin, 1998). With this combined response-guided and randomization approach, the researcher would (a) track the outcome measure(s) until a satisfactory criterion of "stability" is determined (taking into account variability and trend) and then (b) randomly select an intervention point from within a specified range of subsequent outcome measures. This option presents a compromise to investigators who would like to maintain some of the desired features of traditional (response-guided) single-case intervention designs but who wish to enhance the internal and statistical-conclusion validities of their research.

Although incorporating randomization into a response-guided design can improve the study's scientific credibility, the adoption of a recently proposed strategy can also improve the objectivity of the visual-analysis process. In particular, the Ferron and Jones (2006) study illustrates a potentially useful technique for separating the visual analyst from the individual who is implementing the intervention in the context of a multiple-baseline design (see also Ferron & Foster-Johnson, 1998; Mawhinney & Austin, 1999; Chapter 5, this volume). An opportunity for incorporating randomization into single-case designs arises when decisions about the content of an intervention are made by an "interventionist" and the timing of intervention delivery in the design is made by a different person (e.g., a "masked visual analyst"). If this separation of roles is made, the visual analyst would be responsible for assessing when the data in baseline document stability and when a change in the data pattern has been documented, without having been apprised both which phase (baseline or intervention) was actually being represented and which participants were contributing data (e.g., the specific staggered orders of intervention introduction in a multiple-baseline design).

With this approach, the visual analyst (rather than the interventionist) makes decisions about baseline stability and intervention start points for the participants without knowing which particular participant is being administered the intervention at which time period (i.e., the visual analyst is masked with respect to the participants' intervention conditions). In addition, the strategy lends itself to a legitimate randomization statistical test, thereby maintaining the nominal Type I error probability while satisfying the response-guided demands of single-case intervention researchers (again, for details about several "masked visual analyst" response-guided approaches, see Chapter 5, this volume).

Summary and Conclusions

In this chapter we have reviewed the rationale for visual analysis in single-case intervention research and critically examined its longstanding tradition. Visual analysis of single-case data continues to play a prominent role in evidence determination in the majority of published research and research reviews in the fields of psychology and education. The use of visual analysis will likely continue as a prominent data-analytic tool in that major professional groups such as the WWC have endorsed the method for assessing whether single-case outcome data have met evidence criteria (Hitchcock et al., in press; Kratochwill et al., 2010, 2013). In concert with the goals of the chapter, we have (a) reviewed the traditional applications of and arguments for visual analysis in single-case intervention research, noting its pervasiveness in the field of applied behavior analysis research; (b) reviewed research on the reliability and utility of visual analysis, noting limitations of the research investigations in that area; and (c) suggested strategies for improving the visual-analysis process by incorporating recently proposed formal training protocols and supplementary statistical procedures. In particular, building on the work of Horner and Spaulding (2010), Kratochwill and Levin (Chapter 2, this volume), and others (e.g., Ferron & Jones, 2006), we recommend that (a) whenever possible, single-case intervention research be conducted with some appropriate form of randomization in the design; (b) when assessing single-case outcomes, formal training of judges in visual-analysis techniques be adopted; and (c) visual analysis be supplemented with appropriate statistical tests when possible. The combined application of visual and statistical analysis will ultimately enhance the scientific credibility of both single-case individual intervention research studies and integrative reviews of that research.

References

Allison, D. B., Franklin, R. D., & Heshka, S. (1992). Reflections on visual inspection, response guided experimentation, and Type I error rate in single-case designs. *Journal of Experimental Education*, *61*, 45–51. doi:10.1080/00220973.1992.9943848

Allison, D. B., & Gorman, B. S. (1993). Calculating effect sizes for meta-analysis: The case of the single case. *Behaviour Research and Therapy, 31*, 621–631.

Austin, J., & Mawhinney, T. C. (1999). Using concurrent verbal reports to examine data analyst verbal behavior. *Journal of Organizational Behavior Management*, *18*, 61–81. doi:10.1300/J075v18n04_05

Baer, D. M. (1977). Perhaps it would be better not to know everything. *Journal of Applied Behavior Analysis, 10*, 167–172.

Bailey, J. S., & Burch, M. R. (2002). *Research methods in applied behavior analysis.* Thousand Oaks, CA: Sage.

Barlow, D. H. (2010). Negative effects from psychological treatments: A perspective. *American Psychologist, 65*, 13–20.

Barlow, D. H., Hayes, S. C., & Nelson, R. O. (1984). *The scientist practitioner: Research and accountability in clinical and educational settings.* New York, NY: Pergamon.

Barlow, D. H., & Hersen, M. (1984). *Single-case experimental designs: Strategies for studying behavior change* (2nd ed.). New York, NY: Pergamon.

Barlow, D. H., Nock, M. K., & Hersen, M. (2009). *Single-case experimental designs: Strategies for studying behavior change* (3rd ed.). Boston, MA: Allyn & Bacon.

Blanton, H., & Jaccard, J. (2006). Arbitrary metrics in psychology. *American Psychologist, 61,* 27–41.

Bloom, M., Fischer, J., & Orme, J. G. (1999). *Evaluating practice: Guidelines for the accountable professional* (Vol. 1). Boston, MA: Allyn & Bacon.

Borckardt, J. J., Nash, M. R., Murphy, M. D., Moore, M., Shaw, D., & O'Neil, P. (2008). Clinical practice as natural laboratory for psychotherapy research: A guide to case-based time-series analysis. *American Psychologist, 63,* 77–95. doi:10.1037/0003-066X.63.2.77

Box, G. E. P., & Jenkins, G. M. (1970). *Time series analysis: Forecasting and control.* San Francisco, CA: Holden-Day.

Brossart, D. F., Parker, R. I., Olson, E. A., & Mahadevan, L. (2006). The relationship between visual analysis and five statistical analyses in a simple AB single-case research design. *Behavior Modification, 30,* 531–563. doi:10.1177/0145445503261167

Brown-Chidsey, R., & Steege, M. W. (2010). *Response to intervention: Principles and strategies for effective practice* (2nd ed.). New York, NY: Guilford Press.

Browning, R. M., & Stover, D. O. (1971). *Behavior modification in child treatment: An experimental and clinical approach.* Chicago, IL: Aldine-Atherton.

Bulté, I., & Onghena, P. (2012). When the truth hits you between the eyes: A software tool for the visual analysis of single-case experimental data. *Methodology: European Journal of Research Methods for the Behavioral and Social Sciences, 8,* 104–114.

Busk, P. L., & Marascuilo, L. A. (1992). Meta-analysis for single-case research. In T. R. Kratochwill and J. R. Levin (Eds.), *Single-case research design and analysis: New directions for psychology and education* (pp. 159–185). Hillsdale, NJ: Erlbaum.

Campbell, D. T., & Stanley, J. C. (1966). *Experimental and quasi-experimental designs for research.* Chicago, IL: Rand McNally.

Carr, E. G., Horner, R. H., Turnbull, A. P., Marquis, J. G., Magito McLaughlin, D., McAtee, M. L., . . . Doolabh, A. (1999). *Positive behavior support for people with developmental disabilities: A research synthesis.* American Association on Mental Retardation Monograph Series. Washington, DC: American Association on Mental Retardation.

Center, B. A., Skiba, R. J., & Casey, A. (1985–1986). A methodology for quantitative synthesis of intra-subject design research. *Journal of Special Education, 19,* 387–400.

Chassan, J. B. (1967). *Research designs in clinical psychology and psychiatry.* New York, NY: Appleton-Century-Crofts.

Chassan, J. B. (1979). *Research designs in clinical psychology and psychiatry* (2nd ed.). New York, NY: Appleton-Century-Crofts.

Cipani, E. (2009). *Becoming an evidence-based practitioner: Practical research methods for educators.* New York, NY: Springer.

Cook, T. D., & Campbell, D. T. (1979). *Quasi-experimentation: Design and analysis issues for field settings.* Chicago, IL: Rand McNally.

Crosbie, J. (1993). Interrupted time-series analysis with brief single subject data. *Journal of Consulting and Clinical Psychology, 61,* 966–974.

De Prospero, A., & Cohen, S. (1979). Inconsistent visual analysis of intrasubject data. *Journal of Applied Behavior Analysis, 12,* 573–579.

DiNoia, J., & Tripodi, T. (2007). *Single-case design for clinical social workers.* Washington, DC: NASW Press.

Dugard, P., File, P., & Todman, J. (2012). *Single-case and small-n experimental designs: A practical guide to randomization tests* (2nd ed.). New York, NY: Routledge.

DuPaul, G. J., Ervin, R. A., Hook, C. L., & McGoey, K. E. (1998). Peer tutoring for children with attention-deficit/hyperactivity disorder: Effects on classroom behavior and academic performance. *Journal of Applied Behavior Analysis, 31,* 579–592. doi:10.1901/jaba.1998.31-579

Edgington, E. S. (1975). Randomization tests for one-subject operant experiments. *The Journal of Psychology: Interdisciplinary and Applied, 90,* 57–68. doi:10.1080/00223980.1975.9923926

Edgington, E. S. (1992). Nonparametric tests for single-case experiments. In T. R. Kratochwill & J. R. Levin (Eds.), *Single-case research design and analysis* (pp. 133–157). Hillsdale, NJ: Erlbaum.

Edgington, E. S., & Onghena, P. (2007). *Randomization tests* (4th ed.). Boca Raton, FL: Chapman & Hall/CRC.

Fahmie, T. A., & Hanley, G. P. (2008). Progressing toward data intimacy: A review of within-session data analysis. *Journal of Applied Behavior Analysis, 41*, 319–331. doi:10.1901/jaba.2008.41-319

Faith, M. S., Allison, D. B., & Gorman, B. S. (1996). Meta-analysis of single-case research. In R. D. Franklin., D. B. Allison, & B. S. Gorman (Eds.), *Design and analysis of single-case research* (pp. 245–277). Mahwah, NJ: Erlbaum.

Ferron, J., & Foster-Johnson, L. (1998). Analyzing single-case data with visually guided randomization tests. *Behavior Research Methods, Instruments, & Computers, 30*, 698–706. doi:10.3758/BF03209489

Ferron, J., Foster-Johnson, L., & Kromrey, J. D. (2003). The functioning of single-case randomization tests with and without random assignment. *Journal of Experimental Education, 71*, 267–288.

Ferron, J., & Jones, P. K. (2006). Tests for the visual analysis of response-guided multiple-baseline data. *Journal of Experimental Education, 75*, 66–81. doi:10.3200/JEXE.75.1.66-81

Ferron, J., & Ware, W. (1994). Using randomization tests with responsive single-case designs. *Behavior Research and Therapy, 32*, 787–791.

Ferster, C. B., & Skinner, B. F. (1957). *Schedules of reinforcement.* New York, NY: Appleton-Century-Crofts. doi:10.1037/10627-000

Fisch, G. S. (2001). Evaluating data from behavioral analysis: Visual inspection or statistical models. *Behavioural Processes, 54*, 137–154. doi:10.1016/S0376-6357(01)00155-3

Fischer, J. (1978). *Effective casework practice: An eclectic approach.* New York, NY: McGraw-Hill.

Fisher, W. W., Kelley, M. E., & Lomas, J. E. (2003). Visual aids and structured criteria for improving visual inspection and interpretation of single-case designs. *Journal of Applied Behavior Analysis, 36*, 387–406. doi:10.1901/jaba.2003.36-387

Fisher, W. W., Kodak, T., & Moore, J. W. (2007). Embedding an identity-matching task within a prompting hierarchy to facilitate acquisition of conditional discriminations in children with autism. *Journal of Applied Behavior Analysis, 40*, 489–499. doi:10.1901/jaba.2007.40-489

Franklin, R. D., Gorman, B. S., Beasley, T. M., & Allison, D. B. (1997). Graphical display and visual analysis. In R. D. Franklin, D. B. Allison, & B. S. Gorman (Eds.), *Design and analysis of single-case research* (pp. 119–158). Mahwah, NJ: Erlbaum.

Gabler, N. B., Duan, N., Vohra, S., & Kravitz, R. L. (2011). N-of-1 trials in the medical literature: A systematic review. *Medical Care, 49*, 761–768. doi:10.1097/MLR.0b013e318215d90d

Gast, D. L. (2010). *Single subject research methodology in behavioral sciences.* New York, NY: Routledge.

Gentile, J. R., Roden, A. H., & Klein, R. D. (1972). An analysis of variance model for the intrasubject replication design. *Journal of Applied Behavior Analysis, 5*, 193–198.

Gersten, R., Fuchs, L., Compton, D., Coyne, M., Greenwood, C., & Innocenti, M. (2005). Quality indicators for group experimental and quasi-experimental research studies in special education. *Exceptional Children, 71*, 149–164.

Glass, G. V., Willson, V. L., & Gottman, J. M. (1975). *Design and analysis of time series experiments.* Boulder: University of Colorado Press.

Gorsuch, R. L. (1983). Three methods for analyzing time-series (N of 1) data. *Behavioral Assessment, 5*, 141–154.

Greenspan, P., & Fisch, G. S. (1992). Visual inspection of data: A statistical analysis of behavior. In *Proceedings of the annual meeting of the American Statistical Association* (pp. 79–82). Alexandria, VA: American Statistical Association.

Greenwald, A. G. (1975). Consequences of prejudice against the null hypothesis. *Psychological Bulletin, 82*, 1–20. doi:10.1037/h0076157

Hagopian, L. P., Fisher, W. W., Thompson R. H., OwenDeSchryver, J., Iwata, B. A., & Wasker, D. P. (1997). Toward the development of structured criteria for interpretation of functional analysis data. *Journal of Applied Behavior Analysis, 30*, 313–326.

Hammond, D., & Gast, D. L. (2010). Descriptive analysis of single-subject research designs: 1983–2007. *Education and Training in Autism and Developmental Disabilities, 45*, 187–202.

Harbst, K. B., Ottenbacher, K. J., & Harris, S. R. (1991). Interrater reliability of therapists' judgments of graphed data. *Physical Therapy, 71*, 107–115.

Hartmann, D. P. (1974). Forcing square pegs into round holes: Some comments on " An analysis of variance model for the intrasubject replication design." *Journal of Applied Behavior Analysis, 7,* 635–638.

Hayes, S. C. (1981). Single-case experimental designs and empirical clinical practice. *Journal of Consulting and Clinical Psychology, 49,* 193–211. doi:10.1037/0022-006X.49.2.193

Hayes, S. C., Barlow, D. H., & Nelson-Gray, R. O. (1999). *The scientist practitioner: Research and accountability in the age of managed care* (2nd ed.). Needham Heights, MA: Allyn & Bacon.

Hitchcock, J. H., Horner, R. H., Kratochwill, T. R., Levin, J. R., Odom, S. L., Rindskopf, D. M., & Shadish, W. R. (in press). The What Works Clearinghouse "Single-Case Design Pilot Standards": Who will guard the guards? *Remedial and Special Education.*

Hojem, M. A., & Ottenbacher, K. J. (1988). Empirical investigation of visual-inspection versus trend-line analysis of single-subject data. *Journal of the American Physical Therapy Association, 68,* 983–988.

Horner, R., & Spaulding, S. (2010). Single-case research designs. In N. J. Salkind (Ed.), *Encyclopedia of research design* (pp. 1386–1394). Thousand Oaks, CA: Sage. doi:10.4135/9781412961288. n424

Horner, R. H., Carr, E. G., Halle, J., McGee, G., Odom, S., & Wolery, M. (2005). The use of single-subject research to identify evidence-based practice in special education. *Exceptional Children, 71,* 165–179.

Horner, R. H., Sugai, G., & Anderson, C. M. (2010). Examining the evidence base for school-wide positive behavior support. *Focus on Exceptional Children, 42,* 1–14.

James, I. A., Smith, P. S., & Milne, D. (1996). Teaching visual analysis of time series data. *Behavioural and Cognitive Psychotherapy, 24,* 247–262. doi:10.1017/S1352465800015101

Jayaratne, S., & Levy, R. L. (1973). *Empirical clinical practice.* Irvington, NY: Columbia University Press.

Johnston, J. M., & Pennypacker, H. S. (1980). *Strategies and tactics of human behavioral research.* Hillsdale, NJ: Erlbaum.

Johnston, J. M., & Pennypacker, H. S. (1993). *Strategies and tactics of behavioral research* (2nd ed.). Hillsdale, NJ: Erlbaum.

Johnston, J. M., & Pennypacker, H. S. (2009). *Strategies and tactics of behavioral research* (3rd ed.). New York, NY: Routledge.

Jones, R. R., Weinrott, M. R., & Vaught, R. S. (1978). Effects of serial dependency on the agreement between visual and statistical inference. *Journal of Applied Behavior Analysis, 11,* 277–283. doi:10.1901/jaba.1978.11-277

Kahng, S., Chung, K.-M., Gutshall, K., Pitts, S. C., Kao, J., & Girolami, K. (2010). Consistent visual analysis of intrasubject data. *Journal of Applied Behavior Analysis, 43,* 35–45. doi:10.1901/jaba.2010.43-35

Kazdin, A. E. (1977). Assessing the clinical or applied significance of behavior change through social validation. *Behavior Modification, 1,* 427–452. doi:10.1177/014544557714001

Kazdin, A. E. (1982). *Single-case research designs: Methods for clinical and applied settings.* New York, NY: Oxford University Press.

Kazdin, A. E. (2011). *Single-case research designs: Methods for clinical and applied settings* (2nd ed.). New York, NY: Oxford University Press.

Kennedy, C. H. (2005). *Single-case designs for educational research.* Boston, MA: Allyn & Bacon.

Keselman, H. J., & Leventhal, L. (1974). Concerning the statistical procedures enumerated by Gentile et al.: Another perspective. *Journal of Applied Behavior Analysis, 7,* 643–645.

Knapp, T. J. (1983). Behavior analysts' visual appraisal of behavior change in graphic display. *Behavioral Assessment, 5,* 155–164.

Koehler, M. J., & Levin, J. R. (1998). Regulated randomization: A potentially sharper analytical tool for the multiple-baseline design. *Psychological Methods, 3,* 206–217. doi:10.1037/1082-989X.3.2.206

Kratochwill, T. R. (Ed.). (1978). *Single subject research: Strategies for evaluating change.* New York, NY: Academic Press.

Kratochwill, T. R., Alden, K., Demuth, D., Dawson, D., Panicucci, C., Arntson, P., ... Levin, J. (1974). A further consideration in the application of an analysis-of-variance model for the intrasubject replication design. *Journal of Applied Behavior Analysis, 7,* 629–633.

Kratochwill, T. R., Brody, G. H. (1978). Single-subject designs: A perspective on the controversy over employing statistical inference and implications for research and training in behavior modification. *Behavior Modification, 2*, 291–307.

Kratochwill, T. R., Hitchcock, J., Horner, R. H., Levin, J. R., Odom, S. L., Rindskopf, D. M., & Shadish, W. R. (2010). Single case designs technical documentation. In *What Works Clearinghouse: Procedures and standards handbook (Version 2.0)*. Retrieved from http://ies.ed.gov/ncee/wwc/pdf/wwc_procedures_v2_standards_handbook.pdf

Kratochwill, T. R., Hitchcock, J. H., Horner, R. H., Levin, J. R., Odom, S. L., Rindskopf, D. M., & Shadish, W. R. (2013). Single-case intervention research design standards. *Remedial and Special Education, 34*, 26–38. doi:10.1177/0741932512452794

Kratochwill, T. R., & Levin, J. R. (Eds.). (1992). *Single-case research design and analysis: New directions for psychology and education*. Hillsdale, NJ: Erlbaum.

Kratochwill, T. R., & Shernoff, E. S. (2003). Evidence-based practice: Promoting evidence-based interventions in school psychology. *School Psychology Quarterly, 18*, 389–408.

Kratochwill, T. R., & Stoiber, K. C. (2002). Evidence-based interventions in school psychology: Conceptual foundations of the Procedural and Coding Manual of Division 16 and the Society for the Study of School Psychology Task Force. *School Psychology Quarterly, 17*, 341–389.

Lieberman, R. G., Yoder, P. J., Reichow, B., & Wolery, M. (2010). Visual analysis of multiple baseline across participants graphs when change is delayed. *School Psychology Quarterly, 25*, 28–44. doi:10.1037/a0018600

Marriott, F. H. C., & Pope, J. A. (1954). Bias in the estimation of autocorrelations. *Biometrika, 41*, 390–402.

Matyas, T. A., & Greenwood, K. M. (1990). Visual analysis of single-case time series: Effects of variability, serial dependence, and magnitude of intervention effects. *Journal of Applied Behavior Analysis, 23*, 341–351. doi:10.1901/jaba.1990.23-341

Mawhinney, T. C., & Austin, J. (1999). Speed and accuracy of data analysts' behavior using methods of equal interval graphic data charts, standard celeration charts, and statistical process control charts. *Journal of Organizational Behavior Management, 18*, 5–45. doi:10.1300/J075v18n04_02

McGuire, J., Bates, G. W., Dretzke, B. J., McGivern, J. E., Rembold, K. L., Seabold, D. R., . . . Levin, J. R. (1985). Methodological quality as a component of meta-analysis. *Educational Psychologist, 20*, 1–5. doi:10.1207/s15326985ep2001_1

Michael, J. (1974). Statistical inference for individual organism research: Mixed blessing or curse. *Journal of Applied Behavior Analysis, 7*, 647–653.

Moher, D., Hopewell, S., Schulz, K. F., Montori, V., Gotzsche, P. C., Devereaux, P. J., . . . Altman, D. G. (2010). CONSORT 2010 explanation and elaboration: Updated guidelines for reporting parallel group randomized trials. *BMJ, 340*, c869. doi:10.1136/bmj.c869

Morales, M., Dominguez, M. L., & Jurado, T. (2001). The influence of graphic techniques in the evaluation of the effectiveness of treatment in time-series design. *Quality & Quantity: International Journal of Methodology, 35*, 277–289. doi:10.1023/A:1010393831820

Morgan, D. L., & Morgan, R. K. (2001). Single-participant research design: Bringing science to managed care. *American Psychologist, 56*, 119–127.

Morley, S., & Adams, M. (1991). Graphical analysis of single-case time series data. *British Journal of Clinical Psychology, 30*, 97–115. doi:10.1111/j.2044-8260.1991.tb00926.x

National Reading Panel. (2000). *Report of the National Reading Panel: Teaching children to read: An evidence-based assessment of the scientific research literature on reading and its implications for reading instruction*. Jessup, MD: National Institute for Literacy.

Normand, M. P., & Bailey, J. S. (2006). The effects of celeration lines on visual analysis of behavioral data. *Behavior Modification, 30*, 295–314. doi:10.1177/0145445503262406

Ottenbacher, K. J. (1990). When is a picture worth a thousand *p* values? A comparison of visual and quantitative methods to analyze single-subject data. *Journal of Special Education, 23*, 436–449.

Ottenbacher, K. J. (1993). Interrater agreement of visual analysis in single-subject decisions: Quantitative review and analysis. *American Journal on Mental Retardation, 98*, 135–142.

Park, H., Marascuilo, L., & Gaylord-Ross, R. (1990). Visual inspection and statistical analysis in single-case designs. *Journal of Experimental Education, 58*, 311–320.

Parsonson, B. S., & Baer, D. M. (1978). The analysis and presentation of graphic data. In T. Kratochwill (Ed.), *Single subject research* (pp. 101–165). New York, NY: Academic Press. doi:10.1016/B978-0-12-425850-1.50009-0

Parsonson, B. S., & Baer, D. M. (1992). The visual analysis of data and current research into the stimuli controlling it. In T. R. Kratochwill & J. R. Levin (Eds.), *Single-case research designs and analysis: New directions for psychology and education* (pp. 15–40). Hillsdale, NJ: Erlbaum.

Poling, A., Methot, L. L., & LeSage, M. G. (1995). *Fundamentals of behavior analytic research.* New York, NY: Plenum Press.

Reichow, B., Barton, E. E., Sewell, J. N., Good, L., & Wolery, M. (2010). Effects of weighted vests on the engagement of children with developmental delays and autism. *Focus on Autism and Other Developmental Disabilities, 25,* 3–11. doi:10.1177/1088357609353751

Riddoch, J., & Lennon, S. (1991). (Eds.). *Single case research designs.* Hove, England: Erlbaum.

Riley-Tillman, C. T., & Burns, M. K. (2009). *Evaluating educational interventions: Single-case design for measuring response to intervention.* New York, NY: Guilford Press.

Riviello, C., & Beretvas, S. N. (2009). Detecting lag-one autocorrelation in interrupted time-series experiments with small datasets. *Journal of Modern Applied Statistical Methods, 8,* 469–477.

Rosenthal, R. (1979). The "file drawer problem" and tolerance for null results. *Psychological Bulletin, 86,* 638–641. doi:10.1037/0033-2909.86.3.638

Schrandt, J. A., Townsend, D. B., & Poulson, C. L. (2009). Teaching empathy sills to children with autism. *Journal of Applied Behavior Analysis, 42,* 17–32. doi:10.1901/jaba.2009.42-17

Shadish, W. R., Cook, T. D., & Campbell, D. T. (2002). *Experimental and quasi-experimental designs for generalized causal inference.* Boston, MA: Houghton Mifflin.

Shadish, W. R., Rindskopf, D. M., Hedges, L. V., & Sullivan, K. J. (2011). *Empirical Bayes estimates of autocorrelations in single-case designs.* Manuscript submitted for publication.

Shadish, W. R., & Sullivan, K. J. (2011). *Characteristics of single-case designs used to assessment treatment effects in 2008.* Manuscript submitted for publication.

Shavelson, R. J., & Towne, L. (2002). *Scientific research in education.* Washington, DC: National Academies Press.

Sidman, M. (1960). *Tactics of scientific research.* New York, NY: Basic Books.

Skib, R., Deno, S., Marston, D., & Casey, A. (1989). Influence of trend estimation and subject familiarity on practitioners' judgments of intervention effectiveness. *Journal of Special Education, 22,* 433–446.

Skinner, B. F. (1953). *Science and human behavior.* New York, NY: Free Press.

Skinner, C. H. (Ed.). (2004). *Single-subject designs for school psychologists.* New York, NY: Hawthorne Press.

Smith, J. D. (2012). Single-case experimental designs: A systematic review of published research and recommendations for researchers and reviewers. *Psychological Methods, 17,* 510–550. doi:10.1037/a0029312

Sterling, T. D., Rosenbaum, W. L., & Weinkam, J. J. (1995). Publication decisions revisited: The effect of the outcome of statistical tests on the decision to publish and vice versa. *The American Statistician, 49,* 108–112.

Stewart, K. K., Carr, J. E., Brandt, C. W., & McHenry, M. M. (2007). An evaluation of the conservative dual-criterion method for teaching university students to visually inspect AB-design graphs. *Journal of Applied Behavior Analysis, 40,* 713–718.

Stocks, J. T., & Williams, M. (1995). Evaluation of single-subject data using statistical hypothesis tests versus visual inspection of charts with and without celeration lines. *Journal of Social Research, 20,* 105–126.

Sullivan, K. J., & Shadish, W. R. (2011). *An assessment of single-case designs by the What Works Clearinghouse.* Manuscript submitted for publication.

Swoboda, C. M., Kratochwill, T. R., Horner, R. H., & Levin, J. R. (2012). *Visual analysis training protocol: Applications with the alternating treatment, multiple baseline, and ABAB designs.* Unpublished manuscript, University of Wisconsin-Madison.

Swoboda, C. M., Kratochwill, T. R., & Levin, J. R. (2010, November). *Conservative dual-criterion method for single-case research: A guide for visual analysis of AB, ABAB, and multiple-baseline designs* (Working Paper 2010-13). Madison: Wisconsin Center for Education Research. Retrieved from http://www.wcer.wisc.edu/publications/workingPapers/Working_Paper_No_2010_13.php

Tate, R. L., McDonwald, S., Perdices, M., Togher, L., Schultz, R., & Savage, S. (2008). Rating the methodological quality of single-subject designs and n-of-1 trials: Introducing the Single-Case Experimental Design (SCED) scale. *Neuropsychological Rehabilitation*, *18*, 385–401. doi:10.1080/09602010802009201

Tawney, J. W., & Gast, D. L. (1984). *Single subject research in special education*. Columbus, OH: Merrill.

Thoresen, C. E., & Elashoff, J. D. (1974). An analysis-of-variance model for intrasubject replication design: Some additional considerations. *Journal of Applied Behavior Analysis, 7*, 639–641.

Todman, J., & Dugard, P. (1999). Accessible randomization tests for single-case and small-n experiment designs in AAC research. *Augmentative and Alternative Communication*, *15*, 69–82. doi:10.1080/07434619912331278585

Todman, J. B., & Dugard, P. (2001). *Single-case and small-n experimental designs: A practical guide to randomization tests*. Mahwah, NJ: Erlbaum.

Tufte, E. R. (1983). *The visual display of quantitative information*. Cheshire, CT: Graphics Press.

Vannest, K. J., Davis, J. L., & Parker, R. I. (2013). *Single-case research in schools: Practical guidelines for school-based professionals*. New York, NY: Routledge.

Vanselow, N. R., Thompson, R., & Karsina, A. (2011). Data-based decision-making: The impact of data variability, training, and context. *Journal of Applied Behavior Analysis*, *44*, 767–780. doi:10.1901/jaba.2011.44-767

Wainer, H., & Thissen, D. (1993). Graphical data analysis. In G. Keren & C. Lewis (Eds.), *A handbook for data analysis in the behavioral sciences: Statistical issues* (pp. 391–457). Hillsdale, NJ: Erlbaum.

Wampold, B. E., & Furlong, M. J. (1981a). The heuristics of visual inference. *Behavioral Assessment*, *3*, 79–92.

Wampold, B. E., & Furlong, M. J. (1981b). Randomization tests in single-subject designs: Illustrative examples. *Journal of Behavioral Assessment*, *3*, 329–341. doi:10.1007/BF01350836

Weisz, J. R., & Hawley, K. M. (2001, June). *Procedural and coding manual for identification of evidence-based treatments* (Document of the Committee of Science and Practice of the Society for Clinical Psychology, Division 12, American Psychological Association). Washington, DC: American Psychological Association.

Wendt, O., & Miller, B. (2012). Quality appraisal of single-subject experimental designs: An overview and comparison of different appraisal tools. *Education & Treatment of Children*, *35*, 235–268. doi:10.1353/etc.2012.0010

White, D. M., Rusch, F. R., Kazdin, A. E., & Hartmann, D. P. (1989). Applications of meta-analysis in individual subject research. *Behavioral Assessment, 11*, 281–296.

White, O. R. (1972). *A manual for the calculation and use of the median slope: A technique of progress estimation and prediction in the single case*. Eugene, OR: University of Oregon Regional Resource Center for Handicapped Children.

White, O. R., & Haring, N. G. (1980). *Exceptional teaching* (2nd ed.). Columbus, OH: Charles E. Merrill.

Wodarski, J. S. (1981). *The role of research in clinical practice: A practical approach for human services*. Baltimore, MD: University Park Press.

Wolery, M., Busick, M., Reichow, B., & Barton, E. (2010). Comparison of overlap methods for quantitatively synthesizing single-subject data. *Journal of Special Education, 44*, 18–28.

Wolf, M. M. (1978). Social validity: The case of subjective measurement or how applied behavior analysis is finding its heart. *Journal of Applied Behavior Analysis, 11*, 203–214.

Ximenes, V. M., Manolov, R., Solanas, A., & Quera, V. (2009). Factors affecting visual inference in single-case designs. *The Spanish Journal of Psychology*, *12*, 823–832. doi:10.1017/S1138741600002195

4

Non-Overlap Analysis for Single-Case Research

Richard I. Parker, Kimberly J. Vannest, and John L. Davis

This chapter describes the development, refinement, and strengths of non-overlap indices of effects for single-case research (SCR). Non-overlap indices, most of which are directly interpretable as the percent of non-overlapping data between baseline (A) and treatment phase (B) are attractive for several reasons. As "distribution free" indices, they are applicable to score distributions that lack normality or constant variance, yielding robust results in the presence of extreme (outlier) scores. Non-overlap indices also are well suited to interval, ordinal, and even dichotomous or binary scales. Most non-overlap indices can be calculated by hand, and confirmed by visual analysis of graphed data. Until recently, non-overlap techniques had two notable limitations: low statistical power and their inability to address data trend. But some recently proposed innovations have removed those limitations, and the most recent non-overlap techniques can compete with more complex regression models, such as those presented by Faith, Allison, and Gorman (1996).

The smallest level of non-overlap analysis is the phase contrast, usually between phase A (baseline) and phase B (treatment). A number of these A versus B contrasts can be combined to yield an overall or omnibus non-overlap effect size for the full design. The most defensible procedure for combining individual A versus B contrasts appears to be in multi-tier medical studies (Abramson, 2010) and meta-analyses (Hedges & Olkin, 1985). This method essentially obtains a full design effect by using an additive method, starting with the smallest contrast and combining them (while respecting the logic of the SCR design) to represent the entire series of contrasts for the study as a whole.

More sophisticated approaches are also available by multi-level modeling (MLM; Van den Noortgate & Onghena, 2003, 2008), multiple regression (Allison & Gorman, 1993; Huitema & McKean, 2000), and randomization designs and analyses (Chapter 2, this volume). These methods, like non-overlap techniques, have their strengths and limitations. They are efficient but are relatively more

http://dx.doi.org/10.1037/14376-005
Single-Case Intervention Research: Methodological and Statistical Advances, by T. R. Kratochwill and J. R. Levin

complex than non-overlap techniques and in some cases require an a priori set of design criteria that may or may not be well suited to particular practical applications. These are beyond the scope of this chapter but are addressed elsewhere in this book (Chapters 5, 7, and 8, this volume).

This chapter reviews the historical development of nine non-overlap indices in order of development: (a) the Extended Celeration Line (ECL), or "split middle line," of *Precision Teaching* leaders, by White and Haring (1980); (b) the original Percent of Non-overlapping Data (PND) from Scruggs, Mastropieri, and Casto (1987); (c) Ma's Percent of data Exceeding the Median (PEM; Ma, 2006); (d) the Percent of All Non-overlapping Data (PAND), by Parker, Hagan-Burke, and Vannest (2007); (e) The Robust Improvement Rate Difference (IRD) by Parker, Vannest, and Brown (2009); (f) Non-overlap of all Pairs (NAP) by Parker and Vannest (2009); (g) the Percent of data Exceeding the Median Trend (PEM-T; Wolery, Busick, Reichow, & Barton, 2010), and (h) the hybrid non-overlap-plus-trend index, TauU (Parker, Vannest, Davis, & Sauber, 2011). We conclude this chapter with an example of how phase A versus phase B contrasts are selected, calculated, and aggregated to obtain an omnibus, design-wide effect size. Excluded from this review is the Percentage Reduction Data (PRD) measure by O'Brien and Repp (1990), as it is a parametric, means-based method. Also excluded is the Percentage of Zero Data (PZD) measure by Scotti, Evans, Meyer, and Walker (1991), as it can be applied to only certain scales and behavioral goals.[1]

Rationale for Non-Overlap Indices

Non-overlap indices are justified and recommended for several reasons. They are robust enough to handle typical SCR data and do not make assumptions about distributions of the data. They are directly interpretable and appear to be accessible enough for most interventions to use. This in turn maintains the control of the individual working directly with the client in decision making.

Robust and Distribution Free

The first rationale for a non-overlap index is that SCR data frequently do not conform to parametric standards. SCR studies may employ ordinal scales, dichotomous scales, frequency counts, or percentages. Much SCR data are non-normal, skewed, and do not show constant score variance from left to right along the time axis (Parker, 2006). For these datasets, means and standard deviations are poor summaries (Scruggs & Mastropieri, 1998, 2001; Sheskin, 2007). Not only

---

[1]Percentage reduction data (PRD) and Percentage of zero data (PZD) were not included in the current review. Although both are considered non-overlap methods, PRD is a mean-based method that requires distributional and data assumptions (e.g. normality, equal variance, and interval-level measurement) to be met prior to analysis. PZD was also excluded because its calculation relies on a certain score being achieved. This restriction limits the applicability of the method for studies that use measures that do not achieve or include a predetermined score. Although these methods may be appropriate in certain applications, the limitations for both preclude broad application of them.

do these SCR data violate parametric assumptions, but their short lengths make it impossible to fairly test adherence to these assumptions (Draper & Smith, 1998). Even a median-based nonparametric approach may poorly describe a set of scores when they are multi-modal or heavily skewed (Siegel & Castellan, 1988; Wilcox, 2010). Non-overlap, universally termed *dominance*, indices do not assume central tendency nor any particular distribution shape (Cliff, 1993), not even a usefully representative median.

Non-overlap indices may be classified as "complete" or not. A complete non-overlap index (e.g., NAP, Tau-U) equally emphasizes all datapoints, whereas an incomplete index emphasizes particular scores, such as the median (e.g., ECL, PEM) or the highest phase score (e.g., PND). Complete non-overlap indices are calculated from all pairwise data comparisons between Phase A and Phase B (Huberty & Lowman, 2000). From each AB comparison the phase B datapoint is determined to be higher (positive), lower (negative), or tied with the paired phase A datapoint value. The sum of all possible paired comparison results denotes the degree of separation of the two phase "data clouds" (Grissom & Kim, 2005). A complete non-overlap or dominance index of change is the most robust option for nonconforming, atypical, and very short data series, including those containing extreme outlier scores and from a variety of scale types. A complete non-overlap index also possesses the strongest statistical precision power available from nonparametric analysis (Acion, Peterson, Temple, & Arndt, 2006).

Directly Interpretable Effect-Size Measures

The most commonly published (Kirk, 1996) effect sizes R^2 and Cohen's d (or Hedges'g), lack direct, intuitive interpretations for most single-case researchers (Campbell, 2004; May, 2004). An R^2 is the proportion of total variance accounted for by an intervention (assuming a strong design). To understand R^2 requires knowledge of partitioning of sums of squares in a linear model. A similar difficulty arises with Cohen's d or Hedges'g, which are (again assuming a strong design) the magnitude of change due to the intervention, expressed as standard deviation units. The consumer must understand sampling distributions, scaled in standard deviation units. Possessing only partial understanding of R^2 or Cohen's d, applied researchers tend to rely for understanding on Cohen's benchmarks for small, medium, and large effects derived from large-N social science research (Cohen, 1988). SCR effects are generally much larger than group effects, even by a factor of two or three. Thus, adopting group research effect sizes to SCR can confuse rather than clarify magnitude of improvement. The equivalence of effect sizes from group research and from SCR is a topic deserving treatment beyond this chapter. Various points of view and new calculation methods are presented in Chapter 8, this volume.

A non-overlap index is directly interpretable, as the vertical separation of two data clouds, confirmable by a visual scan of a data chart. Differences in exact interpretation do exist among the non-overlap methods. Several non-overlap indices (e.g., PAND, NAP, and TauU) are interpreted as "the percent of data in both phases showing no overlap between phases" (Parker, Vannest, &

Davis, 2011, p. 6); for NAP and TauU only, the percent of datapoints is derived from percent of all pairwise data comparisons across phases. Another difference is that NAP refers to percent of non-overlap, whereas TauU refers to "percent of non-overlap minus overlap" (Parker, Vannest, Davis, & Sauber, 2011, p. 3).

Exact interpretations of other non-overlap indices differ more. For PEM, non-overlap is the percent of Phase B datapoints not overlapping the extended Phase A median line (Ma, 2009) for White's ECL and Wolery's PEM-T, the meaning is the percent of Phase B datapoints not overlapping a Phase A trend line. For IRD (Parker et al., 2009), the meaning is the improvement rate difference between the two phases. And for PND, the meaning is the percent of Phase B datapoints exceeding the single highest Phase A datapoint. From these examples, it is clear that some non-overlap indices rely on additional simple statistical concepts, such as *median line* (PEM), *trend line* (ECL, PEM-T), *highest Phase A datapoint* (PND), and *ratio of two improvement rates* (IRD).

Keeping the Interventionist in Control

Another rationale for a non-overlap index is history. Historical roots in the visual analysis of SCR data, as long practiced in both experimental psychology and applied behavior analysis (ABA), have informed the interpretation and purposes of the data analysis. Visual analysis of non-overlap has been a standard practice of behavior analysts for more than 50 years, valued for its ease of use and its applicability to any type of design, scale, or data type (Parsonson & Baer, 1978). It is a tool that the skilled interventionist has used to judge the existence of functional relationships, and albeit only generally, the amount of behavior change. In the early decades of ABA (1960s–1970s), non-overlap was judged visually but not summarized statistically. A non-overlap statistic (PND) soon followed, but because it lacked a known sampling distribution it possesses unknown precision-power and therefore no protection against chance-level results. Only in the past decade has a quantitative summary of non-overlap been available that possesses a known sampling distribution and has sufficient precision-power to meet the needs of small SCR designs and short phases.

Because non-overlap is contextualized to visual analysis, a statistical summary of non-overlap should support the visual analysis. Visual and statistical analyses are integrated and, at minimum, informed by the interventionist (or person understanding the data, setting, etc.). Our viewpoint is that interventionist control of SCR data analysis is always desirable and often essential. Idiosyncrasies of a study may be known only by the interventionist. Such idiosyncrasies are typically identified by notations on figures or visual graphs as they occur and may not translate to a complex analysis of a data base decontextualized from the knowledge of the interventionist. This information is necessary to inform the analysis at every stage. Visual analysis may reveal unexpected permutations in the data stream potentially due to some confounding external influence. Idiosyncrasies may include unexpected (and undesired) improvement trend in baseline. Visual analysis also may reveal unanticipated slow progress early in a treatment phase, constituting an "acquisition period." Unexpected data trend, or lack of trend where it was expected, also can be revealed through visual analysis. Still other features scanned for in visual analysis are extended absences and the unintended influence or "bleed" of effects across parallel data streams in a design. Finally, the graphic display can show lack of consistent direction of results across multiple-phase contrasts. Consistency of results across key contrasts is required for an overall or omnibus design-wide effect size to be meaningful (i.e., to indicate treatment effectiveness).

Although standard SCR design types exist (e.g., multiple-baseline designs [MBD]), it would be a mistake to proceed with data analysis based on design type alone. A close study of a visual display of data by someone with intimate knowledge of the implementation of the study is a thoughtful and conservative approach to analysis choices. Conversely, a potential obstacle in complex SCR analysis is the need for accurate, detailed communication of idiosyncrasies of a design to statistical experts conducting the analysis. When communication does occur, analysis modifications to model or represent any design changes must be a two-way understanding of the data and the analysis. One without the other could lead to violated assumptions, invalid analytic models, and incorrect conclusions. Unlike group research, where a relatively few design types exist and analysis by template is possible through regression or analysis of variance statistical packages, a wide range of blended SCR designs exist. A final difficulty is that the expression of results (relying on advanced statistical concepts and formulae) may be poorly understood and not readily confirmed by the interventionist. In a worst-case scenario, the interventionist receives results back from the statistician that are poorly understood and cannot be validated against visual scrutiny of the data. These problems build a strong case for interventionist control of SCR data analysis (see also Chapter 5, this volume).

Eight Non-Overlap Indices

Eight distinct non-overlap indices, in order of their first publication dates, are depicted graphically in Figure 4.1 (computation methods for all indices are presented in Table 4.1): (a) ECL or "split middle" method (White & Haring, 1980), which is identical to the later PEM-T (Wolery et al., 2010); (b) PND (Scruggs et al., 1987); (c) PEM (Ma, 2006); (d) PAND (Parker et al., 2007); (e) IRD, which is identical to robust phi (Parker et al., 2009); (f) NAP (Parker & Vannest, 2009); and (g) TauU (Parker, Vannest, Davis, & Sauber, 2011).

The well-accepted ECL method is being periodically reconsidered. The PEM method is a subtype of ECL. When no Phase A trend exists, then PEM equals ECL; thus, ECL subsumes PEM. In this chapter, however, ECL and PEM will be separately described. The more recent PEM-T technique is identical to the earlier ECL. Therefore, in this chapter PEM-T will not be separately considered.

ECL or "Split Middle" Line

This time-honored method (White & Haring, 1980) has for decades been a key tool of the scientist-practitioner. ECL began with the "precision teaching" movement, and spread from there through the field of special education, as

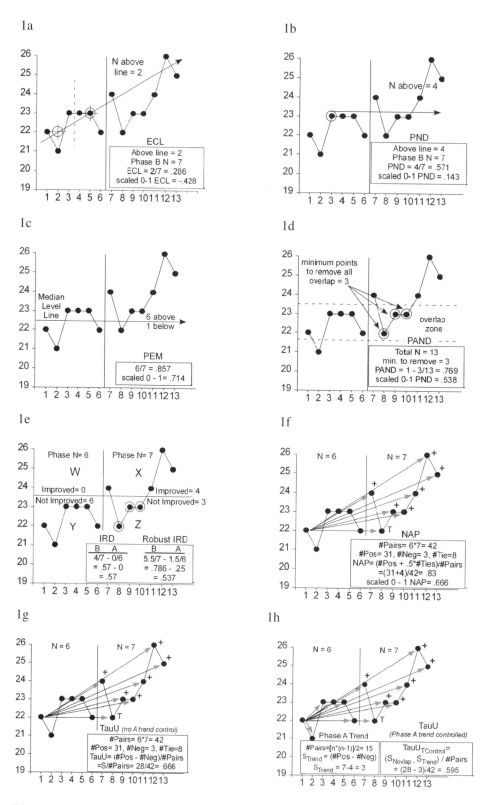

Figure 4.1. Graphic displays demonstrating eight non-overlap indices.

Table 4.1. Computation Summaries of Eight Non-Overlap Methods

Method	Procedure with example data	Significance test
Extended Celeration Line (ECL; White & Haring, 1980)	a. Median-based slope plotted for Phase A, and extended through Phase B. b. Count phase B datapoints above (2) and below (5) trend line. c. Calculate phase B ratio above/total = 2/7 = .286. d. Convert to 0–100 scale for percent of non-overlapping data: (.286 × 2) − 1 = −.428.	Compare above/below ratios for two phases: 3/6 vs. 2/7 in a "two proportions" test. Results: testing that the phase B proportion exceeds the phase A proportion, Fisher's exact one-tailed. $p = .914$.
Percent of Non-Overlapping Data (PND; Scruggs et al., 1987)	a. Find single highest datapoint in Phase A (23), and extend line from it through Phase B. b. In Phase B, take ratio of datapoints above line to total B datapoints: 4/7 = .571.	Statistical test unavailable.
Percent of Phase B Data Exceeding the Phase A Median (PEM; Ma, 2006)	a. Draw flat Phase A Median line (22.5), and extend through Phase B. b. Calculate the proportion of Phase B datapoints above the Median line: PEM = 6/7 = .857. c. Rescale PEM to 0–100: (2 × .857) − 1 = .714, so 71% non-overlapping data.	Mood's Median Test: Overall Median = 23. Above/below median ratio in phase A = 0/6, and in phase B = 4/7. Fisher exact test on 0/6 vs. 4/7 yields two-tailed $p = .069$.
Percent of All Non-Overlapping Data (PAND; Parker et al., 2007)	a. Fewest datapoints removed from Phase A and/or Phase B to eliminate all overlap between phases = 3. b. Calculate: 1− removed/total datapoints = 1 − (3/13) = .769 = PAND. c. Convert to 0–100 scale: (2 × .769) − 1 = .538 = 54% non-overlapping data.	Statistical test unavailable.

(continued on next page)

Table 4.1.   Computation Summaries of Eight Non-Overlap Methods (*Continued*)

Method	Procedure with example data	Significance test
Robust Improvement Rate Difference (R-IRD; Parker et al., 2009)	a. Fewest datapoints removed from Phase A and/or B to eliminate all overlap (3 from phase B). b. Draw horizontal line separating Phase A and B data, creating quadrants: W = 0, X = 4, Y = 6, Z = 3. c. Balance quadrants W = 0 and Z = 3 to create W = 1.5, Z = 1.5, and adjust other two quadrants true to phase Ns: Y = 4.5, X = 5.5. d. Calculate IRD = X/(X + Z) − W/(W + Y) = 5.5/7 − 1.5/6 = .537.	Statistical test unavailable.[a]
Non-Overlap of All Pairs (NAP; Parker & Vannest, 2009)	a. Submit variables Phase (0/1) and Score to ROC analysis (Phase is response variable, Score is criterion variable), yielding "empirical AUC" = .833. b. Rescale to 0–100: (2 × .833) − 1 = .666. *or* a. Submit Phase (0/1) and Score variables to Mann-Whitney U offering full output. b. Large U (U$_L$) = 35; small U (U$_S$) = 7. c. Calculate NAP = U$_L$/(U$_L$ + U$_S$) = 35/42 = .833. (Then rescale to 0–100 as above.)	From ROC analysis, 2-tailed *p value* p = .002 calculated from standard Z scores. From Mann Whitney Test: exact two-tailed p = .038 without correction, p = .046 with correction for ties as calculated from standard Z scores.
TauU (Parker, Vannest, Davis, & Sauber, 2011; without baseline trend control)	a. Calculate #Pairs as n$_A$ × n$_B$ = 6 × 7 = 42. b. Submit Phase (0/1) and Score variables to Kendall Rank Correlation (KRC) module with full output. Output: S$_{novlap}$= 28. c. Calculate TauU: S$_{novlap}$/Pairs = 28/42 = .666, so 67% non-overlapping data. (*Note: The Tau or Tau-b values output will not be accurate so discard them.*)	From KRC: Approx. Z = 2.072, two-tailed p = .038; continuity-corrected p = .045.

TauU (Parker, Vannest, Davis, & Sauber, 2011; with baseline trend control)

a. Calculate #Pairs as $n_A \times n_B = 6 \times 7 = 42$.
b. Submit variables Time and Scores for Phase A only to KRC module with full output. Output: $S_{trend} = 3$.
c. Submit Phase (0/1) and Score variables to Kendall Rank Correlation (KRC) module with full output. Output: $S_{novlap} = 28$.
d. Calculate TauU: $(S_{Novlap} - S_{Trend})/\text{Pairs} = (28 - 3)/42 = .595$, so 60% non-overlapping data after controlling for confounding Phase A trend.

or

a. Make new Phase variable. Make Phase A values reverse time order. Make Phase B values all equal to the next largest Time value. ($A = 6, 5, 4, 3, 2, 1$; $B = 7, 7, 7, 7, 7, 7, 7$).
b. Output: $S = 25$.
c. Calculate TauU = S/Pairs = 25/42 = .595, so 60% non-overlap after Phase A trend control.[b]

From KRC output to non-overlap analysis: Approx. Z: 2.072, two-tailed $p = .038$; continuity-corrected $p = .045$.

[a] Balancing within the 2×2 table creates fractional (decimal) numbers in table cells. Ideally, a small-N exact test would then be used for an inference test of the modified table. However, tests based on the hypergeometric and binomial distributions are applied to frequencies and therefore non-integer values (other than continuity-corrected integers) are not allowed. [b] The previously discussed Tau and Tau-b values output will not be accurate here and so they should be disregarded.

popularized by White and Haring (1980). In ECL, non-overlap is the proportion of Phase B data that do not overlap (exceed) a "median-based trend line," which is plotted from the Phase A data, and then extended into Phase B. ECL can employ any straight trend line, though it was originally published with the median-based line publicized by Koenig and colleagues (Pennypacker, Koenig, & Lindsley, 1972). Commonly used in special education research since the 1970s, it may be less familiar in other fields. A median-based line is created by first dividing all data in a phase into earlier and later halves. Then for each half, find the point that marks its vertical and horizontal middle or median (i.e., coordinates 2, 22 and 5, 23, respectively, in Figure 4.1a). Connecting these two median points yields the median-based trend line. This line is sometimes adjusted slightly up or down (while maintaining it parallel to the original drawn line) to split all of the data evenly, half above and half below the adjusted line.

ECL mixes non-overlap with trend, in attempting to control effects of preexisting baseline improvement trend. Only ECL and one other non-overlap index (TauU) have this trend control capability. A chance-level ECL score is 50% (Phase A slope equally splits Phase B data), so the obtained .286 in Figure 4.1a could be described as 21.4 percent points below chance (.500 − .286 = .214). But a standardized, more useful interpretation is obtained by rescaling the result to a 0 to 100 scale by the formula $Result_{0-100} = (Result_{50-100} \times 2) - 1$. For the same Figure 4.1a results, the transformation is $(.286 \times 2) - 1 = -.428$, so when rescaled 0 to 100, the final index is below chance level, or 43% in the direction of deterioration. So the Figure 4.1a results can be summarized by saying that when Phase A positive trend is controlled, the client evidenced no progress, and even deteriorated. This interpretation may seem extreme, raising a concern with the ECL method of baseline trend control. Many interventionists would not feel comfortable judging that the data had deteriorated, and this type of baseline trend control is open to multiple criticisms that are detailed later in the chapter.

Through its ability to control for potentially confounding improvement trend in the baseline, ECL addresses a major limitation of non-overlap techniques (Wolery et al., 2010). However, the popularity of ECL at the classroom level has not extended to broader use by researchers. Its main limitation for research is the lack of statistical precision-power, a large concern with short phases. ECL relies on the low-powered (Pitman efficiency 60%–65% of a parametric t test) binomial proportions test, which tests the obtained split in Phase B (above vs. below the extended Phase A trend line) against a null hypothesis split of 50%–50% (Hodges & Lehmann, 1956; Sprent & Smeeton, 2001).

Another weakness of the ECL technique is its assumption of linearity (straight line) of improvement trend. In SCR, progress is often not linear, and yet well-established alternatives to linear trend, such as monotonic trend (Anderson & Darling, 1954; Mann, 1945), cannot be used with ECL.

Another limitation is that for variable data and short phases, the Phase A trend line may have very low reliability, for which ECL offers no correction. Extending an unreliable Phase A trend line can easily project it beyond the limits of the Y scale, especially when Phase B is long (Scruggs & Mastropieri, 2001). Any trend line fit to data possesses measurement error, which is not considered within ECL. ECL is typically performed with Koenig's (1972) bi-split (the median-based line described earlier), or Tukey's (1977) tri-split median-based trend lines. These two easy-to-draw lines are convenient but possess the lowest precision-power of any available. In Monte Carlo tests (Johnstone & Velleman, 1985), the bi-split line (Koenig, 1972) falls last in precision-power, beaten by Tukey's (1977) tri-split line, while both are inferior to the newer Theil–Sen (Theil, 1950; Sen, 1968; Wilcox, 2005) nonparametric trend line, which to our knowledge has not yet been used in SCR.

The most appropriate statistical test for ECL appears to be the low-powered test of two independent proportions, the proportions being formed by the number of datapoints above versus below or at the line, for each phase. With this test, as with most others on SCR data, an assumption of data independence between phases, and of independence of one contrast from another, is commonly made, although strictly speaking it is not likely to be true. The best argument for data independence is that the logic of the design requires it to be so. The design is built, and the study is conducted so that Phase A data can vary greatly from Phase B data, and so that each A versus B contrast can be evaluated as separate pieces of evidence toward experimental control. However, a reasonable argument against independence, at least within a single data stream, is that a single subject is emitting all the outcome measures (see Crosbie, 1987; Chapter 5, this volume).

The question of data independence of Phase A from B and, also, of one contrast from another may warrant further discussion. Although some data dependence is likely (see Levin, Marascuilo, & Hubert, 1978), only an assumption of data independence upholds the design logic, and permits statistical analysis with existing analytic techniques (but see Chapter 5, this volume, for a discussion of randomization-test assumptions). For example, in meta-analyses of group-design data from a complex design with multiple important contrasts, those contrasts are specified as dependent or independent from one another (Hedges & Olkin, 1985), and the consequences of that decision on the overall significance test are enormous. If the multiple contrasts are judged to be dependent, then the logic of "experiment-wise" error (e.g., Kirk, 1995) applies and the statistical significance of findings benefits little from several contrasts with individually strong results. Within a SCR framework, this would be saying that repeated demonstrations of intervention effectiveness over multiple A versus B contrasts are not much more convincing than impressive results from a single A versus B contrast. Clearly, that conclusion would violate the logic of SCR designs. Instead, a (qualified) assumption of data independence between contrasts is made, and through arithmetic with the standard errors of the contrasts, the overall p value becomes smaller (more impressive) for each additional contrast that shows a positive result. Thus, although we acknowledge that the data are not fully independent between phases and contrasts, they are enough so conceptually to make that qualified assumption.

In the Figure 4.1a example, for Phase A the "above" versus "equal to or below" split is 3 versus 3, and for Phase B it is 2 versus 5. A proportions test of three sixths versus two sevenths yields a statistically nonsignificant Fisher's exact two-tailed $p = .91$. Results are interpreted as follows: After controlling for confounding Phase A trend, there is no significant improvement from Phase A to B. At the same time, this test of proportions is of limited use with Ns this small because of its low power.

PND

PND (Scruggs et al., 1987), the original index of simple non-overlap, continues to be the most popular. PND is a transformation of the earlier range-based "percent of overlap" (PO) calculations from Tawney and Gast (1984). PND is the positive expression of PO: PND = 100 – PO. PND has been used in dozens of SCR published studies, and in at least 10 meta-analyses (Scruggs & Mastropieri, 2001). PND is interpreted as the percentage of Phase B data exceeding the single highest Phase A datapoint. In Figure 4.1b, the three highest Phase A datapoints (26) are exceeded by four of the seven Phase B datapoints, so PND = 100 × 4/7 = 57.1, or 57%. Hand calculation of PND, assisted by a transparent ruler, is straightforward on uncrowded data sets. On the basis of PND, an intervention's effectiveness can range from 0% to 100% and is interpreted by its authors as follows: >70% is effective, 50% to 70% is questionable effectiveness, and <50% is no observed effect (Scruggs & Mastropieri, 1998). These benchmarks were based on clinical observations of the authors.

PND is perhaps the easiest of all non-overlap indices to calculate by hand. Another asset, confirmed by our own research (Parker et al., 2007), is that PND tends to correlate well with non-quantitative visual judgments. A spirited debate two decades ago revealed most of the strengths (already enumerated) and weaknesses of PND (Allison & Gorman, 1993, 1994; Scruggs et al., 1987; Scruggs & Mastropieri, 1994, 1998, 2001; White, 1986). One of its most serious weaknesses is that PND is calculated from only one Phase A datapoint, which is the most extreme and therefore likely to be the least reliable. A second is that PND effects demonstrate undesirable floor and ceiling effects with a large proportion of published SCR data (Parker et al. 2007).

PND's other serious limitation is seen when it is used to compare results between studies and combing results as in a meta-analysis. PND lacks a sampling distribution, and therefore p values and confidence intervals cannot be calculated to indicate the precision of the result. This is a problem for an individual analysis and the aggregation of results between studies, which should weight the individual effect sizes according to their precision.

PEM

PEM, or the percentage of Phase B datapoints exceeding the median of the baseline phase (Ma, 2006) was developed to improve on PND. Rather than relying on the single most extreme score in Phase A, PEM relies on the more stable and representative Phase A median level. The Phase A median line is extended through Phase B, and the split of Phase B datapoints above and below the line are compared to the line's split of Phase A data, which is always 50/50. In Figure 4.1c, the Phase A median is at 22.5, which is below 6 of the 7 Phase B scores. PEM is 6/7 = .857, and rescaled 0–100 is (PEM × 2) – 1 = .714 or 100 × [(PEM × 2) – 1] = 71.4%. PEM is also reliant on a low power median test, especially when sample sizes are small. PEM improves upon PND by providing a sampling distribution (see below), and by not emphasizing a single extreme Phase A score.

The two pronounced limitations of PEM are its low power and its lack of sensitivity in distinguishing among several datasets. PEM has a severe ceiling effect or attenuation of range that manifests as insensitivity to any overlap between phases that does not extend across the median line. Also, when a median score poorly reflect a score distribution, PEM has little use. In a sample of 165 published graphs, PEM could not discriminate among effects for fully half of the sample—those with stronger effects (Parker & Hagan-Burke, 2007). This lack of discrimination ability then limits PEM's correlation with other effect sizes and with visual judgments. Among all non-overlap indices described in this chapter, PEM's ceiling effect is most severe.

Ma (2006) did not propose a statistical test for PEM, but the most logical would be Mood's Median Test (Siegel & Castellan, 1988), which unfortunately has low precision power. Mood's test begins with the overall median across the two phases (Median$_{overall}$). Mood's test then counts the number of datapoints above Median$_{overall}$ for each phase and those equal to or below Median$_{overall}$. For this example, the median of all 13 observations is 23, and the number of within-phase observations above versus equal to or below the median are Phase A: 0 versus .6, and Phase B: 4 versus .3. For large-sample situations, a chi-square test could be conducted from this 2 × 2 cross-classification. In the case of the present small-sample example, a Fisher exact test yields a two-tailed p value of .098.

PAND

PAND (Parker et al., 2007) was developed to address two weaknesses of PND: overemphasis on a single datapoint and lack of a sampling distribution. PAND is the percentage of data remaining after determining the fewest datapoints that must be removed to eliminate all between-phase overlap. The removal of data-points may be from Phase A or B or from both phases. In Figure 4.1d, the fewest datapoints needing removal to eliminate all overlap equals 3 (circled). PAND equals the number of remaining datapoints, divided by the total N: $[1 - (3/13)]$ or $[(13 - 3)/13] = .769$. PAND is scaled 50–100, where 50 percent is chance level. Conversion to a 0–100 scale is by $(PAND \times 2) - 1$, here $.769 \times 2 - 1 = .538$, or nearly 54 percent. PAND considers all datapoints equally, unlike PND. However, PAND lacks a known sampling distribution and so it was first presented along with the well-established Pearson's Phi, the correlation coefficient for a 2 × 2 table. Phi relied on the same calculations as PAND, but is not a non-overlap index. It was later found that Phi can also be derived directly from a different index, IRD, so Phi is described subsequently, with IRD. Two PAND calculation methods were presented by Parker et al. (2007): hand analysis (as conducted in Figure 4.1d) and Excel sorting. The Excel sorting method is no longer rec-ommended because of the inconsistencies in the seed values of some search engines, as was noted by Shadish, Rindskopf, and Hedges (2008) in their com-mentary on PAND.

Lacking a sampling distribution, PAND is not the complete non-overlap index needed for meta-analysis or other comparisons of results across studies. Its use in meta-analysis (Burns, Codding, Boice, & Lukito, 2010; Schneider, Goldstein, & Parker, 2008) requires the accompanying Phi index. PAND has been superseded by IRD, which follows.

Robust Improvement Rate Difference (R-IRD)

IRD (Parker et al., 2009) was developed to improve on PAND by providing an easily interpretable, reputable effect size index (with a sampling distribution). The result, IRD, is employed in group medical research as "risk reduction" or "risk difference" (Altman, 1990; Cochrane Collaboration, 2006; Sackett, Richardson, Rosenberg, & Haynes, 1997). IRD calculation begins with the same method (fewest datapoints that must be removed to eliminate all overlap) procedure as PAND, but in a second step converts the results to two improvement rates (IR), for Phase A and B respectively. The two IR values are finally subtracted to obtain the "Improvement Rate Difference" (IRD). IRD is interpreted as the difference in the proportion of high or "improved" scores between Phases B and A.

The original IRD article recommended that in the first step, datapoint *removal* "should be balanced across the contrasted phases" (Parker et al., 2009, p. 141) for more robust results. A better robust IRD solution was later described and formalized as "Robust IRD" (R-IRD). R-IRD requires rebalancing (by hand) of a 2×2 matrix (see Figure 4.1e; Parker, Vannest, & Davis, 2011). In Figure 4.1e, the graph quadrants have been labeled W, X, Y, and Z, and can be viewed as constituting 4 cells of a 2×2 matrix. After determining the fewest datapoints that must be removed to eliminate overlap, values are W = 0, X = 4, Y = 6, and Z = 3. The improvement rate (IR) for phase A (IR_A) is calculated as W/(W + Y) = 0/6 = 0, and the IR for phase B (IR_B) as X/(X + Z) = 4/7 = .57, which yields IRD = $IR_B − IR_A$ = .57. The superior R-IRD requires that quadrants W and Z be balanced (to 1.5 each). Balancing allows for a more conservative effect in instances where a large number of datapoints may be removed arbitrarily from one side and a few from the other, which can unduly influence the results. Then values of the remaining two quadrants (X and Y) are also adjusted to maintain the original number of datapoints per phase. Since W was adjusted to 1.5, Y must be reduced to 4.5 to maintain the Phase A N of 6 (1.5 + 4.5). The same logic is applied to Phase B. Balanced quadrant values are: W = 1.5, X = 5.5, Y = 4.5, Z = 1.5. Robust IRD is then calculated as was IRD: for Phase A: W/(W + Y) = 1.5/6 = .25, and for Phase B, X/(X + Z) = 5.5/7 = .786. Finally, R-IRD = .786 − .25 = .536. R-IRD is unbiased in the sense that it does not allow bias in removal of datapoints from A versus B, as some datasets provide two or more equally good removal solutions.

When quadrant values are entered as W/Y, X/Z into a "difference between two proportions" statistical module, a statistical test yields a standard error (*SE*), *p* value, and confidence intervals (CIs). Alternatively, these values can be entered into a 2×2 contingency-table matrix to produce a Phi statistic. It should be noted that *p* values can only be calculated for IRD and not R-IRD. This is because statistical significance test cannot be calculated for non-integer values (e.g., 1.5) within a 2×2 contingency table. IRD possesses only moderate precision-power compared to least squares regression, but more power than ECL or PEM. Thus, IRD was viewed as the best available non-overlap technique in 2009, although still limited by its insensitivity to data trend. IRD has been used in SCR meta-analyses (Ganz, Parker, & Benson, 2009; Vannest, Davis, Davis, Mason, & Burke, 2010; Vannest, Harrison, Temple-Harvey, Ramsey, & Parker, 2011). Most statistical packages (e.g., SPSS, SAS, NCSS, SPlus) can calculate IRD or R-IRD. In addition, meta-analysis software often provides "risk difference" analyses, with Forest plots, which are displays of effect sizes and their confidence intervals across several studies. Software with this capability include StatsDirect (Buchan, 2012), MetaWin (Rosenberg, Adams, & Gurevitch, 2000), and WinPepi software for epidemiologists (Llorca, 2002). The latter program is freely available from a biomedical website (http://www.epi-perspectives.com/content/1/1/6). Ian Buchan, the author of StatsDirect (2006), also provides free interactive web-based calculations from the University of Manchester Medical School (http://www.phsim.man.ac.uk/).

NAP

NAP (Parker & Vannest, 2009) emerged from the search for a nonparametric index supported by established statistics, which also possessed superior precision-power. It was discovered that non-overlap in SCR was identical to "dominance," "non-inferiority," or "stochastic superiority" of one group over another in rank statistics (D'Agostino, Campbell, & Greenhouse, 2006a, 2006b). The term *non-overlap* is even used occasionally by statisticians to describe dominance statistics (Huberty & Lowman, 2000). Dominance statistics include the Mann-Whitney U (MW-U) group test, Kendall's Tau Test of association and the area under the curve (AUC) from a receiver operator characteristic (ROC) Test. A two-group ROC analysis yields NAP directly as "empirical AUC," and NAP can be calculated from MW-U with a little arithmetic. The direct calculation of NAP from raw scores without the prior step of "minimum datapoints removal" gives NAP an advantage over earlier techniques.

NAP is literally the percentage of data that improve from A to B or, operationally, the percentage of all pairwise comparisons from Phase A to B showing improvement or growth. If calculated by hand, NAP begins with all pairwise comparisons (#Pairs = $n_A \times n_B$) between phases. Each paired comparison has one of three outcomes: improvement over time (Pos), deterioration (Neg), or no change over time (Tie). NAP is calculated as (Pos + .5 × Tie)/#Pairs. In Figure 4.1f, #Pairs = 6 × 7 = 42, of which Pos = 31 and Tie = 8. (This calculation is illustrated in Figure 4.1f for Phase A's first observation.) NAP= (31 + 4)/42 = .83 or 83 percent. Because NAP is scaled 0–50, most users will prefer transformation to a 0–100 scale: $NAP_{0-100} = 2 \times .83 - 1 = .666$, or 66.6%. In short time series, a single datapoint can have a consequential influence on NAP. In the present case, for instance, if the A phase had 5 datapoints and the B phase had 5, the greatest influence possible would be a 25%. Also consider the present example with N = 6 and N = 7. If there were no overlap the NAP score would be 100%. If a single data point were extremely out of place (exceeding all other phase data in one direction or the other), the NAP score could go as low as 83%. This difference could be considered nontrivial (an ES of 100% vs. one of 83%) or both of these indices may be interpreted as large effects. Interpretation of ES is a tricky business, with context, social significance, clinical significance, effects of prior studies, and the behaviors under examination all a part of the interpretation (see Onwuegbuzie & Levin, 2003).

Dominance statistics are known for strong precision-power, and MW-U is the most powerful nonparametric statistic for comparing two groups, at 91%

to 94% (Pitman efficiency) that of regression analysis for "well-behaved" data conforming to parametric assumptions. For "ill behaved," nonconforming data, the power of a MW-U analysis can exceed that of regression analysis with a Pitman efficiency rating of 114% (Wilcox, 2010). NAP possessed higher precision-power than any previous non-overlap technique, commending its use with shorter datasets (Parker & Vannest, 2009). This finding, plus NAP's direct interpretability, its identity with nonparametric dominance statistics, and its computation by computer (or with minimal arithmetic), makes NAP a superior non-overlap index. NAP's marked limitation is that it is insensitive to trend in data. Another limitation is that it is not as easy to calculate by hand as is PND, PEM, PAND, or even IRD. NAP has been used in recent meta-analysis of SCR (Bowman-Perrott, Davis, Vannest, Greenwood, & Parker, 2012).

TauU

NAP's major limitation of insensitivity to data trend led to development of a new index that integrates non-overlap and trend: TauU (Parker, Vannest, Davis, & Sauber, 2011). TauU is named for its two origins: Kendall's Rank Correlation (KRC) Tau, and the MW-U Test for two groups. Melding KRC and MW-U may seem strange, but these two different-appearing statistics, with very different applications, are actually transformations of one another, and share the same S sampling distribution. Furthermore, the operational meanings of trend and non-overlap are essentially the same (Newson, 2002).

The hybrid TauU has more than one form. The simplest is non-overlap only, and is calculated from the same pairwise comparisons ($n_A \times n_B$ = #Pairs) across phases as is NAP, resulting in a Pos, Neg, or Tie for each pair. But whereas NAP = (Pos + .5 × Tie)/Pairs, the TauU simple non-overlap form (not considering trend) is TauU = (Pos − Neg)/Pairs (also written as S/Pairs or S_{novlap}/Pairs). Thus, NAP is percent of non-overlapping data, whereas TauU is percent of non-overlapping minus overlapping data. The two are equivalent by simple transformation: 2 × NAP − 1 = TauU. Note that this is the same equivalence formula for transforming NAP from a 0–50 to a 0–100 scale; NAP_{0-100} equals simple TauU without trend. Figure 4.1g shows calculation of TauU without trend. From the $6 \times 7 = 42$ pairwise comparisons across phases, Pos = 31, Neg = 3, and Tie = 8, and TauU = (31 − 3)/42 = .666, the same as the NAP_{0-100} solution in Figure 4.1f.

A more complex form of TauU expands to include control of Phase A monotonic trend, the trend calculated by KRC from two data columns—a time series and a set of scores. Monotonic trend is the tendency for data to go up or improve over time, in any configuration or profile, which may include plateaus, drops, curves and straight line segments. Monotonic trend within a phase can be hand-calculated from all pairwise comparisons made in a "time forward" direction; each datapoint is compared with each later point in time. If a subsequent datapoint is higher than a previous one, a "Pos" is recorded; and if it is lower, a "Neg" is recorded. The formula for monotonic trend is the same as for non-overlap (i.e. [Pos − Neg]/Pairs), except that #Pairs formula for trend is different: n (n − 1)/2. In Figure 4.1h, for Phase A, #Pairs = (6 × 5)/2 = 15, and so the Phase A monotonic trend is $(7 - 4)/15 = .20$, or 20%. The numerator $(7 - 4)$ is termed S or S_{trend}. We can summarize this result by saying that Phase A shows 20% positive monotonic trend, or that 20% of the Phase A data show relative improvement over time. This latter interpretation is literally true, because (a) a net 20% of the paired comparisons are Pos, and (b) each datapoint contributes the same number of paired comparisons to the total. This is the nexus of non-overlap and monotonic trend: both can be measured as percent of paired comparisons that are positive when made in a time-forward direction.

Figure 4.1h shows calculation of a TauU that controls for baseline trend. Calculation begins with the simple non-overlap TauU ratio, then subtracting Phase A S_{trend} from its numerator. Thus, TauU non-overlap with control of confounding baseline trend is $TauU = (S_{novlap} - S_{trend})/Pairs_{novlap}$. The denominator does not change from the simple TauU to TauU with Phase A trend control. Controlling baseline trend reduces TauU from .67 to .60. This technique of baseline trend control subtracts the Phase A trend as a finite amount from the non-overlap. This technique is more conservative than that used by other statistical models (e.g., linear regression) and avoids the unwarranted assumption of linear trend techniques). More liberal trend control techniques (as that used in ECL) assume an errorless Phase A trend line slope, which would continue unabated through Phase B and beyond, ad infinitum—a questionable assumption. The extended baseline control technique yields results that are often severe, unintuitive, and even nonsensical (i.e., beyond the range of the score scale limits). These concerns are our clinical impressions from trend control with hundreds of published datasets, but have not yet been empirically documented.

TauU with baseline trend control can be calculated from a KRC module in a single analysis. A special dummy code is required to replace the Time variable. Phase A is coded in reverse time order (e.g., as 5, 4, 3, 2, 1 for a baseline with five data points). Phase B (say, for 7 data points) is then coded 6, 6, 6, 6, 6, 6, 6, if we want client scores to go up, or 0, 0, 0, 0, 0, 0, 0, if we want client scores to go down. An example is provided in Table 4.1. Much more detail is available in a TauU article by Parker, Vannest, Davis, and Sauber (2011).

Yet another form of TauU includes Phase B trend, with or without control of Phase A trend. That form of TauU has not yet been evaluated by application to a large number of datasets so it is not presented here. However, TauU's inclusion of trend should permit TauU models analogous to regression-based models, such as the best validated model family by Allison and colleagues (Allison & Gorman, 1993). Again, a more detailed explanation of TauU derivation and its various versions is available in the aforementioned article by Parker, Vannest, Davis, and Sauber (2011).

Table 4.1 summarizes calculations for each of the eight non-overlap methods, in reference to the Figure 4.1 sample data.

Additional Discussion of TauU

TauU has implications for use in the design itself and in meta-analysis. There are considerations and decisions to be made in both instances.

Design-Wide Application of TauU

The TauU effect size for a full design is achieved by combining multiple A versus B phase contrasts, each of which has its own calculated TauU and standard error. The algorithm for combining individual TauU values is that recommended by meta-analysts for combining multiple independent effect sizes within a single study (Cooper, Hedges, & Valentine, 2009; Hedges & Olkin, 1985; Lipsey & Wilson, 2001). Each TauU is first weighted by the reciprocal of its *SE* (which for TauU is the same as its standard deviation). The weighted TauU values are then added, and their sum is divided by the sum of the weights. The preferred method for combining standard errors is to square them, add the squares, and then take the root of their sum (Hedges & Olkin, 1985; Shadish & Haddock, 1994). Statistical software for meta-analysis or multi-tier analysis can automatically obtain the overall or omnibus TauU. We have found the most efficient software to be the freely downloadable WinPepi (Abramson, 2010), a program built specifically for epidemiologists and other medical researchers.

Figure 4.2 is a multiple-baseline design across participants, with four series, data streams, or tiers, the top three of which possess "concurrent baseline control" (see Chapter 1, this volume, for discussion of the multiple-baseline design). The fourth tier is for control purposes only, without an intervention; Dave's data are not entered into the analysis but used in determining a functional relationship by having 3 "true" demonstrations of replication of effect. The objective is to calculate an omnibus TauU for the full design. The simple TauU will suffice for Bob and Carol, but for Adam we choose to control for the slight positive trend noted in baseline. Adam's baseline trend has low reliability, given its few datapoints and its considerable bounce, and so applying regression-type trend control would be an excessive correction. However, correction by TauU is conservative and serves well even with examples such as this one.

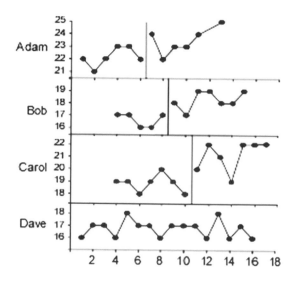

Figure 4.2. Data from a multiple-baseline design data across four subjects, with one control.

Omnibus TauU is calculated piecemeal, tier by tier. Beginning with Bob, first calculate the total number of pairs as $n_A \times n_B = 5 \times 7 = 35$. Next, input Bob's Phase and Score into KRC, saving as output: S = 32 (Concordant – Discordant or Pos – Neg: 32 – 0 = 32), so TauU = S/Pairs = 32/35 = .914. We also need SE_{Tau}, but it might not be provided in the output. If only the SE for S (SE_S) is provided, then calculate $SE_{Tau} = SE_S$/Pairs = 11.9/35 = .34.

The same procedure is used to obtain TauU and SE_{Tau} for Carol, beginning with: Pairs = $7 \times 7 = 49$. From a KRC analysis, Carol's S = (43 – 1) = 42, so TauU = S/Pairs = 42/49 = .857. The output SE_S = 15.09, so $SE_{Tau} = SE_S$/Pairs = 15.09/49 = .308.

For Adam, total Pairs = $6 \times 6 = 36$. We want to control his minor Phase A trend, so a new Time variable with unique coding must be created. Phase A will contain integers in reverse time order: 6, 5, 4, 3, 2, 1. Phase B will be coded all the same, all integers the same and larger than any Phase A integer code: 7, 7, 7, 7, 7, 7. From a KRC analysis, Adam's S = (30 – 10) = 20, so TauU = S/Pairs = 20/36 = .555. The output SE_S = 13.02, so $SE_{Tau} = SE_S$/Pairs = 13.02/36 = .362. Without A trend control, S = (27 – 2) = 25, so Tau = 25/36 = .694.

For an omnibus TauU for the entire design, Tau and SE_{Tau} are entered into a multi-tier analysis module such as offered by the free WinPepi. These values (TauU, SE_{Tau}) are, for Adam: .555, .362; for Bob: .914, .34; for Carol: .857, .308. The WinPepi menu location is: "Compare2" >> "Any of the above using summary measures for each stratum" >> "Proportions or Rates with Standard Errors." Enter each TauU and its SE_{Tau}, and then click "next stratum," until all three pairs are entered. Then click "all strata" to obtain the overall Tau = .79, and its SE_{Tau} = .19. Also provided are confidence intervals at the 90% level [.47, 1.0] and the 95% level [.41, 1.0]. Note the increased precision-power obtained by combining results from three tiers. The omnibus SE_{Tau}=.19 is much smaller than the SE_{Tau} for any one tier, thereby permitting shorter data series.

The WinPepi fixed effects ("precision-based estimates") algorithm for combining TauU values takes their weighted average, where the weight is the reciprocal of the SE_{Tau}. The weighted TauU values are summed and that sum is divided by the sum of the weights. The WinPepi algorithm for combining SE_{Tau} values involves squaring each, adding the squared values, and then taking the root of that sum. These are standard algorithms common in multi-tier and meta-analytic studies. This procedure matches commonly used meta-analytic techniques and should lend credibility to the technique. The additive or comparative method is commonly seen in meta-analyses conducted in related disciplines such as medicine, where multi-tier procedures in interventions are employed and aggregated.

TauU for Meta-Analysis

WinPepi's fixed effects model, for precision-based analysis of multi-tier effects can be applied not only to obtain a full design's omnibus TauU and SE_{Tau}, but also to obtain omnibus values across multiple studies. In other words, omnibus values from three studies can be entered as three tiers, and WinPepi's multi-tier analysis will output a weighted average TauU, and a further reduced average

SE_{Tau}. With sufficiently large numbers of studies, inference testing of the difference between two omnibus results can be carried out with reference to an approximate Z distribution. For example, suppose that we have a moderator variable: "use of negative reinforcement," with two levels, yes and no. Suppose also that the average results for 12 studies employing negative reinforcement are TauU = .66, SE_{Tau} = .18, whereas for 7 studies not employing negative reinforcement, TauU = .31, SE_{Tau} = .11. We test Z = (.66 − .31)/sqrt (.18^2 + .11^2) = .35/.211 = 1.66, which has a two-tailed p = .097, and so the effectiveness of "use of negative reinforcement" is not statistically significant at the .05 level.

Advantages of Non-Overlap Indices for SCR

In this chapter we have reviewed most available nonparametric non-overlap effect-size indices that measure change across phases in an SCR design. Their respective features were compared, with the strengths and weaknesses of each. All non-overlap indices share five advantages, three of which were articulated earlier in this chapter: (a) congruence with visual analysis, (b) simply and directly interpreted, and (c) robust and distribution-free. To those three we now add one more: (d) statistical accessibility.

Statistical Accessibility

As with the permutation and randomization tests discussed in Chapter 5 (this volume), the non-overlap calculations are all more accessible than parametric methods, in that they require no more than basic arithmetic. To conduct inferential statistical tests, the only additional skills required are the ability to square a number and take its root. By comparison, the statistical requirements of multiple regression are sophisticated, and those of multi-level modeling (MLM) are foreboding. Again, like permutation/randomization tests, non-overlap indices also share conceptual simplicity. This approach may lack the efficiency of a single complex omnibus model, but its distinct advantage is accessibility to most interventionists.

Comparing Non-Overlap Indices

It should be clear from the foregoing discussion that we regard the newest non-overlap indices to be superior to their predecessors in most ways. However, the newer indices do sacrifice some of the hand calculation simplicity of the earliest indices. The seven distinct indices, along with ordinary least squares (OLS) regression, will now be subjectively compared by how well they meet seven desirable criteria: (a) integration with visual analysis, (b) simple calculation by hand, (c) direct and simple meaning, (d) applicable to very small studies with short phases, (e) requires minimal statistical expertise, (f) includes trend, and (g) possesses strong precision-power. The four-point rating scale (++, +, −, —), represents "major strength," "strength," "minor weakness," and "major weakness" (see Table 4.2).

Table 4.2. Comparing Seven Non-Overlap Indices and Ordinary Least Squares (OLS) Regression on Seven Quality Criteria

Method	Visual analysis	Hand calculation	Simple meaning	Small study	Minimum stats	Includes trend	Precision-power
OLS Regression (Allison & Gorman, 1993)	−	−	−	+	−	++	++
ECL (White & Haring, 1980)	++	+	−	+	+	++	−
PND (Scruggs et al., 1987)	++	++	++	++	++	−	−
PEM (Ma, 2006)	++	++	++	++	+	−	−
PAND (Parker et al., 2007)	++	++	++	++	++	−	+
R-IRD & Phi (Parker et al., 2009)	++	+	++	++	+	−	++
NAP (Parker & Vannest, 2009)	++	+	++	++	+	−	++
TauU (Parker, Vannest, Davis, & Sauber 2011)	++	−	++	++	−	++	++

Table 4.2 shows that most of the non-overlap indices fare well against OLS regression, when considering all seven criteria. For integration with visual analysis, all seven non-overlap indices were rated high. Simple hand calculation, however, is possible with only three of the earlier indices. Direct and simple meaning is provided by all non-overlap indices, but not with the original ECL and OLS regression. The same is true with suitability for very short datasets. The level of statistical sophistication required is a strength of most of the non-overlap indices, but the newest and strongest (TauU) requires the most statistical sophistication of all. Still, the statistical skills required by TauU are far less than those required for OLS regression. Inclusion of trend is needed for only some datasets, but when needed, most non-overlap indices fall short. Only ECL and TauU include control of baseline trend. Sufficient precision-power to reliably detect medium-size effects in short datasets is a common weakness of non-overlap indices, which has been overcome only by the three most recent indices: IRD, NAP, and TauU. Among these three, only NAP and TauU approach the precision-power of OLS regression. To these seven criteria, an eighth could have been added, which would be "possesses a known sampling distribution for inferential tests." Only PND would not meet that criterion.

The number of non-overlap indices for SCR has greatly expanded over the past decade. The traditional benefits of non-overlap include a simple, robust, and interpretable analysis with direct meaning to most interventionists. Although not without limitations, non-overlap indices are nimble for use with any SCR design or measurement scale. Recently, two key additional benefits have been added: strong precision-power and the ability to integrate trend along with level changes. These recent additional benefits should make non-overlap indices strong contenders among other worthy effect sizes for SCR. Continued development of non-overlap techniques include a recalibration of TauU variance accounted for to total variance. We expect the work of Shadish et al. in Chapter 8 of this volume to further identify the comparability of non-overlap ES indices with more traditional indices such as R^2.

Conclusion

Improvements in SCR analysis are occurring rapidly and noticeably. These improvements are noticed within MLM, randomization models, and various regression models. At present there is not a single preferred analysis method. The questions, the design, the implementation or context, and the data will likely dictate the best fit of any selected analysis.

References

Abramson, J. H. (2010). Programs for epidemiologists-Windows version (WinPepi) [Computer software]. Retrieved from http://www.brixtonhealth.com/pepi4windows.html

Acion, L., Peterson, J., Temple, S., & Arndt, S. (2006). Probabilistic index: An intuitive nonparametric approach to measuring the size of treatment effects. Statistics in Medicine, 25, 591–602. doi:10.1002/sim.2256

Allison, D. B., & Gorman, B. S. (1993). Calculating effect sizes for meta-analysis: The case of the single case. *Behaviour Research and Therapy, 31*, 621–631. doi:10.1016/0005-7967(93)90115-B

Allison, D. B., & Gorman, B. S. (1994). Make things as simple as possible, but no simpler: A rejoinder to Scruggs and Mastropieri. *Behaviour Research and Therapy, 32*, 885–890. doi:10.1016/0005-7967(94)90170-8

Altman, D. G. (1990). *Practical Statistics for Medical Research.* London, England: Chapman & Hall/CRC.

Anderson, T. W., & Darling, D. A. (1954). A test of goodness of fit. *Journal of the American Statistical Association, 49*, 765–769. doi:10.1080/01621459.1954.10501232

Bowman-Perrott, L., Davis, H. D., Vannest, K. J., Greenwood, C., & Parker, R. I. (2012). Academic benefits of peer tutoring: A meta-analytic review of single-case research. *School Psychology Review, 41,* 39–55.

Buchan, I. (2012). StatsDirect [Computer software]. Cheshire, England: StatsDirect Ltd.

Burns, M. K., Codding, R. S., Boice, C., & Lukito, G. (2010). Meta-analysis of acquisition and fluency math interventions with instruction and frustration level skills: Evidence for a skill-by-treatment interaction. *School Psychology Review, 39,* 69–83.

Campbell, J. M. (2004). Statistical comparison of four effect sizes for single-subject designs. *Behavior Modification, 28*, 234–246. doi:10.1177/0145445503259264

Cliff, N. (1993). Dominance statistics: Ordinal analyses to answer ordinal questions. *Psychological Bulletin, 114*, 494–509. doi:10.1037/0033-2909.114.3.494

Cochrane Collaboration. (2006). *Cochrane handbook for systematic reviews of interventions.* Retrieved from http://www.cochrane.org/index_authors_researchers.htm

Cohen, J. (1988). *Statistical power analysis for the behavioral sciences* (2nd ed.). Hillsdale, NJ: Erlbaum.

Cooper, H., Hedges, L. V., & Valentine, J. C. (Eds.). (2009). *The handbook of research synthesis and meta-analysis* (2nd ed.). New York, NY: Russell Sage Foundation.

Crosbie, J. (1987). The inability of the binomial test to control Type I error with single-subject data. *Behavioral Assessment, 9*, 141–150.

D'Agostino, R. B., Campbell, M., & Greenhouse, J. (2006a). The Mann–Whitney statistic: Continuous use and discovery. *Statistics in Medicine, 25*, 541–542. doi:10.1002/sim.2508

D'Agostino, R. B., Campbell, M., & Greenhouse, J. (2006b). Noninferiority trials: Continued advancements in concepts and methodology. *Statistics in Medicine, 25*, 1097–1099. doi:10.1002/sim.2553

Draper, N. R., & Smith, H. (1998). *Applied regression analysis* (3rd ed.). New York, NY: Wiley.

Faith, M. S., Allison, D. B., & Gorman, B. S. (1996). Meta-analysis of single-case research. In D. R. Franklin, D. B. Allison, & B. S. Gorman (Eds.), *Design and analysis of single-case research* (pp. 245–277). Mahwah, NJ: Erlbaum.

Ganz, J. B., Parker, R., & Benson, J. (2009). Impact of the picture exchange communication system: Effects on communication and collateral effects on maladaptive behaviors. *Augmentative and Alternative Communication, 25*, 250–261. doi:10.3109/07434610903381111

Grissom, R. J., & Kim, J. J. (2005). *Effect sizes for research: A broad practical approach.* Mahwah, NJ: Erlbaum.

Hedges, L. V., & Olkin, I. (1985). *Statistical methods for meta-analysis.* San Diego, CA: Academic Press.

Hodges, J. L., & Lehmann, E. L. (1956). The efficiency of some nonparametric competitors of the *t*-test. *Annals of Mathematical Statistics, 27*, 324–335.

Huberty, C. J., & Lowman, L. L. (2000). Group overlap as a basis for effect size. *Educational and Psychological Measurement, 60*, 543–563.

Huitema, B. E., & McKean, J. W. (2000). Design specification issues in time series intervention models. *Educational and Psychological Measurement, 60*, 38–58. doi:10.1177/00131640021970358

Johnstone, I. M., & Velleman, P. F. (1985). The resistant line and related regression methods. *Journal of the American Statistical Association, 80*, 1041–1054. doi:10.1080/01621459.1985.10478222

Kirk, R. E. (1995). *Experimental design: Procedures for the behavioral sciences* (3rd ed.). Pacific Grove, CA: Brooks/Cole.

Kirk, R. E. (1996). Practical significance: A concept whose time has come. *Educational and Psychological Measurement, 56*, 746–759. doi:10.1177/0013164496056005002

Koenig, C. H. (1972). *Charting the future course of behavior.* Kansas City, KS: Precision Media.

Levin, J. R., Marascuilo, L. A., & Hubert, L. J. (1978). N = nonparametric randomization tests. In T. R. Kratochwill (Ed.), *Single subject research: Strategies for evaluating change* (pp. 167–196). New York, NY: Academic Press.

Lipsey, M. W., & Wilson, D. (2001). *Practical meta-analysis.* Thousand Oaks, CA: Sage.

Llorca, J. (2002). Computer programs for epidemiologists: PEPI v. 4.0. *Journal of Epidemiology and Community Health, 56,* 959–960.

Ma, H. H. (2006). An alternative method for quantitative synthesis of single-subject research: Percentage of datapoints exceeding the median. *Behavior Modification, 30,* 598–617. doi:10.1177/0145445504272974

Ma, H. H. (2009). The effectiveness of intervention on the behavior of individuals with autism: A meta-analysis using percentage of datapoints exceeding the median of baseline phase (PEM). *Behavior Modification, 33,* 339–359. doi:10.1177/0145445509333173

Mann, H. B. (1945). Nonparametric tests against trend. *Econometrica, 13,* 245–259. doi:10.2307/1907187

May, H. (2004). Making statistics more meaningful for policy and research and program evaluation. *American Journal of Evaluation, 25,* 525–540.

Newson, R. (2002). Parameters behind "nonparametric" statistics: Kendall's tau, Somers' D and median differences. *The Stata Journal, 2,* 45–64.

O'Brien, S., & Repp, A. C. (1990). Reinforcement-based reductive procedures: A review of 20 years of their use with persons with severe or profound retardation. *Journal of the Association for Persons With Severe Handicaps, 15,* 148–159.

Onwuegbuzie, A. J., & Levin, J. R. (2003). Without supporting statistical evidence, where would reported measures of substantive importance lead? To no good effect. *Journal of Modern Applied Statistical Methods, 2,* 133–151.

Parker, R. I. (2006). Increased reliability for single-case research results: Is the bootstrap the answer? *Behavior Therapy, 37,* 326–338. doi:10.1016/j.beth.2006.01.007

Parker, R. I., & Hagan-Burke, S. (2007). Median-based overlap analysis for single case data: A second study. *Behavior Modification, 31,* 919–936. doi:10.1177/0145445507303452

Parker, R. I., Hagan-Burke, S., & Vannest, K. J. (2007). Percent of all non-overlapping data PAND: An alternative to PND. *The Journal of Special Education, 40,* 194–204. doi:10.1177/00224669070400040101

Parker, R. I., & Vannest, K. J. (2009). An improved effect size for single case research: Non-overlap of all pairs (NAP). *Behavior Therapy, 40,* 357–367. doi:10.1016/j.beth.2008.10.006

Parker, R. I., Vannest, K. J., & Brown, L. (2009). The improvement rate difference for single case research. *Exceptional Children, 75,* 135–150.

Parker, R. I., Vannest, K. J., & Davis, J. L. (2011). Nine non-overlap techniques for single case research. *Behavior Modification, 35,* 303–322. doi:10.1177/0145445511399147

Parker, R. I., Vannest, K. J., Davis, J. L., & Sauber, S. (2011). Combining non-overlap and trend for single case research: Tau-U. *Behavior Therapy, 42,* 284–299. doi:10.1016/j.beth.2010.08.006

Parsonson, B. S., & Baer, D. M. (1978). The analysis and presentation of graphic data. In T. R. Kratochwill (Ed.), *Single-subject research: Strategies for evaluating change* (pp. 101–165). New York, NY: Academic Press. doi:10.1016/B978-0-12-425850-1.50009-0

Pennypacker, H. S., Koenig, C. H., & Lindsley, O. R. (1972). *Handbook of the standard behavior chart.* Kansas City, KS: Precision Media.

Rosenberg, M. S., Adams, D. C., & Gurevitch, J. (2000). MetaWin: Statistical software for meta-analysis (V 2.0) [Computer Software]. Sunderland, MA: Sinauer Associates.

Sackett, D. L., Richardson, W. S., Rosenberg, W., & Haynes, R. B. (1997). *Evidence-based medicine: How to practice and teach EBM.* New York, NY: Churchill Livingstone.

Schneider, N., Goldstein, H., & Parker, R. (2008). Social skills interventions for children with autism: A meta-analytic application of percentage of all non-overlapping data (PAND). *Evidence-Based Communication Assessment and Intervention, 2,* 152–162. doi:10.1080/17489530802505396

Scotti, J. R., Evans, I. M., Meyer, L. H., & Walker, P. (1991). A meta-analysis of intervention research with problem behavior: Treatment validity and standards of practice. *American Journal on Mental Retardation, 96,* 233–256.

Scruggs, T. E., & Mastropieri, M. A. (1994). The utility of the PND statistic: A reply to Allison and Gorman. *Behaviour Research and Therapy, 32,* 879–883. doi:10.1016/0005-7967(94)90169-4

Scruggs, T. E., & Mastropieri, M. A. (1998). Summarizing single-subject research: Issues and applications. *Behavior Modification, 22,* 221–242. doi:10.1177/01454455980223001

Scruggs, T. E., & Mastropieri, M. A. (2001). How to summarize single-participant research: Ideas and applications. *Exceptionality, 9,* 227–244. doi:10.1207/S15327035EX0904_5

Scruggs, T. E., Mastropieri, M. A., & Casto, G. (1987). The quantitative synthesis of single subject research: Methodology and validation. *Remedial & Special Education, 8,* 24–33. doi:10.1177/074193258700800206

Sen, P. K. (1968). Estimates of the regression coefficient based on Kendall's tau. *Journal of the American Statistical Association, 63,* 1379–1389. doi:10.1080/01621459.1968.10480934

Shadish, W. R., & Haddock, C. K. (1994). Combining estimates of effect size. In H. Cooper & L. V. Hedges (Eds.), *The handbook of research synthesis* (pp. 261–284). New York, NY: Sage.

Shadish, W. R., Rindskopf, D. M., & Hedges, L. V. (2008). The state of the science in the meta-analysis of single-case experimental designs. *Evidence-Based Communication Assessment and Intervention, 2,* 188–196. doi:10.1080/17489530802581603

Sheskin, D. J. (2007). *Handbook of parametric and nonparametric statistical procedures* (4th ed.). Boca Raton, FL: Chapman & Hall.

Siegel, S., & Castellan, N. J., Jr. (1988). *Nonparametric statistics for the behavioral sciences* (2nd ed.). New York, NY: McGraw-Hill.

Sprent, P., & Smeeton, N. C. (2001). *Applied nonparametric statistical methods.* Boca Raton, FL: Chapman & Hall/CRC Press.

StatsDirect. (2006). StatsDirect statistical software [Computer software]. Retrieved from http://www.statsdirect.com

Tawney, J. W., & Gast, D. L. (1984). *Single-subject research in special education.* Columbus, OH: Merrill.

Theil, H. (1950). A rank-invariant method of linear and polynomial regression analysis, III. *Proceedings of the Koninklijke Nederlandse Akademie van Wetenschappen A, 53,* 1397–1412.

Tukey, J. W. (1977). *Exploratory data analysis.* Menlo Park, CA: Addison-Wesley.

Van den Noortgate, W., & Onghena, P. (2003). Hierarchical linear models for the quantitative integration of effect sizes in single case research. *Behavior Research Methods, Instruments & Computers, 35,* 1–10. doi:10.3758/BF03759492

Van den Noortgate, W., & Onghena, P. (2008). A multilevel meta-analysis of single subject experimental design studies. *Evidence-Based Communication Assessment and Intervention, 2,* 142–151. doi:10.1080/17489530802505362

Vannest, K. J., Davis, J. L., Davis, C. R., Mason, B. A., & Burke, M. D. (2010). Effective intervention with a daily behavior report card: A meta-analysis. *School Psychology Review, 39,* 654–672.

Vannest, K. J., Harrison, J. R., Temple-Harvey, K., Ramsey, L., & Parker, R. I. (2011). Improvement rate differences of academic interventions for students with emotional and behavioral disorders. *Remedial and Special Education, 32*(6), 521–534. doi:10.1177/0741932510362509

White, O. R. (1986). Precision teaching-Precision learning. *Exceptional Children, 52,* 522–534.

White, O. R., & Haring, N. G. (1980). *Exceptional teaching* (2nd ed.). Columbus, OH: Merrill.

Wilcox, R. R. (2005). *Introduction to robust estimation and hypothesis testing* (2nd ed.). San Diego, CA: Academic Press.

Wilcox, R. R. (2010). *Fundamentals of modern statistical methods: Substantially improving power and accuracy* (2nd ed.). New York, NY: Springer. doi:10.1007/978-1-4419-5525-8

Wolery, M., Busick, M., Reichow, B., & Barton, E. (2010). Comparison of overlap methods for quantitatively synthesizing single-subject data. *The Journal of Special Education, 44,* 18–28. doi:10.1177/0022466908328009

5

Single-Case Permutation and Randomization Statistical Tests: Present Status, Promising New Developments

John M. Ferron and Joel R. Levin

We begin this chapter with a description of permutation and randomization statistical tests, the motivation for their use, and their application to single-case intervention research. We then outline the limitations and concerns associated with these methods, along with the methodological work that has sought to address these concerns. Next, we suggest alternative methods for incorporating randomization (i.e., some form of random assignment) into single-case designs so that the applicability of randomization tests can be extended to a broad range of single-case investigations. More specifically, we (a) consider contexts where previously developed randomization schemes are not sufficient to meet all of a researcher's goals, (b) offer suggestions that would allow the goals to be met while also allowing for the conduct of statistically valid permutation/randomization tests, and (c) illustrate the use of these methods.

Overview of Permutation and Randomization Tests

Permutation tests are nonparametric statistical analyses that can be used to draw treatment-effect inferences from single-case intervention research investigations. Unlike more familiar parametric statistical tests that rely on the comparison of a test statistic to a theoretical distribution (e.g., t or F) derived under a nontrivial set of assumptions (e.g., normality, equality of variance, independence), permutation tests compare the obtained test statistic with an empirical distribution that is formed by either (a) all possible permutations of the dataset, subject to the sample-size constraints of the design, or (b) computing the test statistic over and over (through sampling with replacement) for different permutations of the dataset, again subject to the sample-size constraints

http://dx.doi.org/10.1037/14376-006
Single-Case Intervention Research: Methodological and Statistical Advances, by T. R. Kratochwill and J. R. Levin

of the design. Additionally, when (a) the study incorporates some type of random assignment, as discussed throughout this chapter, and (b) the permissible permutations are restricted to the permutations that coincide with the possible random assignments, then the permutation test is termed a *randomization test* (Edgington & Onghena, 2007; and as is illustrated subsequently)—a distinction that has either been glossed over or not carefully made in previous analysis considerations of single-case data (e.g., Levin, Marascuilo, & Hubert, 1978). In the present chapter, we focus our attention primarily on randomization tests—namely, tests applied to single-case designs that have some type of random-assignment component—but we briefly consider single-case permutation tests along the way as well.

Randomization is widely recognized not only as a defining feature of experimental research, but one that plays a critical role in enhancing the internal validity (Campbell & Stanley, 1966), or scientific credibility (Levin, 1994), of the study. As a result, randomization strengthens the researcher's ability to draw causal inferences involving interventions and outcomes (Edgington, 1996; Kratochwill & Levin, 2010; Shadish, Cook, & Campbell, 2002). Increased adoption of randomization in single-case intervention research would position such research as a more credible contributor to the establishment of a scientific basis for educational and psychological interventions (Kratochwill & Levin, 2010).

In addition, randomization statistical tests enhance statistical conclusion validity (Cook & Campbell, 1979). If a permutation test is applied to a nonrandomized design, the assumption of "exchangeability"—namely that the joint distribution $f(y_1, \ldots, y_N)$ is invariant under permutation of its arguments (Greenland & Draper, 1998)—can be questioned and problems with Type I error control can arise, at least for some situations (Ferron, Foster-Johnson, & Kromrey, 2003; Levin, Ferron, & Kratochwill, 2012; Levin et al., 1978; Manolov & Solanas, 2009; Manolov, Solanas, Bulté, & Onghena, 2009; Sierra, Solanas, & Quera, 2005). In contrast, if a randomization test is applied to a randomized design, the Type I error probabilities associated with assessing intervention effects are well controlled. More specifically, a randomization test is statistically valid (i.e., the Type I error rate will be no greater than the stated a priori significance level) as long as (a) the design includes some appropriate type of randomization scheme, where "some appropriate type" is discussed later in this chapter; (b) the permutations are based on the data divisions that could have resulted from the randomization scheme; and (c) the choice of a test statistic is not influenced by the experimental results (Edgington, 1980b).

Notably absent from the just-provided list of conditions are the standard parametric statistical assumptions of normality, homogeneity of variance, and independence, making randomization tests applicable in contexts where alternative statistical analyses may not be appropriate. For example, in many single-case applications there is concern that the observations (or the corresponding errors of a statistical model) in the time series will be sequentially dependent (*autocorrelated*), rather than independent (Kratochwill et al., 1974; Matyas & Greenwood, 1997). Moreover, the presence of autocorrelation substantially compromises the statistical-conclusion validity of analyses that assume independence, including standard analysis of variance and regression

(Toothaker, Banz, Noble, Camp, & Davis, 1983), which makes preferable an analysis that is free of the independence assumption.

A Single-Case Randomization Test Example

To illustrate the logic of randomization tests and their control over Type I error rates in a single-case intervention research context, consider a simple two-treatment comparison study consisting of a cognitive intervention (A) and a behavioral intervention (B), in which six observations are collected on a single individual, three during the A treatment and three during the B treatment. Further suppose that the three A observations and the three B observations are randomly assigned to the six sequential time periods, 1–6 (e.g., $B_1B_2A_3A_4B_5A_6$)—according to what can be called a *phase-randomization* scheme (and which, for this example, corresponds to an *intervention-randomization* scheme)—yielding one of 20 (6!/3!3! = 20) possible assignments of observations to time periods. Before collecting the data, the researcher would both decide on an acceptable Type I error probability (say, $\alpha = .05$) and define a logical test statistic for the anticipated effect (e.g., $M_B - M_A$ for an anticipated shift in means). Then, after collecting the data, the researcher would construct a randomization distribution by computing the test statistic for each of the 20 ways of dividing the data into two groups of three observations. To test for statistical significance, the obtained test statistic would then be compared to the randomization distribution (see Levin et al., 1978). For the present example, if the obtained test statistic (a) were in the predicted direction (e.g., that the behavioral intervention would produce higher outcomes than the cognitive intervention) and (b) turned out to be the largest of the 20 possible rank-ordered randomization distribution outcomes, the researcher would reject the null hypothesis of no treatment effect at the $\alpha = .05$ level of significance (in that $p = 1/20 = .05$, which is less than or equal to the predesignated one-tailed α).[1]

As a conceptually straightforward explanation of the preceding randomization test, consider the following: In situations where there is no intervention effect, randomly selecting any one of the 20 possible assignments of observations to time periods is tantamount to randomly selecting a test statistic from the randomization distribution. The likelihood of randomly selecting the largest test statistic is quite small, and would therefore be attributable to chance (specifically, 1 in 20 times for this example). Given this small probability (represented by $\alpha = .05$) then, one would incorrectly reject the null hypothesis of no intervention effect and conclude that the difference between the cognitive-intervention and the behavioral-intervention phase observations was attributable to the intervention rather than to chance only 5% of the time.

In the just-discussed example, the ordering of the 3A and 3B phase observations within the time sequence was predetermined on a random basis by the

---

[1]Alternatively, if no a priori prediction of direction had been made (i.e., if a two-tailed statistical test were being conducted), then the randomization distribution outcomes would have to be rank ordered in terms of their absolute (unsigned) values and assessed for statistical significance on that basis.

researcher and the statistical test that followed was based on a model that assumed that such predetermined randomization was implemented. Suppose, however, that for a number of reasons to be discussed shortly, the researcher elected not to assign the phase observations randomly to the six time periods, but rather in a systematically alternating fashion such as ABABAB. Even though the data would be collected and statistically analyzed in exactly the same way as in the preceding example, in this case because of the absence of phase randomization the statistical test would be termed a permutation test. In a later section, we consider the various implications of this distinction in a single-case intervention research context.

Concerns With Permutation and Randomization Tests

Although the value of randomization and the statistical validity of permutation and randomization tests are well established, questions and concerns about these procedures have been raised (e.g., Barlow, Nock, & Hersen, 2009; Kazdin, 1980). The concerns focus on "practicality" and can be loosely placed into four categories: interpretability of results, sensitivity or statistical power, computational demands, and feasibility of randomization. Each of these concerns is now discussed in turn.

INTERPRETABILITY OF RESULTS. Do statistical tests, including randomization tests, lead to meaningful interpretations of single-case outcomes? Or should single-case researchers avoid statistical tests altogether and focus instead on graphical displays and visual-analysis procedures (see Chapter 3, this volume) and effect-size estimates (see Chapters 4 and Chapter 8, this volume)? The visual-versus-statistical analysis question has been a long-time topic of considerable controversy and debate (see Kratochwill, 1978; Kratochwill & Levin, 1992). Regarding the effect-size question, it seems conceptually valuable for researchers first to provide a convincing argument that an observed intervention effect was greater than what would have been expected by chance (something for which randomization tests are well suited) and only then to estimate the magnitude of the effect. (For an analogous argument in the context of conventional "group" designs, see Robinson & Levin, 1997.)

SENSITIVITY OR STATISTICAL POWER. Are single-case intervention researchers able to detect meaningful intervention effects on the basis of randomization tests, relative to both traditional visual-analysis methods (Chapter 3, this volume) and alternative statistical-analysis procedures such as time-series analysis, regression-based methods, and multilevel modeling? Neither we nor any other statistical analyst could in good conscience provide a single definitive response to this question because in several empirical simulation studies that have examined the statistical power of single-case randomization tests, the power has varied widely across applications, from unacceptably low to quite high, as a function of multiple factors. These factors include the type of design used, the randomization method and randomization test adopted, the amount of data collected (e.g., the number of within-phase observations per case and the number of cases in the design), the degree of autocorrelation, and the size of the effect (see Ferron & Onghena, 1996; Ferron & Sentovich, 2002; Ferron & Ware, 1995; Lall & Levin, 2004; Levin et al., 1978, 2012; Levin, Lall, & Kratochwill, 2011; Onghena, 1994). Thus, there is increasing information about the statistical power of randomization tests, but for now the jury is still out on questions concerning the power of single-case randomization tests relative to the statistical power of other statistical-analysis options.

COMPUTATIONAL DEMANDS. To what extent are user-friendly software programs available to aid researchers in conducting randomization tests? Typical statistical software programs do not have "canned" procedures for conducting single-case randomization tests and so to date this has been a limitation for researchers wishing to apply these procedures. Although there are a few applications for which a standard permutation test procedure would be appropriate, most applications of true randomization tests to single-case studies require specialized software or programming scripts. Considerable work has been done to create these scripts. The book *Randomization Tests* by Edgington and Onghena (2007) has a CD that contains Single-Case Randomization Test software; the second edition of *Single-Case and Small-n Experimental Designs* by Dugard, File, and Todman (2012) includes a website with macros to conduct a variety of randomization tests (but see Levin & Ferron, in press); and two articles have been published that illustrate how to conduct a variety of customized single-case randomization tests using the R software package, which is freely available (Bulté & Onghena, 2008, 2009). In addition, Gafurov and Levin's single-case intervention data-analysis *ExPRT* (*Excel Package of Randomization Tests*, detailed in Chapter 6, this volume), can be freely accessed by single-case intervention researchers.

FEASIBILITY OF RANDOMIZATION. How can researchers incorporate randomization, obtain other desirable design features (e.g., reversals, phases of sufficient length), and at the same time meet the practical constraints of the research context? With *phase randomization*, consider a single-case intervention study, similar to the example presented earlier, but in this case where 10 of 20 observations are to be randomly assigned to condition A (a baseline condition) and the other 10 observations to condition B (an intervention condition). Although highly unlikely, it is possible that the assignment could produce an AAAAAAAAAABBBBBBBBBB sequence, and the resulting AB design would generally be considered unacceptable to a researcher who was planning on a systematically alternating treatment design, such as ABABAB . . . AB (discussed later in this chapter). It would also be unacceptable to a researcher planning to implement a traditional single-case ABAB reversal design (represented here by AAAAABBBBBAAAAABBBBB). Although an obvious solution to the problem is for the study to be designed without randomization—so that the researcher has complete control over the assignment of conditions to time—one might wonder whether permutation tests are statistically valid with respect to Type I error control if they are applied to nonrandomized (or *systematic*) single-case studies.

The answer that can be given to date is a qualified "yes" because researchers have examined this issue and are beginning to map out the conditions under which permutation tests for systematic single-case designs do and do not control the Type I error rate (Ferron et al., 2003; Levin et al., 1978, 2012; Manolov & Solanas, 2009; Manolov et al., 2009; Sierra et al., 2005). But why the qualification? For either systematic ABAB . . . AB designs or analogous alternating treatment designs, empirical Type I errors are acceptably controlled (i.e., they are at or less than their nominal levels) when an appropriately constructed two-sample permutation test is applied. The permutation test is appropriately constructed when the alternating A and B phases consist of single observations (as in our earlier six-observation example) and the test is applied to those individual observations. However, when the alternating A and B phases contain multiple observations, the permutation test is appropriately constructed only if the data being analyzed consist of phase summary measures (such as phase means, standard deviations, or slopes) rather than individual observations. Levin et al. (2012) have demonstrated this point for both 24-observation and 12-observation designs, and the present authors have extended it downward for six-observation designs. For the earlier 3A and 3B phase example, if the six observations are taken systematically as ABABAB and analyzed via Levin et al.'s (1978) two-sample permutation test, the Type I error never exceeds the specified .05 level for autocorrelation values that would be expected in single-case intervention research, namely, those ranging from 0 to .60. In contrast, Levin et al. (2012) found that for a six-phase ABABAB design containing six observations per phase, although empirical Type I errors similarly never exceed their nominal levels in the presence of positive autocorrelation when a permutation test is applied to the six phase means, the Type I errors are greatly inflated when the same test is applied to the 24 individual A and B observations.

A second alternative for ensuring the inclusion of desired design elements is to restrict the randomization. Consider again the randomization test originally proposed for single-case data where N_1 observations are randomly assigned to condition A and N_2 observations are randomly assigned to condition B (Edgington, 1967). Researchers who wish to ensure that they obtain an alternating treatment design could restrict the randomization so that there will be no more than n observations of the same condition in a row (Onghena & Edgington, 1994) or so that each sequential pair of observations contains one A and one B observation (Edgington, 1992; Levin et al., 2012). The randomization test could then be conducted by comparing the obtained test statistic to the set of permutations that correspond to the restricted set of possible assignments.

For researchers who wish to implement a systematic AB design, a different type of randomization strategy (*intervention start-point randomization*) is available. Specifically, the *actual* intervention start point(s) can be randomly selected from among some prespecified set of *potential* (or "acceptable") intervention start points (Edgington, 1975). For example, a researcher planning to collect 30 observations for an AB design could randomly select the intervention start point from anywhere between the sixth and 25th observations. Randomly selecting intervention start points from among a restricted set of possibilities can be generalized to accommodate more complex reversal designs such as the ABA, ABAB, or even a multiple-phase alternating treatment design (see Chapter 6, this volume), where the restrictions can be set up to ensure that there are k phases and that each phase has at least N observations (Onghena, 1992).

Replicated AB designs and analyses have also been proposed, for which start-point randomization is independently implemented for each case (Marascuilo & Busk, 1988). In addition, (a) both replicated AB and multiple-baseline designs/analyses have been developed that incorporate *case randomization*, namely, random assignment of cases to the different temporally staggered intervention start points of the multiple-baseline design (Wampold & Worsham, 1986) or by a combination of case randomization and start-point randomization applied to each of the design's staggered start points (Koehler & Levin, 1998); (b) AB-type designs/analyses that compare the effectiveness of two different interventions (e.g., BC designs in the traditional single-case literature) have been developed, in which cases are paired or blocked, with pair/block members randomly assigned to the different intervention conditions and the pairs/blocks randomly assigned to intervention start points (Chapter 6, this volume; Levin, Ferron, & Gafurov, 2014; Levin & Wampold, 1999); and (c) a combination of (a) and (b), discussed later in this chapter, along with a single-case adaptation of the conventional "group" crossover design and analysis (see Levin et al., 1990, Experiment 1). Over the years, a variety of randomization options have been proposed in an attempt to make random assignment practical for a wide range of single-case intervention studies. For additional illustrations of the various randomization approaches, see Dugard et al. (2012), Edgington (1980a, 1992), Edgington and Onghena (2007), Kratochwill and Levin (2010), and Wampold and Furlong (1981).

Is Randomization in Single-Case Intervention Studies Worth the Effort?

In the preceding section, we addressed the question—and common researcher concern—regarding the feasibility of randomization in single-case intervention studies. In so doing, we introduced three different types of randomization that single-case interventionists can consider implementing, either individually or in combination. The three types are phase randomization, intervention start-point randomization, and case randomization. Although each of these randomization types was discussed in conjunction with an accompanying statistical randomization test to enhance the statistical-conclusion validity of the intervention study, here we argue that even without the randomization test (i.e., with either visual analysis or one of the other statistical procedures presented in this volume), including one or more randomization types (including our later-discussed *intervention-order randomization*) is well worth the effort from a methodological standpoint. That is, and as we indicated at the outset of this chapter, if a single-case interventionist elects to incorporate an appropriate form of randomization into the study's design and procedures, the study's internal validity and associated scientific credibility will be considerably enhanced (Kratochwill & Levin, 2010). Specifically, including phase randomization in

ABAB . . . AB-type and alternating-treatment studies counteracts concerns about order-effect issues such as maturation (practice, fatigue), testing, history, and researcher-bias effects (see Kratochwill & Levin, 1980). For replicated ABAB . . . AB designs in which different phase orders or different interventions are randomly assigned to the various cases, in addition to enhancing the study's external validity the just-noted order-effect issues become even more moot. Including intervention start-point randomization, wherein the actual intervention start point is randomly selected from a predesignated interval of start points that is acceptable to the researcher, serves to counteract internal-validity concerns about both regression-toward-the mean effects and researcher bias. These concerns could arise when a researcher adopts a "response-guided" intervention strategy (see the following section as well as Chapter 3, this volume) that could result in an intervention phase beginning immediately following the occurrence of one or more extreme (or intervention-favoring) baseline observations. Again, in replicated designs, randomly determining the intervention start point independently for the different cases would additionally enhance the study's internal validity, especially with respect to history and specific day and time-of-day concerns. Finally, in replicated single-case designs where the intervention start points are decided upon in advance (such as conventional multiple-baseline designs), assigning cases randomly to the various staggered intervention start points clearly removes any concerns about researcher subjectivity and bias with respect to which case is receiving the intervention when.

Response-Guided Interventions and Visual Analysis

Although considerable progress has been made in each of the areas of present concern, a number of unresolved single-case intervention research and data-analysis issues remain. We are especially interested in issues associated with randomization feasibility and the lack of viable randomization schemes for certain single-case intervention studies. A primary purpose in our writing this chapter is to contribute additional randomization schemes and data-analysis strategies, with the aim of both expanding the pool of options available to researchers and extending the range of single-case investigations for which randomization tests are applicable. In this section, we (a) present a context for which previously discussed randomization schemes would not be sufficient to meet all of a single-case interventionist's goals and then (b) describe and illustrate an alternative method that would allow for the goals to be met, while at the same time allowing for the conduct of statistically valid randomization–permutation tests.

Review and Overview

In this section we illustrate how visual-analysis procedures—and, specifically, those procedures that are response guided—can be combined with a novel approach that affords single-case researchers a formal statistical basis for establishing the presence of intervention effects (Ferron & Jones, 2006). The evidence standards developed for the What Works Clearinghouse (WWC) indicate that each phase must show a clear pattern of response so that researchers can extrapolate and project the performance that would have been observed had there been no change in treatment (Kratochwill et al., 2013). The need to make projections is critical for both visual analysis and effect-size estimation, but such projections can present problems for researchers who have elected to incorporate randomization for internal validity and/or statistical-conclusion validity purposes. Suppose, for example, that a researcher randomly selects the eighth observation in the series to be the start point for the intervention. There is no problem with this particular random selection if the first seven observations represent a stable baseline pattern of responses, but what if the seventh observation happens to be an outlier that falls either in the direction of expected change or in the opposite direction? In the former case, if the researcher sticks with the randomly selected start point it is unclear whether, in the absence of intervention, the behavior would have stayed at the level of the seventh observation or would have returned to the earlier baseline levels. In the latter case, an outlying seventh observation in the opposite direction of the expected change would be predicted to produce an eighth observation that has regressed back to the mean of the preceding six baseline observations. As a result, if instead of intervening the researcher adopts a response-guided approach and extends the baseline to resolve this outlying observation concern, the randomization process and the validity of the associated statistical test are both compromised.

The challenge is to provide a randomization scheme that not only ensures the desired design type, the desired number of phases, and the desired minimum phase lengths, but also ensures that each phase exhibits a consistent response pattern. Initial work along these lines has led to the suggestion that researchers could randomly select an intervention start point only after a stable baseline pattern has been established (Edgington, 1975; Ferron & Ware, 1994; Koehler & Levin, 1998; Kratochwill & Levin, 2010). Unfortunately, a potential limitation of this approach is that the pattern may be lost before the intervention is implemented. Suppose, for example, that a researcher observes a stable baseline after five observations and then randomly selects the intervention start point from between the sixth through the tenth observations. The eighth observation may be selected, but the seventh observation could be an outlier, or the fifth, sixth, and seventh observations could align to suggest a trend either in the direction of or opposite to the expected change.

MULTIPLE-BASELINE DESIGN WITH FOUR PARTICIPANTS. To counteract these unfortunate possibilities, Ferron and Jones (2006) illustrated a more flexible approach, which includes a *masked visual analyst* (MVA)—someone with expertise in the single-case intervention research domain of interest but who is "blind" (or "masked") with respect to the execution particulars of the present study. The general process of including an MVA is depicted in Figure 5.1. In the specific example given by Ferron and Jones, the planning stage (Stage 1) led to agreement about conducting a multiple-baseline study with four participants, requiring at least five observations in each baseline phase; randomly assigning the participants to the different temporally staggered intervention

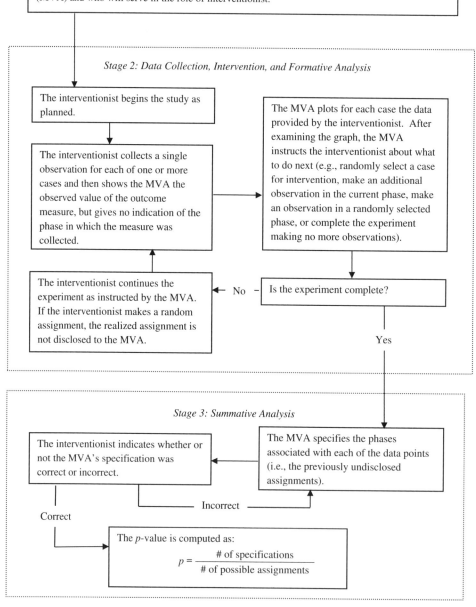

Figure 5.1. Flow chart depicting the process for including a masked visual analyst (MVA).

start points; and designating who would serve as the MVA and who would serve as the interventionist. The data collection, intervention, and formative analysis stage (Stage 2) began with the interventionist gathering baseline data on each participant and sending those baseline observations to the MVA. The MVA plotted the observations and indicated at what point the baselines were stable and the intervention could begin. The interventionist then randomly selected a participant for intervention, began the intervention for that participant, and gathered more data. The values of the outcome measure continued to be sent to the MVA but the MVA was not informed which participant had been selected for intervention. The MVA used the emerging outcome data to select the time for each of the successive intervention start points. At each step of Stage 2, the participant was selected randomly by the interventionist and the outcome of the random selection was not disclosed to the MVA. The interventionist continued gathering data and sending the values of the outcome measure to the MVA. The MVA continued to plot the data and when ample data had been gathered the MVA signaled the end of the experiment.

In the summative analysis stage (Stage 3), the MVA specified what she believed to be the intervention order. In this example, there were 4! = 24 possible assignments, and thus the MVA would have a one in 24 chance of identifying the correct intervention order if there were no systematic pattern in the data and she were simply guessing. The 1/24 = .0417 value can alternatively be thought of as the Type I error probability (α) associated with this exercise. Accordingly, with a correct intervention-order specification by the MVA, the experiment's outcome ($p = .0417$) would be statistically significant if $\alpha = .05$ had been specified as the *a priori* Type I error probability. Visual displays that have been masked so that treatment assignment is not revealed have been previously discussed (Ferron & Foster-Johnson, 1998; Mawhinney & Austin, 1999) and it is their use during data collection that allows researchers who prefer the adoption of a response-guided intervention process to "have their cake and eat it too." That is, with the present MVA approach researchers can employ visual analysis to ensure an acceptable baseline pattern of responding while at the same time incorporating randomization both to enhance the research's internal validity and to produce a valid inferential statistical test. We now extend the idea of coupling randomization with an MVA to provide statistically valid approaches for other single-case designs.

REVERSAL DESIGN. Consider a single-case context where the research team wishes to use a reversal design (an ABAB . . . AB-type design with at least four phases) to examine the effect of an intervention that was developed to reduce the disruptive behavior of a child with a severe emotional disturbance. The research team further wants the study to be consistent with the single-case design standards put forth by the WWC (Kratochwill et al., 2013) but also would like to incorporate random assignment. To meet the design standards without reservations, the design would have to include at least four phases, or three phase changes (e.g., ABAB or ABABA, but not ABA), and a minimum of five observations per phase. In addition, the phase changes would need to occur at times where the phases showed a clear pattern of responding. One could ensure at least three phase changes, a minimum of five observations per phase, and a bona fide randomization scheme by randomly selecting a triplet of phase-change points from among the triplets of "acceptable" phase-change points based on each phase needing to contain at least five observations (Chapter 6, this volume; Onghena, 1992). To ensure that each phase exhibits a clear pattern of responding, the more interactive response-guided approach is needed, and thus one member of the research team would be designated as the MVA.

The MVA examines a plot of the data as the study unfolds. After each successive observation is graphed the MVA decides whether the data pattern within the phase is sufficiently clear for a phase change to occur. If not, the phase is extended. If so, the MVA has the interventionist do one of the following: (a) gather the next observation under the A condition, (b) gather the next observation under the B condition, or (c) randomly determine whether the next observation will be under the A condition or the B condition. If conditions are determined randomly, the outcome of the random assignment is not disclosed to the MVA.

Hypothetical data for this study are shown in Figure 5.2. The MVA has the interventionist begin the study by gathering the first five baseline observations, the minimum acceptable number for ABAB . . . AB-type designs according to the WWC design standards and to the research team. The MVA examines the graph of the five baseline observations and thinks it presents a sufficiently clear pattern to consider intervening. Accordingly, the interventionist is asked to flip a coin to determine whether the next observation will be a continuation of baseline or the first intervention observation. The interventionist flips the

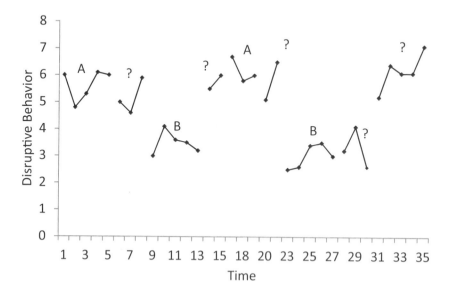

Figure 5.2. Graphical display of hypothetical data for an ABAB/ABABA reversal design in which groups of observations were collected under the baseline condition (A), under the intervention condition (B), or under a randomly selected condition, A or B (?). For this study, the five ?s in fact represent, respectively, Phases A, A, A, B, and A.

coin, does not disclose the outcome of the coin flip, gathers another observation, and sends the value of this observation to the MVA. The MVA adds the value to the graph, marking the first five observations as being part of the first A phase and the sixth observation with a question mark, indicating that it is either a continuation of the A phase or the beginning of the first B phase. If the MVA cannot decide whether the sixth observation represents the beginning of the B phase or a continuation of the A phase, the interventionist is asked to gather a second question-marked observation under the same condition, and the examination process (based on all seven observations) is repeated. At this point, if it is still not clear to the MVA whether these question-marked observations were a continuation of the first A phase or the beginning of the first B phase, then a third observation of the same condition is gathered (as is done here). After the first eight observations in Figure 5.1 have been plotted, the MVA suspects that the group of the last three observations was a continuation of the first A phase, and the interventionist is asked to gather five observations under the intervention condition (B).

After this is done and the observations have been communicated to the MVA, the MVA adds the observations to the graph and concludes that it would be an appropriate time to change phases. Again the interventionist is asked to flip a coin to decide whether the next set of observations will be made under the A or B condition, and again the interventionist does not reveal the result of the coin flip to the MVA. Observations are successively gathered and plotted under this condition. Suppose that after two observations have been plotted under this condition the MVA suspects that a second A phase has been started. The MVA asks the interventionist to gather the next set of observations under the A condition. After three more observations have been plotted, the MVA believes the last five observations were gathered for the second A phase. If so, the phase is sufficiently long and the pattern of responding is sufficiently clear to switch to the second B phase. Instead of asking for the next observations to be gathered under the B condition, the MVA again asks the interventionist to flip a coin to choose the condition and then to gather additional observations. This process is completed and the observations are added to the graph, again using a question mark to indicate that the condition was decided randomly.

Suppose that after two observations have been plotted, the MVA suspects that those observations were an extension of the second A phase. In addition, the MVA knows that at least one more phase shift is required and thus asks the interventionist to gather five observations for the second B phase, which the interventionist does. At this point the design is suspected to have four phases (i.e., ABAB) and each suspected phase has at least five observations and a pattern that is sufficiently clear. The MVA recognizes that to obtain statistical significance based on $\alpha = .05$ there need to be at least 20 potential randomization (in this context, binomial) distribution outcomes so that the MVA's "chance" probability of being correct on all indicated phase changes is less than or equal to $1/20 = .05$. To this point in the study, however, there have been only eight (or 2^3) potential outcomes, namely two potential outcomes for each of the three designated sets of observations, representing sets 6–8, 14–15, and 19–20. Therefore, the study must be extended and the MVA asks the interventionist to flip a coin to decide the subsequent phase/condition and to gather additional observations.

After visually examining the graph with two more observations, the MVA suspects that the two observations were a continuation of B but is concerned about the upward trend through this suspected B phase. The MVA therefore asks the interventionist to gather another question-marked observation. After this observation is gathered and plotted, the MVA is more convinced that these question-marked observations were an extension of the second B phase and concludes that this suspected B phase now presents an acceptably clear pattern. The MVA then asks the interventionist again to flip a coin to decide the subsequent phase–condition and to gather additional observations. After three more observations are gathered, the MVA believes that these observations were likely part of a third A phase. Not wanting to have any phases with less than five observations, the MVA asks the interventionist to gather two more observations under the same condition. This then completes the graph in Figure 5.1 and ends the study.

The MVA now has the task of correctly identifying the conditions corresponding to the groups of observations marked with question marks. The MVA suggests that the five groups were gathered under the conditions A, A, A, B, A, respectively. For the present example, this is a completely correct designation, and because there are $2^5 = 32$ potential randomization outcomes, the Type I error probability (and reported p-value) for the visual randomization test would be 1/32, or .03125. Because the sets of observations are gathered only when the preceding observations have demonstrated acceptable patterns and because the groups can be extended by the MVA until their pattern also becomes clear, the task of correctly identifying the conditions should be possible when the intervention has an effect. When the intervention has no effect, however, the task becomes difficult. In that case, the data contain no information about which condition was randomly selected at each choice point, and thus viewing the data does not alter the MVA's probability of correctly specifying which conditions were randomly selected. Correctly specifying all five of the randomly determined conditions therefore has a probability of $.5^5$, which equals .03125.

MULTIPLE-BASELINE DESIGN WITH THREE PARTICIPANTS. Consider next a context where a research team wishes to examine the effect of an intervention to increase prosocial behaviors in children with autism spectrum disorder. Suppose the research team adopts a multiple-baseline design with three participants. Given that this design allows for three demonstrations of the effect at three different points in time and can be constrained to have at least five observations per phase, it would meet single-case research WWC design standards (Kratochwill et al., 2013). If the research team wants to incorporate randomization, the participants could receive the intervention in a randomly determined staggered order (Wampold & Worsham, 1986), but this would lead to only 3! = 6 potential assignments of participants to orders. Alternatively the researchers could both randomize the participant order and also randomize the intervention start point for each participant (Koehler & Levin, 1998). With the latter incorporated, however, it is possible that the randomly selected start points will not occur at times when the baseline data show acceptable stability patterns, therefore resulting in data that do not meet the evidence criteria for single-case research. Although Ferron and Jones (2006) illustrated the use of an MVA to work in a response-guided format (thereby ensuring that all baseline phases exhibited acceptable stability patterns), their hypothetical multiple-baseline study required four participants in order to yield a Type I error probability that was less than or equal to .05 (namely, 1/4! = 1/24 = .042).

Here we present an alternative randomization scheme, mentioned briefly by Ferron and Jones (2006), which can produce a valid randomization statistical test based on $\alpha \leq .05$, with only three multiple-baseline participants. The MVA is shown the data as the study is being conducted. Hypothetical data for the study are presented in Figure 5.3. After the first five observations have been made, the MVA requests that all participants' baseline phases be extended as a result of the outlying observation for Marie. After three more observations

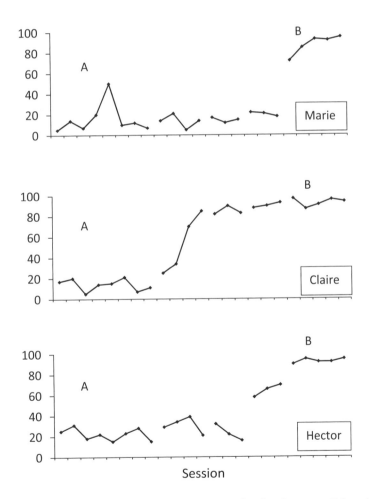

Figure 5.3. Graphical display of hypothetical data for the three-participant multiple-baseline example, where the intervention start for each participant is selected randomly from the four potential intervention start points (breaks in the series) with the restriction that each participant has a unique start point.

have been collected, the MVA judges the baseline patterns to be acceptable for all participants, and the interventionist is asked to randomly select from one of four options: (a) Start the intervention with Marie, (b) start the intervention with Claire, (c) start the intervention with Hector, or (d) start the intervention with no one. The interventionist does so, but the result of the random selection is not shared with the MVA.

Observations continue to be gathered and graphed, but the graph does not indicate which, if any, of the participants is in the intervention phase. Suppose that after two post-randomization observations it is unclear to the MVA who, if anyone, is in the intervention phase. After three observations it appears that both Claire and Hector have data patterns suggesting a trend toward improvement. After four observations it is clearer to the MVA that Claire is the one who was selected to start the intervention. Because Claire's data pattern has now been judged as indicating an apparent B phase, and because the other participants' baseline phases reveal acceptably clear patterns, the interventionist is asked to randomly select from the remaining three options.

The interventionist does so, again not revealing to the MVA the outcome of the random selection. Observations are again gathered and plotted. After an additional three observations, the MVA suspects that no new participant (i.e., Marie or Hector) was selected for intervention this round, and so the interventionist is asked to make the next random selection from the two remaining options (namely, starting the intervention for either Marie or Hector). Again data are gathered and plotted. After three post-randomization observations, the MVA suspects that Hector has entered the intervention phase and requests that the final operation be made (i.e. to start the intervention for Marie). After five more observations are collected in order to meet minimum observations-per-phase standards, the MVA indicates that sufficient data have been gathered and the study is concluded.

The MVA then tries to identify the intervention assignment, and suggests that the intervention assignments were Claire, no one, Hector, Marie. Assuming that this is a correct specification, then a p-value of .04167 would be reported. This probability was obtained by dividing the MVA's single specification by the $4! = 24$ ways of ordering the four options from which the interventionist randomly selected. Because the probability is less than or equal to $\alpha = .05$, the null hypothesis of no treatment effect would be rejected and it would be concluded that the intervention produced its desired staggered multiple-baseline effect.

MULTIPLE-PROBE DESIGN. Suppose that a research team wishes to incorporate randomization into a multiple-probe design, a variation of the multiple-baseline design. Like the multiple-baseline design, the start of the intervention is staggered over time across participants; but unlike the multiple-baseline design, observations are not collected at all points in time for all participants. The substitution of probing for continuous measurement is helpful when it is not feasible to collect data at each point in time for each participant. Given the similarities between multiple-probe and multiple-baseline designs, one may initially contemplate random assignment of participants to baseline lengths and a visual test that paralleled the one for the multiple-baseline design. This, however, is not a viable option, because the multiple-probe design results in different observation schedules for the different participants. Specifically, observations are collected more frequently early in the study on the participant who is intervened with first, whereas observations are collected more frequently later in the study for the participant who is intervened with last. Consequently, the pattern of data collection indicates the order of intervention and thus graphs cannot be created that effectively mask the intervention order. More generally, because observation frequency and intervention order are related, any randomization test procedure based on order would be compromised because the data for alternative random assignments of the participant cases to intervention orders are not available.

Although case randomization creates difficulties, phase randomization can be effectively used in a multiple-probe design. Consider the design and hypothetical data shown in Figure 5.4. After the first five observations have been collected for Dave, the MVA concludes that the baseline pattern is sufficiently clear and asks the interventionist to flip a coin to randomly decide whether the next observations will be gathered under the A or B condition. The interventionist flips the coin, does not disclose the outcome of the coin flip to the MVA, gathers two observations, and shares these observed values with the MVA. (The research team had previously decided that there would always be at least two observations in a randomly determined condition so that specifications did not hinge on a single, potentially outlying, observation.) The MVA adds these values to the graph such that for Dave, the first five observations are marked as being part of the first A phase and the sixth and seventh observations are marked with a question mark, indicating that those observations are either a continuation of the A phase or the beginning of the first B phase. The MVA suspects that Dave is in the B condition and notes that Dave has not only shown substantial change relative to baseline, but that the shift was observed only for Dave—not for John or Bob, who were still in baseline. As a result of this analysis, the MVA asks the interventionist to end the question mark phase for Dave, and to begin the question-mark phase for John.

After two question-marked observations have been gathered for John, the MVA asks for a third observation to be gathered in this phase because if these observations were a continuation of baseline, the last three baseline observations would present a trend in the direction of expected change. After the third questioned-marked observation has been gathered and plotted, the MVA suspects that John is still in baseline. If so, the baseline presents a sufficiently clear pattern and so, the MVA requests that the question-marked phase be ended and B observations be gathered. At this point, Bob remains in the baseline phase, so that shifts for John can be assessed relative to Bob, Dan, and Theresa, who are still in the baseline phase. After a few more observations, the desired pattern is presented, and so the MVA asks that the question-marked phase begin for Bob. The study continues in this manner until all the data shown in Figure 5.3 have been collected. The MVA then specifies the five question-marked groups of observations as B, A, B, B, A. This is the correct designation and because there are $2^5 = 32$ potential randomization outcomes, the Type I error probability (and reported p value) for the visual randomization test would be 1/32, or .03125.

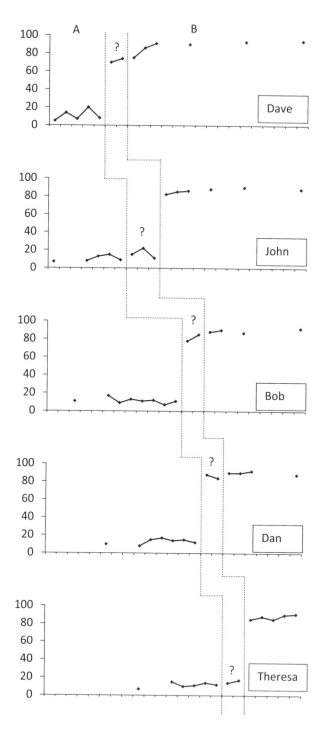

Figure 5.4. Graphical display of hypothetical data for the multiple-probe example, where the observations were collected under the baseline condition (A), under the intervention condition (B), or under a randomly selected condition, A or B (?). For this study, the five ?s in fact represent, respectively, Phases B, A, B, B, and A.

ALTERNATING TREATMENT DESIGN. As a final example of response-guided experimentation, randomization, and a statistical test, consider an alternating treatment design used to determine whether a novel intervention (B) is more effective than the standard intervention (A) with respect to the time on task of a third-grade child with attention problems. The research team plans to use a blocked-pairs random assignment procedure (Levin et al., 2012), where within each successive pair of observations, one observation is randomly assigned to A and the other to B. The response-guided experimentation comes in because the research team does not want to designate a priori how many pairs of observations will be gathered. They know they need at least five pairs of observations to obtain statistical significance at the .05 level, but they are not certain that five pairs will be sufficient to discriminate between the two treatments. Instead of designating the length of the study in advance, they designate one of the research team members as an MVA and let the decision be made based on the emerging data pattern.

The hypothetical data for this study are displayed in Figure 5.5. With the awareness that Intervention B was posited to be superior to Intervention A, after five pairs of observations have been plotted the MVA suspects that the assignment in the second pair was BA, the third pair was AB, the fourth pair was AB, and the fifth pair was BA. Unfortunately, the observations in the first pair are very close together and it is not at all clear to the MVA which was A and which was B. Rather than ending the experiment, the MVA asks the interventionist to collect another pair of observations. In this sixth pair, there is differentiation between the two points and the MVA suspects the assignment was AB.

At this point, the MVA could choose not to specify the first pair of observations and specify just the last five pairs. There are 32 possible assignments

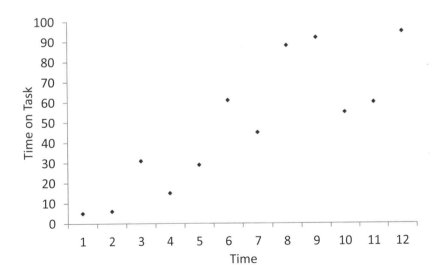

Figure 5.5. Graphical display of hypothetical data for the alternating treatments example, where within each successive pair of observations, one observation is randomly assigned to Intervention A and the other to Intervention B. In this study the intervention assignment was BABAABABBBAAB.

for the last five pairs, and thus correct specification of these would result in a probability of $1/32 = .03125$. Alternatively, the visual analyst could elect to specify all six pairs. If the specification were correct, the probability would be $1/64 = .015625$. If the specification was incorrect, the MVA would be asked to try again, with in the present case likely switching the specified order of the first pair. If this second specification were correct, the probability would be $2/64 = .03125$. Given that a p-value less than .05 can be obtained as long as the last five pairs were correctly specified, the MVA decides that sufficient data have been collected and asks that the study be concluded.[2]

For the present example, the MVA elects to specify all six pairs of observations, and considers the two possible assignments of the first pair, or more specifically the possible six-pair assignment of ABBAABABBAAB versus the possible assignment of BABAABABBAAB. This was done by creating a graph for each possible assignment, where the data points within the same condition were connected and the two resulting lines were compared. Although the second observation is a little higher than the first observation, the lines are more visually distinct when the first pair is specified as BA as opposed to AB. Based on this, the MVA makes the specification BABAABABBAAB, which is the correct designation, and thus the resulting p value is $1/64 = .015625$.

Suppose for a moment that the specification had been incorrect. What would happen next? The interventionist would indicate that the specification was incorrect but would not indicate which part of the specification was incorrect. The MVA would then make a second specification, and for this example starting with AB as opposed to BA. If this second specification (i.e., ABBAABABBAAB) had been the actual assignment, the reported p value would have been $2/64 = .03125$. Gathering the additional pair of observations ensured that a p-value less than .05 could be obtained, even if the first pair was initially specified incorrectly. If there had been two pairs of observations for which the discrimination was difficult, the study could have been extended to include a seventh pair, with the MVA allowed either to specify only five of the seven pairs completely correctly ($1/32 = .03125$), six of the seven pairs with two attempts to get all six correct ($1/64 = .015625$ for the first attempt, $2/64 = .03125$ for the second), or all seven pairs with up to six specifications before the p-value exceeded .05 (i.e., $6/128 = .047$, whereas $7/128 = .055$).

Proposed New Single-Case Randomization Tests

Just as quantitative methods based on permutations are being developed in the visual-analysis domain, the same can also be said of new permutation and randomization techniques as applied to the statistical analysis of single-case

---

[2]It is essential that the masked visual analyst be permitted to execute only one of these two options, (i.e., either a single specification for five pairs or up to two specifications for six pairs). Otherwise, the actual Type I error probability associated with the process will exceed the researcher's desired nominal α. More generally, the MVA procedure may well invite "Do over" or "Are you sure?" requests from the interventionist to the masked visual analyst. Such requests not only compromise the validity of the statistical test but also represent a form of unethical data-reporting behavior (see Panter & Sterba, 2011).

intervention data. In this section, we present several promising randomization-test adaptations and extensions for various single-case design options based on one or more cases.

Although the basic single-case two-phase A (baseline)–B (intervention) design is not acceptable according to WWC design standards, the design gains scientific credibility when A and B consist of two alternative interventions and either the order of intervention administration or the point at which the intervention is introduced (the intervention start point) is randomly determined. Scientific credibility is further enhanced when these procedures are replicated across multiple cases. What follows is a consideration of such designs, along with rationales presented for the application of randomization tests to the analysis of their data.

Intervention Randomization With Fixed Intervention Start Points: Replicated AB, ABAB . . . AB, and Alternating Treatment Designs

Suppose that six participants are to receive two different interventions, A and B. (For ease of presentation, we are designating the two different interventions A and B here, rather than the previously noted traditional single-case designation of B and C.) For each participant a coin is flipped to determine the order of intervention administration, either AB or BA. A straightforward statistical test is based on the binomial distribution. Specifically, if the two interventions do not differ in their effectiveness, then for half of the participants the mean outcomes will be higher in the A intervention condition than in the B intervention condition, and for the other half of the participants the reverse will be true. That is, the across-participants probability of Intervention A being more effective than Intervention B is .50. Further suppose that Intervention A is predicted to be more effective than Intervention B (i.e., a one-tailed alternative). According to a binomial (or sign) test with a "success" probability of .50 and $\alpha =$ .05, if all six of the participants were to exhibit a higher mean outcome following Intervention A than following Intervention B, it can be concluded that there is a statistical difference favoring Intervention A because the significance probability (p-value) is equal to $.50^6 = 1/64 = .016$. (With five participants, if all five performed better with Intervention A than with Intervention B, then the p-value would be $1/32 = .031$; and with seven participants, the p value associated with seven out of seven is $1/128 = .008$.) With eight participants, if either seven or eight of the participants exhibited a higher mean outcome with Intervention A than with Intervention B, that result would be statistically significant with a p value of $9/256 = .035$.

The most important reason for presenting the preceding binomial-test possibility is to contrast it with an alternative simple statistical strategy that is more attractive, namely a one-sample randomization test applied to the N mean A-B differences (i.e., the difference between the average of the B series observations and the average of the A series observations for each of the N participants)—for additional discussion of this approach, see Chapter 6 (this volume). The reason that a randomization test (or the analogous Wilcoxon signed-rank test) is more attractive than a binomial-based sign test is that the former possesses a distinct statistical power advantage (and related "relative efficiency") relative to the latter (a) as the number of participant replicates increases from five and especially (b) when it is expected that even though the expected intervention effect (in the present context, favoring Intervention A) might not be experienced by all participants, those who do benefit from the favored intervention will exhibit larger effects relative to participants who benefit from the competing (or control) intervention (here, Intervention B). For theoretical underpinnings and computational examples, see Chapters 3 and 4, this volume, as well as Bradley (1968), Lehmann (1975), and Marascuilo and McSweeney (1977).[3]

To make the foregoing discussion more concrete, consider a replicated single-case AB design in which a behavioral intervention (A) for reducing fear responses in phobic adults is expected to produce more, and larger, benefits in comparison to a cognitive intervention (B). Eight participants are recruited for the study and for the purposes of the present example, suppose that exactly five of the participants were randomly determined (via a coin flip) to receive the two interventions in an AB order and the remaining three to receive the interventions in a BA order. Repeatedly throughout the study, the amount of self-rated fear on a 7-point scale (with larger numbers representing greater rated fear) is collected from all participants during the administration of each intervention. The participants' B-A mean differences are tabulated and evaluated statistically based on $\alpha = .05$. The B-A mean differences produced by the eight participants were as follows:

$$+3.0 + 3.5 - 1.5 + 2.0 + 4.5 + 3.5 - 2.0 + 4.0.$$

Note that six of the participants rated their amount of fear higher for the B intervention than for the A intervention, as indicated by the six plus signs. A binomial test applied to the set of positive and negative signs yields a one-tailed p-value of $37/256 = .145$, which exceeds the pre-determined Type I error probability value of .05 and therefore leads to a "no intervention effect" conclusion.[4] In contrast, a one-sample randomization test applied to the actual signed mean differences yields an observed average B-A mean difference of +2.125, a value that is the ninth largest difference (specifically, a difference exceeded by five of the outcomes and tied with three others) in a randomization distribution consisting of the $2^8 = 256$ possible ways in which + and − signs can be attached to the eight observed mean differences. This yields a one-tailed p-value of $9/256 = .035$, which in turn leads to the conclusion that there is a statistically significant effect favoring Intervention A over Intervention B. The corresponding p-value associated with a Wilcoxon signed-rank test conducted on the rank-ordered data is .023, which supports this conclusion.

---

[3]From an internal-validity standpoint, a better-controlled variation of this single-case AB intervention comparison is a to-be-discussed crossover design, wherein cases receive both interventions in counterbalanced orders (i.e., exactly half are randomly assigned the two interventions in an AB order and half in a BA order)—see Levin et al. (1990, Experiment 1).

[4]Recall from three paragraphs ago that for the binomial test to detect a statistically significant result with eight participants, in this hypothetical study at least seven of the participants would be required to have rated the B intervention higher than the A intervention.

The preceding randomization-test arguments and procedures extend directly to AB . . . AB and alternating-treatment designs for which the B-A mean differences are based on the combined same-phase means (i.e., the combined B phase means minus the combined A phase means). Thus, in the commonly implemented single-case ABAB reversal design, the test statistic would consist of each case's averaged two B phase means minus the averaged two A phase means.[5] In the replicated single-case AB, ABAB, and alternating-treatments design intervention literature that the present authors have examined, we have not encountered application of either a one-sample randomization test or a Wilcoxon signed-rank test to phase-level data as described here. We therefore recommend its consideration as a useful statistical tool in such contexts.

AB Designs With Intervention Start-Point Randomization[6]

Arguably the most ingenious randomization contribution to the single-case design-and-analysis literature was Eugene Edgington's (1975) suggested random intervention start-point methodology and associated randomization test for the AB design, which was described earlier in this chapter. In contrast to the traditional single-case intervention research procedure of either predetermining the intervention start point in advance of data collection (a fixed intervention start point) or adopting a response-guided intervention start-point approach (as discussed in an earlier section), Edgington proposed that if the intervention start point were randomly selected from within a pre-designated range of potential (or "acceptable") start points, then a distributionally sound randomization test could be applied to the resulting set of time-series outcomes.[7] Edgington's original procedure for a one-case AB design has since been extended to replicated AB designs (Marascuilo & Busk, 1988), ABAB designs (Onghena, 1992), and multiple-baseline designs (Koehler & Levin, 1998), among others. Edgington's randomized intervention start-point approach is illustrated in the newly proposed procedures that follow.

AB DESIGN REPRESENTING TWO INTERVENTIONS, WITH RANDOM DETERMINATION OF INTERVENTION-ADMINISTRATION ORDER. In Edgington's (1975) random intervention start-point model for a one-case AB design it is assumed that the A phase consists of a baseline series and the B phase consists of an intervention series and that the former always precedes the latter. With those assumptions, the number of possible outcomes (B-A mean differences) in the randomization

---

[5]Levin et al. (2012) and Levin et al. (1978) provide discussion and examples of within-case phase aggregations.

[6]The material presented in this section is derived from a series of research investigations that are now in progress (Levin et al., 2014).

[7]An additional, yet often overlooked, advantage of this procedure is that the study's internal validity is enhanced in that a random determination of the intervention-start point lessens the potential effects of researcher bias, regression toward the mean, and specific time-related factors on the outcomes. At the same time, and as we discussed in the section on response-guided interventions, offsetting the methodological strengths of incorporating a randomly selected intervention start point are substantive concerns and practical disadvantages that single-case researchers have expressed in relation to adopting such an approach.

distribution is k, the number of potential intervention start points. Accordingly, with one case, 20 total observations, and $k = 10$ potential intervention start points, if the actual B-A mean difference produced were the largest of the 10 and in the predicted direction, then the one-tailed significance probability of that outcome would be $p = 1/10 = .10$. To achieve statistical significance at a conventional $\alpha = .05$ level (one-tailed), one would need to include $k = 20$ potential intervention start points in the randomization distribution (i.e., so that if the most extreme mean difference in the predicted direction were obtained, then p would equal $1/20 = .05$).

An improved adaptation of Edgington's (1975) original AB-design model is possible, however, and one that is applicable in a number of single-case intervention investigations. To illustrate, suppose that instead of A representing a baseline or control phase, it represented one type of experimental intervention, such as our previously discussed behavioral intervention for combatting a phobia. In contrast, B might represent a cognitive intervention targeting the same phobia. In this context, each case will receive both interventions. However, to have a scientifically credible comparison of Intervention A and Intervention B, it is imperative that the order in which the two interventions are administered is randomly determined on a case-by-case basis (as in our previously discussed example in which a coin was flipped for each case). The preceding statement applies whether the investigation includes only one case or multiple cases.

With intervention-order randomization built into the just-discussed one-case example based on 20 total observations and 10 potential intervention start points, in addition to the start points associated with the conventional AB order of intervention administration, one would also need to consider the possibility that Intervention B had been randomly selected to be administered first. If that were the case, there would be a corresponding 10 potential intervention start points for the BA order of intervention administration, resulting in a total of $k = 20$ outcomes that would need to be included in the complete randomization distribution. These 20 possibilities can be depicted as follows for potential intervention points beginning with Observation 6 through Observation 15, where each A and each B refer to either a single observation or a block of observations associated with the designated phase (see Levin et al., 2012):

1. AAAAABBBBBBBBBBBBBBB
2. AAAAAABBBBBBBBBBBBBB
3. AAAAAAABBBBBBBBBBBBB
4. AAAAAAAABBBBBBBBBBBB
5. AAAAAAAAABBBBBBBBBBB
6. AAAAAAAAAABBBBBBBBBB
7. AAAAAAAAAAABBBBBBBBB
8. AAAAAAAAAAAABBBBBBBB
9. AAAAAAAAAAAAABBBBBBB
10. AAAAAAAAAAAAAABBBBBB
11. BBBBBAAAAAAAAAAAAAAA
12. BBBBBBAAAAAAAAAAAAAA
13. BBBBBBBAAAAAAAAAAAAA
14. BBBBBBBBAAAAAAAAAAAA

15. BBBBBBBBBBAAAAAAAAAAA
16. BBBBBBBBBBBAAAAAAAAAA
17. BBBBBBBBBBBBAAAAAAAAA
18. BBBBBBBBBBBBBAAAAAAAA
19. BBBBBBBBBBBBBBAAAAAAA
20. BBBBBBBBBBBBBBBAAAAAA

As noted previously (see footnote 7), the present approach enhances the internal validity of a single-case AB design by virtue of its removing bias stemming from intervention-order effects. But how does including in the randomization distribution outcomes from both intervention-administration orders result in a practical advantage for single-case intervention researchers?

First, with the original Edgington (1975) one-case AB model, a researcher would need to designate 20 potential intervention start points (based on at least 21 total observations) to produce a randomization test that is capable of detecting an intervention effect with a one-tailed Type I error probability less than or equal to .05. With the present procedure, a researcher would need to designate only half as many potential intervention start points (here, 10, based on a total of 11 total observations) to detect an intervention effect in the predicted direction. Moreover, with two independent case replicates, for Marascuilo and Busk's (1988) extension of the Edgington model, at least five potential intervention start points would need to be designated for each replicate to obtain a one-tailed p that is less than or equal to .05. In general, with N replicates, for any number of potential intervention start points the present approach produces 2^N more randomization-distribution outcomes than would the Marascuilo-Busk model (for further discussion, see Chapter 6, this volume). To illustrate, with five potential intervention start points a comparison of the total number of possible randomization-distribution outcomes for the Marascuilo-Busk and present models, respectively, are five versus 10 for $N = 1$, 25 versus 100 for $N = 2$, 125 versus 1,000 for $N = 3$, 625 versus 10,000 for $N = 4$, and 3,125 versus 100,000 for $N = 5$.[8]

A related reason why the present procedure has practical value for single-case intervention researchers is that, relative to the original Edgington (1975) model, the present application produces nontrivial statistical-power advantages for one-tailed tests. Here we provide a few illustrations based on some recent Monte Carlo simulation results by Levin et al. (2014). Consider a one-case 25-observation design comparing Interventions A and B, with an intervention-transition point randomly selected from 20 acceptable ones, beginning with Observation 4 and ending with Observation 23. When no intervention effect is present in the series, for all autocorrelation values ranging from −.30 to +.60 both procedures (Edgington's and the present one based on randomizing the order of

---

[8]Alternatively, with $N = 2$, if the researcher elected to designate a different number of potential intervention points for each replicate, any combination for which the product is at least 20 (e.g., 5 for one replicate and 4 for the other) would be required to obtain $p \leq .05$, one-tailed. In contrast, with the present randomized order procedure with its 2^N more randomization-distribution outcomes, any combination of the k_i for which the product is at least 5 would suffice (e.g., 3 for one replicate and 2 for the other).

A and B intervention administration) demonstrate empirical Type I error probabilities that are in accord with the nominal .05 level. However, when intervention effects are built into the series, the present procedure exhibits one-tailed test powers that are generally anywhere from .10 to .20 higher than those for the original procedure. For example, the following comparative powers were obtained with an autocorrelation of .30 and intervention effects given by Cohen's ds greater than 1.0, which, judging from the single-case intervention literature, are not uncommon parameter values (Levin et al., 2012). With $d = 1.5$, powers for the Edgington model and the present modification are .32 and .48, respectively; with $d = 2.0$, the respective powers are .44 and .63; and with $d = 2.5$, they are .55 and .74.

Of course, and as the Levin et al. (2014) investigation is documenting, these powers and relative power differences steadily increase as more cases are included in the study. Specifically, one of the more interesting findings of our simulation work is that a randomized-order AB design based on three cases is uniformly more powerful than a fixed-order AB design based on six cases. Thus, for no more expense than a coin to flip, a single-case researcher will invariably reap methodological, statistical, and pragmatic benefits by adopting the present procedure rather than either the original Edgington (1975) model or the Marascuilo and Busk (1988) replication extension of it.

With A and B representing two alternative intervention conditions, the present randomized intervention-order procedure can also be adapted to a multiple-case staggered AB (or multiple-baseline) design with either fixed or random intervention start points (as a close cousin to a traditional staggered multiple-baseline design for which A = baseline and B = intervention). By including the two randomized orders and fixed intervention staggers, one can increase the number of Wampold and Worsham (1986) permutations by a factor of 2^N in exactly the same way that they can be increased with the Koehler and Levin (1998) procedure based on two potential intervention start points for each case. This additional application (a) should be of use to researchers who might object to randomly selecting an intervention start point but who would have no objection to a random determination of the intervention-administration order; and (b) attends to Intervention × Maturation and Intervention × History effects by providing opportunities for intervention-effect replications at different points in time.

TRADITIONAL AB DESIGN REPRESENTING BASELINE AND INTERVENTION CONDITIONS, WITH RANDOM DETERMINATION OF THE TWO CONDITIONS' ORDER. It is worth noting that A and B need not refer only to two competing interventions. Rather, suppose that A represents a baseline, standard, or control condition and B an intervention condition. As has been suggested previously (e.g., Chapter 2, this volume; Kratochwill & Levin, 2010), further suppose that prior to the experiment proper one or more mandatory baseline (or adaptation/warm-up) observations (A') are collected for all cases. With A' included, it would then be possible—and of practical importance, presumably acceptable to single-case researchers—to begin the experiment proper by randomizing each case's subsequent A and B phase (i.e., an A first means that the case remains in the baseline condition, followed by the B intervention condition; and a B first means that the case begins with the intervention condition, followed by a return to the A baseline condition). Accordingly, the proposed randomization-order procedure is applicable in either one- or two-intervention AB designs to improve both the design (internal validity) and analysis (statistical-conclusion validity) of single-case intervention studies. Extensions of the present approach to ABAB designs with acceptable start points designated for each of the three phase transitions, A_1B_1, B_1A_2, and A_2B_2 (Chapter 6, this volume; Onghena, 1992) are straightforward as are other single-case design applications of the approach, which are currently being explored.

AB Two-Intervention Crossover Design With Random Assignment of Intervention-Administration Order to Paired Case Members. The crossover design is a fundamental investigative strategy in conventional group educational intervention research (see Jones & Hall, 1982; and Levin et al., 1990, Experiment 1). In addition to within-case comparisons, with a crossover design it is possible to compare two intervention conditions (or an intervention and a nonintervention control condition) in two independent groups that also receive both intervention conditions in counterbalanced orders. Although various single-case designs allow for a single case to receive two or more treatments, the within-case structuring and/or rapid alternation of treatments does not provide an adequate parallel to capture the essence of the crossover design. With a little conceptual tweaking, however, the Levin and Wampold (1999) simultaneous start-point model's design and comparative intervention test can be adapted to capture that essence.

In particular, the same more powerful modification of the Edgington model and Marascuilo-Busk extension is possible when a "case" consists of a pair of participants, classrooms, schools, etc., as in Levin and Wampold's (1999) simultaneous intervention start-point model. With that model applied to an A (baseline phase)–B (intervention phase) design, pairs consisting of individuals, small groups, classrooms, etc. are created, with one member of the pair randomly assigned to Intervention X and the other to Intervention Y. Applying Levin and Wampold's "comparative intervention-effectiveness" randomization test, a researcher can test the hypothesis that the amount of change from the baseline phase to the intervention phase is the same in the two intervention conditions, versus the alternative that the amount of change is greater in one intervention condition than in the other.

In the present context, suppose that X and Y represent two competing interventions that are administered to both pair members and Order 1 and Order 2 represent the two possible orders of intervention administration (Order 1 = Intervention X in the A phase followed by Intervention Y in the B phase and Order 2 = Intervention Y followed by Intervention X). Within the pair, it is randomly determined which pair member is assigned Order 1 and which Order 2. The design then becomes the single-case equivalent of a conventional group crossover design, for which as was mentioned earlier, each case receives two different interventions in a counterbalanced order across cases (Chapter 6, this volume; Levin et al., 2014). The focal statistical hypothesis of interest is that the two interventions are equally effective while controlling for possible order effects. Augmenting the Levin-Wampold model with the two different possible orders of treatment included in the randomization distribution, the present approach can be readily applied to produce a more powerful test of the same hypothesis. In addition, (a) order effects and the Intervention × Order interaction can be similarly assessed with the present procedure; and (b) as with the Marascuilo-Busk model, the present procedure generalizes directly to incorporate two or more paired cases (Levin et al., 2013).

MULTIPLE-BASELINE COMPARATIVE-INTERVENTION DESIGN BASED ON CASE PAIRS, WITH PAIR MEMBERS RANDOMLY ASSIGNED TO INTERVENTIONS, AND PAIRS RANDOMLY ASSIGNED TO BOTH MULTIPLE-BASELINE STAGGERS AND INTERVENTION START POINTS. As an alternative to the just-discussed crossover design, we conclude with a newly proposed comparative-intervention multiple-baseline design that effectively incorporates three of the four randomization variations discussed in this chapter (Levin et al., 2014). Consistent with Levin and Wampold's (1999) simultaneous intervention start-point model, this one is applicable for comparing two different interventions, X and Y, within the context of a baseline-phase (A) versus intervention-phase (B) design. In the present multiple-baseline application, from a total of N available individual cases, $N/2$ case pairs are created, with one member of the pair randomly assigned to Intervention X and the other to Intervention Y (intervention randomization). As in the Koehler and Levin (1998) model, each pair is then randomly assigned to both the $N/2$ different stagger positions within the multiple-baseline design (case randomization) and the potential intervention start points associated with that stagger position (start-point randomization). A unique internal-validity characteristic of this single-case model is that it allows for an unconfounded between-pair-member comparison of intervention effectiveness across multiple pairs at systematically staggered different points in time. The high scientific credibility of both this design and the crossover design should make them attractive to single-case researchers.

Summary and Final Thoughts

In this chapter we have provided a description of permutation and randomization statistical tests, and their application in single-case intervention research. We considered concerns that have been voiced and previous methodological work that has aimed to address those concerns. We also provided several new approaches for incorporating randomization into single-case designs and illustrated the associated randomization and permutation tests. Our motivation for proposing these alternatives stems from the recognition that the methodological benefits of randomization can be realized only if researchers are amenable to incorporating various forms of randomization in their designs. By increasing the range of alternative randomization options, we hope to increase the likelihood that single-case researchers will be able to find a randomization method that is compatible with both the specific goals and practical constraints of their studies.

References

Barlow, D. H., Nock, M. K., & Hersen, M. (2009). *Single case experimental design: Strategies for studying behavior change* (3rd ed.). Boston, MA: Pearson.

Bradley, J. V. (1968). *Distribution-free statistical tests.* Englewood Cliffs, NJ: Prentice-Hall.

Bulté, I., & Onghena, P. (2008). An R package for single-case randomization tests. *Behavior Research Methods, 40,* 46–478. doi:10.3758/BRM.40.2.467

Bulté, I., & Onghena, P. (2009). Randomization tests for multiple-baseline designs: An extension of the SCRT-R package. *Behavior Research Methods, 41,* 477–485. doi:10.3758/BRM.41.2.477

Campbell, D. T., & Stanley, J. C. (1966). *Experimental and quasi-experimental designs for research.* Chicago, IL: Rand McNally.

Cook, T. D., & Campbell, D. T. (1979). *Quasi-experimentation: Design and analysis issues for field settings.* Chicago, IL: Rand McNally.

Dugard, P., File, P., & Todman, J. (2012). *Single-case and small-n experimental designs: A practical guide to randomization tests* (2nd ed.). New York, NY: Routledge.

Edgington, E. S. (1967). Statistical inference from N = 1 experiments. *The Journal of Psychology, 65,* 195–199. doi:10.1080/00223980.1967.10544864

Edgington, E. S. (1975). Randomization tests for one-subject operant experiments. *Journal of Psychology: Interdisciplinary and Applied, 90,* 57–68. doi:10.1080/00223980.1975.9923926

Edgington, E. S. (1980a). Random assignment and statistical tests for one-subject experiments. *Behavioral Assessment, 2,* 19–28.

Edgington, E. S. (1980b). Validity of randomization tests for one-subject experiments. *Journal of Educational Statistics, 5,* 235–251. doi:10.2307/1164966

Edgington, E. S. (1992). Nonparametric tests for single-case experiments. In T. R. Kratochwill & J. R. Levin (Eds.), *Single-case research design and analysis: New directions for psychology and education* (pp. 133–157). Hillsdale, NJ: Erlbaum.

Edgington, E. S. (1996). Randomized single-subject experimental designs. *Behaviour Research and Therapy, 34,* 567–574. doi:10.1016/0005-7967(96)00012-5

Edgington, E. S., & Onghena, P. (2007). *Randomization tests* (4th ed.). Boca Raton, FL: Chapman & Hall.

Ferron, J., & Foster-Johnson, L. (1998). Analyzing single-case data with visually guided randomization tests. *Behavior Research Methods, Instruments, & Computers, 30,* 698–706. doi:10.3758/BF03209489

Ferron, J., Foster-Johnson, L., & Kromrey, J. D. (2003). The functioning of single-case randomization tests with and without random assignment. *Journal of Experimental Education, 71,* 267–288. doi:10.1080/00220970309602066

Ferron, J., & Jones, P. K. (2006). Tests for the visual analysis of response-guided multiple-baseline data. *Journal of Experimental Education, 75,* 66–81. doi:10.3200/JEXE.75.1.66-81

Ferron, J., & Onghena, P. (1996). The power of randomization tests for single-case phase designs. *Journal of Experimental Education, 64,* 231–239. doi:10.1080/00220973.1996.9943805

Ferron, J., & Sentovich, C. (2002). Statistical power of randomization tests used with multiple-baseline designs. *Journal of Experimental Education, 70,* 165–178. doi:10.1080/00220970209599504

Ferron, J., & Ware, W. (1994). Using randomization tests with responsive single-case designs. *Behaviour Research and Therapy, 32,* 787–791. doi:10.1016/0005-7967(94)90037-X

Ferron, J., & Ware, W. (1995). Analyzing single-case data: The power of randomization tests. *Journal of Experimental Education, 63,* 167–178. doi:10.1080/00220973.1995.9943820

Greenland, S., & Draper, D. (1998). Exchangeability. In P. Armitage & T. Colton (Eds.), *Encyclopedia of biostatistics.* London, England: Wiley.

Jones, B. F., & Hall, J. W. (1982). School applications of the mnemonic keyword method as a study strategy by eighth graders. *Journal of Educational Psychology, 74,* 230–237. doi:10.1037/0022-0663.74.2.230

Kazdin, A. E. (1980). Obstacles in using randomization tests in single-case experimentation. *Journal of Educational Statistics, 5,* 253–260. doi:10.2307/1164967

Koehler, M. J., & Levin, J. R. (1998). Regulated randomization: A potentially sharper analytical tool for the multiple-baseline design. *Psychological Methods, 3,* 206–217. doi:10.1037/1082-989X.3.2.206

Kratochwill, T., Alden, K., Demuth, D., Dawson, D., Panicucci, C., Arntson, P., . . . Levin, J. (1974). A further consideration in the application of an analysis-of-variance model for the intrasubject replication design. *Journal of Applied Behavior Analysis, 7,* 629–633. doi:10.1901/jaba.1974.7-629

Kratochwill, T. R. (Ed.). (1978). *Single subject research: Strategies for evaluating change.* New York, NY: Academic Press.

Kratochwill, T. R., Hitchcock, J. H., Horner, R. H., Levin, J. R., Odom, S. L., Rindskopf, D. M., & Shadish, W. R. (2013). Single-case intervention research design standards. *Remedial and Special Education, 34,* 26–38. doi:10.1177/0741932512452794

Kratochwill, T. R., & Levin, J. R. (1980). On the applicability of various data analysis procedures to the simultaneous and alternating treatment designs in behavior therapy research. *Behavioral Assessment, 2,* 353–360.

Kratochwill, T. R., & Levin, J. R. (Eds.). (1992). *Single-case research design and analysis: New directions for psychology and education.* Hillsdale, NJ: Erlbaum.

Kratochwill, T. R., & Levin, J. R. (2010). Enhancing the scientific credibility of single-case intervention research: Randomization to the rescue. *Psychological Methods, 15,* 124–144. doi:10.1037/a0017736

Lall, V. F., & Levin, J. R. (2004). An empirical investigation of the statistical properties of generalized single-case randomization tests. *Journal of School Psychology, 42,* 61–86. doi:10.1016/j.jsp.2003.11.002

Lehmann, E. L. (1975). *Nonparametrics: Statistical methods based on ranks.* San Francisco, CA: Holden-Day.

Levin, J. R. (1994). Crafting educational intervention research that's both credible and creditable. *Educational Psychology Review, 6,* 231–243. doi:10.1007/BF02213185

Levin, J. R., & Ferron, J. M. (in press). Review of Dugard, File, and Todman's *Single-case and small-n designs: A practical guide to randomization tests* (2nd ed.). *American Statistician.*

Levin, J. R., Ferron, J. M., & Gafurov, B. S. (2014). *Improved randomization tests for a class of single-case intervention designs.* Manuscript in preparation.

Levin, J. R., Ferron, J. M., & Kratochwill, T. R. (2012). Nonparametric statistical tests for single-case systematic and randomized ABAB . . . AB and alternating treatment intervention designs: New developments, new directions. *Journal of School Psychology, 50,* 599–624. doi:10.1016/j.jsp.2012.05.001

Levin, J. R., Lall, V. F., & Kratochwill, T. R. (2011). Extensions of a versatile randomization test for assessing single-case intervention effects. *Journal of School Psychology, 49,* 55–79. doi:10.1016/j.jsp.2010.09.002

Levin, J. R., Levin, M. E., Cotton, J. W., Bartholomew, S., Hasty, K., Hughes, C., & Townsend, E. A. (1990). What do college students learn from and about an innovative vocabulary-learning strategy? In S. A. Biggs (Ed.), *Innovative learning strategies, 1989–1990* (pp. 186–206). Pittsburgh, PA: College Reading Improvement Special Interest Group of the International Reading Association.

Levin, J. R., Marascuilo, L. A., & Hubert, L. J. (1978). *N* = nonparametric randomization tests. In T. R. Kratochwill (Ed.), *Single subject research: Strategies for evaluating change* (pp. 167–196). New York, NY: Academic Press. doi:10.1016/B978-0-12-425850-1.50010-7

Levin, J. R., & Wampold, B. E. (1999). Generalized single-case randomization tests: Flexible analyses for a variety of situations. *School Psychology Quarterly, 14,* 59–93. doi:10.1037/h0088998

Manolov, R., & Solanas, A. (2009). Problems of the randomization test for AB designs. *Psicológica, 30,* 137–154.

Manolov, R., Solanas, A., Bulté, I., & Onghena, P. (2009). Data-division–specific robustness and power of randomization tests for ABAB designs. *Journal of Experimental Education, 78,* 191–214. doi:10.1080/00220970903292827

Marascuilo, L. A., & Busk, P. L. (1988). Combining statistics for multiple-baseline AB and replicated ABAB designs across subjects. *Behavioral Assessment, 10,* 1–28.

Marascuilo, L. A., & McSweeney, M. (1977). *Nonparametric and distribution-free methods for the social sciences.* Monterey, CA: Brooks/Cole.

Matyas, T. A., & Greenwood, K. M. (1997). Serial dependency in single-case time series. In R. D. Franklin, D. B. Allison, & B. S. Gorman (Eds.), *Design and analysis of single-case research* (pp. 215–243). Mahwah, NJ: Erlbaum.

Mawhinney, T. C., & Austin, J. (1999). Speed and accuracy of data analysts' behavior using methods of equal interval graphic data charts, standard celeration charts, and statistical control charts. *Journal of Organizational Behavior Management, 18,* 5–45. doi:10.1300/J075v18n04_02

Onghena, P. (1992). Randomization tests for extensions and variations of ABAB single-case experimental designs: A rejoinder. *Behavioral Assessment, 14*, 153–171.

Onghena, P. (1994). *The power of randomization tests for single-case designs*. Unpublished doctoral dissertation, Katholieke Universiteit Leuven, Belgium.

Onghena, P., & Edgington, E. S. (1994). Randomization tests for restricted alternating treatments designs. *Behaviour Research and Therapy, 32*, 783–786. doi:10.1016/0005-7967(94)90036-1

Panter, A. T., & Sterba, S. (Eds.). (2011). *Handbook of ethics in quantitative methodology*. New York, NY: Taylor & Francis.

Robinson, D. H., & Levin, J. R. (1997). Reflections on statistical and substantive significance, with a slice of replication. *Educational Researcher, 26*, 21–26.

Shadish, W. R., Cook, T. D., & Campbell, D. T. (2002). *Experimental and quasi-experimental designs for generalized causal inference*. Boston, MA: Houghton Mifflin.

Sierra, V., Solanas, A., & Quera, V. (2005). Randomization tests for systematic single-case designs are not always appropriate. *Journal of Experimental Education, 73*, 140–160. doi:10.3200/JEXE.73.2.140-160

Toothaker, L. E., Banz, M., Noble, C., Camp, J., & Davis, D. (1983). N = 1 designs: The failure of ANOVA-based tests. *Journal of Educational Statistics, 8*, 289–309. doi:10.2307/1164914

Wampold, B., & Worsham, N. (1986). Randomization tests for multiple-baseline designs. *Behavioral Assessment, 8*, 135–143.

Wampold, B. E., & Furlong, M. J. (1981). Randomization tests in single-subject designs: Illustrative examples. *Journal of Behavioral Assessment, 3*, 329–342.

6

The Single-Case Data-Analysis *ExPRT* (*Excel Package of Randomization Tests*)

Joel R. Levin, Anya S. Evmenova, and Boris S. Gafurov

In Chapter 5 of this volume, Ferron and Levin describe the logic and procedural aspects of single-case randomization and permutation tests while providing illustrative examples of different test variations. In this chapter we introduce a statistical software package that is capable of conducting a vast array of randomization tests (including some older ones and others newly developed) within a user-friendly Microsoft Excel environment. As was mentioned in Chapter 5 (this volume), other single-case randomization-test software has been produced over the years (e.g., Bulté & Onghena, 2008, 2009; Dugard, File, & Todman, 2012; Edgington & Onghena, 2007; Koehler & Levin, 2000). We certainly do not claim that the to-be-described software package is the "best," but as will be seen, it is able to conduct randomization tests for a vast assortment of single-case intervention designs and possesses several novel features and output options.

The Single-Case Data-Analysis *ExPRT* (*Excel Package of Randomization Tests*)

Gafurov and Levin (2013) have developed a set of Microsoft Office 2010 Excel-based programs, namely, the single-case data-analysis *ExPRT* (*Excel Package of Randomization Tests*), for a wide variety of single-case intervention designs that incorporate one or more randomization variations. *ExPRT* (Version 1.1, October 2013), which benefitted from suggestions by colleagues Thomas Kratochwill and Robert Horner as well as by Kent McIntosh and students in a single-case design-and-analysis course at the University of Oregon, is freely available to single-case researchers for downloading (at http://code.google.com/p/exprt). This versatile package consists of an extensive set of macros for (a) generating and displaying complete randomization distributions, (b) conducting randomization statistical

http://dx.doi.org/10.1037/14376-007
Single-Case Intervention Research: Methodological and Statistical Advances, by T. R. Kratochwill and J. R. Levin

tests on single-case intervention data, and (c) providing outcome summaries in both graphical and numerical formats.

Specifically, features of the programs include (a) designs based on either one or multiple cases (replications), with "cases" consisting of either individuals/groups or paired individuals/groups; (b) capability of handling several hundred total outcome observations for up to 15 cases; (c) exact nonparametric statistical analyses based on some type of randomization; (d) either random or fixed intervention start-point options; (e) analyses conducted with either raw or standardized data; (f) allowance for cases' differing series lengths and missing data; (g) user-defined α level for either one- or two-tailed tests; (h) statistical decision (reject, do not reject) and significance probability (p value); (i) summary distribution of all possible outcomes; (j) calculation of either mean (level) or slope (trend) summary measures; (k) editable graph of the outcomes for each case, which includes the mean and slope lines for each phase; (l) effect-size estimate(s) for each case; and (m) an intervention start-point randomization routine for planned studies.

We now describe and provide illustrations of *ExPRT*'s procedures, as applied to the four single-case intervention design frameworks (AB, ABA, ABAB, and multiple baseline) that are currently incorporated into Gafurov and Levin's randomization-test package. Each design, along with its variations and extensions, will be discussed in turn. At this writing, randomization-test procedures for additional single-case designs (e.g., multiple-phase ABAB . . . AB, alternating treatment, multiple probe) are under development. Moreover, we remind the reader that the current version of the *ExPRT* program is in a fluid state and so the specific labels and procedures referred to here may well have changed between this writing and the date at which the chapter appears in print.

For *ExPRT's* programs/macros to run as intended, the user must go into "Trusted Locations" in Microsoft Office 2010 Excel's Trust Center (File/Options/Trust Center/Trust Center Settings . . . /Trusted Locations) and add the microcomputer path location that contains the *ExPRT* programs. On the first run of each Excel file, the user must allow macros to be executed when a warning appears. On subsequent runs the Excel file should proceed without such a warning.

AB Designs

As has been noted in previous chapters, the two-phase AB design is the simplest single-case intervention design. It involves the repeated outcome-measure assessment of one or more cases during two adjacent phase conditions—typically baseline (A) and intervention (B), but also Intervention A and Intervention B (Chapter 2, this volume; Sidman, 1960). With the former variation, Phase A is often characterized as the baseline or control phase, while the outcome of interest continues to be measured after the intervention is introduced during the B phase. If the outcome patterns (levels, trends, and/or variability) in the two phases differ, the researcher seeks to attribute the difference/change to the intervention. As the current *What Works Clearinghouse* (WWC) *Standards* indicate, however, because the basic AB design is associated with too many potential extraneous variables (i.e., threats to internal validity), it cannot be considered a scientifically "credible" (Levin, 1992, 1994) single-case intervention design with respect to its documenting a functional relation between the intervention and the targeted outcome measures (see also Chapters 1 and 2, this volume; Gast, 2010; Kratochwill et al., 2013).

At the same time, it is possible to enhance the scientific credibility of the basic AB design (a) through the inclusion of multiple cases (i.e., independent replications) and (b) when the A and B phases consist of different interventions administered to the cases in different random orders—as, for example, in a conventional group crossover design (see also Chapter 5, this volume). Both of these enhanced credibility features are incorporated into the *ExPRT* package, the specific AB-design components of which include the following:

- Basic time-series design
- Baseline/Control (A) versus Intervention (B)
- Intervention start-point randomization procedure: Edgington (1975) model; Marascuilo–Busk (1988) model; Levin–Wampold (1999) simultaneous start-point model for case pairs—comparative-effectiveness and general-effectiveness tests; Levin, Ferron, and Gafurov's (2014a) intervention-order randomization and pair-member randomization additions to these models
- Levin et al.'s (2014a) single-case crossover design model: intervention-effect and time-effect tests
- Correlated-sample permutation test for designs with no random intervention start points

Marascuilo–Busk (1988) Model and Levin et al.'s (2014a) Additions

Referring to Figures 6.1 to 6.3, we now illustrate the *ExPRT* program's handling of a replicated AB design with a random intervention start for each case (replicate), according to Marascuilo and Busk's (1988) extension of Edgington's (1975) model.[1] The data contained therein are Marascuilo and Busk's adaptation of Wampold and Worsham's (1986) hypothetical example based on four cases providing 20 outcome observations apiece, where a decrease in the outcome measure was predicted between Phase A and Phase B. In Figure 6.1 (*ExPRT*'s Data sheet), the observation numbers 1–20 are entered by the program user in Row 1 and the four cases' outcomes are entered in Rows 2 through 5. In designs where the "cases" are pairs—as in Levin and Wampold's (1999) simultaneous intervention start-point model—each pair of row data is separated by a single empty row and the use of that model would be designated in Column O of

---

[1]Even though Marascuilo and Busk (1988) and Bulté and Onghena (2008) referred to their procedures and examples as "multiple-baseline," in both instances that is actually a misnomer. In the former's procedure, the repeated application of Edgington's (1975) model with the same potential intervention start points for each case does not guarantee the systematic stagger of a multiple-baseline design; and, similarly in the latter's example, the potential intervention start points for each case are allowed to be partially overlapping. Furthermore, the Marascuilo-Busk procedure is more properly regarded as a "replicated AB" design with independently randomized intervention start points for each case that does not include the case-randomization component of either Wampold and Worsham's (1986) or Koehler and Levin's (1998) multiple-baseline procedures.

1	2	3	4	5	6	7	8	9	10	11	12	13	14	15	16	17	18	19	20
8	7	6	7	4	5	6	6	8	4	5	4	4	3	4	5	4	3	2	2
6	7	8	7	5	7	6	8	6	5	4	4	4	3	5	5	3	4	3	2
5	5	4	6	5	5	6	7	4	5	6	5	2	3	2	4	1	0	2	6
8	6	7	7	8	5	7	7	7	6	7	8	5	6	8	8	6	4	4	5

Figure 6.1.   The *ExPRT* data sheet for Marascuilo and Busk's replicated AB design example. Data from Marascuilo and Busk (1988).

A	B	C	D	E	F	G	H	I	J	K	L	M	N	O	P	Q	R	S	T	U
1st pot interv stpnt	# pot stpnts	# units	max # pnts	act interv stpnt	Data: 1:Original, 2:Standardized	alpha	Tails (1,2)	1:A>B or T1>T2, 2:B>A or T2>T1	Sig.	∏pnts, ordr perms, tot	output (yes/no)	1:Mean, 2:Slope	Missing Code	If Pairs Test: 1.Gen, 2.Comp, 3.Comp(Rnd XY)	Design: 1.Std, 2.Cross	If Cross: 1.Cond 2.Time	Order: 1.Fixed 2.Rand	Actual Order	Run 1st	Then Plot
5	13	4	20	5	1	0.05	1	1	1 Sig. p<0.001	28561 no		1	1		N/A, Ind Mode	1	1 N/A in AB d	1 AB		
5	13			9					Rank = 6 of 28561	1								AB	Run	Plot
5	13			13						28561								AB		
5	13			17														AB		

time elapsed - 4.5 sec

Figure 6.2.   The *ExPRT* interventions sheet for Marascuilo and Busk's replicated AB design example. Data from Marascuilo and Busk (1988).

A	B	C	D	E
1st pot intv stpnt	# pot stpnts	# units	max # pnts	act interv stpnt
4	13	4		11
4	13			8
4	13			5
4	13			11

Figure 6.3. The *ExPRT* randomizer sheet.

the Interventions sheet in Figure 6.2, as is illustrated in a later example. For the present example, the same 13 potential intervention start points (Observations 5 through 17 inclusive) were designated for all four cases, but in general both the number of potential intervention start points designated and the actual start points selected can vary from case to case. After the analysis has been conducted (on the Interventions sheet), the program highlights in yellow on the Data sheet the potential intervention start points that were designated for each case.

Figure 6.2 (the Interventions sheet) shows the "design and analysis" portion of the *ExPRT* package. Each of the required and provided operations will now be described, column by column. At the outset, however, we note that the various Interventions sheet options available to *ExPRT* users, as well as the specific columns in which those options appear, vary from one single-case design to the next—namely, AB, ABA, ABAB, and multiple baseline.

In Column A, *1st pot interv stpnt* (first potential intervention start point), the user enters the first designated potential ("acceptable") observation for which the intervention could be in effect (here, the fifth observation for each case).

In Column B, *# pot stpnts* (number of potential start points), the total number of designated potential intervention start points is entered (here, 13 for each case).

Columns C and D are left blank and are provided by the program during the analysis. Column C, *# units*, indicates the number of cases (here, 4) and Column D, *max # pts* (maximum number of points) indicates the maximum number of outcome observations possible (here, 20).

In Column E, *act interv stpnt* (actual intervention start point), the user inputs the actual intervention start point that was randomly selected for each case. In the hypothetical Marascuilo-Busk (1988) example, these turned out to be Observations 5, 9, 13, and 17 for Cases 1 through 4, respectively.

AB Designs With a Single Predetermined Intervention Start Point. For AB designs in which there is no intervention start-point randomization, the potential and actual initial intervention start points for each case (Columns A and E, respectively) would be the same; and the total number of designated potential intervention start points (Column B) would be 1 for each case. In such situations, *ExPRT* conducts (a) a one-sample permutation test on the N phase-mean (or slope) differences when cases have been assigned to a single fixed AB order of intervention administration or (b) a one-sample randomization test on the N phase-mean (or slope) differences when the cases have been randomly assigned to either an AB or BA intervention-administration order (see Chapter 5, this volume; and our description of Column R later in this chapter).

INTERVENTION START-POINT RANDOMIZER. An additional feature of *ExPRT*, an intervention start-point randomizer routine for planned studies, may be seen on the Randomizer sheet in Figure 6.3. To apply the routine, the researcher specifies the design characteristics, including the earliest potential intervention start point for each case (here, Observation 5 in Column A) and the number of potential intervention start points for each case (13 here, from Observation 5 through Observation 17). The researcher then clicks on the Randomize button and is provided a randomly selected intervention start point for each case in Column E. From Figure 6.3's Column E it may be seen that, were the same study being planned for a new set of 4 cases, the intervention would commence immediately before Observations 11, 8, 5, and 11, for Cases 1–4 respectively. Note that with a replicated AB design, it is possible for the same intervention start point to be selected for two or more cases—something that is not permissible in *ExPRT*'s systematically staggered multiple-baseline design that is discussed later. A click on the "Copy to Interven" button in Figure 6.3 copies these randomly selected intervention start points to Column E of the Interventions sheet.

In Column F of Figure 6.2's Interventions sheet (*Data: 1. Original, 2. Standardized*), the user indicates whether the "original" (typically unstandardized) data are to be analyzed or whether they should first be standardized on a case-by-case basis (with an across-observations mean of 50 and standard deviation of 10 for each case). The latter procedure might be considered in situations where a researcher anticipates either differing between-case outcome variability or outlying observations and therefore hopes to counteract the effect of such occurrences by placing each case's set of observations on the same T-score scale ($M = 50$, $SD = 10$). For the present example, the analysis will be conducted on the original unstandardized observations and so a 1 is entered in Column F. We later provide an example with both unstandardized and standardized outcomes to illustrate situations in which the user's basing the randomization test on the latter might be both desired and, presumably, advantageous.

In Column M, the researcher specifies whether the randomization test is to be performed on the means (1) or the slopes (2) of the A and B phases. The former would be selected when a change/difference in the phases' average levels is of interest to the researcher and the latter when a change/difference in the phases' linear trends is the focus (see Chapter 3, this volume). The latter (slopes) test is sensitive to a change in slopes only when such a change is not accompanied by an abrupt A-to-B phase change in levels. (Note that in Version 1.2 of *ExPRT*, which will be available at the time this book has been published, a test of variability change/difference will also be incorporated.) In order to conduct a slopes/trend test, for every potential intervention-point designation in Column B (here, 13) there must be at least two observations associated with each A phase and each B phase. In the present example, a 1 is entered to request a test of phase-mean differences.

In Column G, the researcher specifies the desired Type I error probability (α) for the randomization test, which here is .05 for testing that the observed mean difference between the A and B phases is not greater than what would have been expected by chance (i.e., not among the five percent most extreme differences in the distribution of all possible differences associated with this randomization test). In Column H, 1 is entered for a one-tailed (directional) test of the hypothesis and 2 for a two-tailed (nondirectional) test of the hypothesis; for the present example, a one-tailed test was requested. If a one-tailed test is specified in Column H, then entering a 1 in Column I indicates that the observed A-phase mean/slope is predicted to be greater than the observed B-phase mean/slope whereas entering a 2 indicates the reverse. Here, it was predicted that the A-phase mean would exceed the B-phase mean and so a 1 appears in Column I.

The *T1/T2* in Column I represents "Time 1/Time 2" and is associated with a different AB-design variation, the crossover design (see Chapter 5, this volume), as would be indicated in Column P (*Design: 1. Std, 2. Cross*). For the present example, a 1 is entered in Column P, specifying that a "standard" replicated AB design is in effect, for which all four cases receive the A phase first and the B phase second. Had a crossover design been desired with two different interventions (A and B) and for which both AB and BA intervention orders are implemented, this would be indicated by entering a 2 in Column P. In the latter situation, a 1 in Column Q (*If Cross: 1. Cond, 2. Time*) requests a test of the difference between Intervention A's and Intervention B's outcomes whereas a 2 in Column Q requests a test of the time effect (i.e., the difference between the Time 1 and Time 2 phase outcomes, regardless of the particular intervention [A or B] received). These two tests are analogous to a 2 (conditions) $\times$ 2 (times: e.g., pretest–posttest) conventional "group" repeated measures design's test of the condition and time main effects, respectively. The "Pairs Test" specifications in Column O are also associated with a different AB-design variation: namely, the Levin-Wampold simultaneous intervention start-point model, which is illustrated in the next major section.

A 1 in Column R (*Order: 1. Fixed, 2. Rand*) indicates that it was predetermined by the researcher that the A phase would come first, followed by the B phase. Entering a 2 in Column R would indicate that for each case the researcher had randomly determined the order in which the A and B phases were administered, with each case's specific phase ordering indicated in Column S—see Chapter 5 (this volume) and our later examples. As was indicated in Chapter 5, with N representing the number of cases and k_i representing the number of potential intervention start points for Case i, with a fixed AB order of intervention administration for each case, there is a total of $\prod_{i=1}^{N} k_i$ outcomes in the randomization distribution (or k^N when the number of potential intervention points is the same for all cases). In contrast, with a random order of intervention administration for all cases, the total number of randomization-distribution outcomes increases to $2^N \times \prod_{i=1}^{N} k_i$ [or $2^N \times k^N = (2k)^N$ when k is the same for all cases].

When a crossover design has been specified in Column P, (a) the design must include at least two cases; (b) the Column R order is set either to 1 (Fixed) or 2 (Rand); and (c) for the actual orders indicated in Column S, one or more cases must be represented in each of the two possible orders, AB and BA. If a Random order of AB administration has been specified (a 2 in Column R): For an even number of cases (N), then exactly half of these (x) are assumed to be randomly assigned to each of the two orders (AB and BA) and the total number of possible outcomes in the randomization distribution is augmented by a factor of $\binom{N}{x} = N!/x!(N-x)!$, where N is the total number of cases and x is the number of cases that are to be randomly assigned to each of the two administration orders. For an odd number of cases, it is assumed that (a) the researcher has randomly assigned as close to half of these as possible to each order (i.e., resulting in $N/2+.5$ cases in one order and $N/2-.5$ cases in the other) and (b) the particular order (AB or BA) that received the one additional case was also randomly determined. Following this dual random-assignment process, the total number of possible outcomes in the randomization distribution is augmented by a factor of $2 \times \binom{N}{x} = 2 \times N!/x!(N-x)!$ For example, with 4 cases, N would be 4 and x would be 2, with the augmentation factor equal to 6; and with 5 cases, N would be 5 and x would be 3, with the augmentation factor equal to 2 x 10 = 20.

In Column L, the user specifies whether the output from all outcomes in the randomization distribution should be displayed on the Output sheet ("yes") or suppressed ("no"). The choice here will not affect the analysis per se, but for designs that produce larger numbers of randomization-distribution outcomes (such as for the present example) the difference in analysis time to completion will be noticeable—and even considerable. Here, with $k = 13$ potential start points for each of the $N = 4$ cases, there is a total of k^N, or $13^4 = 28,561$, possible randomization-distribution outcomes. With no output requested (see Column L), an analysis of phase-mean differences took about two seconds to complete on one of the present authors' PCs; whereas with output requested, it took about 10.5 seconds.

In Column N, the researcher has the option of indicating whether there are any missing data in the data file by specifying a code (consisting of any letters, numbers, or symbols, as well as blanks) to represent missing observations. In *ExPRT's* programs it is assumed that missing data are missing at random and not in accord with the researcher's planned observation-collection schedule (as with a multiple-probe design). Missing-data cells are omitted in the calculation of each phase mean or slope and no missing data are allowed within the designated intervention start-point interval.[2] The latter is required because with missing observations in that interval, the number of actual randomization-distribution outcomes will be less than those on which the planned randomization test was based and, therefore, the test itself could be rendered invalid. Even though missing observations are permitted in *ExPRT* analyses, it is important that the missing data are unsystematically interspersed throughout the entire baseline and intervention phases. Otherwise, interpretation of the randomization-test results is compromised because of a potential confounding of outcomes and time periods.

In *ExPRT*, "missing data" are distinguished from "cases' different series lengths," for which the cells associated with the unmeasured time periods are simply left blank. All end-of-series blank cells must be completely empty and cannot contain hidden spaces. For designs in which there are no missing data

---

[2]For recent efforts to improve the estimation of single-case intervention effects when there are missing data, see Smith, Borckardt, and Nash (2012).

but all cases do not have the same series lengths, it is not necessary to specify a missing-data code in Column N. In the present example, all cases have the same series lengths (20), and there are no missing data.

The analysis begins with the user clicking on the *Run* button in Column T, with output then appearing in several places. First, the number of cases/units is reported in Column C (# *units;* here, 4) and the series length in Column D (*max # pnts;* here, 20). In Column K is reported the total number of outcomes in the randomization distribution, which for this AB design variation is based on the number of cases and the number of potential intervention start points for each case (and specifically for the present example, as was noted above, is 28,561). In Column J appear the results of the randomization test, including both a statistical decision ("Sig" or "NS") and a significance probability (*p* value). For the present example, the test yielded a statistically significant result (Sig), in that the difference between the A- and B-phase means was in the predicted direction (A > B) and the difference was among the 5% most extreme in the complete randomization distribution. In fact, the actual difference turned out to be the sixth most extreme of all 28,561 possible differences, which yields a *p* value of 6/28,561 = .00021.[3]

When output is requested in Column L, the result (not included in a figure here) may also be seen by clicking on the Output tab, where the following randomization-distribution information associated with the actually obtained difference is highlighted: 6.463 (A-phase mean), 3.708 (B-phase mean), –2.755 (B-A mean difference, the difference direction consistently applied by *ExPRT*), and 6 (the rank of that difference among all 28,561 B-A mean differences). In situations where there are tied differences, the method of midranks (the average of the ranks in question) is applied. Had a two-tailed test been called for, all randomization-distribution outcomes would have been rank-ordered on the basis of their absolute (rather than their signed) values and the randomization test would have been based on those. Finally, if a one-tailed test had been requested here with the designation in Column I that B > A (i.e., in the opposite direction to what actually occurred), then the result in Column J that would appear is simply "NS, A > B", to dissuade users from even thinking about statistical significance or *p*-values in such wrong-sided prediction situations.

A click on the *Plot* button in Column U begins an Excel graphing routine for the case-by-case outcomes. The output that appears by clicking on the Graphs tab is presented in Figure 6.4, but because of present space limitations, without displaying here the complete numerical data series for each case (which is also provided by *ExPRT*). In addition to the graphical plots of each case's outcomes delineated by phases, for a test of phase-mean differences other standard *ExPRT* output may be seen in Figure 6.4 and includes for each case the A- and B-phase means (along with a dotted line to depict each); the A-phase estimated population standard deviation (i.e., based on $N - 1$ in the denominator); and Busk and Serlin's (1992) "no assumptions model" *d* effect-size measure, which is defined as

---

[3]In Marascuilo and Busk's (1988) analysis of this example, a large-sample normal approximation was used to conduct the randomization test. With that approximation, although the same statistical decision was reached (namely, that the A-phase mean exceeded the B-phase mean), the approximation test's *p* value was .0007, compared with the present exact *p* value of .0002.

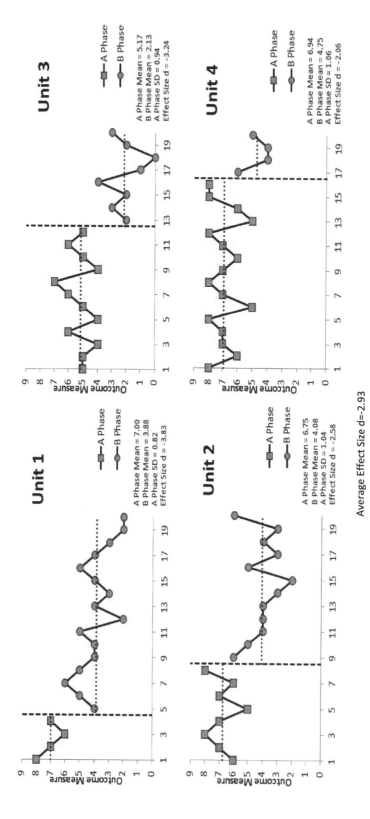

Figure 6.4. The *ExPRT* graphs sheet for Marascuilo and Busk's replicated AB design example. Data from Marascuilo and Busk (1988).

the B-phase mean minus the A-phase mean (typically, though not invariably, representing a baseline or standard-treatment phase), divided by the A-phase standard deviation (or in other design variations to be discussed, the standard deviation of the initial phase). A summary across-cases d measure is also reported, which is the simple average of the individual case ds. For the present example, the average d may be seen to be –2.93 (i.e., the average mean decrease between Phase A and Phase B amounted to almost three A-phase standard deviations).

In every *ExPRT* program and for whichever randomization test variation is implemented, (a) the plotted graphs display all of the actual A- and B-phase observations and (b) the d effect sizes are calculated in the manner just described. As is mentioned throughout this volume (see Chapters 3, 4, and 8), in that there is no consensus in the field about how best to conceptualize or report single-case intervention effect sizes, the present d measure seems to be a reasonable one to provide. Of course, with the complete set of outcome observations made available by *ExPRT*, researchers are able to calculate whichever effect-size measures they deem to be most appropriate (including the various non-overlap indices detailed in Chapter 4, this volume).

For a test of phase-slope differences (requested by entering a 2 in Column M of the Interventions sheet), standard *ExPRT* output includes the A- and B-phase slopes for each case (along with a dotted line to depict each). Because there currently are no commonly applied measures of single-case effect size for slope differences, none is offered by *ExPRT*. However, two summary measures for interpreting the slope difference both for each case and for the across-cases average, are provided by *ExPRT*: the simple difference in slopes (B-phase slope minus A-phase slope) and the ratio of the two slopes (B-phase slope divided by A-phase slope).

Finally, it should be noted that if an individual case's baseline (A) standard deviation is exactly equal to zero, then (a) the mean-difference effect size (d) cannot be calculated for that particular case and (b) the case is excluded in the across-cases average d measure that is provided.[4] The same exclusions apply to the slope-ratio measure (though not to the slope-difference measure) when a case's baseline slope is exactly equal to zero.

RANDOM ORDER OF A AND B ADMINISTRATION. As a curiosity, the present example was rerun with a random order of intervention administration specified for each case (Levin et al., 2014a; see Chapter 5, this volume, for a discussion of that model), by entering a 2 in Column R and assuming that an AB intervention order had been randomly selected for all $N = 4$ cases. With these modifications, there are 456,976 randomization outcomes (2^N, or $2^4 = 16$ times more than the previous 28,561 for the fixed-order design). Again it was concluded that the A-phase mean was statistically greater than the B-phase mean, but this

---

[4]In such situations, if a researcher elects to use some other standard deviation to yield a d (such as the B-phase standard deviation or the second A-phase standard deviation in ABA or ABAB designs), then Excel's Statistical Functions on the Formulas menu can be selected to assist with the calculations.

time with an exact p-value equal to 6/456,976 = .000013 (compared to the previous p of 6/28,561 = .00021).[5] With no output requested (a "no" in Column L), the random-order analysis took about 16 seconds to complete (compared to the previously reported 2 seconds for a fixed-order analysis); and with output requested (a "yes" in Column L), the analysis took a whopping 1 minute and 35 seconds, as compared to the previously reported 10.5 seconds).

UNSTANDARDIZED AND STANDARDIZED DATA EXAMPLE. To complete this section we provide a hypothetical example for which the outcome data are analyzed in both their original (unstandardized) and standardized forms, as would be specified in Column F of the Interventions sheet. Rather than representing a typical (or even a random) dataset, the example has been strategically crafted for "significant" purposes. In particular, the replicated AB design example includes 20 outcome observations, two cases (both receiving the intervention in a fixed AB order), and each case with (a) 10 potential intervention start points beginning at Observation 6 and (b) a randomly determined intervention start point of Observation 11. As may be appreciated from the plotted unstandardized data in Figure 6.5, there is considerably more variability in the second case's within-phase outcomes than in the first case's. Although not shown in the Figure 6.5 summary statistics, this is reflected in the second case's pooled within-phase standard deviation of 1.67 compared with the first case's standard deviation of .72, resulting in a variance ratio of $1.67^2/.72^2 = 5.38$ (i.e., the second case's pooled within-phase variance is more than five and one third times larger than that of the first case). The consequence of this situation is that with the Marascuilo and Busk (1988) simple additive combination of cases for the AB-design randomization test of mean differences, the second case's outcomes will "count more" (i.e., will be weighted more heavily) than the first case's—even though, as may be seen from the summary statistics, the intervention effect size is actually greater for the first case than for the second ($d = 3.39$ vs. 2.60, respectively).

In contrast, when the outcomes for both cases are standardized, based on a mean of 50 and standard deviation of 10, the graphical plot in Figure 6.6 results. From that figure it is visually apparent that the variability in the two cases' outcomes is now more similar than it was for the unstandardized outcome data, with the pooled within-phase standard deviations equal to 4.92 and 5.83, respectively, yielding a variance ratio = $5.83^2/4.92^2 = 1.40$ (i.e., the second case's pooled within-phase variance is now only 1.4 times larger than that of the first case, as opposed to 5.4 times larger previously). Although the individual effect sizes are not affected by the standardization process ($d = 3.39$ and 2.60 for Cases 1 and 2, respectively), the randomization distribution and associated

[5]It should not be concluded that the random intervention-order p value will always be reduced by a factor exactly proportional to the increased number of randomization outcomes of the random order relative to the fixed order (here, 6/456,976 = .000013 vs. 6/28,561 = .00021, with the former exactly $2^4 = 16$ times smaller than the latter). Although that relationship holds for the two present random- versus fixed-order examples, in our development of the *ExPRT* programs and subsequent research (Levin et al., 2014a) we have found it not to be a general relationship but one that depends on the randomization specifications associated with the data being analyzed.

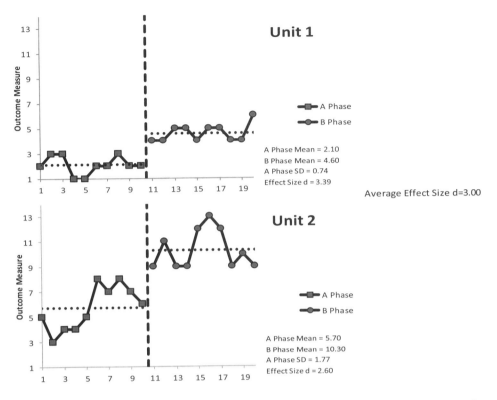

Figure 6.5.   The *ExPRT* graphs sheet for a hypothetical replicated AB design example based on unstandardized scores.

statistical test (for which the two cases' outcomes are additively combined) are. In the present example, standardizing works to increase the likelihood that the combined difference between the A- and B-phase means is not due to chance. In particular, of the 100 total randomization-distribution phase-mean differences, without standardization the actual B-A mean difference was the eighth largest ($p = .08$) whereas with standardization it is now the fourth largest ($p = .04$). Thus, for the present hypothetical example, if a one-tailed Type I error probability of .05 had been selected, then standardizing the data would have yielded a (statistical) difference relative to not standardizing: namely, that the B-phase mean statistically exceeded the A-phase mean in the former situation but not in the latter.

Levin–Wampold (1999) Simultaneous Intervention Start-Point Model

Finally, we provide an example that illustrates Levin and Wampold's (1999) simultaneous intervention start-point model as applied to units/cases consisting of one or more pairs. In such applications, one pair member (X) receives one intervention or condition and the other pair member (Y) receives a different

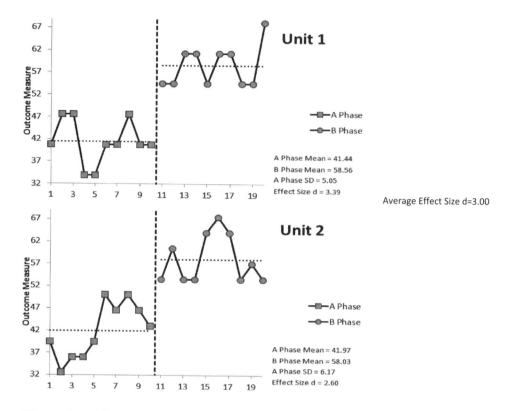

Figure 6.6. The *ExPRT* graphs sheet for a hypothetical replicated AB design example based on standardized scores.

intervention or condition.[6] In the example presented here for *ExPRT* analysis, we describe a novel within-case application variation that fits the Levin–Wampold model, namely one in which X represents an individual's performance on one outcome measure and Y represents the same individual's performance on a different outcome measure. Specifically, Shabani et al. (2002) conducted a single-case intervention study in which three children with autism were administered a social imitation intervention (a tactile prompt in the form of a vibrating paging device) that was designed to increase both the children's verbal initiations (X) and their verbal responses (Y). Their design was actually an

---

[6]If, in addition, the members within each pair are *randomly* assigned to the two intervention conditions (by specifying Option 3 in Column O of the Interventions sheet), *ExPRT* capitalizes on that additional randomization component to increase the original Levin-Wampold comparative intervention-effectiveness test's statistical power (Levin et al., 2014a). With such pair-member randomization, k_i representing the number of potential intervention start points for each pair, and N representing the number of pairs, as with the earlier-discussed improved AB randomized-order procedure the total number of possible randomization-distribution outcomes increases from the

original $\prod_{i=1}^{N} k_i$ (or k^N when the number of potential intervention start points is the same for all pairs)

to $2^N \times \prod_{i=1}^{N} k_i$ (or $2^N \times k^N = (2k)^N$ in the "same k for all pairs" situation).

ABAB design but only the first A (Baseline) and first B (Tactile Prompt) phases of the study are considered here.

In Shabani et al.'s (2002) Figure 1, there are two sets of plotted points in each panel of the graph, one set for the percentage of children's verbal initiations and the other for the percentage of children's verbal responses. Although those two outcome measures were treated separately by Shabani et al., for present purposes suppose that in addition to expecting increases in both measures following the pager intervention (Levin and Wampold's [1999] "general intervention effectiveness" hypothesis), the researchers also had predicted that the effect of the intervention would be manifested more strongly for the verbal initiations measure (X) than for the verbal responses measure (Y)—or that the B-A difference would be larger for Outcome X than for Outcome Y (Levin and Wampold's "comparative intervention effectiveness" hypothesis). The latter hypothesis is equivalent to a within-subjects measures-by-time interaction in a conventional group design and the former hypothesis is equivalent to a within-subjects time main effect. As will be seen, the *ExPRT* program is able to test both hypotheses.

The *ExPRT*-entered data for the first two phases of Shabani et al.'s (2002) study may be found on the Data sheet presented in Figure 6.7. The data are entered in pairs of rows for each child, with an empty row between each child's two sets of outcome observations (for the present example, percentage of verbal initiations [X] and percentage of verbal responses [Y], respectively, during free-play sessions). In *ExPRT*, the first row of each pair must always contain the set of X observations and the second row the set of Y observations. The series lengths differed for the three children: 7 for the first child (Mike), 8 for the second (Nathan), and 6 for the third (John). Accordingly, Mike's cell corresponding to the eighth observation and John's corresponding to the seventh and eighth observations are left completely blank.

The design-and-analysis portion of the Shabani et al. (2002) study from *ExPRT*'s Intervention sheet is shown in Figure 6.8. For purposes of the present random intervention start-point adaptation of the study, we decided that each child could have been assigned three potential intervention start points (Column B), from right before Observation 3 (Column A) to right before Observation 5. In Shabani et al.'s study, the actual intervention start points for the three children were Observations 5, 5, and 4, respectively (Column E). The original (unstandardized) data were analyzed (Column F) and a one-tailed Type I error probability of .05 was selected (Columns G and H) for the Levin–Wampold general intervention-effectiveness test (a 1 in Column O), with the prediction that averaged across the X and Y outcome measures, there would be an increase in mean performance between the baseline and intervention phases (a 2 in Column I). The following design-and-analysis options were also specified: a standard AB design (a 1 in Column P) based on a fixed AB intervention order for each child (a 1 in Column R), with a test of phase-mean differences to be conducted (a 1 in Column M). Had the intervention order been randomly determined for each child, then entering a 2 in Column R would incorporate Levin et al.'s (2014a) order-randomization addition into the analysis.

With the preceding specifications ($k = 3$ potential intervention start points for each child and $N = 3$ pairs of observations) there are $3^3 = 27$ possible across-

1	2	3	4	5	6	7	8	9	10	11	12	13	14	15	16	17	18	19	20
15	15	20	5	80	45	90	70												
10	0	0	0	20	10	30	50												
0	0	0	0	85	85	45	70												
0	0	0	0	45	70	35	50												
0	0	0	100	75	90														
0	0	0	0	20	55														

Figure 6.7. The *ExPRT* data sheet for the initial AB portion of Shabani et al.'s (2002) study. Data from Shabani et al. (2002).

A	B	C	D	E	F	G	H	I	J	K	L	M	N	O	P	Q	R	S	T	U
1st pot interv stpnt	# pot stpnts	# units	max # pnts	act interv stpnt	Data: 1:Original, 2:Standardized	alpha	Tails (1,2)	1:A>B or T1>T2, 2:B>A or T2>T1	Sig.	Πpnts, ordr perms, tot	output (yes/no)	1:Mean, 2:Slope	Missing Code	If Pairs Test: 1.Gen, 2.Comp, 3.Comp(Rnd XY)	Design: 1.Std, 2.Cross	If Cross: 1.Cond 2.Time	Order: 1.Fixed 2.Rand	Actual Order	Run 1st	Then Plot
3	3	3	8	5	1	0.05	1	1	2 Sig. p=0.0370	27	no	1	1	1	1	1 N/A in AB c	1	AB		
3	3	3		5					Rank = 1 of 27	1								AB	Run	Plot
3	3	3		4						27								AB		

time elapsed - 2 sec
Missing Data Detected. See output for random intervals and points selected.

Figure 6.8. The *ExPRT* interventions sheet associated with the Levin-Wampold General Effectiveness Test applied to the initial AB portion of Shabani et al.'s study. Data from Shabani et al. (2002).

measures B-A phase-mean differences in the resulting randomization distribution. A click on the *Run* button produces the results shown in Column J, namely, that the actual B-A mean difference was the largest of all 27 possible differences, thereby leading to a rejection of the general effectiveness hypothesis based on a one-tailed α of .05 and significance probability of $p = 1/27 = .037$. A click on the *Graphs* tab displays the summary data for each child on the Graphs sheet (Figure 6.9). The mean lines for Subunit X (verbal initiations) are represented by dots and for Subunit Y (verbal responses) by dashes.

For the Levin–Wampold model, *ExPRT* calculates the individual standardized effect sizes based on the case's pooled Phase A standard deviation. For the general intervention-effectiveness test, it may be seen that averaged across the two outcome measures all three children exhibited a much higher level of Phase B (tactile prompt) performance than mean Phase A (baseline) performance, with "B Phase Gen Mean"–"A Phase Gen Mean" differences of about 38%, 61%, and 57% for Child 1 (Mike), Child 2 (Nathan), and Child 3 (John), respectively. In the present context, this corresponds to an intervention main effect (mean B-A difference, averaged across measures), which when "properly scaled" (Levin, 1997), is calculated as the average of the two B-phase measures minus the average of the two A-phase measures. When this difference is divided by Mike's pooled Phase A standard deviation, the difference amounts to a Busk-Serlin (1992) "no assumptions" effect size d of 6.64; because the pooled Phase A standard deviation was 0 for Nathan and John, no standardized effect size could be calculated for those two children.

To conduct Levin and Wampold's (1999) comparative intervention-effectiveness test, namely that the baseline-to-intervention phase change (i.e., the B-A mean difference) was of comparable magnitude for the two outcome measures, verbal initiations (X) and verbal responses (Y), the user would return to the Interventions sheet of Figure 6.8 and enter a 2 in Column O (i.e., the "Comp" option).[7] For the present example, it was predicted that the intervention effect would be larger for verbal initiations than for verbal responses, based on a one-tailed α of .05. The two latter values are entered in Columns G and H as before for the general intervention-effectiveness test. By entering a 2 in Column I (i.e., B > A), the user is indicating that the mean difference between the first listed outcome measure, verbal initiations (X), and the second

---

[7]Because in this example the X and Y paired observations represent two different (nonrandomly assigned) outcome measures, Column O's Option 2 (Comp) must be selected for the comparative intervention-effectiveness test. Similarly, if the pairs were to consist of two different individuals representing some "status" variable (such as gender, age, ability, etc.), for which random assignment to X and Y is not possible, then Option 2 in Column O must also be selected. With pairs consisting of two different individuals (or other entities) and X and Y representing two different intervention types or experimental conditions, if the two interventions are *not* randomly assigned to the members of each pair, then again Option 2 in Column O must be selected. For that design variation, Option 3 [Comp (Rnd XY)] is applicable only when the members of each pair have been randomly assigned to the X and Y intervention conditions. The nature of the XY factor and the associated within-pair assignment process has no bearing on the general intervention-effectiveness test (Option 1 in Column O). Conversely, in situations where X and Y are two different intervention conditions and pair members have been randomly assigned to those conditions (i.e., when Option 3 in Column O is called for), whether the AB intervention order is fixed or random (as specified in Column R) has no bearing on the comparative intervention-effectiveness test.

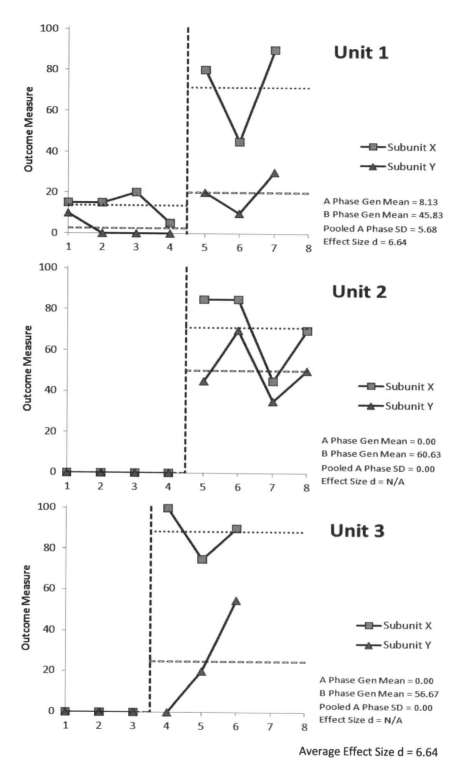

Figure 6.9. The *ExPRT* graphs sheet associated with the General Effectiveness Test applied to the initial AB portion of Shabani et al.'s study. Data from Shabani et al. (2002).

listed outcome measure, verbal responses (Y), is predicted to be larger during the B phase than during the A phase (i.e., that there would be an increase in the X-Y mean difference from Phase A to Phase B). This is equivalent to predicting that the intervention effect will be more pronounced for verbal initiations than for verbal responses. Alternatively, if it had been predicted that the increase between Phase B and Phase A would be greater for verbal responses than for verbal initiations, then the X-Y mean difference would be expected to decrease (or increase negatively) and so a 1 (A > B) would have been entered in Column I.

With the former specification here (i.e., a 2 in Column I to indicate that B > A), a click on the *Run* button yields the same statistical outcome for the comparative intervention-effectiveness test as was obtained for the general intervention-effectiveness test, namely a statistically significant result with $p = 1/27 = .037$. Then, clicking on the *Plot* button produces the summary data that are presented in Figure 6.10. There it can be seen that, consistent with predictions, there are larger mean differences between the dotted lines representing Subunit X (verbal initiations measure) and the dashed lines representing Subunit Y (verbal responses measure) during the intervention phase (B) than during the baseline phase (A). Again, with the pooled A-Phase standard deviation as the effect-size denominator, the properly scaled measures-by-intervention interaction (X-Y by B-A) is represented as the average of Phase B, Measure X and Phase A, Measure Y minus the average of Phase B, Measure Y and Phase A, Measure X, which is equivalent to half the Phase B X-Y mean difference minus half the Phase A X-Y mean difference. For Mike, Nathan, and John, the respective "B Phase Cmp Mean" – "A Phase Cmp Mean" differences are about 20%, 10.5%, and 32%. The effect-size d for Mike is 3.56 and none is calculated for either Nathan or John because of the all-zero scores for both outcome measures during the baseline phase.

ABA and ABAB Designs

Although at one time the three-phase A (Baseline)–B (Intervention)–A (Baseline) design was considered to be a methodological improvement over the two-phase AB design, it still leaves too many potentially confounding doors open for it to satisfy the current WWC Standards (Chapter 1, this volume; Kratochwill et al., 2013). As with the AB design, incorporating an independent replication component would help to elevate the ABA design's methodological status somewhat. That said, many single-case intervention researchers continue to use the ABA design today and so randomization tests for that design, without and with replication, were developed by Gafurov and Levin (2013) to become part of the *ExPRT* package.

Most of *ExPRT*'s previously described basic components for the AB design are also part of its programs for the ABA and ABAB designs. Additional specific components include (a) intervention start-point randomization (Onghena, 1992, model and Levin et al., 2014a, randomized-intervention order addition to that model) and (b) overall test, separate two-phase tests, and a predicted-pattern test (Levin, Marascuilo, & Hubert, 1978) based on either interval- or ordinal-scale predictions.

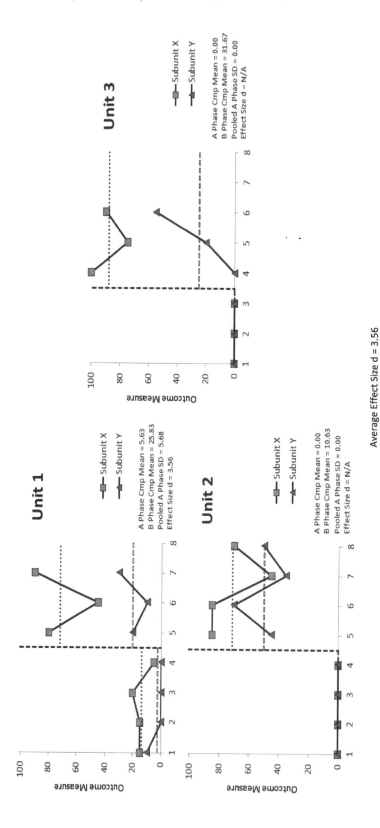

Figure 6.10. The *ExPRT* graphs sheet associated with the comparative effectiveness test applied to the initial AB portion of Shabani et al.'s study. Data from Shabani et al. (2002).

Onghena (1992) Model and Levin et al.'s (2014a) Additions

Onghena (1992) proposed an inventive approach for extending Edgington's (1975) random intervention start-point model beyond the single two-phase AB design. The general formula underlying Onghena's approach is:

$$\text{total number of randomization-distribution outcomes} = \begin{pmatrix} N - \sum_{i=1}^{I} n_i + k \\ k \end{pmatrix}$$

where in this context N = the total number of outcome observations, n_i = the minimum number of required observations for each of the I phases, k = the number of phase transitions in the design (which is one fewer than the number of phases), and the curved parentheses are again combinatorial notation for representing the number of ways in which k phase transitions can be chosen from the numerator value.

ABA DESIGN. Consistent with this model, for the ABA design (or A_1BA_2 for ease of explication), the researcher must specify two a priori permissible phase transitions (i.e., $k = 2$): one for the beginning of the B phase, as with the previously discussed Edgington (1975) AB model, and a second one for the beginning of the second A phase (A_2). The researcher must also specify the minimum number of observations required for each of the three phases, A_1, B, and A_2. In *ExPRT's* ABA design program (which allows for replication across cases), the user also specifies whether a fixed or random order of intervention administration was adopted; if the latter, then the user indicates which of the two permissible orders (ABA or BAB) was randomly selected for each case.[8]

For each of the possible randomization-distribution outcomes, the difference between the mean of the B-phase observations and the mean of the two A-phase observations is calculated. In *ExPRT*, the latter is represented by the unweighted A-phase mean (the simple average of the two A-phase means). As before, the significance probability is based on the extremity of the mean difference associated with the actually selected start-point division within the distribution of all possible differences. The same procedure is also applied to the test of slope differences. In addition to the overall (omnibus) test of B-A phase differences, *ExPRT* also allows for a test of two individual phase-transition effects (based on means or slopes), namely the intervention effect (Phase 1 vs. Phase 2) and the "reversal" or "return to baseline" effect (Phase 2 vs. Phase 3), each with its own user-designated Type I error probability. No illustrations of the ABA program are presented here because the setup and analysis parallel those for the ABAB design, for which we provide an example.

ABAB DESIGN. The ABAB design is the first of the ABAB . . . AB class to be "acceptable" from a "single-case design intervention standards" perspective

---

[8]In *ExPRT's* ABA and ABAB design programs, the two possible orders of intervention administration take into account the terminology used to characterize the design-and-transition aspects that are specified in the initial Intervention sheet columns. Specifically, in the ABA design, P1 (Phase 1), P2 (Phase 2), and P3 (Phase 3) refer respectively to either A_1BA_2 or B_1AB_2 intervention-administration orders; and in the ABAB design, with the addition of P4 (Phase 4) they refer to either $A_1B_1A_2B_2$ or $B_1A_1B_2A_2$ orders.

(Kratochwill et al., 2013), in that it affords researchers opportunities to demonstrate three effects that are under their systematic control: (a) an initial intervention effect during the A_1-to-B_1 phase transition, (b) a return to baseline during the B_1-to-A_2 phase transition, and (c) a within-case replication of the intervention effect during the A_2-to-B_2 phase transition (Chapters 1 and 2, this volume). Without trying to sound like a broken record, including two or more independent cases would again add valuable replication and internal-validity enhancing features to this design. The *ExPRT* program includes randomization tests for ABAB intervention designs without and with replication.

We now apply *ExPRT*'s replicated ABAB randomization-test procedure to an intervention study conducted by Carnine (1976), to which we have added a hypothetical random intervention start-point process.[9] In that study, two low-achieving first graders were administered a reading-instruction intervention under two different rates of teacher presentation, slow (A) and fast (B) in that order, for both children.

It was anticipated that in comparison to the slow rate of presentation, the fast presentation rate would produce a higher percentage of correct responses, the outcome measure of interest here. For this four-phase ABAB example, the specifications are: $I = 4$, $k = 3$, $N = 33$, and min $n_1 =$ min $n_2 =$ min $n_3 =$ min $n_4 = 6$ (i.e., $n = 6$) so that $\sum_{i=1}^{l} n_i = I \times n = 4 \times 6 = 24$. Applying Onghena's general formula with these specifications, the total number of possible intervention start-point combinations (and hence, randomization-distribution outcomes) for each child is equal to: $\binom{33 - 24 + 3}{3} = \binom{12}{3} = 220$. With two children (i.e., two independent replicates) and the above specifications the same for both children, the total number of randomization-distribution outcomes is equal to the one-child number of randomization-distribution outcomes squared, or $220^2 = 48,400$.

A listing of the 33 sessions (outcome observations) for each child may be seen in *ExPRT*'s Data sheet presented in Figure 6.11. A few things need to be mentioned about those observations, however, in relation to the to-be-discussed ABAB randomization-test analysis. First, Carnine's (1976) "% Answering Correctly" Figures 2 and 3 were closely approximated through the use of special graph-digitization software, *UnGraph*™ (Biosoft, 2004), rounded to one decimal place. Second, from Figure 6.11 it should be noted that the fourteenth outcome observation of 82.8 for the first child (Row 2, Column N in the Data sheet) has been highlighted in a bold larger font). In Carnine's study the first child's fourteenth observation was missing and because *ExPRT* does not allow for missing data within selected intervals (see our previous discussion), for purposes of this example that child's missing score had to be estimated here. Because the first child's Observations 13 and 15 were 82.9 and 82.7, respectively, using the mean of these (namely, 82.8) for Observation 14 can be regarded as not too much of a stretch.

The Interventions sheet (Figure 6.12) includes the design-and-analysis portion of Carnine's (1976) study. As was noted earlier, for the present random

---

[9]Carnine's study actually consisted of a six-phase ABABAB design but for convenience (including the current capabilities of *ExPRT*) we consider the data only from the initial 4-phase ABAB portion of the design.

	1	2	3	4	5	6	7	8	9	10	11	12	13	14	15	16	17	18	19	20	21	22	23	24	25	26	27	28	29	30	31	32	33
	20.4	13.8	23.6	35.0	30.4	49.3	53.8	21.4	25.9	11.0	40.2	43.6	82.9	82.8	82.7	84.7	89.6	81.0	84.7	32.3	50.9	43.1	15.9	13.4	23.5	25.5	31.5	72.5	82.0	78.6	91.2	73.8	63.9
	86.1	76.5	85.1	72.0	98.4	70.0	93.5	95.9	82.7	95.5	95.6	88.1	94.6	97.1	94.5	101.3	89.6	92.0	93.8	88.9	35.6	60.6	79.3	83.6	39.7	56.1	59.7	81.3	97.6	102.8	99.4	101.5	81.3

Figure 6.11.   The *ExPRT* data sheet for Carnine's replicated ABAB design. Data from Carnine (1976).

A	B	C	D	E	F	G	H	I	J	K	L	M	N	O	P	Q	R	S	T	U	V
min Ph1, >1	min Ph2, >1	min Ph3, >1	min Ph4, >1	N	actual ini Ph2	Ph2 lngth, >1	actual ini Ph4	Data:1 Orig. 2 Stnd	alpha	Tails (1,2)	1:A>B, 2:B>A	Sig.	Пprnts, ordr perms, tot	output (yes/no)	1:Mean, 2:Slope	Overall Test	Test: 1 Ph1vsPh2, 2 Ph2vsPh3, 3 Ph3vsPh4	Order: 1.ABAB 2.Rand	If Rand: act order	Missing Code	Run 1st Then Plot
6	6	6	6	33	12	9	28	1	0.05	1	1	2 Sig. p=0.0018	48400	no	1	1	1 Omitted	1	1		
6	6	6	6	6	12	9	28					Rank = 86 of 48400	1								
													48400								

time elapsed - 6.984375 sec

Figure 6.12.   The *ExPRT* interventions sheet for Carnine's replicated ABAB design. Data from Carnine (1976).

intervention start-point adaptation of the study, we required a minimum of six observations for each of the four phases (Columns A–D) and the rest of the design incorporated Carnine's actual phase lengths. Specifically, the first A phase included 11 observations; the first B phase, nine observations; the second A phase, seven observations; and the second B phase, six observations. Given that 33 total observations had been specified in Row 1 of the Data sheet (Figure 6.9), these phase observation numbers dictated the values that are entered in Columns F, G, and H of Figure 6.12. In Figure 6.12, it has been further specified that with $\alpha = .05$ (Column J), a directional test (a 1 in Column K) of overall (i.e., the average of the two B-phase means vs. the average of the two A-phase means) phase-mean differences (1s in Columns P and Q) will be conducted, with the prediction that the two combined B-phase means will exceed the two combined A-phase means (a 2 in Column L).[10]

The results of the randomization test, seen in Column M, prove to be statistically significant, with a significance probability given by a p value of $86/48,400 = .0018$. The outcomes for each child are summarized on the Graphs sheet (Figure 6.13). For both children it may be seen that the percentage of correct reading responses under the fast presentation rate (the two combined B-phase means) was considerably higher than under the slow presentation rate (the two combined A-phase means), resulting in respective ds of 3.53 and 2.04 (average $d = 2.79$).

RANDOM ORDER OF A AND B ADMINISTRATION. As was noted earlier, *ExPRT*'s ABA and ABAB programs are conducive to researchers randomly determining which of two alternating orders the A and B conditions are administered: ABA or BAB and ABAB or BABA (see Chapter 5, this volume). In Carnine's (1976) study, both children received the reading-instruction intervention in an ABAB order, with A and B referring to slow and fast teacher presentation rates, respectively. To illustrate the application of *ExPRT*'s intervention-order option, we reconsider the study under the assumption that the researcher randomly determined for each child the order in which the reading-instruction intervention was administered, either ABAB or BABA. Let us further assume that the random determination resulted in an ABAB order for each child, the order that was actually implemented by Carnine in his study. With this "random order" addition (not presented in a figure here), the 1 in Column S of Figure 6.12 would be changed to a 2 and an ABAB order would be indicated for each child in Column T. In comparison to a fixed order of intervention administration with its 48,400 total number of possible randomization outcomes, with a random order this number increases by a factor of 4, or 2^2, to 193,600. A randomization-test analysis with these random-order

---

[10]As can be inferred from Column R of Figure 12, randomization tests of the three adjacent phase-mean or phase-slope changes (Phase 1 vs. Phase 2, Phase 2 vs. Phase 3, and Phase 3 vs. Phase 4) are also available for researchers seeking separate documentations of the ABAB (or BABA) design's initial intervention effect, the reversal effect, and the replicated intervention effect, respectively. In that case, Column Q would be left empty and a 1, 2, or 3 would be entered in Column R to indicate which of the three tests is to be conducted.

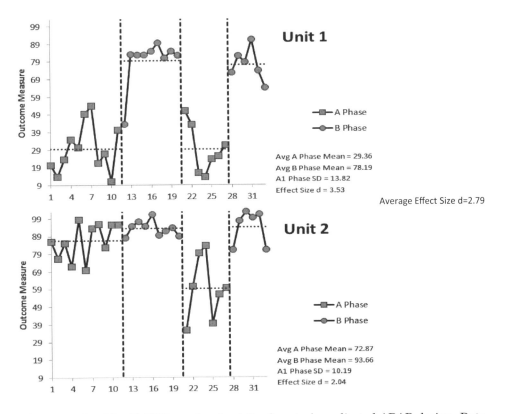

Figure 6.13. The *ExPRT* graphs sheet for Carnine's replicated ABAB design. Data from Carnine (1976).

specifications yields a one-tailed significance probability of $p = 86/193,600 = .00044$, 4 times lower than the previous fixed-order one-tailed p value of .0018 (but see Footnote 5).

Multiple-Baseline Designs

The multiple-baseline design augments the internal validity of the preceding designs by allowing for a replicated comparison of the outcomes in baseline and intervention phases in a staggered (across time periods) fashion within the same study (Chapters 1 and 2, this volume; Kratochwill et al., 2013; Richards, Taylor, Ramasamy, & Richards, 1999). Typical replication variations of the design are based on different "cases" consisting of either individuals/groups, settings, or behaviors/skills, with the first variation (individuals/groups) argued to be the most convincing from a scientific credibility standpoint (Levin, 1992). The collection of baseline data starts simultaneously for all cases, with at least three replicates required to meet the WWC Standards. Then, following either a predetermined or "response-guided" (Chapter 5, this volume) number of baseline observations, the researcher introduces the intervention to the first case while the other cases remain in the baseline phase. Again after some number of observations, implementation of the intervention begins with the second case while continuing the intervention with the first case. The process continues, so that each subsequent case is introduced to the treatment in this staggered fashion. Experimental control is documented if (a) the target outcome measure changes in the predicted manner when the intervention is introduced to a particular case while (b) measures for the nonintervened cases remain at or near a baseline level (Cooper, Heron, & Heward, 1987; Kratochwill et al., 2013; McReynolds & Kearns, 1983; Poling, Methot, & LeSage, 1995; Revusky, 1967)—a pattern that considerably bolsters the discriminant validity of the intervention (Campbell & Fiske, 1959; Levin, 1992). Multiple-baseline designs have been recommended for situations in which more than one case would benefit from an intervention, when withdrawal of the intervention in the ABAB design is unethical, or when the achieved target outcome cannot be reversed (Alberto & Troutman, 2008; Baer, Wolf, & Risley, 1968; Hersen & Barlow, 1976; Kennedy, 2005).

In addition to the already described general components of the *ExPRT* program, specific components for the multiple-baseline design include (a) case randomization (Wampold & Worsham's [1986] "within-case comparison" model), (b) combined case randomization and intervention start-point randomization (Koehler & Levin's [1998] regulated randomization "within-case comparison" model), (c) case-pair simultaneous intervention start-point randomization extension of the Koehler–Levin model (Levin et al. 2014a) general-effectiveness and comparative-effectiveness tests, and (d) sequential "between-case comparison" models (modified Revusky, 1967, procedure and the modification and intervention start-point randomization extension of Levin, Ferron, & Gafurov, 2014b).

Wampold–Worsham (1986) and Koehler–Levin (1998) "Within-Case Comparison" Models

With cases randomly assigned to the N staggered positions of the multiple-baseline design (see Footnote 1), for the Wampold–Worsham model there is a total of $N!$ B-A phase-mean differences in the randomization distribution. By also incorporating staggered intervention start-point randomization (again see Footnote 1), with k_i potential start points for the i-th case the Koehler–Levin regulated-randomization multiple-baseline design model augments the Wampold–Worsham number by the product of the individual k_i, $\prod_{t=1}^{N} k_i$, resulting in a total number of randomization-distribution outcomes equal to $N! \prod_{i=1}^{N} k_i$.

With the same number of potential intervention start points, k, for all cases, this quantity simplifies to $N! \times k^N$. By allowing for multiple potential intervention start points, the Koehler–Levin model affords a statistically more powerful test of multiple-baseline intervention effects in comparison to Wampold and Worsham's single start-point model (Ferron & Sentovich, 2002).

In *ExPRT's* multiple-baseline randomization-test program, the N replicated cases must be listed in their naturally ascending sequential-intervention order (i.e., beginning with the case for which the intervention is introduced first and ending with the case for which the intervention is introduced last). For the Wampold–Worsham and Koehler–Levin models (which are referred to in *ExPRT* as "within-case comparison" procedures), missing data and unequal series lengths are permitted, but under two restrictions because of the randomization-test requirements of cases having to be assigned to stagger positions within the multiple-baseline design. First, all cases must have data associated with each of the $\prod_{i=1}^{N} k_i$ potential intervention start-point observation periods. For example, with 20 observations and $N = 3$ cases associated with potential start points of 3–5, 8–9, and 12–14, respectively all units must have data for each of those $3 + 2 + 3 = 8$ potential intervention start-point intervals. Second, for a test of mean differences, all units must have (a) at least one A-phase observation prior to the earliest potential intervention start point (here, Observation 3) and (b) at least one B-phase observation coincident with or following the latest potential intervention start point (here, Observation 14). For a test of slope differences, each case must have at least two observations within the just-specified intervals.

In addition to providing randomization-test analyses for both the Wampold–Worsham and Koehler–Levin models, *ExPRT* also accommodates the previously described Levin–Wampold case-pair approach in which pair members are randomly assigned to two different intervention conditions (X or Y). With that methodological variation, the scientific credibility of single-case multiple-baseline designs is further strengthened (Chapter 5, this volume; Levin et al., 2014a). An example of this case-pair application may be found in a federally funded school-intervention team problem-solving study that is currently underway (Kratochwill & Asmus, 2013).

We now provide an example that applies *ExPRT's* multiple-baseline randomization test procedure to the Koehler–Levin model and hypothetical example (Koehler & Levin, 1998) in which an intervention is administered to three classrooms in a multiple-baseline design, with 10 outcome observations collected for each classroom (see Figure 6.14). In the example, a 1 in Column P indicates that a within-series comparison for the Wampold–Worsham and Koehler–Levin models will be applied (rather than a between-series comparison for the to-be-described Revusky, 1967, and Levin et al., 2014b, models), with the

1	2	3	4	5	6	7	8	9	10
4	3	5	7	6	7	7	8	9	7
6	7	5	6	6	7	10	9	10	10
9	9	7	10	10	8	9	12	11	14

Figure 6.14. The *ExPRT* data sheet for Koehler and Levin's multiple-baseline design example. Data from Koehler and Levin (1998).

information in Column Q discussed below in relation to the latter models. As can be seen in Columns A and B of the Interventions sheet in Figure 6.15, the researcher considered it acceptable to begin the intervention just prior to either Observation 2 or 3 for one of the classrooms, just prior to either Observation 5 or 6 for another classroom, and just prior to Observation 8 or 9 for the final classroom, with classrooms randomly assigned to these three multiple-baseline stagger positions. Accordingly, there are $N = 3$ classroom "cases" and $k = 2$ potential intervention start points for each case, resulting in a total of $3! \times 2^3 = 48$ possible randomization-distribution outcomes. In the conduct of the hypothetical study, coin flips determined that the intervention for the three classrooms would start just prior to Observations 3, 6, and 8, respectively (Column E of Figure 6.15).

With a baseline-to-intervention-phase improvement in mean outcome performance expected for all classrooms (Column I) based on a Type I error of .05 (Column G), the rest of the design specifications in Figure 6.15 are straightforward, as is the randomization-test result reported in Column J. Specifically, the actually obtained outcome was the most extreme, in the predicted direction, of all 48 outcomes in the randomization distribution, leading to the conclusion that the A-to-B phase-mean increase was statistically significant, with a one-tailed significance probability given by $1/48 = .021$. The summary data (on the Graphs sheet with the plotted data, individual case means and standard deviations, and effect size-information) for the hypothetical study are presented in Figure 6.16, where it may be determined that the across-cases mean B-A difference was 3.43 raw-score units, representing an average standardized effect size of $d = 4.30$.

Levin et al.'s (2014b) Modification and Extension of the Revusky (1967) "Between-Case Comparison" Procedure

As an alternative to the Wampold–Worsham (1986) and Koehler–Levin (1998) multiple-baseline randomization models, *ExPRT* includes Revusky's (1967) much earlier suggested sequential vertical model (and which we refer to as a "between-case comparison" procedure).[11] The test has particular utility for situations in which the sequentially introduced B-phase intervention for each case does not (or cannot) continue for the maximum number of outcome observations that are indicated in Column D of *ExPRT's* Interventions sheet. That is, in certain multiple-baseline contexts, the researcher may elect to discontinue an earlier case's B phase at some point in time before the later cases have completed theirs. For situations where the cases' series lengths are not all equal, the Revusky procedure is applicable whereas the Wampold–Worsham

---

[11]Technically speaking, Revusky's (1967) procedure conducts a between-case comparison of within-case differences. However, in *ExPRT* the procedure is referred to simply as a "between-case comparison" to distinguish it from the just-discussed Wampold and Worsham (1986) and Koehler and Levin (1998) approaches.

A 1st pot interv stpnt	B # pot stpnts	C # units	D max # pmts	E act interv stpnt	F Data: 1:Original, 2:Standardized	G alpha	H Tails (1,2)	I 1:A>B, 2:B>A	J Sig.	K #pnts, units/, X	L output (yes/no)	M 1:Mean, 2:Slope	N Pairs Test: 1.Gen, 2.Comp	O Missing Code	P Series Comp: W/in, 2 Btwn	Q 1 If W/in, Diff. Simp	R Run 1st	S Then Plot
2	2	3	10	3	1	0.05	1	2	Sig. p=0.0208		no		1 N/A, Ind Mode			1	Run	Plot
5	2			6					Rank = 1 of 48									
8	2			8														

time elapsed - 0.765625 sec

Figure 6.15. The *ExPRT* interventions sheet for Koehler and Levin's multiple-baseline design example (within-case comparison). Data from Koehler and Levin (1998).

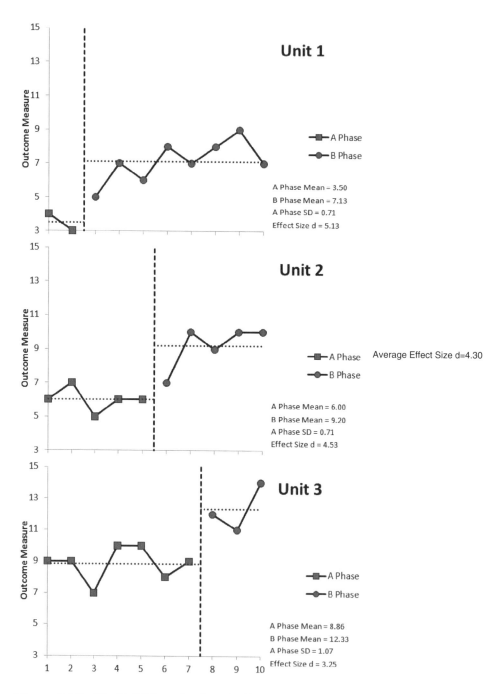

Figure 6.16.   The *ExPRT* graphs sheet for Koehler and Levin's multiple-baseline design example. Data from Koehler and Levin (1998).

and Koehler–Levin procedures might not be (see our earlier discussion of the required conditions) and so the former has been included as one of *ExPRT's* multiple-baseline randomization-test options.

Although the original Revusky (1967) procedure allows for only a single staggered intervention start point for each of the N cases, Levin et al. (2014b) have developed an extension analogous to the Koehler–Levin (1998) procedure, wherein more than one potential intervention start point can be specified for each case. Identical to the Koehler–Levin procedure, for the Levin et al. extension, the total number of randomization-distribution outcomes can be calculated to be $N! \prod_{i=1}^{N} k_z$ according to the general formula, where k_i = the number of potential intervention start points for the i-th case; and for the special situation in which all k_i are equal to k, this formula reduces to $N! \times k^N$.

In addition to this extension, Levin et al. (2014b) have proposed a modification of Revusky's (1967) procedure, which is incorporated into *ExPRT*. In particular, the original Revusky procedure is based on rank-ordering the mean B-A differences for each of N "subexperiments" (or steps) and then calculating the sum of the ranks associated with the intervened cases. Levin et al.'s modified Revusky procedure is based on calculating a common set of mean B-A differences at each step, forming a distribution of the combined across-step differences, and then determining the rank associated with the actually intervened cases within that distribution. Whether this modification produces a more powerful test than the original Revusky procedure is a focus of Levin et al.'s (2014b) current empirical investigation.

Finally, in contrast to Revusky's (1967) hypothetical multiple-baseline example with its single post-intervention observation, Levin et al. (2014b) recommend that researchers include at least a few outcome observations in each case's intervention (B) phase both: (a) so that more than one post-intervention observation point is included for each case in the analysis and (b) to allow for the possibility of detecting either gradual or delayed intervention effects. Specifically, at each step (a) the mean of the actually intervened case's A-phase observations is compared with the mean of its B-phase observations up to but not including the next case's first potential intervention start point (B-A), (b) the corresponding means of the remaining cases are compared as well, and (c) all of those are included in the distribution of ranked mean differences.

With those preliminary comments, we now turn to *ExPRT's* reanalysis of Revusky's (1967) example. In that example, a poison was sequentially introduced to five rats over a 10-day period, with the effect of the poison on the rats' avoidance performance measured. One change between Revusky's analysis and what was analyzed here should be noted. Revusky included a constant number of baseline observations (namely, 5) for each of the five sequential steps. Thus, the first rat was measured for five baseline days prior to its poison injection on Day 6; and even though the subsequent four rats were measured from six to nine baseline days prior to their poison injections on Days 7 through 10, only the outcomes from the five days immediately preceding their injections were included in the analysis. In contrast, in *ExPRT's* reanalysis of those data, all baseline observations preceding the given step's first post-intervention

1	2	3	4	5	6	7	8	9	10
1570	1470	1490	970	1130	740				
1180	1040	1210	1120	970	990	490			
640	680	590	580	530	890	990	770		
890	780	970	1010	930	890	770	980	710	
930	900	840	960	860	750	1130	980	860	390

Figure 6.17. The *ExPRT* data sheet for Revusky's multiple-baseline design example. Data from Revusky (1967).

observation were included (i.e., from five to nine baseline observations for the first through the fifth rat injected, respectively)—see Figure 6.17 for *ExPRT's* Data-sheet listing of Revusky's example.

We begin the Interventions sheet in Figure 6.18 by entering a 2 in Column P (*Series Comp: 1.W/in, 2.Btwn*) to indicate that this multiple-baseline analysis will follow the between-series comparison format of the Revusky (1967) and Levin et al. (2014b) procedures. Revusky additionally recommended that in many situations, rather than comparing the simple A- and B-phase mean differences, comparing the relative differences, or proportional gains/losses (i.e., (B-A)/A) would be advisable—especially when the different cases are starting at different baseline levels. In *ExPRT*, for the between-series comparison models, such a choice between simple and relative differences is possible and is indicated, respectively, by inputting either a 1 or a 2 in Column Q. For the present example, we follow Revusky's lead and conduct the analysis on the relative differences (i.e., a 2 in Column Q). It should be noted, however, that analysis of the relative differences (a) cannot be conducted when at least one of the cases has baseline (A) data consisting of all zeroes and (b) will be misleading if the underlying outcome-observation scale does not have a true zero point.

With a one-tailed Type I error of .05 selected and specifying an A-to-B performance decrease (Columns G, H, and I), in Column J it can be seen that the actual mean difference is statistically significant in that it represents the third most extreme outcome, in the predicted direction, out of 120 outcomes in the randomization distribution (i.e., $p = 3/120 = .025$). Although Revusky (1967) did not provide an exact significance probability in his analysis of this example, he did indicate on page 324 that the outcome was statistically significant with $p < .05$, one-tailed. He also indicated that had the simple differences (rather than the relative differences) been analyzed instead, the result would have been statistically significant with $p < .01$ (one-tailed). Our reanalysis using simple differences (a 1 in Column Q) based on *all* of each rat's baseline observations (rather than Revusky's constant number of 5) reveals that the actually obtained outcome is the second most extreme, in the predicted direction, out of 120, yielding a one-tailed p value of $2/120 = .0167$.

Summary

In this chapter we have introduced Version 1.1 of the single-case data-analysis *ExPRT*, an Excel Package of Randomization Tests that was developed by present authors Boris S. Gafurov and Joel R. Levin. The package currently contains

A	B	C	D	E	F	G	H	I	J	K	L	M	N	O	P	Q	R	S
1st pot interv stpnt	# pot stpnts	# units	max # pnts	act interv stpnt	Data: 1:Original, 2:Standardized	alpha	Tails (1,2)	1:A>B, 2:B>A	Sig.	#pnts, unitsl, X	output (yes/no)	1:Mean, 2:Slope	Pairs Test: 1.Gen, 2.Comp	Missing Code	Series Comp: W/In, 2 Btwn	1 If Btwn, Diff: 1.Simp 2.Rel	Run 1st	Then Plot
6	1	5	10	6	1	0.05	1	1	1 Sig. p=0.0250		no		1 N/A, Btwn Comp		2	2	Run	Plot
7	1			7					Rank = 3 of 120									
8	1			8														
9	1			9														
10	1			10														

time elapsed - 0.359375 sec

Figure 6.18. The *ExPRT* interventions sheet for Revusky's multiple-baseline design example (between-case comparison). Data from Revusky (1967).

randomization statistical tests that are applicable to a vast array of single-case intervention designs and design variations, including AB, ABA, ABAB, and multiple-baseline. Several detailed *ExPRT* data-analysis illustrations were provided in the present chapter. Additional single-case designs (such as multiple-phase ABAB . . . AB, alternating treatment, and multiple-probe) and data-analysis options will continue to be developed and incorporated into future *ExPRT* versions. It is believed that user-friendly *ExPRT* will be a versatile and valuable data-analysis tool to single-case intervention researchers.

References

Alberto, P. A., & Troutman, A. C. (2008). *Applied behavior analysis for teachers* (8th ed.). Upper Saddle River, NJ: Prentice Hall.

Baer, D. M., Wolf, M., & Risley, R. (1968). Some current dimensions of applied behavior analysis. *Journal of Applied Behavior Analysis, 1,* 91–97. doi:10.1901/jaba.1968.1-91

Biosoft. (2004). *UnGraph for Windows* (Version 5.0). Cambridge, England: Author.

Bulté, I., & Onghena, P. (2008). An R package for single-case randomization tests. *Behavior Research Methods, 40,* 467–478. doi:10.3758/BRM.40.2.467

Bulté, I., & Onghena, P. (2009). Randomization tests for multiple-baseline designs: An extension of the SCRT-R package. *Behavior Research Methods, 41,* 477–485. doi:10.3758/BRM.41.2.477

Busk, P. L., & Serlin, R. C. (1992). Meta-analysis for single-case research. In T. R. Kratochwill & J. R. Levin (Eds.), *Single-case research design and analysis* (pp. 187–212). Hillsdale, NJ: Erlbaum.

Campbell, D. T., & Fiske, D. W. (1959). Convergent and discriminant validation by the multitrait-multimethod matrix. *Psychological Bulletin, 56,* 81–105. doi:10.1037/h0046016

Carnine, D. W. (1976). Effects of two teacher-presentation rates on off-task behavior, answering correctly, and participation. *Journal of Applied Behavior Analysis, 9,* 199–206. doi:10.1901/jaba.1976.9-199

Cooper, J. O., Heron, T. E., & Heward, W. L. (1987). *Applied behavior analysis.* Columbus, OH: Merrill.

Dugard, P., File, P., & Todman, J. (2012). *Single-case and small-n experimental designs: A practical guide to randomization tests* (2nd ed.). New York, NY: Routledge.

Edgington, E. S. (1975). Randomization tests for one-subject operant experiments. *The Journal of Psychology: Interdisciplinary and Applied, 90,* 57–68. doi:10.1080/00223980.1975.9923926

Edgington, E. S., & Onghena, P. (2007). *Randomization tests* (4th ed.). Boca Raton, FL: Chapman & Hall/CRC Press.

Ferron, J., & Sentovich, C. (2002). Statistical power of randomization tests used with multiple-baseline designs. *Journal of Experimental Education, 70,* 165–178. doi:10.1080/00220970209599504

Gafurov, B. S., & Levin, J. R. (2013). *The single-case data-analysis ExPRT (Excel Package of Randomization Tests),* Version 1.1). Retrieved from http://code.google.com/p/exprt

Gast, D. L. (2010). *Single subject research methodology in behavioral sciences.* New York, NY: Routledge.

Hersen, M., & Barlow, D. H. (1976). *Single-case experimental designs: Strategies for studying behavior change.* New York, NY: Pergamon.

Kennedy, C. H. (2005). *Single case designs for educational research.* Boston, MA: Allyn & Bacon.

Koehler, M. J., & Levin, J. R. (1998). Regulated randomization: A potentially sharper analytical toll for the multiple-baseline design. *Psychological Methods, 3,* 206–217. doi:10.1037/1082-989X.3.2.206

Koehler, M. J., & Levin, J. R. (2000). RegRand: Statistical software for the multiple-baseline design. *Behavior Research Methods, Instruments & Computers, 32,* 367–371. doi:10.3758/BF03207807

Kratochwill, T. R., & Asmus, J. M. (2013). *System-level analysis of evidence-based intervention implementation by problem solving teams* (Grant FDA 84.324). Washington, DC: U.S. Department of Education.

Kratochwill, T. R., Hitchcock, J. H., Horner, R. H., Levin, J. R., Odom, S. L., Rindskopf, D. M., & Shadish, W. R. (2013). Single-case intervention research design standards. *Remedial and Special Education, 34,* 26–38. doi:10.1177/0741932512452794

Levin, J. R. (1992). Single-case research design and analysis: Comments and concerns. In T. R. Kratochwill & J. R. Levin (Eds.), *Single-case research design and analysis: New developments for psychology and education* (pp. 213–224). Hillsdale, NJ: Erlbaum.

Levin, J. R. (1994). Crafting educational intervention research that's both credible and creditable. *Educational Psychology Review, 6*, 231–243. doi:10.1007/BF02213185

Levin, J. R. (1997). Overcoming feelings of powerlessness in "aging" researchers: A primer on statistical power in analysis of variance designs. *Psychology and Aging, 12*, 84–106. doi:10.1037/0882-7974.12.1.84

Levin, J. R., Ferron, J. M., & Gafurov, B. S. (2014a). *Improved randomization tests for a class of single-case intervention designs.* Unpublished manuscript, University of Arizona, Tucson.

Levin, J. R., Ferron, J. M., & Gafurov, B. S. (2014b). *Modification and extension of Revusky's rank test for single-case multiple-baseline designs.* Unpublished manuscript, University of Arizona, Tucson.

Levin, J. R., Marascuilo, L. A., & Hubert, L. J. (1978). N = nonparametric randomization tests. In T. R. Kratochwill (Ed.), *Single subject research: Strategies for evaluating change* (pp. 167–196). New York, NY: Academic Press.

Levin, J. R., & Wampold, B. E. (1999). Generalized single-case randomization tests: Flexible analyses for a variety of situations. *School Psychology Quarterly, 14*, 59–93. doi:10.1037/h0088998

Marascuilo, L. A., & Busk, P. L. (1988). Combining statistics for multiple-baseline AB and replicated ABAB designs across subjects. *Behavioral Assessment, 10*, 1–28.

McReynolds, L. V., & Kearns, K. P. (1983). *Single-subject experimental designs in communicative disorders.* Baltimore, MD: University Park Press.

Onghena, P. (1992). Randomization tests for extensions and variations of ABAB single-case experimental designs: A rejoinder. *Behavioral Assessment, 14*, 153–171.

Poling, A., Methot, L. L., & LeSage, M. G. (1995). *Fundamentals of behavior analytic research.* New York, NY: Plenum Press.

Revusky, S. H. (1967). Some statistical treatments compatible with individual organism methodology. *Journal of the Experimental Analysis of Behavior, 10*, 319–330. doi:10.1901/jeab.1967.10-319

Richards, S., Taylor, R. L., Ramasamy, R., & Richards, R. Y. (1999). *Single subject research: Applications in educational and clinical settings.* San Diego, CA: Singular Publishing Group.

Shabani, D. B., Katz, R. C., Wilder, D. A., Beauchamp, K., Taylor, C. R., & Fischer, K. J. (2002). Increasing social initiations in children with autism: Effects of a tactile prompt. *Journal of Applied Behavior Analysis, 35*, 79–83. doi:10.1901/jaba.2002.35-79

Sidman, M. (1960). *Tactics of scientific research: Evaluating experimental data in psychology.* New York, NY: Basic Books.

Smith, J. D., Borckardt, J. J., & Nash, M. R. (2012). Inferential precision in single-case time-series data streams: How well does the EM procedure perform when missing observations occur in autocorrelated data? *Behavior Therapy, 43*, 679–685. doi:10.1016/j.beth.2011.10.001

Wampold, B., & Worsham, N. (1986). Randomization tests for multiple-baseline designs. *Behavioral Assessment, 8*, 135–143.

7

Using Multilevel Models to Analyze Single-Case Design Data

David M. Rindskopf and John M. Ferron

Much of the discussion of statistical models for single-case designs (SCDs) has focused on the application of single-level models (e.g., regression and time-series models) that have been developed to analyze the interrupted time-series data from a single case (e.g., Glass, Willson, & Gottman, 1975; Huitema & McKean, 2000; Maggin et al., 2011). In many single-case studies, however, there are actually multiple cases (Shadish & Sullivan, 2011), such as with multiple-baseline, replicated ABAB, or replicated alternating treatment designs (see Chapter 1, this volume). When time-series data from multiple cases are available, a separate single-level analysis could be made for each case, but it is also possible to examine all cases simultaneously using a multi-level model, where part of the model describes the behavior of each case and another part of the model describes the commonalities and differences among cases (e.g., Nugent, 1996; Shadish & Rindskopf, 2007; Shadish, Rindskopf, & Hedges, 2008; Van den Noortgate & Onghena, 2003a, 2007).

In doing so, multilevel modeling allows researchers to answer a wider range of research questions than single-level models. In addition to address-ing questions about how large the treatment effect is for a particular case and how the treatment effect changes over time for that case, multilevel models also allow researchers to address questions about the average treatment effect and how that average effect changes over time. Furthermore, questions can be addressed about the degree to which the treatment effect varies across cases and whether this variation can be explained by characteristics of the cases. The ability to address a variety of specific questions can also be seen as an advantage of multilevel models over randomization tests (Chapter 5, this volume). Single-case randomization tests lead to general inferences about whether there was an intervention effect, but not to more specific inferences

The first author gratefully acknowledges support from Institute of Educational Sciences Grants R305D100046 and H324U050001, and the second author gratefully acknowledges support from Institute of Educational Sciences Grant R305D110024.

http://dx.doi.org/10.1037/14376-008
Single-Case Intervention Research: Methodological and Statistical Advances, by T. R. Kratochwill and J. R. Levin

about the size of the effect, how the effect changes over time, and how the effect varies across persons.

A limitation of multilevel models is that to obtain these more specific inferences, a set of distributional assumptions needs to be made. For example, (a) is the variance the same in baseline and treatment phases? (b) Is the variance the same across participants? (c) Can a normal distribution be assumed? (d) Can the residuals within a case be considered independent or is a dependent error structure more appropriate? Ideally, researchers know the answers to questions like these a priori, but if not, they may turn to their data for guidance. Unfortunately, in many situations the data available are not sufficient to provide definitive answers to these types of questions. In such circumstances, researchers may use sensitivity analyses to estimate the model multiple times under alternative plausible sets of assumptions. If the inferences of interest remain substantially the same across the different plausible sets of assumptions, the conclusions are strengthened.

Note that multilevel models not only require more assumptions than randomization tests, but also require more assumptions than the single-level models. By making additional assumptions across cases, multilevel models not only extend the range of research questions that can be addressed, but they capitalize on similarities among the cases, which can lead to better inferences about the specific cases, particularly when the additional assumptions are accurate. Also of note, multilevel models have the flexibility to accommodate a variety of modeling challenges that may arise in single-case studies, such as (a) the need to account for outcomes that are counts or proportions, (b) the need to consider potential dependencies among errors (e.g., autocorrelation), and (c) the need to model linear or nonlinear trends. The recognition of the flexibility of these models and their compatibility with the research goals of many single-case researchers motivated the writing of this chapter.

Our focus is on analyses of data from primary studies, as opposed to meta-analyses, and thus we focus on two-level models, where observations are nested within cases, such as what would result from a multiple-baseline design, a replicated ABAB design, or a replicated alternating treatments design. Those interested in meta-analytic multilevel models for single-case data are referred to extensions of the two-level models to three levels, where observations are nested within cases and cases are nested within studies (Moeyaert, Ugille, Ferron, Beretvas, & Van den Noortgate, 2013; Owens & Ferron, 2012; Van den Noortgate & Onghena, 2008), and to multilevel analyses where effect-size measures are computed for each case and these effect sizes are then modeled as nested within studies (Ugille, Moeyaert, Beretvas, Ferron, & Van den Noortgate, 2012; Van den Noortgate & Onghena, 2003b, 2008).

In the course of this discussion we frequently refer to the effect size of a treatment. This reference typically means the treatment effect in terms of raw score units, or rates, proportions, or odds. These units allow researchers to represent results in terms that are easily understandable. A different perspective is needed when the results of many studies are combined; then the effects need to be expressed in standardized units so that studies using different outcomes can be appropriately compared. One such effect size for combining studies is d, the effect size discussed in other chapters of this book.

We begin our treatment of multilevel models with a relatively simple two-level model, which could be used for analyzing data from a multiple-baseline design, where the outcome is continuous and there are no trends in either the baseline or treatment phases. We then move through a series of increasingly more complex applications where we illustrate the inclusion of trends, accommodations for designs with more than two phases, extensions to adapt the model for counts (using the Poisson distribution) and proportions (using the binomial distribution), a Bayesian model to solve some of the problems of small sample size, and a method for examining gradual change between phases using a non-linear model. By considering a wide range of SCD applications and various levels of complexity, we hope to highlight both the advantages and limitations of multilevel models and, in doing so, facilitate the consideration of these models by SCD researchers. Those who would like to see examples illustrating statistical software commands and the resulting output are referred to Nagler, Rindskopf, and Shadish (2008).

Model With No Time Effect and Two Phases

Let us consider a simple example of a multiple-baseline design with several participants. Each person has a baseline phase and a treatment phase, begun at different time points to satisfy the replication requirement of this design. Suppose that during each phase there is no trend up or down over time, but that there is a jump going from one phase to another. We treat first the case of a continuous outcome that is normally distributed within each phase. Data consistent with this general scenario are presented graphically in Figure 7.1.

We begin with the model for each individual's behavior; for person j we let y_{ij} be the response at time i. Similarly for each time point we let x_{ij} be the phase of person j at time i, which will be a value of 0 for the baseline phase points, and 1 for treatment phase points. In other words, x_{ij} is a dummy variable representing phase. We let r_{ij} be the residual. The level-1 model is written

$$y_{ij} = \beta_{0j} + \beta_{1j} x_{ij} + r_{ij}. \quad (7.1)$$

During baseline phase, $x_{ij} = 0$, and so the expected response for the jth person during baseline is β_{0j}. This is illustrated graphically in Figure 7.1, where the baseline level for the first participant is 70 ($\beta_{01} = 70$), for the second participant 60 ($\beta_{02} = 60$), and for the third participant 65 ($\beta_{03} = 65$). During treatment phase, $x_{ij} = 1$, so the expected response for the jth person is $\beta_{0j} + \beta_{1j}$, which means that β_{1j} is the jump between phases for the jth person. This jump can be thought of as the person-specific treatment effect. In Figure 7.1 we see the treatment effects for the three participants are –50, –40, and –55, respectively (i.e., $\beta_{11} = -50$, $\beta_{12} = -40$, and $\beta_{13} = -55$).

The residual r_{ij} is the difference between the observed value at the ith point in time for the jth person and what would be expected given the model. These residuals can be seen visually in Figure 7.1 as the vertical gaps between the points in the graph (observed values) and the lines (expected values based on

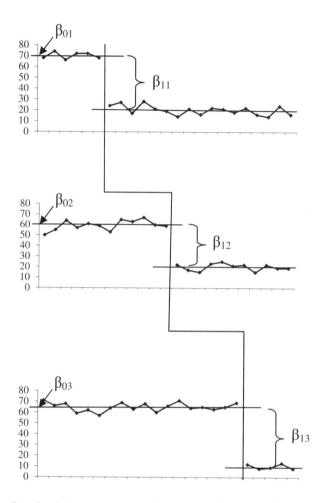

Figure 7.1. Graph of data for a hypothetical multiple-baseline study illustrating parameters in the multilevel model.

the model), i.e., $r_{ij} = y_{ij} - (\beta_{0j} + \beta_{1j}x_{ij})$. For example, the first observation for the first participant in Figure 7.1 is 68, but the expected baseline level is 70, and thus the residual for this observation is −2. With a continuous outcome variable, like we are currently considering, the residuals are typically assumed to be sampled independently from a normal distribution with variance σ^2. If so, there is a single variance parameter (i.e., σ^2) to be estimated for the level-1 model.

There are situations, however, where a more complex level-1 error structure may be warranted. For example, the treatment may be expected not only to shift the level of responding, but also to reduce the variance in responding, in which case the treatment phase variance would be different from the baseline variance. In other contexts the variance may be assumed to differ across participants. Multilevel models that group the level-1 residuals and provide separate variance estimates for the different groups have been proposed and illustrated (Baek & Ferron, 2013).

Another type of complexity is encountered when researchers assume nonindependent, as opposed to independent, residuals. Researchers may think, for example, that for each participant the residuals that are closer together in time are more likely to be similar than the residuals that are further apart in time, suggesting a nonindependent (or autocorrelated) error structure. In such circumstances, researchers using multilevel models can choose from a variety of possible error structures, including first-order autoregressive, Toeplitz, and banded Toeplitz structures (Baek & Ferron, 2013; Ferron, Bell, Hess, Rendina-Gobioff, & Hibbard, 2009).

Just because it is possible to model the error structure as autocorrelated doesn't mean that researchers should. There is no agreement among methodologists regarding whether residuals from behavioral time-series should be, or are, autocorrelated (Ferron, 2002; Huitema & McKean, 1998; Kratochwill et al., 1974; Matyas & Greenwood, 1997; Shadish & Sullivan, 2011), and thus no consensus about how the level-1 error structure should be modeled. Furthermore, residuals that are independent can appear to be autocorrelated as a result of misspecifying another part of the model (e.g., modeling a nonlinear trend as linear), and conversely, residuals that are autocorrelated may appear to be independent because of imprecision in the estimation. Our advice is to think carefully about the case being studied, the behavior being observed, and the spacing between the observations, and to ask whether there is reason to believe that residuals should be independent or autocorrelated, and then to model accordingly. If it is unclear, researchers could consider a sensitivity analysis to assess the degree to which the primary inferences of the study (e.g., inferences about the size of the treatment effect) are sensitive to the assumptions made about the level-1 error structure. (In a sensitivity analysis, one changes a peripheral aspect of the analysis and sees how much the main results are affected. For example, one could make different assumptions about the value of the autocorrelation and see whether the effect size or standard errors are greatly affected.)

Now that we have considered specification of the level-1 model, we turn to the level-2 model that allows us to model the variation between participants. The values of β_{0j} and β_{1j} may be the same across participants, or they may vary. A simple level-2 model that allows for differences among participants, but does not attempt to explain that variation, is used as a starting point. There is one equation for each β:

$$\beta_{0j} = \gamma_{00} + u_{0j} \quad (7.2)$$

$$\beta_{1j} = \gamma_{10} + u_{1j} \quad (7.3)$$

The γ parameters are the average values. More specifically, γ_{00} is the average baseline level (referring to Figure 7.1 it would be the average of β_{01}, β_{02}, and β_{03}), and γ_{10} is the average treatment effect (referring to Figure 7.1 it would be the average of β_{11}, β_{12}, and β_{13}). Thus, the estimate of γ_{10} could be used to address questions regarding the size of the average treatment effect. Each equation in this level-2 model also has a residual term, where u_{0j} is the difference between the jth person's baseline level (β_{0j}) and the average baseline level (γ_{00}), and u_{1j} is the difference between the jth person's treatment effect (β_{1j}) and the average treatment effect (γ_{10}), and therefore the u_{ij} show that an individual might vary above or below that average. It is typically assumed that pairs of level-2 residuals (u_{0j}, u_{1j}) are sampled independently from a multivariate normal distribution. The u_{0j} have variance τ_{00}, the u_{1j} have variance τ_{11}, and their covariance is τ_{01}.

To some degree we are limited by the small sample size in explaining differences across participants, and may not be able to explain variation among them, but if the sample size is large enough, we could include an explanatory variable (either categorical or continuous) to explain variation in the β_{0j} or β_{1j}. Suppose we think that age is a factor that explains variation, and that the average participant is 10 years old. We center age by defining Age10 = Age − 10, and add Age10 as a predictor:

$$\beta_{0j} = \gamma_{00} + \gamma_{01}Age10_{ij} + u_{0j}; \quad (7.4)$$

$$\beta_{1j} = \gamma_{10} + \gamma_{11}Age10_{ij} + u_{1j}. \quad (7.5)$$

In these equations γ_{01} is the amount of change in the baseline level for each year of age, and γ_{11} is the change in treatment effect for each year of age.

Fixed Versus Random Effects

Unexplained variation (residuals) among participants (subjects) is represented by a random effect u_{0j} (with variance τ_{00}) for intercepts and u_{1j} (with variance τ_{11}) for slopes. Problems with this assumption include (a) the residuals may not be normally distributed, as is often assumed; (b) they may be not be well-estimated if there are only a few participants (say two or three); and (c) it may be questionable whether we consider the participants to be a random sample from any population. An alternative is to consider subjects as fixed; instead of fitting a multilevel model, we would fit an ordinary regression model to all the observations, and have variables (either dummy coded or effects coded) representing subjects. Further, we could have interactions of treatment phase with subjects to test whether the effect of treatment is the same across all participants.

Normally, using variables for subjects in this way would waste degrees of freedom and would suggest that multilevel models be used; however, with two or three participants it makes little difference and does not require the assumptions of normality that multilevel models usually implement. We can make inferences about the participants in a study, and whether each is similar to the others in the study. We lose some accuracy in doing this, as Bayesian methods make use of all the data without restricting the estimate to be the same for each person.

The basic two-level model that we have presented here has been studied using Monte Carlo simulation methods for a variety of multiple-baseline study conditions (e.g., four cases with 20 observations per case). The results of these simulation studies suggest that when the model is correctly specified, (a) the estimates of the average treatment effect (and other γ coefficients) are unbiased and that the corresponding inferences are accurate when either the Satterthwaite or Kenward–Roger method (Kenward & Roger, 1997) is used to estimate degrees of freedom, but (b) the restricted maximum likelihood estimates of the variance parameters tend to be biased (Ferron et al., 2009). In addition, the empirical Bayes estimates of the individual effects (β_{1j}) are biased as expected, but the interval estimates for these individual effects are accurate, assuming that the model is correctly specified and the Kenward-Roger approach is used for making the inferences (Ferron, Farmer, & Owens, 2010).

Adding a Time Trend

Adding a time trend is straightforward (statistically) if it is a constant time trend, that is, it does not change across phases. As will be seen, there are conceptual difficulties with including trend, but in terms of the equations it just means adding a time trend to the equation for individuals:

$$y_{ij} = \beta_{0j} + \beta_{1j}x_{ij} + \beta_{2j}t_{ij} + r_{ij}. \qquad (7.6)$$

In this equation t_{ij} represents the time (generally session number) for the observation at time i for person j. Consequently, β_{2j} represents the slope of the growth trajectory for person j, or the expected change in the outcome for each unit increase in time. The common slope across phases is illustrated in Figure 7.2, which provides a graphical display and visual representation of each of the regression coefficients in Equation 7.6. Because the baseline and treatment slopes are assumed to be equal, the vertical gap between the two parallel lines in Figure 7.2 stays constant over time. This gap represents the treatment effect, or shift in behavior that occurred with treatment, and is indexed by β_{1j}.

Finally, β_{0j} is the expected response when both the treatment variable and the time variable are equal to zero. In Figure 7.2, time is coded such that 0 corresponds to the first baseline observation and the treatment variable is dummy coded so that baseline observations are coded 0. Consequently, β_{0j} is the expected response at the start of the study. If the researcher wanted β_{0j} to represent the baseline measure at the end of baseline period, we have to scale time separately for each individual by subtracting the time at which the phase changes. For example, if time is measured in number of sessions, and the first person has 12 baseline sessions before changing to treatment, then we must calculate $t12 = t - 12$, so that $t12$ will be zero when $t = 12$. Of course, in a multiple-baseline design every person will have the phase change at a different session, and will need a different constant subtracted to produce the right transform of time.

Most SCDs will not include a constant time trend, because a baseline phase should continue until a trend is no longer present. However, it is possible for a flat baseline to be followed by a trend during treatment phase, or a trend in

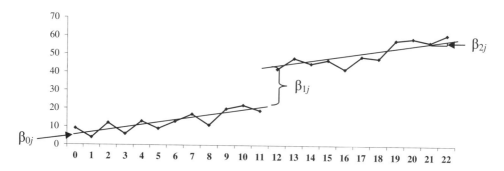

Figure 7.2. Graph of data for the jth participant, showing the parameters defining the growth trajectory defined in Equation 7.6, which models a shift in levels between phases and a constant linear change within each phase.

baseline to be followed by a different (or no) trend in the treatment phase. Therefore, allowing for a change in trend would be necessary under those conditions. This assessment can be accomplished by adding an interaction term to the model that allows the time effect to depend on treatment. More specifically, we would create a new variable representing the product of the dummy-coded variable representing phase (x_{ij}) and a centered version of the time variable ($t_{ij} - k_j$):

$$y_{ij} = \beta_{0j} + \beta_{1j}x_{ij} + \beta_{2j}\left(t_{ij} - k_j\right) + \beta_{3j}x_{ij}\left(t_{ij} - k_j\right) + r_{ij}. \quad (7.7)$$

A visual representation of the parameters in this model is provided in Figure 7.3. For this illustration we coded the variables as follows: t_{ij} is coded 1 at the beginning of the study, and k_j corresponds to the value of t_{ij} for the first observation in the treatment phase for person j, so that $t_{ij} - k_j = 0$ for the first treatment observation. With this coding, β_{0j} is the projected baseline value for person j at the time point that coincides with the first treatment observation, β_{1j} is the expected immediate shift in behavior for person j (i.e., the vertical gap between the extension of the baseline trajectory and the treatment phase trajectory at the time of the first treatment observation), β_{2j} is the slope during baseline for person j, and β_{3j} is the change in slope that occurs with treatment for person j.

A trend will not continue forever and so it is an oversimplification to use this model; we will see that nonlinear models sometimes offer a better solution. If we do use this oversimplified model, we have to consider what measure of treatment effect we want. In our illustration we have two parameters related to the treatment effect: β_{1j} is the immediate treatment effect, and β_{3j} provides information on how the treatment effect changes with time. In Figure 7.3 we see that the gap between the baseline extension and the treatment phase trajectory increases with time, indicating that the effect of the treatment is greater at the end of the study then it was one observation into treatment. At what point in time should we measure the effect of treatment? Should we have measured the effect at the end of all treatment sessions as opposed to measuring it after a

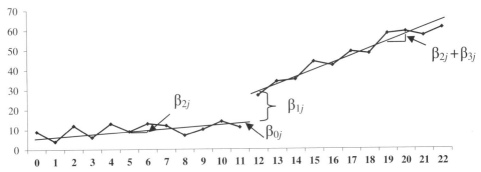

Figure 7.3. Graph of data for the jth participant, showing the parameters defining a growth trajectory as defined in Equation 7.7, which models a change in level and a change in slope.

single treatment session? Perhaps in many cases, five sessions into treatment would be reasonable, but in all cases some judgment is required on the part of the researcher. Whatever the choice, it is implemented by centering time at the point decided on; for example, if the phase change is at Session 7 for person j and we want to go 5 sessions beyond to measure treatment effect, then we code $t_{ij} - k_j$ as $t_{ij} - 12$.

Changing time effects within a phase involves problems, both statistical and conceptual. In general, it is difficult to think of a trend that would continue for any length of time; generally one expects behavior to level off. Also, many measures are limited by zero at the lower end, and frequently have upper limits as well. For a short time period, behavior may show a linear trend, but we cannot project that linear behavior very far into the future.

Other Designs

With a more complicated design, handling the coding of time becomes more complicated also. The most common design besides the multiple-baseline is ABAB, which we will write as A1 B1 A2 B2 in order to track the change from the first AB sequence to the second. The most obvious way to code phases in this design is to have one dummy variable for baseline versus treatment, another dummy variable for first sequence versus second sequence, and the product of these for the interaction. If there is no trend, or if trend is constant across phases, then this works well; if there is varying trend, then this coding is problematic. Some options are considered later.

Another common SCD is the alternating treatment design. In this design, treatments are changed frequently, perhaps chosen by a coin flip for each session. There are no long phases, and so one cannot model change in trend within phases. The simplest trend would be an overall trend line, or in more complicated cases perhaps a quadratic (degree two polynomial) to allow a curve over time. A model with linear trend is analogous to an analysis of covariance; the lines for the different treatments are parallel, so the difference between the lines (effect of treatment) is a constant. If the lines are not parallel, the analyst must decide at what time point to measure the treatment effect. For example, if there are 15 time points, and the desired assessment of treatment effect is the end of the study, compute sess15 = session − 15, and use sess15 instead of session as the time variable. More complicated cases would require treatment-by-trend interactions to allow the lines to have different slopes for different treatments.

Issues About Coding Phases of Treatment

With ABAB (and more complicated) designs the most obvious way to code phases is to have a main effect for treatment (A vs. B), a main effect for whether the first AB pair is observed or second AB pair, and an interaction. These effects are traditionally coded using effects coding (1/0/−1 coding in general, and 1/−1 with only two conditions).

The coding for this design would be

$$
\begin{bmatrix} \mu_{A1} \\ \mu_{B1} \\ \mu_{A2} \\ \mu_{B2} \end{bmatrix} = \begin{bmatrix} 1 & 1 & 1 & 1 \\ 1 & -1 & 1 & -1 \\ 1 & 1 & -1 & -1 \\ 1 & -1 & -1 & 1 \end{bmatrix} \begin{bmatrix} \beta_0 \\ \beta_1 \\ \beta_2 \\ \beta_3 \end{bmatrix}, \quad (7.8)
$$

where the four columns of the model matrix represent the intercept, the treatment main effect, the main effect of first versus second set of phases, and the interaction of treatment and phase set.

Such coding can be useful, but other methods should be considered as well. First, suppose that we want to represent the difference between the two baselines, and the difference between the two treatment effects. To represent the coding, we will use matrix notation first, then expand that to individual equations to better see the interpretation. The coding is written in matrix form as

$$
\begin{bmatrix} \mu_{A1} \\ \mu_{B1} \\ \mu_{A2} \\ \mu_{B2} \end{bmatrix} = \begin{bmatrix} 1 & 0 & 0 & 0 \\ 1 & 1 & 0 & 0 \\ 1 & 0 & 1 & 0 \\ 1 & 1 & 1 & 1 \end{bmatrix} \begin{bmatrix} \beta_0 \\ \beta_1 \\ \beta_2 \\ \beta_3 \end{bmatrix}. \quad (7.9)
$$

The separate equations are

$$\mu_{A1} = \beta_0 \quad (7.10)$$

$$\mu_{B1} = \beta_0 + \beta_1 \quad (7.11)$$

$$\mu_{A2} = \beta_0 + \beta_2 \quad (7.12)$$

$$\mu_{B2} = \beta_0 + \beta_1 + \beta_2 + \beta_3 \quad (7.13)$$

We recognize this coding as the usual main effects and interaction, but using dummy coding rather than effects coding. β_0 is the first baseline average; β_1 the jump at the introduction of the first treatment; β_2 is the difference between A1 and A2 (the two baseline phases); and through rearrangement and substitution of terms β_3 can be seen to be the difference between the first treatment effect (B1 − A1) and the second treatment effect (B2 − A2):

$$(\mu_{B2} - \mu_{A2}) - (\mu_{B1} - \mu_{A1}) =$$

$$\mu_{A1} - \mu_{B1} - \mu_{A2} + \mu_{B2} =$$

$$\beta_0 - (\beta_0 + \beta_1) - (\beta_0 + \beta_2) + (\beta_0 + \beta_1 + \beta_2 + \beta_3) =$$

$$\beta_3.$$

As this example illustrates, changing from one type of coding to another changes the interpretation of the parameters. For this reason, one should always proceed from the effects wanted to the coding; by first specifying what the parameters should mean, one can write the coding to represent them correctly (see Serlin & Levin, 1985).

Next consider coding that would represent differences between successive phases. For successive changes, the coding is

$$\begin{bmatrix} \mu_{A1} \\ \mu_{B1} \\ \mu_{A2} \\ \mu_{B2} \end{bmatrix} = \begin{bmatrix} 1 & 0 & 0 & 0 \\ 1 & 1 & 0 & 0 \\ 1 & 1 & 1 & 0 \\ 1 & 1 & 1 & 1 \end{bmatrix} \begin{bmatrix} \beta_0 \\ \beta_1 \\ \beta_2 \\ \beta_3 \end{bmatrix}. \qquad (7.14)$$

When written as separate equations, this becomes

$$\mu_{A1} = \beta_0 \qquad (7.15)$$

$$\mu_{B1} = \beta_0 + \beta_1 \qquad (7.16)$$

$$\mu_{A2} = \beta_0 + \beta_1 + \beta_2 \qquad (7.17)$$

$$\mu_{B2} = \beta_0 + \beta_1 + \beta_2 + \beta_3 \qquad (7.18)$$

From this representation, it is clear that β_0 represents the level during Phase A1; β_1 is the change in going from Phase A1 to Phase B1; β_2 the change from B1 to A2; and β_3 the change from A2 to B2.

For alternating treatment designs with three or more conditions, there is a choice of coding methods. For example, if there is a baseline and two treatment conditions (B, T1, and T2), one might code two dummy variables, one for T1 compared to baseline and the other for T2 compared to baseline. Another possibility would be to have one dummy variable for treatment versus baseline (with T1 and T2 coded 1, baseline coded 0), and an effect-coded term comparing treatment 1 with treatment 2 (with B coded 0, T1 coded 1/2, and T2 coded –1/2). This would result in the model

$$\mu_B = \beta_0$$

$$\mu_{T1} = \beta_0 + \beta_1 + .5\beta_2 \qquad (7.19)$$

$$\mu_{T2} = \beta_0 + \beta_1 - .5\beta_2$$

where it is easy to see that $\beta_0 = \mu_B$, and adding the second and third equations and dividing by two, and subtracting equation one, one sees that $\beta_1 = \dfrac{\mu_{T1} + \mu_{T2}}{2} - \mu_B$ and subtracting equation three from equation two results in $\beta_2 = \mu_{T1} - \mu_{T2}$.

Issues in Coding Subjects as Fixed Effects

With few participants, we are faced with a choice of using multilevel models (in which case variations among subjects are random effects), or models in which subjects are fixed effects. In the latter case we must code the subjects to reflect differences among them. Suppose there are three subjects; we could use dummy coding (0/1 coding) to represent subjects (e.g., let S1 = 1 if Subject 1, 0 if Subject 2 or 3). If an intercept is included in the model, we would use only two of the three dummy variables, say S2 and S3, letting the intercept represent S1 (and S2 and S3 the difference between Subjects 2 and 3 and Subject 1).

As seen in an example here, it sometimes makes more sense to use effects (1/0/–1) coding, even though it is not as transparent in interpretation. For example, let the three subjects be coded as follows:

$$\begin{bmatrix} \mu_1 \\ \mu_2 \\ \mu_3 \end{bmatrix} = \begin{bmatrix} 1 & 0 & 0 \\ 1 & 0 & 0 \\ 1 & -1 & -1 \end{bmatrix} \begin{bmatrix} \beta_0 \\ \beta_1 \\ \beta_2 \end{bmatrix}. \qquad (7.20)$$

Written out as separate equations, this is

$$\mu_1 = \beta_0 + \beta_1$$

$$\mu_2 = \beta_0 + \beta_2 \qquad (7.21)$$

$$\mu_3 = \beta_0 - \beta_1 - \beta_2$$

Adding the three equations together and dividing by 3, we see that β_0 is the average for the three subjects. Taking the first equation and subtracting β_0 from both sides, we see that β_1 is the amount by which Subject 1 differs from the average of all subjects; similarly β_2 is the amount by which Subject 2 differs from the overall average. This coding is particularly useful when we want to compare the random effects multilevel model to the comparable fixed effects model.

Dependent Variables That Are Counts

A frequent outcome variable in SCD research is counts, either over a time period or out of some total number of trials. Count outcomes are often disguised as rates or proportions and treated as continuous. Under some circumstances, treating counts (or transforms of counts) as continuous does not create severe problems, but other times it results in major errors in analysis. First, the measures should not result in floor or ceiling effects. For example, counts that cluster around zero, or percentages near zero or 100 percent, result in nonlinearity and heterogeneity of variance. Counts can display heterogeneity of variance if small counts have small variance and large counts have larger variance. Because there are so many ways in which counts can create problems, it is best to treat counts correctly rather than assume normality and analyze them as continuous measures.

First let us consider the case of counts for a period of time, for example, the number of times that a child hits another child during the period of observation. We suppose for this example that the time of observation is the same for each period and the same for each child, but if it is not, then a simple adjustment can be made to this method. Consider again the multiple-baseline design with no effect of time (zero slope). The model is now expressed in terms of the natural logarithm of the counts, F_{ij}, for individual i observed in session j:

$$\ln(F_{ij}) = \beta_{0j} + \beta_{1j}x_{ij}, \qquad (7.22)$$

whereas before x_{ij} indicates whether this child is in the baseline or treatment phase. There is no residual in this equation because F_{ij} is the expected frequency, and the observed count y_{ij} has a Poisson distribution with mean F_{ij}.

The parameters are now interpreted in the logarithmic scale; to translate back into the original scale we must exponentiate. For example, if $\beta_{0j} = 3$ for child j, and $\beta_{1j} = -2$, then the average baseline count for the child would be $\exp(3) = 20.09$, and the average during treatment phase would be $\exp(3\text{-}2) = \exp(1) = 2.72$. Another way to express this is to note that

$$F_{ij} = \exp(\beta_{0j} + \beta_{1j}x_{ij})$$
$$= \exp(\beta_{0j})\exp(\beta_{1j}x_{ij})$$
$$= \exp(3)\exp(-2)$$
$$= (20.09)(0.13533) = 2.718$$

In other words, the original behavior was about 20 hits per session, which was reduced by treatment to .135 of its original value, becoming a rate of under three hits per session.

For data in the form of percentages or proportions, the modeling is of the raw counts. One must go back to the form of actual counts (e.g., 6 events out of 10 trials, not 60%). After all, 60 percent could be 3 out of 5, or 300 out of 500, and one is much less precisely estimated than the other. The statistical model for each individual is expressed in the form

$$\pi_{ij} = F_{ij}/n_{ij}$$

$$\ln\left(\frac{\pi_{ij}}{1-\pi_{ij}}\right) = \beta_{0j} + \beta_{1j}x_{ij},$$

(7.23)

where is n_{ij} the number of trials, and F_{ij} is the number of trials on which the behavior of interest was observed. As with continuous outcomes, we can add a time trend, or we can extend the model to handle an ABAB design.

Another type of dependent variable closely related to count data is ordinal data. Perhaps each respondent is rated on a scale from 0 to 3, with 0 being *no problems* and 3 being *major problems*. This type of data is easily analyzed by common multilevel programs; the assumption is that a continuous normally distributed unobserved variable underlies the observed categorical variable. It is an extension of the logistic regression model, for which each possible cut of "low" and "high" is used as a dependent variable. For example, the possible divisions for a 0 to 3 scale would be {0} vs. {1, 2, 3}, {0, 1} vs. {2, 3}, and {0, 1, 2} vs. {3}. A logistic regression is conducted for each possible division; the usual restriction made is that all of the logistic regressions have the same slopes, but different intercepts. The model is usually written as

$$\ln\left(\frac{\pi_{low}}{1-\pi_{low}}\right) = \beta_{0j} - \eta,$$

(7.24)

where η is a linear combination of the predictor variables, and where "low" indicates being at or below category j of the outcome variable. Note that η is subtracted instead of added, because the model is (usually) expressed in terms of responding in a low category rather than a higher category, which is usually an undesirable response (in the example below, a low grade rather than a higher grade). A positive value of η means a lower logit, and thus a lower probability of a low grade (a higher probability of a higher grade).

An example comes from Hall, Cristler, Cranston, and Tucker (1970), who studied the effect of treatment (after-school tutoring for students getting a D or F on daily assignments) on quiz score in French assignments. Quizzes were graded with the usual grades of A to F that were coded for data analysis as A = 4, B = 3, C = 2, D = 1, and F = 0. The study involved a multiple-baseline design with three participants, and each participant was observed for 25 days. The data and code for the analyses using the statistical package R are presented in Appendix 7.1. The data are plotted in Figure 7.4.

A visual analysis of the data in Figure 7.4 leads to the conclusion that there is a functional relationship between the intervention and grades. The treatment effect is demonstrated at three separate points in time, first for Dave, then for Roy, and finally for Deb. The data patterns are similar for the three participants. During the baseline phase each participant primarily has grades

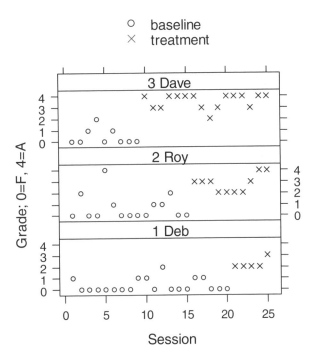

Figure 7.4. An ordered outcome in a multiple-baseline design study. Data from Hall, Cristler, Cranston, and Tucker (1970).

of D and F with an occasional higher grade and no trend toward improvement. The implementation of intervention is followed immediately by a shift to higher grades, with no intervention phase grades below C for any of the participants. Multilevel modeling provides a complement to the visual analysis by allowing us to quantify the size of the intervention effect and to index the uncertainty in our effect inferences.

We first fit two simple models to these data; one is a random effects model, the other a fixed effects model. Both assume that the effect of treatment is the same for all participants. The random effects model assumes that the intercepts may differ across the participants, so that their baselines may differ. The results are presented in Table 7.1.

The threshold coefficients are the intercepts for different dichotomizations of the response variable. The treatment effect is 5.7 on the logit scale, which is exp(5.7) = 297; this is the change in the odds of having a higher versus lower grade (for any dividing point), a very large treatment effect. For example, in the baseline period the "average" participant would have had an odds of exp(1.97) = 7.17 of having a grade of D or F (i.e., 1|2 = grade division of {0, 1} vs. {2, 3, 4}); this corresponds to a probability of exp(1.97)/[1 + exp(1.97)] = 7.17/8.17 = .88. During treatment, that changes to a logit of 1.97 − 5.695 = −3.725, an odds of exp(−3.725) = .024, and a probability of .024/1.024 = .024 of

Table 7.1. Random Effects Analysis of French Quiz Grade Data

Random effects:

	Var	SD
id	0.202	0.4494

Coefficients:

	Estimate	SE	z value	Pr(>|z|)
trt	5.695	1.129	5.042	(.0001

Threshold coefficients:

	Estimate	SE	z value
0|1	0.5743	0.4205	1.366
1|2	1.9717	0.5472	3.603
2|3	4.9382	1.1247	4.391
3|4	6.2675	1.1747	5.335

getting a D or F. From the complementary perspective, during baseline students had a probability of .12 of getting a C or higher; during treatment this increased to a probability of .976.

The variance of the intercepts among participants is .202, corresponding to a standard deviation of .45. If we take seriously the idea that participants might have been randomly selected from some population, then about 95 percent would be within .90 logits (i.e., 2 standard deviations) of the average logit.

The fixed effects version of this model uses effects coding for the respondents (1/0/–1); this version is to ensure that the intercepts (thresholds) represent the average person. The results for the model with main effects only for subjects are presented in Table 7.2. Note that the treatment effect and intercepts have nearly the same estimates, standard errors, and t values as in the random effects model, and so the interpretation is the same. The effect for e1 is Participant 1, who is greater (than the average participant) by about .81, meaning a greater probability of a lower grade during both baseline and treatment. (Remember that these effects are subtracted, changing the sign, so it will enter the equation as –.81.) To determine the effect for Participant 3, note that the effects must sum to zero, so the effect is –(.81-.05) = –.76. To get the standard error, we would have to change the coding to include Participant 3; to get an approximate standard error, we could assume that it would be about the same as for the other participants' effect-coding standard errors, or about .33.

As a test of whether the effect of treatment is the same for all three participants, we will fit the fixed effects model with treatment by subject interactions. The results are presented in Table 7.3. The quantity labeled "Residual Deviance" can be thought of as measure of goodness of fit (more properly, badness of fit: big is worse). By itself, it cannot be interpreted intuitively, but if we subtract the deviance of a model that is less restricted from the deviance from a model

Table 7.2. Fixed Effects Results for French Quiz Data

Coefficients:

	Value	SE	t value
trt	5.62426	1.1298	4.9783
e1	0.80655	0.3362	2.3988
e2	−0.05175	0.3244	−0.1595

Intercepts:

	Value	SE	t value
0|1	0.4992	0.3334	1.4972
1|2	1.9126	0.4841	3.9505
2|3	4.9467	1.1023	4.4876
3|4	6.3646	1.1556	5.5078

Note. Residual Deviance: 146.5151; AIC: 160.5151

that is more restrictive, the difference has a chi-square distribution with degrees of freedom equal to the number of parameters dropped in the more restricted model. Comparing this model with the model that omits interaction terms gives a result of 146.52 − 140.14 = 6.38, which just exceeds the critical value of 5.99 with two degrees of freedom. This overall test tells us that the treatment effects differ among respondents. Examining the two effects individually, we see that Participant 1 (Deb) is clearly different from the average in her treatment effect.

Table 7.3. Fixed Effects Model With Treatment × Subject Interactions for French Quiz Data

Coefficients:

	Value	SE	t value
trt	5.87684	1.1526	5.0989
e1	−0.06885	0.5196	−0.1325
e2	0.35371	0.4490	0.7878
trt:e1	1.80586	0.7517	2.4024
trt:e2	−0.49750	0.6819	−0.7296

Intercepts:

	Value	SE	t value
0|1	0.6256	0.3367	1.8579
1|2	2.0184	0.4876	4.1397
2|3	5.3118	1.1602	4.5784
3|4	7.0531	1.2588	5.6032

Note. Residual Deviance: 140.1422; AIC: 158.1422

Of course, going from an average that is already so big does not have much of a practical effect.

Bayesian Models

Bayesian ideas provide many benefits, both theoretical and practical. One important aspect in which Bayesian methods improve prediction is in estimating parameters with small amounts of data but when there is auxiliary evidence to aid prediction. For example, sometimes similar quantities must be estimated for all participants, and although each has a separate estimate, the estimates for all participants might be similar. The effect of treatment on each individual is one such quantity. We can "borrow strength" from the other participants when estimating each participant's value of the parameter. In classical statistics we would have to choose between using each participant's data by themselves (with the small sample size) or pooling the data to get one estimate for all participants (losing individual estimates). This issue was referred to above in the discussion of fixed versus random effects.

Another way in which Bayesian estimation is an improvement is by its taking into account all sources of uncertainty in estimation. In most estimation procedures for multilevel models, some quantities are estimated first (usually variances), and then other quantities (typically the fixed effects) are estimated conditional on the variances. This process assumes that the variances are estimated well, which is not so with small sample sizes (number of participants or cases). Autocorrelation is another quantity that is typically estimated and then assumed known in the next stage of estimation, even though autocorrelations are usually poorly estimated in SCDs. Bayesian methods do not require these assumptions.

One does not have to know a lot about Bayesian theory to use Bayesian methods. Two aspects are crucial: prior distributions and posterior distributions. The likelihood function that is used in classical statistics also plays a central role in Bayesian methods. The prior distribution (*prior*) of a parameter summarizes the analyst's beliefs, before seeing any data, about possible values of the parameter. We can make the prior noninformative, meaning that we have no idea about likely values of the parameter, to make the analysis as objective (and similar to the classical analysis) as possible. (In practice, we must make the priors nearly, but not totally, noninformative; this has no practical effect on the model.)

The posterior distribution (*posterior*) combines information about the data (expressed through the likelihood) with information from the prior; if the prior is (relatively) noninformative, the posterior resembles the likelihood. The difference is the interpretation. Because the prior and posterior summarize one's beliefs about a parameter (or several parameters), they are probability distributions and can be interpreted as such. For example, one can calculate the probability that the parameter is greater than zero, or the probability that one treatment is more effective than another, and a 95% interval (called a *credible interval* in Bayesian terminology) can be interpreted as "there is a 95% probability that the parameter is in the interval."

One practical benefit of Bayesian modeling using variants of the BUGS program (WinBUGS [Lunn, Thomas, Best, & Spiegelhalter, 2000]; OpenBUGS [Lunn, Spiegelhalter, Thomas, & Best, 2009]; JAGS [Plummer, 2003]) is that one can fit a wide variety of models that are not standard (see Chapter 8, this volume). This option includes the nonlinear model with floor and ceiling effects that are described in the next section. It is often simple to write a special model that is appropriate for the situation but is not available in standard statistical software.

For categorical data, Bayesian models have the advantage of being able to deal with extreme results (if somewhat informative, rather than uninformative, priors are used). Extreme results (e.g., all zero counts during baseline) can lead to infinite parameter estimates in several kinds of models; a slightly informative prior can modify this to a finite number. This condition not only affects the estimate of the baseline, but also the estimate of the treatment effect, which is the difference between the two phases.

Another practical benefit of these software programs is their ability to keep track of derived quantities, and not only get an estimate of them, but also a standard error (and for that matter to investigate their entire distribution, which may not be normal). As an example, if one wanted to estimate the final level in a multiple-baseline design, one could track the values of $\beta_{0j} + \beta_{1j}$ as separate quantities. Other examples are given in the following section on nonlinear models.

Nonlinear Models

Seldom do data immediately jump to a new steady level when the phase changes. If only one or two sessions are required for the change, we can adapt by leaving those data points out of the analysis. If this is too wasteful of data, or if the change is very gradual, we must consider different models. For example, when the outcome is binomial, as in a previous section, we might expect the data to start at one proportion, then gradually shift and settle down at a new proportion. The flat lines that the proportions settle down to are not likely to be zero and one, so a typical logistic regression model will not work. Instead the lower level (the floor) and the higher level (the ceiling) will have to be estimated in the model. Analysts who are familiar with item response theory (IRT) will recognize the floor effect; it is analogous to the guessing parameter in a three-parameter IRT model. The ceiling effect is similar, but at the top.

Consider the data plotted in Figure 7.5; they are based on data from Horner et al. (2005). The figure shows data from three participants in a multiple-baseline design. A visual analysis of the data in Figure 7.5 leads to the conclusion that there is a functional relationship between the intervention and the proportion of correct trials. The data patterns for the three participants are similar. Each baseline shows a relatively low proportion of correct trials, little variation, and no trend toward improvement. Once the intervention is implemented there is a change in the trend, with each participant showing gradual increases in the proportion of correct trials. Furthermore, the upward trend occurs first with Participant A, second with Participant B, and third with Participant C, mirroring the order that

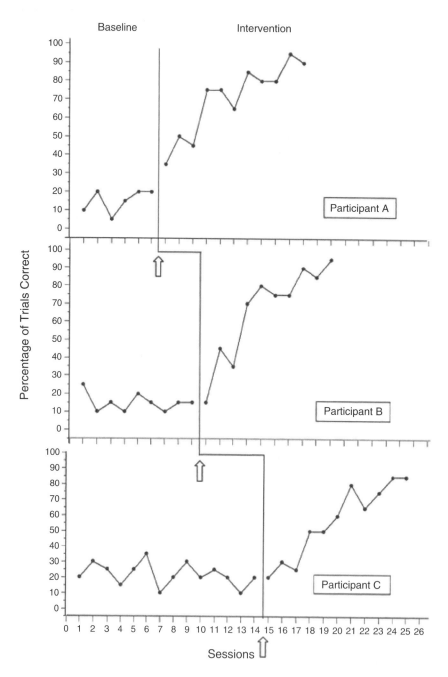

Figure 7.5. Nonlinear trajectories. Arrows indicate the three demonstrations of effect at three different points in time. From "The Use of Single-Subject Research to Identify Evidence-Based Practice in Special Education," by R. H. Horner, E. G. Carr, J. Halle, G. McGee, S. Odom, and M. Wolery, 2005, *Exceptional Children, 71*, p. 170. Copyright 2005 by Council for Exceptional Children. Reprinted with permission.

the intervention was implemented. Multilevel modeling allows us to quantify the size of the intervention effects and also to quantify the uncertainty in our inferences. For example, we would like to be able to index the uncertainty in the effect estimates and the uncertainty in the inference that the order the participants changed matches the order that the intervention was implemented.

To build the model, we start with the usual way of writing the dependent variable:

$$L_{ij} = \beta_{0j} + \beta_{1j} X_{ij}. \quad (7.25)$$

(In the usual logistic regression model, L would be the logit, or log-odds, and it would be that here if it were not for floor and ceiling effects.)

The equation for individual behavior can be expressed as

$$\pi_{ij} = f_j + (c_j - f_j)\exp(L_{ij})/\{1 + \exp(L_{ij})\}, \quad (7.26)$$

where f_j is the floor, c_j is the ceiling, and π_{ij} is the probability of observing the behavior of interest.

This way of writing the model (Equation 7.25) would be fine if we were not interested in the place on the curve where the response occurs. As in IRT, we are interested in the time for which the response has gone halfway between the floor and ceiling. In IRT this is the item difficulty; here we will use H for "halfway point." The halfway point occurs at the value of X that makes $L = 0$; solving for X gives $X = -\beta_{0j}/\beta_{1j}$. We would like to rewrite the equation so that this is a parameter of the model. Rewriting Equation 7.25 gives

$$\begin{aligned} L_{ij} &= \beta_{1j}\{(\beta_{0j}/\beta_{1j}) + X_{ij}\} \\ &= \beta_{1j}(X_{ij} - H_j) \end{aligned} \quad (7.27)$$

Again, this is similar to the form of IRT models. Notice that H is important for determining whether the change occurs at the right time, but that $c - f$ is important because it indicates the size of the effect (change from baseline level to treatment condition level).

Table 7.4 contains the results of fitting the model with floor and ceiling effects to the Horner et al. (2005) data. The ceilings are all around .8 or so, and the floors around .2, with little variation across respondents in either. The treatment effect is the rise from the floor to the ceiling; these effects vary from .57 to .72, again showing similar and large values. An important indicator that change was due to treatment is that the halfway points are in the right places and in the right order. For the first participant the halfway point is between Sessions 8 and 9; for the second, about Session 12; and for the third between Sessions 18 and 19; these are all consistent with when the phase changed. Further, the 95% credible intervals (similar to the confidence interval in classical inference) are fairly narrow, so there is little possibility that the ordering is wrong. This outcome can be directly checked in Bayesian models; the quantities gt21, gt31, and gt32 are based on the number of times in the 25,000 simulations that the

Table 7.4. Results of Fitting a Nonlinear Model With Floor and Ceiling to Horner et al.

Node	M	SD	MC error	2.5%	Mdn	97.5%
ceiling[1]	0.8322	0.04401	0.002131	0.7457	0.8315	0.9203
ceiling[2]	0.874	0.0464	0.002514	0.7828	0.874	0.9637
ceiling[3]	0.7941	0.05725	0.002796	0.6893	0.7919	0.9103
floor[1]	0.168	0.03486	6.979E-4	0.1055	0.1657	0.2412
floor[2]	0.1566	0.02644	4.972E-4	0.1075	0.1553	0.2119
floor[3]	0.2199	0.024	3.586E-4	0.1748	0.2193	0.2683
effect[1]	0.6642	0.05588	0.002501	0.552	0.6649	0.7726
effect[2]	0.7175	0.05381	0.002845	0.6097	0.7187	0.8194
effect[3]	0.5743	0.0616	0.002982	0.4586	0.5722	0.6991
half[1]	8.547	0.6156	0.01462	7.325	8.529	9.769
half[2]	12.29	0.5014	0.01175	11.33	12.3	13.31
half[3]	18.59	0.7197	0.02454	17.22	18.56	20.05
gt21	1.0	0.0	1.0E-12	1.0	1.0	1.0
gt31	1.0	0.0	1.0E-12	1.0	1.0	1.0
gt32	1.0	0.0	1.0E-12	1.0	1.0	1.0
mu0	−19.28	5.7	0.3198	−29.05	−19.63	−8.429
mu1	0.8945	0.4117	0.03188	0.4128	0.7776	1.815
mu2	8.01	6.122	0.5549	−2.542	9.472	18.74
sd0	5.7	8.523	0.4003	0.0663	3.774	24.79
sd1	0.2293	0.4204	0.01807	0.02791	0.1259	1.024
sd2	2.315	4.388	0.2346	0.03385	0.9758	11.95

Note. Data from Horner et al. (2005).

halfway point for Participant 2 is greater than for Participant 1, and so on. The proportion of times is calculated (and rounded to two decimal places) as 1.00 in all cases, showing near certainty that these participants responded in the right order.

Final Perspectives

The use of statistical methods (in general) and multilevel models (in particular) can offer SCD researchers many benefits. They can make valid probability statements about their results and generate quantitative estimates of the effects of their treatment. They can capture the important qualities of their results in these models. They can account for influences that would be difficult or impossible without statistics, such as autocorrelation or the ability to predict the performance of respondents over time (and help determine how bad such prediction might be). They can test whether trends are really in the data, or whether they are illusions.

Statistical methods have drawbacks, but generally these drawbacks are as bad or worse for visual-analysis methods. Phases can begin with points that are nonrepresentative, due to a sudden change in conditions. Unmeasured influences can occur (such as illnesses not noted, or events that make the participants more or less active generally). If these influences are known or suspected, they can be modeled. But in the end, statistical models are ways to assess what we do and do not know, as well as the precision with which we have estimated important quantities. Such capabilities are beyond the scope of most visual analyses.

Appendix 7.1: Code for the Analyses Using the Statistical Package, R WinBUGS

R Program for Ordered Data

```
# SCD ordered categorical data

# from Hall, et al, JABA, 1970, 3, 247-255.
# quiz score grades, 0=F, 4=A

dave <- c(0,0,1,2,0,1,0,0,0, 4,3,3,4,4,4,4,3,2,3,4,4,4,3,4,4)
roy <- c(0,2,0,0,4,1,0,0,0,0,1,1,2,0,0, 3,3,3,2,2,2,2,3,4,4)
deb <- c(1,0,0,0,0,0,0,0,0,1,1,0,2,0,0,0,1,1,0,0,0, 2,2,2,2,3)

trt1 <- c(rep(0,9),rep(1,16))
trt2 <- c(rep(0,15),rep(1,10))
trt3 <- c(rep(0,20),rep(1,5))

id <- rep(1:3,each=25)
sess <- rep(1:25,3)

s2 <- as.numeric(id==2)
s3 <- as.numeric(id==3)

y <- c(dave,roy,deb)
trt <- c(trt1,trt2,trt3)

data <- c(id,y,sess,trt,s2,s3)
data.m <- matrix(data,ncol=6,byrow=F)
data.fr <- data.frame(data.m)
attach(data.fr)

# Fixed effects models

library(polr)
summary(polr(as.ordered(y) ~ trt + s2 + s3))

summary(polr(as.ordered(y) ~ trt*s2 + trt*s3))

# Effects Coding
```

```
e1 = (id==1) - (id==3)
e2 = (id==2) - (id==3)

summary(polr(as.ordered(y) ~ trt + e1 + e2))
summary(polr(as.ordered(y) ~ trt*e1 + trt*e2))

# Random effects model

library(ordinal)
library(ucminf)

model.2 <- clmm(as.ordered(y) ~ trt + (1|id))
summary(model.2)
```

WinBUGS Program for Nonlinear Model

```
model {
for( i in 1:61) {
n.right[i] <- p.right[i]/5 # change percent to number
n.right[i] ~ dbin(prob[i],20)
logit(yhat[i]) <- b0[person[i]] + b1[person[i]] * sess.10[i] +
b2[person[i]] *phase[i]
prob[i] <- floor[person[i]] + (ceiling[person[i]] - floor[person[i]]) * yhat[i]

n.right[i] ~ dbin(prob[i],20)
}

for( j in 1:3) {
b0[j] ~ dnorm(mu0, prec0)
b1[j] ~ dnorm(mu1, prec1)
b2[j] ~ dnorm(mu2, prec2)
floor[j] ~ dbeta(2,1)
ceiling[j] ~ dbeta(1,2)
effect[j] <- ceiling[j] - floor[j]
half[j] <- -1*(b0[j] + b2[j])/b1[j] }

mu0 ~ dnorm(.1,.001)
mu1 ~ dnorm(-.1,.001)
mu2 ~ dnorm(.02,.001)

prec0 ~ dgamma(.001,.001)
prec1 ~ dgamma(.001,.001)
prec2 ~ dgamma(.001,.001)

sd0 <- 1/sqrt(prec0)
sd1 <- 1/sqrt(prec1)
sd2 <- 1/sqrt(prec2)
```

```
# how often is halfway point higher in person 2 than 1, etc.?
gt21 <- step(half[2] - half[1])
gt32 <- step(half[3] - half[2])
gt31 <- step(half[3] - half[1])


}
```

References

Baek, E. K., & Ferron, J. M. (2013). Multilevel models for multiple-baseline data: Modeling across participant variation in autocorrelation and residual variance. *Behavior Research Methods*, *45*, 65–74. doi:10.3758/s13428-012-0231-z

Ferron, J. (2002). Reconsidering the use of the general linear model with single-case data. *Behavior Research Methods, Instruments & Computers*, *34*, 324–331. doi:10.3758/BF03195459

Ferron, J. M., Bell, B. A., Hess, M. R., Rendina-Gobioff, G., & Hibbard, S. T. (2009). Making treatment effect inferences from multiple baseline data: The utility of multilevel modeling approaches. *Behavior Research Methods*, *41*(2), 372–384. doi:10.3758/BRM.41.2.372

Ferron, J. M., Farmer, J., & Owens, C. (2010). Estimating individual treatment effects from multiple-baseline data: A Monte Carlo study of multilevel modeling approaches. *Behavior Research Methods*, *42*, 930–943. doi:10.3758/BRM.42.4.930

Glass, G. V., Willson, V. L., & Gottman, J. M. (1975). *Design and analysis of time-series experiments*. Boulder, CO: Colorado Associated University Press.

Hall, R. V., Cristler, C., Cranston, S. S., & Tucker, B. (1970). Teachers and parents as researchers using multiple baseline design. *Journal of Applied Behavior Analysis*, *3*, 247–255. doi:10.1901/jaba.1970.3-247

Horner, R. H., Carr, E. G., Halle, J., McGee, G., Odom, S., & Wolery, M. (2005). The use of single-subject research to identify evidence-based practice in special education. *Exceptional Children*, *2*, 165–179.

Huitema, B. E., & McKean, J. W. (1998). Irrelevant autocorrelation in least-squares intervention models. *Psychological Methods*, *3*, 104–116. doi:10.1037/1082-989X.3.1.104

Huitema, B. E., & McKean, J. W. (2000). Design specification issues in time-series intervention models. *Educational and Psychological Measurement*, *60*, 38–58. doi:10.1177/00131640021970358

Kenward, M. G., & Roger, J. (1997). Small sample inference for fixed effects from restricted maximum likelihood. *Biometrics*, *53*, 983–997. doi:10.2307/2533558

Kratochwill, T., Alden, K., Demuth, D., Dawson, D., Panicucci, C., Arntson, P., . . . Levin, J. (1974). A further consideration in the application of an analysis-of-variance model for the intrasubject replication design. *Journal of Applied Behavior Analysis*, *7*, 629–633. doi:10.1901/jaba.1974.7-629

Lunn, D., Spiegelhalter, D., Thomas, A., & Best, N. (2009). The BUGS project: Evolution, critique, and future directions. *Statistics in Medicine*, *28*, 3049–3067. doi:10.1002/sim.3680

Lunn, D. J., Thomas, A., Best, N., & Spiegelhalter, D. (2000). WinBUGS: A Bayesian modelling framework: Concepts, structure, and extensibility. *Statistics and Computing*, *10*, 325–337. doi:10.1023/A:1008929526011

Maggin, D. M., Swaminathan, H., Rogers, H. J., O'Keefe, B. V., Sugai, G., & Horner, R. H. (2011). A generalized least squares regression approach for computing effect sizes in single-case research: Application examples. *Journal of School Psychology*, *49*, 301–321. doi:10.1016/j.jsp.2011.03.004

Matyas, T. A., & Greenwood, K. M. (1997). Serial dependency in single-case time series. In R. D. Franklin, D. B. Allison, & B. S. Gorman (Eds.), *Design and analysis of single-case research* (pp. 215–243). Mahwah, NJ:. Erlbaum.

Moeyaert, M., Ugille, M., Ferron, J., Beretvas, T., & Van den Noortgate, W. (2013). The three-level synthesis of standardized single-subject experimental data: A Monte Carlo simulation study. *Multivariate Behavioral Research*, *48*, 719–748. doi:10.1080/00273171.2013.816621

Nagler, E., Rindskopf, D., & Shadish, W. (2008). *Analyzing data from small N designs using multilevel models: A procedural handbook*. Unpublished manuscript.

Nugent, W. (1996). Integrating single-case and group comparison designs for evaluation research. *Journal of Applied Behavioral Science, 32*, 209–226. doi:10.1177/0021886396322007

Owens, C. M., & Ferron, J. M. (2012). Synthesizing single-case studies: A Monte Carlo examination of a three-level meta-analytic model. *Behavior Research Methods, 44*, 795–805. doi:10.3758/s13428-011-0180-y

Plummer, M. (2003, March). *JAGS: A program for analysis of Bayesian graphical models using Gibbs sampling.* Paper presented at the Proceedings of the 3rd International Workshop on Distributed Statistical Computing, Vienna, Austria.

Serlin, R. C., & Levin, J. R. (1985). Teaching how to derive directly interpretable coding schemes for multiple regression analysis. *Journal of Educational Statistics, 10*, 223–238. doi:10.2307/1164794

Shadish, W. R., & Rindskopf, D. M. (2007). Methods for evidence-based practice: Quantitative synthesis of single-subject designs. *New Directions for Evaluation, 113*, 95–109. doi:10.1002/ev.217

Shadish, W. R., Rindskopf, D. M., & Hedges, L. V. (2008). The state of the science in the meta-analysis of single-case experimental designs. *Evidence-Based Communication Assessment and Intervention, 2*, 188–196. doi:10.1080/17489530802581603

Shadish, W. R., & Sullivan, K. J. (2011). Characteristics of single-case designs used to assess intervention effects in 2008. *Behavior Research Methods, 43*, 971–980. doi:10.3758/s13428-011-0111-y

Ugille, M., Moeyaert, M., Beretvas, T., Ferron, J., & Van den Noortgate, W. (2012). Multilevel meta-Analysis of single-subject experimental designs: A simulation study. *Behavior Research Methods, 44*, 1244–1254. doi:10.3758/s13428-012-0213-1

Van den Noortgate, W., & Onghena, P. (2003a). Combining single-case experimental data using hierarchical linear models. *School Psychology Quarterly, 18*, 325–346. doi:10.1521/scpq.18.3.325.22577

Van den Noortgate, W., & Onghena, P. (2003b). Hierarchical linear models for the quantitative integration of effects sizes in single-case research. *Behavior Research Methods, Instruments & Computers, 35*, 1–10. doi:10.3758/BF03195492

Van den Noortgate, W., & Onghena, P. (2007). The aggregation of single-case results using hierarchical linear models. *The Behavior Analyst Today, 8*, 196–209.

Van den Noortgate, W., & Onghena, P. (2008). A multilevel meta-analysis of single subject experimental design studies. *Evidence-Based Communication Assessment and Intervention, 2*, 142–151. doi:10.1080/17489530802505362

8

Analyzing Single-Case Designs: d, G, Hierarchical Models, Bayesian Estimators, Generalized Additive Models, and the Hopes and Fears of Researchers About Analyses

William R. Shadish, Larry V. Hedges,
James E. Pustejovsky, David M. Rindskopf,
Jonathan G. Boyajian, and Kristynn J. Sullivan

New approaches to the analyses of single-case designs are proliferating, which some single-case design researchers welcome and others view with skepticism. In this chapter we describe some of the analyses that we have been exploring, all of which can be conceptualized as versions of hierarchical models as a unifying framework. The approaches include a d statistic for the $(AB)^k$ design that estimates the same parameter as the usual between-groups d statistic, Bayesian approaches to the same and similar models, hierarchical generalized linear models that model outcomes as binomial or Poisson rather than the usual assumptions of normality, and semi-parametric generalized additive models that allow diagnosis of trend and linearity. Throughout, we illustrate the analyses using a common example and show how the different analyses provide different insights into the data. We conclude with a discussion of potential criticisms and skepticism expressed by some researchers about such analyses, along with reasons why the field is increasingly likely to develop and use such analyses despite the criticisms.

In 2004, three authors of this chapter (Shadish, Hedges, and Rindskopf) were members of the Technical Advisory Group (TAG) of the What Works Clearinghouse (WWC), which at that time was newly funded to help the U.S. Department of Education identify effective educational practices. An early task

This research was supported in part by Institute for Educational Sciences, U.S. Department of Education Grants R305D100046 and R305D100033 and by a grant from the University of California Office of the President to the University of California Educational Evaluation Consortium.

http://dx.doi.org/10.1037/14376-009
Single-Case Intervention Research: Methodological and Statistical Advances, by T. R. Kratochwill and J. R. Levin

was to determine which research methods provided acceptable evidence of a treatment effect. TAG members all agreed that the randomized experiment did so, as did both the regression discontinuity design and nonrandomized experiments where groups were equated at pretest—although not all members agreed about what the latter meant.

Notably missing from this list was single-case design (SCD) methodology. When we raised the question of this methodology to the TAG, most members were skeptical. That skepticism had many sources, ranging from unfamiliarity with the design in many research and policy circles to doubts that a methodology based on single-cases could ever rise high in the pantheon of designs. But the most compelling objection was much simpler—how would data from these designs be analyzed, and how would analytic results be compared to those from between-groups designs? At that time, WWC was conceived largely as a meta-analytic enterprise where the coin of the realm was an effect-size estimate, especially one with well-known statistical properties and with widespread acceptance among researchers, such as the standardized mean difference statistic, the correlation coefficient, or the odds ratio. No TAG member could provide a credible response to this objection. So WWC decided not to include SCDs in its evidence-based practice reviews, a decision that is only recently and slowly changing (Kratochwill et al., 2010). The research in this chapter arose from this early TAG discussion.

The paucity of analytic methods for SCDs in 2003 is not surprising. With a few exceptions, most SCD researchers follow a visual-analysis tradition within which inferential statistical methods are eschewed (see Chapter 3, this volume). In recent years, however, a number of researchers have developed such analyses, and several authors have reviewed them (Maggin et al., 2011; Parker, Vannest, & Davis, 2011; Parker, Vannest, Davis, & Sauber, 2011; Shadish & Rindskopf, 2007; Shadish, Rindskopf, & Hedges, 2008). In general, the analyses fall into two classes: effect-size indices and methods based on the general linear model or its extensions. The effect-size indices provide a common metric to synthesize cases within and across studies but have unclear statistical properties. The general linear model approaches rely on well-developed statistical techniques but usually fail to provide a common metric across studies and outcomes.

The problems with the effect-size indices are most significant. Prior reviews, especially Maggin et al. (2011), provide some details that we do not include here due to space constraints. Rather, we focus on the most salient problems. First, all of these effect-size indices (see Parker, Vannest, & Davis, 2011, for a comprehensive list) lack formal statistical derivation so that their statistical properties (e.g., distributions, standard errors) are unknown or incorrectly described. This could and probably should be remedied by collaboration between the pertinent authors and statisticians. The results could well be very beneficial for the field. Second, these effect-size indices are frequently but incorrectly described as "nonparametric;" an effect size by Parker, Vannest, Davis, and Sauber (2011) is an exception that does seem to be nonparametric (see also Chapter 4, this volume). We have made this mistake ourselves (Shadish & Rindskopf, 2007) by following others' descriptions, but the label "ad hoc" is probably more accurate than the label "nonparametric." Third, most or all of these indices ignore autocorrelation (serial dependence) of time points within cases, sometimes using the erroneous rationale that nonparametric statistics do not make the independence assumption. Reference to any introductory statistics text on chi-square will make clear the latter rationale is wrong. For those effect-size indices that do propose standard errors and significance tests, the failure to take autocorrelation into account renders those tests even more problematic. Fourth, many authors propose a novel effect-size index that they then convert to a more commonly used index such as the standardized mean difference statistic (d), the correlation coefficient (r), or the odds ratio (o). However, because the underlying novel statistics suffer from the previously described problems, the resulting converted statistics are not comparable to their counterparts from between-groups experiments. We know little about exactly how different they are from the usual effect sizes used in statistics. Fifth, nearly all of these effect-size indices assume no trend (see Chapter 4, this volume; Parker, Vannest, Davis, & Sauber, 2011, for exceptions), but the presence of trend in SCD data has yet to be thoroughly studied. This problem may be the most easy to address, however, by removing trend using detrended residuals from regressions. Removing trend is challenging because SCD researchers rarely know the functional form of the trend to be removed; but failure to take trend into account is an even worse solution. In short, this list of problems is quite substantial, and thus it is quite unfortunate that these effect-size indicators are the most widely used approaches to the analysis and meta-analysis of SCDs. They may give some rough sense of relative ordering of treatment effectiveness, but they otherwise do not provide trustworthy point estimates of known parameters or their standard errors.

SCD analysis methods based on general linear models rely on well-developed statistical theory so that parameter estimation and statistical inference are far more credible. The analyses use either regression or multilevel models. The former are easier for many SCD researchers to learn but the latter are more flexible in their capacity to model error structures and multiple cases within studies simultaneously. Each particular approach has its own unique features that need not much concern us here. Among the regression approaches, Huitema's (2011) is an exemplar in conducting model comparisons with and without autocorrelations and trend terms. Van den Noortgate and Onghena (2003a, 2003b, 2007, 2008) are exemplars of the multilevel modeling approaches. However, these approaches do not (yet) yield an effect size that is equivalent to the usual between-groups effect sizes. The latter is not necessary, by any means, but it is very useful for comparing results of SCDs to the randomized and nonrandomized between-groups studies that dominate discussions of evidence-based practice in entities like the WWC and the Institute for Education Sciences (IES).

Some authors have proposed effect-size estimates that use the same labels as the usual between-groups estimates, but that does not mean they actually are the same. Busk and Serlin (2005) used a standardized mean difference formula to compute effect size estimate (ES) for each case:

$$ES = \frac{M_b - M_t}{s_b},$$

where M_b is the mean of a case's baseline observations, M_t is the mean of the treatment observations, and s_b is the standard deviation of the baseline observations. They note this ES can be pooled with the usual between-groups d-estimator, which might suggest to some readers that the two estimators are comparable. But this is not the case, because the denominators are very different for the two estimators and so they are not estimating the same parameter. SCD researchers can compute this ES, but it is not comparable to the usual between-groups d and so pooling is of questionable validity.

Similarly, Parker, Hagan-Burke, and Vannest (2007) proposed a phi correlation coefficient from single-case designs (see Chapter 4, this volume). They start by creating various versions of a fourfold table with the columns being whether the observation is from the baseline or treatment phase, and with the rows being a prediction of which phase the observation should be in if the treatment is effective. From that fourfold table, several methods can be used to create a correlation or an odds ratio, either of which can be converted to a d-estimator if desired (though not without assumptions). Again, however, this estimator is not in the same metric as the usual between-groups d-estimator, in this case because the underlying data are autocorrelated, whereas the effect-size estimators associated with the usual fourfold tables assume the data points are independent. Other examples are Beretvas and Chung (2008), whose estimators suffers from the same problem as that of Busk and Serlin (2005), and Van den Noortgate and Onghena (2008), who explicitly stated that their d-estimator is not the same as the usual d for a host of reasons.

Maggin et al.'s (2011) generalized least squares regression approach yields a d that may come closest to approximating the usual between-groups d-statistic. For instance, it is based on a between-cases variance in the denominator and it takes autocorrelation into account. However, as the reader will note shortly in the next section of this chapter, formal development of such a d may require considerably more detailed derivation from general principles about d, and also attention not just to the autocorrelation but also to the number of cases, the number of time points within cases and the ratio of between-case variance to total (between-case plus within-case) variance (assuming that our derivation is itself correct). Of course, it is an empirical question whether Maggin et al.'s d, or any other of these effect sizes, actually produce similar numbers to the d in this chapter.

In summary, then, past approaches suffered from either or both of two problems, lack of formal statistical derivation, and lack of an effect-size metric comparable to those used in between-groups designs. The research in this chapter attempts to address these problems. We have been fortunate to obtain two grants from the IES to develop appropriate statistical models to use in the analysis and meta-analysis of SCDs. By the end of the first grant in 2008 we had developed an initial version of a d-statistic that would be in the same metric as the usual between-groups d (Shadish et al., 2008), and we had developed an extensive manual outlining how to apply multilevel models to various kinds of SCDs with various kinds of outcome metrics. (The metric issue is still mostly ignored in the SCD literature where the predominant outcome is a count best modeled with Poisson or binomial distributions rather than with a distribution requiring the usual assumptions of normality.) At the time of this writing, in the 3rd year of our second grant, we have completed the statistical derivation of the d-statistic for multiphase reversal (ABAB) designs and applied it to several cases, extended our work to implement a version of this d-statistic in a fully Bayesian context, and developed several other analytic approaches not originally envisioned in the grant.

At heart, all of the analyses we develop in this chapter are based on the framework of hierarchical models, either linear models that assume normal error distributions or generalized linear models that allow greater flexibility in this assumption. In our hierarchical conception, individual measurements over time are nested within individual cases. This is a very common approach to thinking about longitudinal data generally (Singer & Willett, 2003), and has received greater attention in the single-case research community, notably in the work of Van den Noortgate and Onghena (2003a, 2003b, 2007, 2008; see also Jenson, Clark, Kircher, & Kristjansson, 2007). It also helps to show that the effect-size approaches and the general linear model approaches are closely related and might someday yield a unified approach to the analysis of SCDs that provides the benefits of both.

In this chapter, we summarize some of our recent work that builds on this hierarchical framework. First, we describe a simple hierarchical linear model and use it to define a d-statistic for the $(AB)^k$ design (where k indicates the number of AB phase pairs) that is comparable to the d from a between-groups design. Second, we elaborate on the first simple model and demonstrate how to estimate the same effect-size parameter in a Bayesian framework. Third, we present a hierarchical generalized linear model (HGLM) that better accounts for the outcome distribution and that allows different parameterizations of the $(AB)^k$ design; and we show how the same $(AB)^k$ design can be coded in different ways to reflect different subtleties in the interpretation of effects. Finally, we use semi-parametric generalized additive models (Wood, 2006, 2010) to test assumptions of trend, linearity, and autocorrelations. We conclude with discussion of the future of data analyses for the field of SCD research.

A word of caution about the statistics in this chapter: Much of what we present is more complex than previous statistical analyses applied to single-case designs. In some cases the development of simple computer programs will ameliorate that complexity. For instance, for the d-statistic developed in the next section, some formulas are complex, but we are developing an SPSS macro to compute d that is very simple to use with no knowledge of the underlying formulas at all (though one hopes to presume some knowledge of what a d-statistic is). In other cases, such as the use of Bayesian statistics, HGLMs, or generalized additive models, reduction to simple programs is a bit further away in time, though we provide model syntax. This will inevitably raise questions about the usefulness and purpose of complex statistics in the single-case research community, in which there is a principled skepticism of the capacity of such statistics to capture the nuances of SCD research. This concern is quite serious for the field, and we attempt to address it in the discussion section of this chapter. In the meantime, the reader with little interest in statistics can simply skip the formulas with no loss of the major conceptual points in the examples, while the reader who is intrigued by the statistical possibilities will have the necessary leads to pursue such interests.

An Effect Size for the (AB)^k Design

Effect size measures are often a supplement to hypothesis tests and a way to provide a quantitative representation of study results. They also make more comparable the results of studies using somewhat different designs and outcome measures, and so they provide the basis of formal quantitative syntheses of results across studies in systematic reviews. This section summarizes a new effect size measure (and corresponding estimate) for SCDs of the (AB)^k type, that is, where baseline (A) and treatment (B) phases are paired, and repeated k times. The measure can be conceptualized as a simple hierarchical linear model that entails certain assumptions. Specifically, we consider a certain stable pattern of outcomes: fluctuation around a constant value, with common mean within phases and common residual variance within phases. The model does not consider time trends, either linear or nonlinear. We present the hierarchical model and derive an effect size parameter that corresponds to the standardized mean difference from a between-subjects experiment (Cohen's d and Hedges' g). We give expressions for the approximate mean and variance of the estimate; derivations and related simulation work are provided in Hedges, Pustejovsky, and Shadish (2012).

Conceptual Hierarchical Model

To simplify exposition, we begin by considering a two-phase (AB)^1 design. Let Y_{ti} be the tth observation from the ith case, where there are an even number $m = 2a > 2$ cases and let $t = 1, \ldots, n$ be observations in the baseline period and $j = n + 1, \ldots, 2n$ correspond to observations in the treatment period. Thus the data are $Y_{ti}, i = 1, \ldots, m; t = 1, \ldots, 2n;$ Figure 8.1 portrays the entire data layout. We broaden this to the more general case shortly.

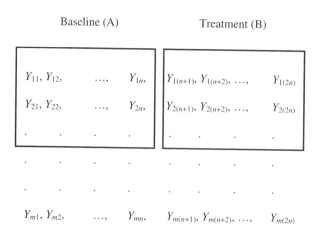

Figure 8.1. Data layout for a two period AB^1 single-case design with outcome Y, m participants and n observations per phase.

We consider a structural model that is broad enough to encompass both a between-subjects experiment and an SCD with replications across cases. The level-1 model for case i is

$$Y_{ti} = \pi_{0i} + \pi_{1i}X_{ti} + \varepsilon_{ti}, \quad (8.1)$$

where π_{0i} is the mean outcome for case i during the baseline phase, $j = 1, \ldots, n$; X_{ti} is an indicator variable for baseline or treatment, equal to 0 for $t = 1, \ldots, n$ and 1 for $t = n + 1, \ldots, 2n$; and π_{1i} is the treatment effect, that is, the difference in mean outcomes between the treatment phase and the baseline phase. Following convention for statistical analysis of single-case designs, we assume that the error terms ε_{sh} and ε_{ti} have variance σ^2 and first order autocorrelation φ within cases, so that

$$\mathrm{Cov}\{\varepsilon_{sh}, \varepsilon_{ti}\} = \begin{cases} 0 & \text{if } h \neq i \\ \phi^{|t-s|}\sigma^2 & \text{if } h = i \end{cases}.$$

To complete the model, we need level-2 assumptions about the distribution of the coefficients π_{0i} and π_{1i} across cases. Here, we assume that the mean outcomes during baseline may vary across cases, but that the treatment effect is constant:

$$\begin{aligned} \pi_{0i} &= \beta_{00} + r_{0i}, \\ \pi_{1i} &= \beta_{10}, \end{aligned} \quad (8.2)$$

where r_{0i} is normally distributed with mean 0 and variance τ^2. In the above, β_{00} is the mean baseline outcome across all m cases, β_{10} represents the treatment effect, and τ^2 is the across-case variance.

Because this model is hierarchical, encompassing variation both within- and between-cases, it becomes possible to identify a parameter that is a conventional effect size (the standardized mean difference or d-index) from between-subjects design. In a between-subjects design, Cohen's d is the difference between the mean of the treatment group and the mean of the control group, divided by the standard deviation of the control group. Based on the above model, if we had conducted a between-groups experiment, the mean of the control group would be β_{00}, while the mean of the treatment group would be $\beta_{00} + \beta_{10}$. The variance of the control group would be $\sigma^2 + \tau^2$, because at any given point in time, there is both within-case and between-case variation in the outcome. Thus, the effect size parameter is defined as

$$\delta = \frac{\beta_{10}}{\sqrt{\sigma^2 + \tau^2}}. \quad (8.3)$$

This definition of the effect size is precisely the standardized mean difference (Cohen's d-index) that is widely used in between-subjects experiments. As we discuss below, this effect size parameter can be estimated from within-subjects experiments, and specifically from $(AB)^k$ designs, as long as there are replications across cases (that is $m > 1$), although at least $m = 3$ cases are usually needed to estimate the variance of the estimate.

Model for the (AB)ᵏ Design With Unequal Numbers of Observations

We now present the model for a more general design, allowing $2k$ phases with unequal numbers of observations in each phase and each case. Following this model, we give formulas for estimating the more general model; estimators for the simpler case of an $(AB)^1$ design are a special case of these. Suppose that a study uses an $(AB)^k$ design, so that there are $2k$ phases, and m cases. We allow that each case may have a different number of observations in each phase. Let n_i^a, $a = 1, \ldots, 2k$, $i = 1, \ldots, m$ be the number of observations in the ath phase for the ith case, and define $n_i^0 = 0$ for all $i = 1, \ldots, m$. Because the number of observations within phases is not the same across cases, we need a notation that can denote the first, second, etc. observation within each phase for each case. Define the total number of observations (j-values) for the ith case through the ath phase to be N_i^a, so that

$$N_i^a = n_i^0 + n_i^1 + \cdots + n_i^a,$$

and define $N_\bullet$ to be the total number of observations (the sum of the n_i^a) so that

$$N_\bullet = \sum_{i=1}^{m} N_i^{2k} = \sum_{i=1}^{m} \sum_{a=1}^{2k} n_i^a.$$

Thus the ath phase for the ith case includes the j-values between $N_i^{a-1} + 1$ and $N_i^{a-1} + n_i^a = N_i^a$ inclusive. Thus the observations in the ath phase are

$$Y_{ti}, i = 1, \ldots, m; t = N_i^{a-1} + 1, \ldots, N_i^{a-1} + n_i^a$$

for $a = 1, \ldots, 2k$.

The same stochastic model, as given in Equations 8.1 and 8.2, can be applied to the more general design by appropriately adapting the treatment indicator variable. Let

$$X_{ti} = \tfrac{1}{2}\left[1 + (-1)^a\right],$$

for $t = N_i^{a-1} + 1, \ldots, N_i^{a-1} + n_i^a, a = 1, \ldots, 2k$, and $i = 1, \ldots, m$. The expression in square brackets just assures that the indicator is zero in odd numbered phases (baseline phases) and that the indicator is one in even numbered phases (treatment phases). The interpretation of level-1 and level-2 coefficients remains the same as before, as does the effect size parameter. Consequently, we are implicitly assuming that the mean of the outcomes during the first baseline phase is the same as the mean during all later baseline phases, and similarly that the mean outcome during the treatment phases remains constant. This is a consequence of the underlying assumption that the SCD contains no trend. This is not as much an obstacle as it might seem because the researcher can detrend the data using residuals from a regression modeling trend, and then compute d on the residuals. We are currently working on a version of the d-statistic that deals with trend in more elegant ways. Furthermore, we assume that the treatment effect is constant across cases.

There are many ways that one could estimate this simple hierarchical model. For instance, one could use maximum likelihood methods to generate estimates of the component parameters (using widely available statistical software, such as SPSS, SAS, Stata, or HLM), and form a treatment effect estimate by substituting these estimates for the corresponding parameter values. However, maximum likelihood methods are justified based on asymptotic approximations (meaning that they will perform well when sample sizes are sufficiently large), but they may be biased in the small samples typical of single-case designs. An alternative approach is to use a fully Bayesian approach, calculating the posterior distribution of the effect size parameter, given the model and the data. We pursue this approach in the following section. In this section, however, we present an effect-size estimator that is specialized to the model, that is nearly unbiased in small samples, and that can be expressed using only algebraic formulas (albeit somewhat involved ones); in contrast, maximum likelihood methods do not generally have closed-form expressions, and have to be calculated using iterative computer algorithms.

We now provide an approach for estimating the effect-size parameter based on the data from an $(AB)^k$ design. The denominator of the effect-size estimate is based on the sample variance across cases for each timepoint, averaged over timepoints. Because each case can have a different number of observations within each phase, there may not be a complete set of m observations for some time points. The contribution to the variance for a time point is computed only if there is an observation at that time point for every case. Define the minimum number of observations for any case in the ath phase by M^a, so that $M^a = \text{Minimum}\ \{n_1^a, \dots, n_m^a\}$, and define $M^\bullet$ to be the sum of the $M^\bullet$, so that $M^a = M^1 + \dots + M^{2k}$. The variance pooled across phases and across cases is

$$S^2 = \frac{1}{M^\bullet(m-1)} \sum_{a=1}^{2k} \sum_{t=N_i^{a-1}+1}^{N_i^{a-1}+M^a} \sum_{i=1}^{m} \left(Y_{ti} - \bar{Y}_{t\bullet}\right)^2, \quad (8.4)$$

where $\bar{Y}_{t\bullet}$ is the average across cases of the tth observations within cases, given by

$$\bar{Y}_{t\bullet} = \frac{1}{m} \sum_{i=1}^{m} Y_{ti}.$$

The numerator of the effect size is the unweighted mean difference between phases A and B, defined as

$$\bar{D} = \frac{1}{mk} \sum_{i=1}^{m} \sum_{a=1}^{k} \left(\bar{Y}_{\bullet i}^{2a} - \bar{Y}_{\bullet i}^{2a-1}\right) = \frac{1}{mk} \sum_{i=1}^{m} \sum_{a=1}^{k} \left(\frac{1}{n_i^{2a}} \sum_{t=N_i^{2a-1}+1}^{N_i^{2a}} Y_{ti} - \frac{1}{n_i^{2a-1}} \sum_{t=N_i^{2a-2}+1}^{N_i^{2a-1}} Y_{ti} \right). \quad (8.5)$$

Define the effect size estimate ES to be

$$ES = \frac{\bar{D}}{S}, \quad (8.6)$$

where $\bar{D}$ is given in Equation 8.5 and S^2 is given in Equation 8.7.

Define the auxiliary constant A via

$$A = \frac{1}{k^2} \sum_{i=1}^{m} \sum_{a=1}^{2k} \sum_{b=1}^{2k} \left(\frac{(-1)^a (-1)^b}{n_i^a n_i^b} \sum_{s=N_i^{a-1}+1}^{N_i^a} \sum_{t=N_i^{b-1}+1}^{N_i^b} \phi^{|s-t|} \right), \qquad (8.7)$$

and the auxiliary constants B, C, and D via

$$B = \sum_{i=1}^{m} \sum_{a=1}^{2k} \sum_{b=1}^{2k} \sum_{s=1}^{M^a} \sum_{t=1}^{M^b} \phi^{|N_i^{a-1}-N_i^{b-1}+s-t|}, \qquad (8.8)$$

$$C = \sum_{i=1}^{m} \sum_{a=1}^{2k} \sum_{b=1}^{2k} \sum_{s=1}^{M^a} \sum_{t=1}^{M^b} \phi^{2|N_i^{a-1}-N_i^{b-1}+s-t|}, \qquad (8.9)$$

and

$$D = \sum_{a=1}^{2k} \sum_{b=1}^{2k} \sum_{s=1}^{M^a} \sum_{t=1}^{M^b} \left(\sum_{i=1}^{m} \phi^{|N_i^{a-1}-N_i^{b-1}+s-t|} \right)^2, \qquad (8.10)$$

The expected value of $\bar{D}$ is β_{10} and the variance of $\bar{D}$ is

$$V\{\bar{D}\} = \frac{A\sigma^2}{m^2}. \qquad (8.11)$$

The expected value of S^2 is $\sigma^2 + \tau^2$ and the variance of S^2 is

$$\frac{2(\sigma^2+\tau^2)^2}{(M^\bullet)^2(m-1)} \left[(M^\bullet)^2 \rho^2 + 2\rho(1-\rho)\left(\frac{B}{m}\right) + \frac{(1-\rho)^2}{m-1}\left\{ \left(\frac{m-1}{m}\right)C + \frac{D}{m^2} \right\} \right]. \qquad (8.12)$$

where ρ is the intraclassroom correlation defined as

$$\rho = \frac{\tau^2}{\tau^2 + \sigma^2},$$

representing the between-person variance τ^2 as a fraction of the total variance $(\tau^2 + \sigma^2)$. Proof of these facts is given in Hedges et al. (2012).

If $\bar{D}$ and S^2 are independent, it follows by Box's (1954) theorem that the sampling distribution of ES is approximately a constant θ times a noncentral t-distribution with υ degrees of freedom, where θ is given by

$$\theta = \sqrt{\frac{V\{\bar{D}\}}{\tau^2+\sigma^2}} = \frac{\sqrt{A(1-\rho)}}{m} \qquad (8.13)$$

and υ is given by

$$\upsilon = \frac{(M^\bullet)^2(m-1)^2}{(M^\bullet)^2(m-1)\rho^2 + 2\rho(1-\rho)\left(\frac{m-1}{m}\right)B + (1-\rho)^2\left[\left(\frac{m-2}{m}\right)C + \frac{D}{m^2}\right]}. \qquad (8.14)$$

It follows from results in Hedges (1981) that the bias in *ES* can be corrected by multiplying *ES* by the correction factor J(v) defined as

$$J(v) = 1 - \frac{3}{4v - 1} \qquad (8.15)$$

So that the effect size

$$G = J(v)ES \qquad (8.16)$$

is an approximately unbiased estimator of δ. It also follows that the variance of *G* is approximately

$$V\{G\} = J(v)^2 \left[\frac{v\theta^2}{v - 2} + \delta^2 \left(\frac{v}{v - 2} - \frac{1}{J(v)^2} \right) \right]. \qquad (8.17)$$

As a caveat, it should be noted that independence of $\bar{D}$ and S^2 might not hold in unbalanced (AB)^k designs where the number of data points per phase is unequal across cases. Still, unless the degree of imbalance is severe, these approximations should remain fairly accurate. Hedges et al. (2012) also report results of an extensive simulation study verifying the finite-sample properties of this estimator.

Example

Here we analyze data from an unbalanced (AB)^2 design reported by Lambert, Cartledge, Heward, and Lo (2006), digitized using methods described in Shadish et al. (2009). In this study, researchers assessed the effects of a response card program on the disruptive behavior and academic responding of students in two elementary school classrooms (Figure 8.2). The data analyzed in this section represent instances of disruptive behavior during baseline single-student responding (SSR; phase A), where the teacher called on students one at a time as they raised their hands, and during the response card treatment condition (RC; phase B), where every student wrote a response to each question on a laminated board and presented them simultaneously. Both phases were repeated a second time, resulting in an ABAB design. Data collection focused on nine fourth-grade students (four boys, five girls) with a history of disciplinary issues. Each student was observed for ten 10-second intervals during each observation session. A partial interval recording technique was used, where the number of intervals during which disruptive behaviors were observed was recorded (with a maximum of ten for each session). Between five and ten sessions were recorded for each phase.

The minimum number of timepoints for the first phase is $M^1 = 4$ and the minimum numbers of timepoints for the second through fourth phases are $M^2 = 7$, $M^3 = 6$, and $M^4 = 6$, so that $M^\bullet = 23$. About 10% of the data are missing, scattered intermittently across cases and phases. For present purposes, missing data are ignored in the computations. The weighted average difference

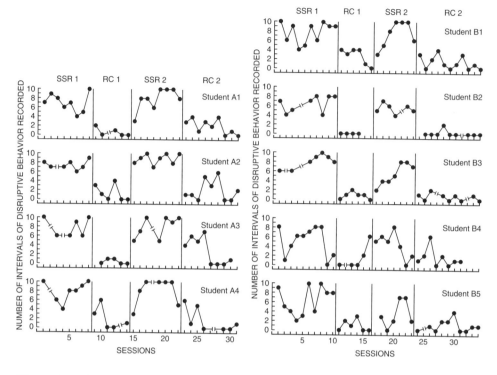

Figure 8.2. Number of disruptive behaviors during single-student responding (SSR: baseline) and response card (RC: treatment) conditions for the target students in Classrooms A (left) and B (right). From "Effects of Response Cards on Disruptive Behavior and Academic Responding During Math Lessons by Fourth-Grade Urban Students," by M.C. Lambert, G. Cartledge, W. L. Heward, and Y. Lo, 2006, *Journal of Positive Behavior Interventions, 8,* pp. 93–94. Copyright 2006 by Sage Publications. Adapted with permission.

between phases is $\bar{D} = -5.458$, $S^2 = 4.674$, and $S = 2.162$. The estimate of effect size (before bias correction) is therefore

$$ES = \frac{-5.458}{2.162} = -2.525$$

Knowledge of the autocorrelation can be used to correct for the estimation bias of *ES* as well as its variance. Because the number of cases in this example is relatively large for SCDs, the bias correction has little effect; however, this will not be true for many SCDs where the number of cases is small. Following the methods described in Hedges et al.'s (2012) Appendix C, the autocorrelation is $\hat{\phi} = 0.225$; and the within-case variation $\hat{\sigma}^2 = 4.534$. Combining this with $S^2 = 4.674$, we obtain an estimate of 0.030 for the intraclassroom correlation ρ. Using the autocorrelation φ = 0.225, the values of the auxiliary constants are $A = 1.754$, $B = 294.751$, $C = 223.488$, and $D = 2002.444$. Inserting the value ρ = 0.030 and the values of the auxiliary constants B, C, and D into Equation 8.4, we obtain $\upsilon = 164.492$ degrees of freedom. This value of the degrees of freedom permits us to compute G, the bias-corrected estimate of effect size. Using $ES = -2.525$ and inserting 164.492 degrees of freedom into Equation 8.16, we obtain $G = -2.513$. Inserting the value of the auxiliary constant A and $\rho = 0.030$ into Equation 8.13, we obtain the value $\theta = 0.145$. Finally, inserting the values v, θ, and $\delta = G = -2.513$ into Equation 8.17, we obtain $V\{G\} = 0.041$, corresponding to a standard error of 0.20. Further details are provided in Hedges et al. (2012).

Summary

In this section we have presented an effect size estimate based on a simple hierarchical linear model that is in the same metric as the usual d-statistic in between-groups designs. It allows one to summarize results from a study using an $(AB)^k$ design and containing at least three SCDs in a single effect size estimate, accompanied by an estimate of the estimate's sampling variance. That effect can stand alone as a summary of one study's results, or can be combined with results from similar studies—both SCDs and between-groups studies such as randomized experiments—in a meta-analysis of research on a common topic.

We hope to develop this line of research considerably more in future years. We have recently completed a version of this estimator specific to the multiple-baseline design, using the same underlying stochastic model. We hope to extend this approach further to alternating treatment designs (Hedges, Pustejovsky, & Shadish, 2013), changing criterion designs, and studies that combine more than one of these in a single SCD such as a multiple-baseline design with alternating treatments. The current model assumes a normal error distribution for a continuous outcome, and so it needs to be extended to distributions appropriate to all the versions of count data that SCDs report (Shadish & Sullivan, 2011). This model also assumes no trend, and so another task is adapting it to SCDs that display various kinds of trend. The current model can be used if trend is suspected by detrending data using a regression with a trend term and then applying this d to the residuals. However, this solution is not fully satisfactory because it still assumes trend does not change after treatment. We are currently working to extend this d to such cases.

More complex multilevel models can address many of these limitations. However, adding more complex modeling assumptions requires re-evaluation of our approach to estimation, because the methods presented in this section are tailored to the specific, very simple model that we used. In the following section, we present a Bayesian approach to estimation using a slightly more general model. Following that, we illustrate the use of a hierarchical generalized linear model that can account for non-normal error distributions.

A Bayesian Estimate of the *d*-Statistic Using WinBUGS

We are currently exploring the use of fully Bayesian methods to analyze SCDs because they have two interesting advantages. One is that they may produce more accurate answers in small datasets that are often characteristic of SCDs. Second, programs for computing fully Bayesian estimates like WinBUGS (Lunn, Thomas, Best, & Spiegelhalter, 2000; Spiegelhalter, Thomas, Best, & Lunn, 2004) are flexible enough to estimate a d effect size such as that described in the previous section, while allowing for more complex models. We illustrate this point by fitting a model similar to the one presented in the previous section, but allowing the treatment effect to vary across cases. This research is very much a work in progress meant to illustrate and intrigue more than to be of immediate practical application.

We use the data from Lambert et al. (2006) so we can compare results from WinBUGS to the d-statistic results that were presented earlier in the chapter. Because the purpose is to see if WinBUGS can yield a d-statistic that matches the one previously developed, we model the data in WinBUGS assuming normality and linearity, but in future work will loosen those assumptions to allow for nonlinearity and more appropriate outcome metrics. Specifically, we assume the following model. At level 1, we assume that

$$Y_{ti} = \pi_{0i} + \pi_{1i}X_{ti} + \varepsilon_{ti}, \quad (8.18)$$

just as before. For simplicity, we assume that the errors are independent rather than auto-correlated. At level 2, we assume that

$$\pi_{0i} = \beta_{00} + r_{0i},$$
$$\pi_{1i} = \beta_{10} + r_{1i}, \quad (8.19)$$

where (r_{0i}, r_{1i}) is multivariate-normally distributed with mean $(0,0)$ and covariance matrix

$$T = \begin{bmatrix} \tau_0^2 & 0 \\ 0 & \tau_1^2 \end{bmatrix},$$

meaning that the baseline intercept and treatment effects are assumed to be independent for each case in their prior distributions. However, the posterior distributions are allowed to covary.

The nine cases yield 264 observations. Exhibit 8.1 translates the model into WinBUGS code, annotated to explain what each command does, with further explanations in the paragraphs that follow. As in the previous model, level 1 models observations over time within case, with one level 1 equation for each case (nine total), whereas level 2 models variation over the 9 cases in slope and intercept. In WinBUGS code, the variable y is the outcome, the frequency of disruptive behavior at each time point for each case. The variable "phase" is the baseline (0) or treatment (1) phases of the experiment and is a time-varying covariate at level-1. The b's in WinBUGS level-1 models are parallel to the π's in HLM notation and can vary across the nine cases (cases are denoted by [subj[i]]); b0[j] is person j's estimated average disruption count at the baseline phase and b1[j] is person j's estimated average change in disruption count from baseline to treatment phase.

A fully Bayesian model treats parameters such as b as variable rather than fixed in the population. As such they can be characterized by two distributions, the prior and the posterior. The prior reflects previous data and/or researcher beliefs before gathering data about how parameters might be distributed. The posterior adjusts the prior given the data, and is the primary result of interest. Here the b[j] have a normal distribution (b[j] ~ dnorm(mu, prec)), and mu and prec have diffuse hyperpriors (mu ~ dnorm(0, .001); prec ~ dgamma(.01, .01)). *Diffuse*

Exhibit 8.1. WinBUGS Code to Estimate Between-Groups d From Single-Case Designs for Lambert Data

---

```
#LAMBERT MODEL: y = intercept + slope(phase)

model {

for (i in 1:264){                    #264 total observations
    theta[i] <- b0[subj[i]] + b1[subj[i]]*phase[i]    #level 1 model

    y[i] ~ dnorm(theta[i],prec)      #count outcome modeled normally.
}

for (j in 1:9){                      #9 cases
    b0[j] ~ dnorm(mu0, prec0)        #intercept treated as a random effect

    b1[j] ~ dnorm(mu1, prec1)        #treatment treated as a random effect

    disrupt.0[j] <- b0[j]            #disruptions expected during baseline
    disrupt.1[j] <- b0[j]+b1[j]      #disruptions expected during treatment
}

mu0 ~ dnorm(0, .001)                 #hyperpriors on hyperparameters
mu1 ~ dnorm(0, .001)
prec ~ dgamma(.01, .01)
prec0 ~ dgamma(.01, .01)
prec1 ~ dgamma(.01, .01)
sig <- 1/sqrt(prec)                  #standard deviation of outcome
sig0 <- 1/sqrt(prec0)                #standard deviation of intercept
sig1 <- 1/sqrt(prec1)                #standard deviation of phase effect
var <- 1/prec                        #within-person variance
var0 <- 1/prec0                      #between-person variance
eff.size <- mu1/sqrt(var + var0)     #effect size measure (d statistic)
}
```

Note. Data from Lambert, Cartledge, Heward, and Lo (2006).

means that the researcher knows little about prior distributions; the b's are normally distributed with mean of mu and precision to be specified as a distribution in a subsequent equation; mu is normally distributed with mean of zero and low precision of .001 (variance of 1000); and prec follows a gamma distribution with mean of $.01/.01 = 1$ and variance of $.01/.01^2 = 100$. Precision is the inverse of variance; the lower the precision, the higher the variance. Low precision means the researcher cannot locate the parameter very precisely given prior information (it could be nearly anywhere in a very wide distribution with high variance), accurately reflecting a lack of much prior knowledge. Of course, if the researcher has more prior information, the distribution shape, mean, and precision could be changed to reflect that. Finally, disrupt.0[j] and disrupt.1[j] are calculated, where disrupt.0[j] is child j's estimated average disruptions count for the baseline phase and is equal to b0[j], and disrupt.1[j] is the estimated average disruptions count for the treatment phase, the sum of b0[j] and the treatment effect b1[j].

The WinBUGS results from the Lambert et al. (2006) data are in Table 8.1. Before getting to the d effect size estimate, we consider other lines in this output. First, mu0 is the estimated average disruption count during baseline over cases

Table 8.1.   Results of WinBUGS Analysis of Lambert Data

Node	Mean	SD	2.5%	Median	97.5%
eff.size	−2.366	0.214	−2.758	−2.375	−1.915
mu0	6.834	0.377	6.090	6.832	7.597
mu1	−5.453	0.311	−6.080	−5.449	−4.840
sig	2.106	0.096	1.926	2.102	2.305
sig0	0.915	0.349	0.432	0.853	1.765
sig1	0.422	0.309	0.081	0.339	1.207
var	4.445	0.407	3.711	4.420	5.312
var0	0.959	0.927	0.186	0.728	3.114
disrupt.0[1]	7.171	0.399	6.406	7.169	7.971
disrupt.0[2]	7.589	0.422	6.787	7.581	8.451
disrupt.0[3]	7.503	0.439	6.666	7.498	8.386
disrupt.0[4]	7.520	0.429	6.699	7.507	8.374
disrupt.0[5]	7.344	0.388	6.588	7.340	8.123
disrupt.0[6]	6.075	0.426	5.220	6.082	6.895
disrupt.0[7]	6.577	0.411	5.777	6.575	7.388
disrupt.0[8]	5.775	0.454	4.832	5.795	6.618
disrupt.0[9]	5.963	0.418	5.098	5.975	6.762
disrupt.1[1]	1.636	0.434	0.778	1.638	2.493
disrupt.1[2]	1.986	0.435	1.106	1.995	2.826
disrupt.1[3]	2.001	0.452	1.116	2.003	2.897
disrupt.1[4]	2.010	0.456	1.116	2.009	2.918
disrupt.1[5]	1.861	0.403	1.066	1.862	2.647
disrupt.1[6]	0.475	0.467	−0.463	0.486	1.365
disrupt.1[7]	0.982	0.431	0.112	0.990	1.807
disrupt.1[8]	0.767	0.502	−0.162	0.745	1.816
disrupt.1[9]	0.727	0.425	−0.085	0.717	1.584

Note. Data from Lambert, Cartledge, Heward, and Lo (2006).

(mu0 = 6.834) and mu1 is the estimated mean effect of treatment on disruption count (mu1 = −5.45); that is, disruption decreased substantially. The remaining columns for each line reflect information about the estimated posterior distribution for the parameter. Most important, the sd column is the standard deviation of the parameter, analogous to the standard error in classical statistics, which is easily used to construct 95% credible intervals around the parameter if the posterior distribution is symmetric (analogous to confidence intervals but with a slightly different interpretation). With reference again to the rows, sig0 is the standard deviation of each case's estimated average disruption count during baseline around the mean disruption count over all cases; sig1 is the standard deviation of each case's estimated average change in disruption count during treatment around the mean change over all cases; var is the estimated within-person variance; and var0 is the estimated between-person variance. All four estimates have their own distributions, reflecting the uncertainty the Bayesian allows in the model about estimating the parameters. The Bayesian estimates of disrupt.0[j] and disrupt.1[j] are each case's average disruption count during baseline and treatment, respectively. In a longer presentation we would use Bayesian tools such as trace plots to show how the distribution of effects over cases vary depending on uncertainty in other parameters such as the estimates of the variances around those parameters.

We now move to the main estimate of interest. The effect size parameter is defined to be mu1 (the treatment effect, or the mean change in disruption count moving from baseline to treatment phase) divided by the square root of the sum of the within-person variance (var) and the between-person variance (var0), just as in Equation 22 from the previous section. In the Bayesian approach, an estimate of the effect size is formed by averaging over the joint posterior distribution of the component parameters to arrive at the marginal posterior distribution of the effect size parameter. WinBUGS reports this d-statistic in the row labeled eff.size: the posterior mean $d = -2.37$ (sd = 0.21). The 95% credible interval (-2.76 to -1.92) does not include zero, so the effect is "statistically significant" (alternatively, there is greater than a 2.5% probability that the effect is less than zero). This compares to a bias-corrected effect size estimate of $G = -2.513$, $sd\{G\} = 0.20$ (that is, treatment reduced disruptive behavior) for the same data computed using the d-statistic earlier in this chapter. So the d and its standard deviation produced by WinBUGS are quite similar to that produced earlier. Differences may be due to not taking the autocorrelation into account in the Bayesian estimate, using different estimation algorithms, allowing effects to vary randomly over cases in the Bayesian estimate, and incorporating greater uncertainty in Bayesian parameter estimation through the information in the prior distributions.

Using Nonnormal Distributions for Hierarchical Analyses of SCDs

As noted previously, hierarchical linear models have attracted increased attention for analysis of SCDs. However, HGLMs have yet to be explored. HGLMs have a number of useful features, being already well-developed for diverse outcome metrics, allowing flexible modeling of nonlinear functional forms, and allowing exploration of sources of variability among cases within a study. Here we develop an HGLM for the Lambert et al. (2006) data. We estimate the model using the HLM 6.0 computer program (Raudenbush, Bryk, Cheong, Congdon, & du Toit, 2004), which uses maximum likelihood with a high-degree Laplace approximation (Raudenbush, Yang, & Yosef, 2000). Our analysis extends past work in two ways. First, the dependent variable in this dataset is a proportion (number of trials with occurrences of disruptive behavior out of 10 total trials) for each session. We show how this type of dependent variable may be accommodated by using a binomial distribution. Second, analysis of effects of ABAB designs can be coded in several different ways, and we illustrate two of them. Further details are in Kyse, Rindskopf, and Shadish (2012).

Model With Level-1 Predictors

The level-1 specification in our analysis is a generalized linear model that describes the mean and variance of the outcome variable. In this case, the outcome variable is a proportion, so the variance is a direct function of the mean. Let $P_{ti} = E(Y_{ti})$ be the expected proportion of intervals within a session in which a disruptive behavior was exhibited. The model for the mean is described by the log-odds of P_{ti}:

$$Log\left(\frac{P_{ti}}{1-P_{ti}}\right) = \pi_{0i} + \pi_{1i}a_{1ti} + \pi_{2i}a_{2ti} + \pi_{3i}a_{3ti} + \pi_{4i}(a_{2ti}a_{3ti})$$

$$+ \pi_{5i}(a_{1ti}a_{2ti}) + \pi_{6i}(a_{1ti}a_{3ti}) + \pi_{7i}(a_{1ti}a_{2ti}a_{3ti}),$$

(8.20)

where session (a_{1ti}) was centered before analysis so that 0 represented the final session of the first baseline phase, a_{2ti} is a dummy code for phase (0 = baseline, 1 = treatment), a_{3ti} is a dummy variable to express whether a phase was part of the first AB pair (0) or the second AB pair (1), and the product terms represent the interactions among these main effects. By virtue of centering, the intercept denotes the proportion of trials in which the target behavior was observed during the final session of the first baseline. Intercepts for the computed models are long odds at the phase change. The Level-1 specification is completed by assuming that the variance of the outcomes is as follows:

$$Var(Y_{ti}) = P_{ti}(1-P_{ti})/10. \qquad (8.21)$$

The division by 10 is because the outcome is a proportion out of 10 possible intervals per session.

The unconditional (i.e., without predictors) Level-2 model is then

$$\pi_{0i} = \beta_{00} + r_{0i}$$

$$\pi_{1i} = \beta_{10} + r_{1i}$$

$$\pi_{2i} = \beta_{20} + r_{2i}$$

$$\pi_{3i} = \beta_{30} + r_{3i}$$

$$\pi_{4i} = \beta_{40} + r_{4i} \qquad (8.22)$$

$$\pi_{5i} = \beta_{50} + r_{5i}$$

$$\pi_{6i} = \beta_{60} + r_{6i}$$

$$\pi_{7i} = \beta_{70} + r_{7i}$$

The HLM software produced the following fixed-effect estimates for this model:

$$\pi_{0i} = 0.61 + r_{0i}$$

$$\pi_{1i} = -0.05 + r_{1i}$$

$$\pi_{2i} = -5.97* + r_{2i}$$

$$\pi_{3i} = 0.75 + r_{3i}$$

$$\pi_{4i} = 5.97* + r_{4i} \qquad (8.23)$$

$$\pi_{5i} = 0.69 + r_{5i}$$

$$\pi_{6i} = 0.01 + r_{6i}$$

$$\pi_{7i} = -0.82 + r_{7i}$$

Statistically significant ($p < .05$) terms are indicated with an asterisk (*). To get a more parsimonious model, we removed non-significant terms one-by-one until we found a model in which all estimated fixed effects were significant. In the final model only the treatment effect (a_{2ti}) remained significant at Level-1. This is nearly identical to the model from the d-estimator section. The only differences are that (a) the errors are binomially distributed, (b) there is no allowance for autocorrelation, and (c) the treatment effect is allowed to vary across cases, rather than being held fixed. Output from this analysis is

$$\pi_{0i} = 0.61^* + r_{0i}, \qquad \tau_{00} = 0.12^*$$
$$\pi_{2i} = -2.36^* + r_{2i}, \qquad \tau_{22} = 0.17^{\cdot}$$

During baseline, the overall average log odds of exhibiting a disruptive behavior during a 10-second observation period is 0.6129, which converts to an odds of exp(0.6129) = 1.8458, and to a probability of 1.8458/2.8458 = 0.6460. The expected probability of observing a disruptive behavior during the baseline phase intervals is therefore 0.65. The average change in log odds as a student switches from baseline to treatment is –2.3638, which converts to an odds of a disruptive act of exp(0.6129 – 2.3638) = exp(–1.7509) = 0.1736, and a probability of 0.1736/1.1736 = 0.1479.

Model With Level-2 Predictors

Because the between-student variance of intercepts in the last model is statistically significant, with $\tau_{00} = 0.1191$, indicating that students differ by more than chance on their average baseline frequencies of disruptive behavior, we explored whether student characteristics (Level-2 variables) might account for some of the between-student variation found. Exploration involved looking at age, ethnicity, prior mathematics grade, and classroom (Classroom A = 0 or B = 1) one variable at a time; only the last variable was significant. We then used the Level-1 model,

$$\ln\left(\frac{P_{ti}}{1 - P_{ti}}\right) = \pi_{0i} + \pi_{2i}a_{2ti}, \qquad (8.24)$$

with terms defined as in Equation 8.20, and the Level-2 model,

$$\pi_{0i} = \beta_{00} + \beta_{01}x_{0i} + r_{0i}$$
$$\pi_{2i} = \beta_{20} + r_{2i} \qquad , \qquad (8.25)$$

where x_{0i} is whether student i was in Classroom A or B.

Results were

$$\pi_{0i} = 0.94^* - 0.58^* x_{0i} + r_{0i}, \qquad \tau_{00} = 0.09^*$$
$$\pi_{2i} = -2.35^* + r_{2i}, \qquad \tau_{22} = 0.13^{\cdot}$$

During baseline, the average log odds of exhibiting a disruptive behavior for a student in Classroom A is 0.9383, which converts to an odds of exp(0.9383) = 2.5556, and to a proportion of 2.5556/3.5556 = 0.7188. Thus, the expected probability of observing a disruptive behavior during baseline for a student in Classroom A is about 0.72. For a student in Classroom B during baseline, the average log odds of exhibiting a disruptive behavior is $\hat{\beta}_{00} + \hat{\beta}_{01} = 0.9383 - 0.5777 = 0.3606$. This converts to an odds of $\exp(0.3606) = 1.4342$, and a probability of $1.4342/2.4342 = 0.5892$, so the expected probability of observing a disruptive behavior during baseline for a student in Classroom B is about 0.59. The average change in log odds as a student switches from baseline to treatment is significant; $\hat{\beta}_{20} = -2.3638$. For Classroom A, the odds are $\exp(0.9383 - 2.3513) = \exp(-1.413) = 0.2434$, and the probability is $0.2434/1.2434 = 0.1958$ of observing a disruptive behavior during the treatment phase. For Classroom B, the odds are $\exp(0.9383 - 0.5777 - 2.3513) = \exp(-1.9907) = 0.1366$ and the probability is $0.1366/1.1366 = 0.1202$ of observing a disruptive behavior during the treatment phase. Thus, a student in Classroom A is expected to display disruptive behavior more often than one in Classroom B in both phases (probability = 0.72 in baseline, 0.20 in treatment for Classroom A; 0.59 in baseline, 0.12 in treatment for Classroom B). Estimates of the variance components for this model indicate that there may still be significant between-student variation in estimates of the intercept. However, that variation has been reduced and the term for classroom in the model for the intercept did significantly contribute to the estimation of the outcome. Further reduction (if this is possible) would require additional Level-2 predictors.

The estimated effect from the multilevel analysis is similar to that estimated by visual and descriptive analyses in the original publication. However, the multilevel analyses found a small but statistically significant difference between the two classrooms, not in treatment effect but in starting level (baseline). Also, the original authors (Lambert et al., 2006) assumed they could average across phases A1 and A2 and across phases B1 and B2, and that the trend lines within each phase were flat. They were right, as the multilevel analyses confirmed by the non-significant terms in (25), but multilevel modeling provides a test of these assumptions.

Alternative Methods of Coding Phases in ABAB Designs

To code the four phases in an ABAB design, the most natural idea is to code for a main effect for treatment (A vs. B), a main effect for the first pair of AB phases compared with the second pair of AB phases, and an interaction to see whether the effect of treatment is the same in both AB phase changes of the study. Many other codings are possible, however, depending on what quantities are of interest. Here we illustrate a nonstandard but potentially useful coding method, which we call step coding. It resembles dummy coding, in that it uses only the numbers 0 and 1, but the coding is different in other respects.

Suppose that we want the intercept to represent behavior during the baseline phase of the study, and we want other effects to measure the changes as we go from one phase to another. That is, one effect should measure the change from A1 (the first A phase) to B1 (the first B phase); another effect should measure the next change, from B1 to A2 (the second A phase); and the final effect should measure the final change, from A2 to B2 (the second and final B phase)—see Chapter 6 (this volume) for a discussion of this three-transition approach in the context of single-case randomization statistical tests. This process requires three dummy variables that start with the value 0 and then change to 1 with successive changes in phases. The first dummy variable d1 = 0 during phase A1, and then d1 = 1 for phases B1, A2, and B2. Variable d2 = 0 for phases A1 and B1, then d2 = 1 for phases A2 and B2. Finally, d3 = 0 for phases A1, B1, and A2, and d3 = 1 for phase B2. Thus they form a pattern resembling steps. The meaning of these effects depends on all of them being present in the model; removing any of them changes the meanings of the remaining effects because they are not orthogonal. In the following models, we also included a term s for session, to allow for time trend, coded so that 0 is the last session in the first phase of the study (phase A1).

This coding then allows us to specify the following multilevel model. At Level-1,

$$\ln\left(\frac{P_{ti}}{1-P_{ti}}\right) = \pi_{0i} + \pi_{1i}d_{1ti} + \pi_{2i}d_{2ti} + \pi_{3i}d_{3ti} + \pi_{4i}s_{ti}, \qquad (8.26)$$

where the terms are as described above, and the variance assumption remains the same. The unconditional Level-2 equations are now

$$\pi_{0i} = \beta_{00} + r_{0i}$$
$$\pi_{1i} = \beta_{10} + r_{1i}$$
$$\pi_{2i} = \beta_{20} + r_{2i} \ . \qquad (8.27)$$
$$\pi_{3i} = \beta_{30} + r_{3i}$$
$$\pi_{4i} = \beta_{40} + r_{4i}$$

This model says that (a) the logarithm of the odds of showing disruptive behavior is a function of a linear trend, as well as changes due to shifts between phases, and (b) each of these effects may vary across cases, and their posterior distributions are allowed to covary.

The results for this model are

$$\pi_{0i} = 0.40 + r_{0i}, \qquad \tau_{00} = 0.50^*$$
$$\pi_{1i} = -1.81^* + r_{1i}, \qquad \tau_{11} = 2.71^*$$
$$\pi_{2i} = 2.58^* + r_{2i}, \qquad \tau_{22} = 0.79 \ .$$
$$\pi_{3i} = -2.24^* + r_{3i}, \qquad \tau_{33} = 0.84$$
$$\pi_{4i} = -0.05 + r_{4i}, \qquad \tau_{44} = 0.01^*$$

The average log odds in the first baseline phase was .400; exponentiating this gives exp(.400) = 1.492, which is the odds of showing disruptive behavior. To interpret this, consider it as the ratio (approximately) 1.5:1, or 3:2, which means that for every three disruptive observation periods there were two observation periods in which no disruption occurred. How did this change over sessions? The term for sessions is small and not significant, meaning that within phases the behavior was relatively consistent for the average child, with no general trend up or down. However, the average change going from one phase to another was significant for each such change: A1 to B1, B1 back to A2, and A2 to B2. For the first AB change, the (multiplicative) change in odds was $\exp(-1.81) = .164$, meaning that the odds of disruptive behavior dropped by about 84%. For the average child, this would mean that the odds dropped to $1.492(.164) = .245$, or about .25 to 1, which is equivalent to 1:4. That is, for every observation during which there is a disruptive behavior, there are 4 observations with no disruptive behavior, a very large change from baseline. The next phase change (from B1 back to A2) changes the odds by an average of $\exp(2.58) = 13.20$ times, which results in an odds of disruptive behavior well above the original baseline. The final phase change (back to B2) reduces the odds by a factor of $e(-2.24) = .107$, or to about 11% of what they were during the previous A phase; again this is a large change in behavior. Finally, the random effects show that intercepts, slopes, and A1-B1 effects all vary significantly across cases, but B1-A2 and A2-B2 changes do not.

We next investigate whether there is a difference between the two classrooms, now with alternative coding. We will test each effect in the design to see whether the classrooms differ in their general trend over session, in their status during the first phase, or during changes between adjacent phases. The Level-1 model is the same as in the preceding model, and the Level-2 model adds a dummy variable for classroom to each of the equations in

$$\pi_{0i} = \beta_{00} + \beta_{01}x_i + r_{0i}$$
$$\pi_{1i} = \beta_{10} + \beta_{11}x_i + r_{1i}$$
$$\pi_{2i} = \beta_{20} + \beta_{21}x_i + r_{2i} \ . \qquad (8.28)$$
$$\pi_{3i} = \beta_{30} + \beta_{31}x_i + r_{3i}$$
$$\pi_{4i} = \beta_{40} + \beta_{41}x_i + r_{4i}$$

The results were

$$\pi_{0i} = -0.20 + 1.08x_i + r_{0i}, \qquad \tau_{00} = 0.25$$
$$\pi_{1i} = -0.34 - 2.65{}^{*}x_i + r_{1i}, \qquad \tau_{11} = 0.95$$
$$\pi_{2i} = 3.71{}^{*} - 1.91{}^{*}x_i + r_{2i}, \qquad \tau_{22} = 0.04 \ . \qquad (8.29)$$
$$\pi_{3i} = -1.69{}^{*} - 1.01x_i + r_{3i}, \qquad \tau_{33} = 0.78$$
$$\pi_{4i} = -0.17{}^{*} + 0.21{}^{*}x_i + r_{4i}, \qquad \tau_{44} = 0.00$$

The first equation in Equation 8.29 suggests that during baseline, there is a large difference between the classrooms in disruptive behavior, although this effect is not statistically significant at the .05 level. In Classroom A, the average odds of disruptive behavior was $\exp(-0.20) = 0.82$, or about four periods of disruptive behavior for every five periods of nondisruptive behavior. In Classroom B, the average odds were $(.82)(\exp(1.08) = 2.94) = 2.41$, or nearly five periods of disruptive behavior for every two of nondisruptive behavior.

The second equation indicates that the classrooms also differed significantly on the change from phase A1 to B1. In Classroom A, the odds of disruptive behavior decreased by a factor of $\exp(-0.34) = .71$, or a little over two thirds. In Classroom B, the odds decreased much more, by a factor of $\exp(-.034 - 2.65) = 0.05$ below their baseline, or to about one twentieth of their baseline rate.

The third equation indicates that, for the return to baseline (change from phase B1 to A2), Classroom A increased disruptive behavior by an average factor of about $\exp(3.71) = 40.85$ times, while Classroom B rebounded a smaller amount: $\exp(3.71 - 1.91) = 6.04$. This is a large difference, and is statistically significant. From the fourth equation, the final change from A2 to B2 was again a large drop in the average odds for Classroom A of $\exp(-1.69) = .18$ and a somewhat larger (though not significantly different) drop for Classroom B to $\exp(-1.69 - 1.01) = 0.07$. The fifth equation suggests that classrooms significantly differ in their average trend across sessions within phases. For Classroom A, disruptive behavior is slowly decreasing across time, regardless of phase: Each successive session has the odds decrease by a factor of $\exp(-.17) = .84$, or about 16%. On the other hand, for Classroom B there is no time trend given that $\exp(-0.17 + 0.21) = 1.04$. Finally, the variance components show that there is large variability among students within each classroom, but none of these is statistically significant.

Testing Assumptions About Trend and Linearity With Generalized Additive Models

The model for the d-statistic developed at the start of this chapter assumes no trend over time, as did the Bayesian implementation of it. The HGLM analyses tested that assumption, and found no linear trend over time, but did not look at nonlinear trends over time. Even with the HGLM analysis, however, the researcher has to choose the trend to impose on the data, a choice that is often unclear. This section uses a semi-parametric regression called a generalized additive model (GAM) that allows the data to inform the researcher about trend, and so to test whether assumptions about trend and nonlinearity are valid (Wood, 2006). Here we summarize the work that will soon appear in longer form (Sullivan, Shadish, & Steiner, in press).

GAMs are like generalized linear models (GLM) but they replace one or more of the usual terms of a GLM with a predictor that consists of a sum of smoothing functions (Wood, 2006). So GAM estimates both parametric and nonparametric terms. Terms with nonparametric smoothers (explained in more detail shortly) are used to test assumptions about trend, for instance to see if the outcome is changing over time, whether change is linear, quadratic, or some other form, and whether the treatment effect remains constant over time as phases change. In principle, GAMs can be applied jointly to a set of several cases, incorporating random effects terms as in other hierarchical models, to assess the effects of an intervention on all cases in a study. However, we currently know too little about how to do this, and its strengths and weaknesses, to recommend GAM for that purpose in more than an exploratory sense. So here we focus on using GAMs to model each case separately. Our approach is consistent with the goal of using GAMs as a tool for model development and assumption checking rather than for summarizing results across an entire study. That approach will likely change as we learn more.

Within the GAM framework, the smoothing terms have to be represented in such a way that the GAM becomes a linear model. Imagine a simple case, in which you have one smoothed predictor: $Y_i = s(x_i) + \varepsilon_i$. Imagine further that you knew that s should result in a quadratic relationship. The equation for s would be: $s = \beta_0 + x\beta_1 + x^2\beta_2$. Substituting that in to the model equation, you get $Y_i = \beta_1 + x_i\beta_2 + x_i^2\beta_3 + \varepsilon_i$, which is a linear model in the same fashion that all GLM predictors are linear, even in the presence higher order polynomial terms. The problem is that in the real world one doesn't know the true order of s. So, one chooses a basis, or a set of linearly independent vectors, that defines a functional space. These vectors, when linearly combined, can represent any potential vector in the basis space. All of the potential smoothing terms of the model are an element, or basis function, of the chosen basis. So, any potential smoothing term is some linear combination of linearly independent vectors in the basis. Choosing a basis allows the estimation of a nonlinear term from the data, but constrains the geometrical space from which they can be estimated (e.g., so that the smoothing does not result in an unrealistic value, such as a 100th-order polynomial smoother).

There are many potential basis options. A common basis is penalized cubic regression splines (CRS). Spline bases relate the smoothing function to the entire domain of data rather than a single point of the data. CRSs are constructed from pieces of cubic polynomial curves joined together into a continuous function. The curves are joined together at the knots of the data set; knots are the places where an inflection in the curve appears. CRSs are computationally efficient, and their results are easily interpretable. They also can be implemented on small data sets. With CRSs, the researcher has to specify where to place knots, or the location of the potential bends in the functional relationship. One can choose to equally space these knots across the span of the data. Generally, the computer program default spaces the knots evenly across the data, so this is not an arduous process.

Introducing smoothing parameters requires estimating the degree of smoothing necessary for each covariate, for example, the degree of smoothing necessary for the trend term in the present case. Each s term of a GAM model contains a smoothing parameter. The smoothing parameter estimates the optimal amount of smoothing to fit the data while simultaneously adding a penalty for increased "wiggliness" of the smoothing function. Adding a penalty matrix to the least squares estimation model avoids over-fitting the smooth to the data. Within this framework, s approaches a straight line as the smoothing parameter approaches infinity. The optimal degree of smoothness can be estimated directly from the data. GAMs are maximized by penalized iteratively reweighted least squares (P-IRLS). The optimal smoothing parameter is chosen by calculating a generalized cross-validation (GCV) score of each iteration. The underlying idea is to remove one data point from the data set, reestimate the model, and then estimate the predicted value of the removed data point, based on the new model. The observed data point is subtracted from the predicted value, and the deviations are squared. This process is repeated for every data point, and the squared deviations are averaged. The resulting average is the cross validation score. However, this process is computationally tedious. An equivalent score calculation is

$$V = n \sum\nolimits_{(i=1)^n} \equiv \left(y_i - \hat{f}_i \right)^2 \Big/ [\mathrm{tr}(\mathbf{I} - \mathbf{A})]^2$$

y_i is the observed data point, $\hat{f}_i$ is the predicted value of that data point, $\mathbf{I}$ is the identity matrix of the full model, and $\mathbf{A}$ is the model influence matrix, a matrix that maps the vector of observed values, $\mathbf{y}$, to the vector of predicted or fitted values, $\mathbf{f}$, and describes the influence that each observed value has on each fitted value. $\text{Tr}(\mathbf{I} - \mathbf{A})$ is the trace, or sum of the matrix diagonals, of the matrix that results from of the model influence matrix, $\mathbf{A}$, subtracted from $\mathbf{I}$, the identity matrix. The smaller the GCV score, the better the model fit. Models can be compared using their GCV scores, illustrated in the examples that follow.

The model output also lists the effective degrees of freedom of the smoothing term. The effective degrees of freedom is defined as the trace of $\mathbf{A}$, the model influence matrix (recall that the influence matrix is a matrix that maps the vector of observed values to the vector of predicted or fitted values and describes the influence that each observed value has on each fitted value). Estimated degrees of freedom equal to one is a linear effect (Wood, 2006). As the effective degrees of freedom increase, the parameter smooth becomes wigglier. When using cubic regression splines, effective degrees of freedom are very roughly equivalent to the polynomial order of the smoother plus one. That is, effective degrees of freedom of 4 would roughly imply a third-degree polynomial smoothing term for the covariate being tested (Hothorn & Everitt, 2010). This makes interpretation of the nonlinearities of the predictors more intuitive, although the effective degrees of freedom are rarely whole numbers. This is also an extremely approximate rule of thumb, and as the effective degrees of freedom approach one, this rule of thumb no longer applies.

To simplify notation, we omit the subscript i used in previous sections to index each case, retaining only the index for time t. The basic model for a single case is

$$Log\left(\frac{P_t}{1-P_t}\right) = \mathbf{X}_t\theta + s_1(x_{1t}) + s_2(x_{2t}) + s_3(x_{3t}) + \cdots + \varepsilon_t, \quad (8.30)$$

where $Log\left(\frac{P_t}{1-P_t}\right)$ is the logit link function for the proportion outcome as before, $\mathbf{X}_t\theta$ is the design matrix and corresponding parameter vector (i.e., any of the regression components that one wishes to continue to treat in the usual parametric fashion), $s_1(x_{1t}), \ldots, s_p(x_{pt})$ are smoothing functions for each predictor (x) that one wishes to smooth nonparametrically, and ε_t is an error term with a binomial distribution.

We examined four GAM models on each case of the Lambert et al. (2006) data, all modeled in R using the mgcv package (Wood, 2010). Each model includes (a) an intercept, or the participant's initial outcome level; (b) a continuous time (trend) variable X_t measured as calendar time across sessions (e.g., two sessions conducted one day apart would be 1, 2; two sessions one week apart would be 1, 8); (c) a dummy-coded treatment variable z_t (0 for baseline, 1 for treatment); and (d) a Time × Treatment interaction:

$$[X_t - (n_1 + 1)]z_t,$$

where n_1 is the time of the last data point in the first baseline phase (the data point directly preceding the initial introduction of treatment). This interaction captures the change in slope beginning at the start of treatment (Huitema & McKean, 2000).

The first GAM model is a linear model with no smoothers (Model 1):

$$Log\left(\frac{P_t}{1-P_t}\right) = \beta_0 + \beta_1 X_t + \beta_2 z_t + \beta_3 [X_t - (n_1 + 1)] z_t + \varepsilon_t. \quad (8.31)$$

This model yields identical results to a GLM with binomial errors; it will differ somewhat from a GLM that assumes normality, the latter being a common but incorrect analysis for this kind of outcome. The second GAM model applies a smoother to the interaction term (Model 2):

$$Log\left(\frac{P_t}{1-P_t}\right) = \beta_0 + \beta_1 X_t + \beta_2 z_t + s_3 ([X_t - (n_1 + 1)] z_t) + \varepsilon_t. \quad (8.32)$$

The third model applies the smoother to the trend term (Model 3):

$$Log\left(\frac{P_t}{1-P_t}\right) = \beta_0 + s_1 (X_t) + \beta_2 z_t + \beta_3 [X_t - (n_1 + 1)] z_t + \varepsilon_t. \quad (8.33)$$

The fourth model applies a smoother to both the interaction term and the trend term (Model 4):

$$Log\left(\frac{P_t}{1-P_t}\right) = \beta_0 + s_1 (X_t) + \beta_2 z_t + s_3 ([X_t - (n_1 + 1)] z_t) + \varepsilon_t. \quad (8.34)$$

Each GAM analysis gives standard regression output (i.e. regression coefficient, standard error, t test of the coefficient, p value) for each parametric term. For smoothed terms, output lists the effective degrees of freedom. The effective degrees of freedom are a rough measure of the complexity of the fitted spline model; edf = 1 corresponds to a linear model, and as edf increases towards edf = k, the spline model is approximately as complex as a polynomial of degree k − 1 (Hothorn & Everitt, 2010). Smoothed terms also have a corresponding F statistic and p value that are conservative and approximate. To determine which model fits the data best, one compares various model fit statistics (R^2, deviance) along with examining significance tests (more details are in Sullivan, Shadish, & Steiner, in press).

Consider Case A2 from the Lambert et al. (2006) study (Figure 8.2). Visual analysis might suggest (a) a clear treatment effect; (b) no trend in baseline, with deviations around a horizontal trend line being plausibly attributed to chance; and (c) more variability in the outcome during treatment, with a possible nonlinear trend. The latter implies a possible trend by treatment interaction, with the trend varying depending on phase.

Exhibit 8.2 presents the input (boldface) and output for applying each of the GAM models to case A2; in that table, x is time (trend), z is treatment, and int is the interaction of x and z. Model 1 (no smoothers; equivalent to a GLM analysis with binomial errors) suggests a treatment effect, no trend, and no interaction. Model 2 (smoothed interaction) suggests a treatment effect, a linear trend that is not significant ($p = .066$) with a non-significant smoothed interaction ($p = .181$). The estimated degrees of freedom are 8.22, implying a very high (around a 7th order) smooth. Model 3 (smoothed trend) is like Model 1 with a

Exhibit 8.2. GAM Input and Output for Models 1 Through 4 Applied to Case A2

Model 1

gam1 <- gam(y~x+z+int, family=quasibinomial, weights=trial)
> summary (gam1)

Parametric coefficients:

	Estimate	Std. Error	t value	Pr(>|t|)
(Intercept)	0.83864	0.48802	1.718	0.0976.
x	0.07525	0.04707	1.599	0.1220
z	−3.22804	0.69529	−4.643	8.63e-05***
int	−0.05082	0.06258	−0.812	0.4241

Signif. codes: 0 '***' 0.001 '**' 0.01 '*' 0.05 '.' 0.1 ' ' 1

R-sq.(adj) = 0.802   Deviance explained = 71.7%
GCV score = 2.5053   Scale est. = 2.1713 $n = 30$

Model 2

gam2 <- gam(y~x+z+s(int, bs="cr"), family=quasibinomial, weights=trial
> summary (gam2)

Parametric coefficients:

	Estimate	Std. Error	t value	Pr(>|t|)
(Intercept)	−0.25632	0.73701	−0.348	0.7319
x	0.07525	0.03859	1.950	0.0663.
z	−2.19494	0.86034	−2.551	0.0196*

Signif. codes: 0 '***' 0.001 '**' 0.01 '*' 0.05 .' 0.1 ' ' 1

Approximate significance of smooth terms:

	edf	Ref.df	F	p-value
s(int)	8.222	8.822	1.621	0.181

R-sq.(adj) = 0.872   Deviance explained = 86.2%
GCV score = 2.3318   Scale est. = 1.4596 $n = 30$

Model 3

gam3 <- gam(y~s(x, bs="cr")+z+int, family=quasibinomial, weights=trial
> summary (gam3)

Parametric coefficients:

	Estimate	Std. Error	t value	Pr(>|t|)
(Intercept)	1.92976	0.44774	4.310	0.000208***
z	−3.22803	0.69530	−4.643	8.63e-05***
int	−0.05082	0.06258	−0.812	0.424117

Signif. codes: 0 '***' 0.001 '**' 0.01 '*' 0.05 '.' 0.1 ' ' 1

Approximate significance of smooth terms:

	edf	Ref.df	F	p-value
s(x)	1	1	2.555	0.122

R-sq.(adj) = 0.802   Deviance explained = 71.7%
GCV score = 2.5053   Scale est. = 2.1713 $n = 30$

(continued on next page)

Exhibit 8.2.   GAM Input and Output for Models 1 Through 4 Applied
to Case A2 *(Continued)*

Model 4

gam4 <– gam(y~s(x, bs="cr")+z+s(int, bs="cr"), family=quasibinomial, weights=trial)
> summary (gam4)

Parametric coefficients:

	Estimate	Std. Error	t value	Pr(>|t|)
(Intercept)	0.8348	0.5128	1.628	0.1202
z	–2.1949	0.8603	–2.551	0.0196 *

Signif. codes: 0 '***' 0.001 '**' 0.01 '*' 0.05 '.' 0.1 ' ' 1

Approximate significance of smooth terms:

	edf	Ref.df	F	p-value
s(x)	1.000	1.000	3.801	0.0663 .
s(int)	8.222	8.822	1.621	0.1811

Signif. codes: 0 '***' 0.001 '**' 0.01 '*' 0.05 '.' 0.1 ' ' 1

R-sq.(adj) = 0.872   Deviance explained = 86.2%
GCV score = 2.3318   Scale est. = 1.4596   n = 30

Note. R input is in boldface, output is not. Variables are x = time (trend), z = treatment, and
int = interaction between x and z.

treatment effect, no trend, and no interaction. Model 4 (smoothed trend and interaction) suggests a treatment effect, a smoothed linear trend that is not significant ($p = .066$), and a non-significant smoothed interaction ($p = .181$). All four models agree that there is a treatment effect; but it is unclear whether the variability in the treatment phases reflects a trend by treatment interaction.

One can compare these models using a combination of model comparison tests, fit indices, comparison to visual analysis, and substantive knowledge. Fit statistics include the usual R^2 (proportion of variance accounted for), percent deviance explained (larger is better) and GCV score (smaller is better). The fit indices indicate Models 2 (smoothed interaction) and 4 (smoothed trend and interaction) fit best. Model comparison tests use the R analysis of variance function to test whether the difference between the residual deviances from two models is significant using a chi-square difference test. Those comparisons (Exhibit 8.3) suggest Models 2 and 4 that both fit significantly better than Model 1; but Model 4 (smoothed trend and interaction) does not significantly improve the fit of Model 2 (smoothed interaction). Note that the comparison of Models 2 to 4 shows that both models have identical residual deviances and degrees of freedom; the significant chi-square is an artifact of rounding error since both the chi-square difference tests and degrees of freedom are vanishingly close to zero. The same is true for the comparison of Models 1 and 3.

The analysis suggests that Model 2 (significant treatment effect, trend significant only at $p = .066$, smoothed trend by treatment interaction non-significant at $p = .181$) is a strong candidate for the best model. It suggests a clear treatment effect, but also that disruptive behavior shows a very slight average increase over time (the regression coefficient is $b = .075$), with a tendency for the effect of

Exhibit 8.3.   Model Comparisons for Case A2

Model 1, Model 2

> anova(gam1,gam2, test="Chisq")
Analysis of Deviance Table

Model 1: y ~ x + z + int
Model 2: y ~ x + z + s(int, bs = "cr")

	Resid. Df	Resid. Dev	D	Deviance	Pr(>Chi)
1	26.000	56.454			
2	18.778	27.407	7.2221	29.046	0.00668 **

Model 1, Model 3

> anova(gam1,gam3, test="Chisq")
Analysis of Deviance Table

Model 1: y ~ x + z + int
Model 2: y ~ s(x, bs = "cr") + z + int

	Resid. Df	Resid. Dev	Df	Deviance	Pr(>Chi)
1	26	56.454			
2	26	56.454	1.6388e-05	2.4249e-05	9.437e-05***

Model 1, Model 4

> anova(gam1,gam4, test="Chisq")
Analysis of Deviance Table

Model 1: y ~ x + z + int
Model 2: y ~ s(x, bs = "cr") + z + s(int, bs = "cr")

	Resid. Df	Resid. Dev	Df	Deviance	Pr(>Chi)
1	26.000	56.454			
2	18.778	27.407	7.2221	29.046	0.00668**

Model 2, Model 4

> anova(gam2,gam4, test="Chisq")
Analysis of Deviance Table

Model 1: y ~ x + z + s(int, bs = "cr")
Model 2: y ~ s(x, bs = "cr") + z + s(int, bs = "cr")

	Resid. Df	Resid. Dev	Df	Deviance	Pr(>Chi)
1	18.778	27.407			
2	18.778	27.407	1.1435e-05	8.8527e-06	6.934e-05 ***

Model 3, Model 4

> anova(gam3,gam4, test="Chisq")
Analysis of Deviance Table

Model 1: y ~ s(x, bs = "cr") + z + int
Model 2: y ~ s(x, bs = "cr") + z + s(int, bs = "cr")

	Resid. Df	Resid. Dev	Df	Deviance	Pr(>Chi)
1	26.000	56.454			
2	18.778	27.407	7.2221	29.046	0.00668**

Note. R input is in boldface, output is not. Variables are x = time (trend), z = treatment, and
int = interaction between x and z.

treatment to be somewhat lower in later phases than earlier ones. The significance test says the latter trend and variability in treatment effect may be due to chance, even though the model comparison says that modeling that variation would improve the fit of the model.

Another way to use GAMs is to ask how sensitive conclusions about treatment effects derived from the usual parametric GLM analysis are to the assumption of linear trend. If models with GAM smoothers give essentially the same answer as an ordinary linear analysis, SCD researchers can be more confident that their conclusions are correct. The treatment effect was significant in both the GLM and best-fitting GAM model for cases A1, A2, A3, B2, and B3; and it was not significant in both models for cases A4 and B4. For the remaining cases (B1, B5), the GLM showed a significant treatment effect but the best-fitting GAM did not. Even in the latter cases, however, the direction and magnitude of the effect were similar across models, suggesting that taking nonlinearities into account may change significance levels but not necessarily the visual conclusion about the presence of an effect.

In summary, GAMs did not change the conclusion of GLM about treatment effectiveness in seven cases, but did change it in two cases. In the two cases that did change, an effect that was significant at $p < .05$ became plausibly due to chance. GAMs also provided increased subtlety to the interpretation of effects. Where Lambert et al. (2006) called the effect "dramatic" (p. 93), GAM also identifies general increases or decreases in disruptive behavior over time, possible carryover effects from phase to phase, a suggestion that treatment effects in the AB^2 part of the study may be smaller than in the AB^1 part, and some treatment effects that are not clearly different from chance in two of nine cases.

Finally, it is possible to take serial dependence (autocorrelation) into account in GAM models. One way is to use generalized additive mixed models (GAMMs), but this application requires large numbers of data points, which is not reasonable to expect in most SCDs. Another way is to use the best-fitting GAM to estimate residuals, and then compute the autocorrelation on them. We have done so, and the resulting autocorrelations tend to be greatly shrunken compared to their counterparts based on ordinary GLM, probably shrunken so much that they may not pose much of a problem for estimating the effect or its variance. In theory it should also be possible to use the autocorrelations based on GAM residuals as input to a subsequent GAM model that includes an autoregressive component, but the mgcv program currently does not allow this.

In summary, then, a perennial question in SCD research is whether trend and nonlinearities exist, and if so, whether they would change the conclusions about treatment effects. To judge from this one study with nine cases, the answer to the first part of the question is affirmative. The nonlinearities may be of quite high order (third- to seventh-order polynomials in these data) if not always statistically significant. Regarding the second part of the question, the nonlinearities do not much change the conclusions from GLM, at least in this one example. GAMs give the SCD researcher a useful tool for exploring questions concerning assumptions about trend. We hope to extend this work to larger samples of SCDs to see how well treatment effects are sensitive to trend more generally, and to summarizing GAM results over cases within studies to reach conclusions about study-level treatment effects.

Discussion

This is an exciting time for SCD researchers as SCDs begin to receive belated but well-deserved attention from a wider array of researchers and policymakers as a credible methodology for understanding what works for practice and policy. The WWC, long devoted exclusively to including only between-groups and especially randomized experiments in evidence-based practice reviews for education, has now issued standards for how SCDs might provide acceptable evidence for such purposes (Kratochwill et al., 2010). Further, in the U.S. Department of Education's IES grant proposals, SCDs can now be implemented not only for development studies but also for efficacy studies under some conditions. A recent review of the medical literature found hundreds of studies using SCDs, typically called *N-of-1 trials* in that context, to test the effects of medical interventions (Gabler, Duan, Vohra, & Kravitz, 2011), with very interesting new statistics being developed for them (Zucker, Ruthazer, & Schmid, 2010). Reflecting their interest, medical researchers are now extending the CONSORT standards for reporting randomized experiments to reporting standards for N-of-1 trials (Shamseer et al., 2012).

For those of us interested in statistical analysis of SCDs, the times are doubly exciting. There are so many opportunities to contribute to a field that traditionally makes little use of statistics that many researchers could generate long-term programs of research on the topic. The research in this chapter, and no doubt in the volume as a whole, gives some idea of the breadth and possibilities such research could embrace. SCD analysis is now in a stage of proliferating such ideas; most of the approaches, like those in this chapter, are still under active development. It may take some time before we know the strengths and weakness of all these approaches, fully develop them, and are in a position to make best-practice recommendations about how to analyze and meta-analyze SCDs. So there is plenty of time and work for all.

As we noted in the introduction, however, some SCD researchers have raised questions about the usefulness and purpose of newly introduced statistics, or sometimes any statistics at all. Their questions and criticisms express the principled skepticism that has long existed in the SCD research community regarding the capacity of such statistics to capture the nuances of SCD research. While some SCD researchers (e.g., Chapter 2, this volume) are eager to embrace even the more complex new developments, others are reticent. For example, Parker and Vannest (2012) have suggested that

> interventionists should be cautious about analyses that are not easily understood, are not governed by a "'wide 'lens" visual analysis, do not yield intuitive results, and remove the analysis process from the interventionist, who alone has intimate understanding of the design logic and resulting data patterns. (p. 254)

See also Chapter 4, this volume. These comments contain much truth. Statisticians must learn the needs, practices, and conceptual underpinnings of SCD research in order to have meaningful, constructive impact. Statisticians should not expect a uniformly enthusiastic welcome when they present work that is unfamiliar to

SCD researchers, work that might not yet fully capture every complexity and nuance in each SCD, or work that is so inaccessible that even statistically enthusiastic SCD researchers would have a hard time using it.

Yet each of the objections that Parker and Vannest (2012) raised is amenable to discussion. Consider them in order. First, the starting word of this quote from those authors, *interventionists*, is important to the rest of their sentence. Although some fields such as clinical psychology pride themselves on producing interventionists who are scientist-practitioners, even for them it may be unrealistic to expect primary care providers using SCDs to learn complex statistics, especially if those statistics are not made easily accessible with user-friendly computer programs. That being said, no doubt exists that many SCD authors view their work through a research lens, whether in addition to or instead of an interventionist lens. Indeed, it is hard to view the prolific statistical work of authors like Parker and many others as not having that lens. Perhaps we should hold SCD researchers to different standards than SCD interventionists.

Second, it is not clear how to distinguish between analyses that are not easily understood and researchers who have not yet taken the time to learn approaches that are well-accepted and widely-used in other fields. Traditional SCD research has failed to adopt statistical methods for such a long period of time that SCD researchers should anticipate that a nontrivial learning curve will apply: You have to learn to walk before you can run.

Third, visual analysis is consistent in principle with statistical analyses of all sorts. Of course, we have yet to achieve in practice what is possible in principle. Developing accessible and intuitive methods for presenting the results of statistical analysis in graphical form is a fruitful and badly needed area for future work. On the other hand, it is not clear that the interpretation of SCD data should be governed by visual analysis, which can be more misleading than sometimes appreciated. For instance, with count data a Poisson distribution predicts more large observations by chance than many appreciate, and so letting visual analysis govern interpretation is likely to lead to too many Type I errors (see also Chapter 5, this volume). As in so many other fields, visual and statistical analyses should be used to complement each other, not govern each other.

Fourth, intuition most often results from repeated exposure to an approach, and is hindered by avoidance of it, although clear presentation by the statistician helps facilitate intuition greatly. This works both ways, of course. Statisticians will need repeated exposure to SCDs to gain an intuitive understanding of that research.

Fifth, Parker and Vannest (2012) have argued that the analysis process should never be removed from the interventionist. This assertion conflicts with the working methods of many scientific disciplines where there is real concern that confirmation biases and self-interest might lead to selective analyses and reporting of results. We contend that the analyst and the interventionist should be partners (see the "masked visual analyst" discussion in Chapter 5, this volume). That being said, an interesting feature of SCD research is that studies typically present the raw data in graphs. It is not so much that analysts are removing the process from interventionists as it is that interventionists are giving their data away by making it publicly available for all to use.

Sixth, no one is alone in having an intimate understanding of the design and data. SCDs can be complex, but they are not rocket science. Indeed, the exemplary transparency in the presentation of methods and results in SCD research makes them among the easiest to understand. No obvious reason exists to think statisticians cannot have an intimate understanding of SCD research.

Finally, it is the nature of statistical models, and indeed of all scientific theory, to simplify. Statistical models will never fully reflect the complexity of the data; their aim is to capture the most salient features, making it possible to summarize results and to generalize from specific study operations to general constructs. This is true with all research designs, not just SCDs but also, for example, randomized experiments and epidemiological studies. Sometimes models simplify too much, and it is not yet clear which SCD analyses do so, nor which can be improved to reflect important features better. Clearly, for example, some of the analyses in the present chapter simplify too much.

A number of reinforcing consequences are likely to encourage SCD researchers to learn and incorporate quantitative data analyses into their practices. One is the expectations of the larger evidence-based practice communities who want findings communicated in commonly used statistical languages before agreeing to include SCDs in evidence-based practice reviews. Regression, hierarchical models, and meta-analysis with well-accepted effect size measures are examples of those languages. Ad hoc effect-size estimators with unclear statistical properties or clear statistical errors are not. Of course, so-called "nonparametric" effect sizes (it is not clear they really are nonparametric), which are widely used in SCD research, could be developed more formally (see also Chapter 4, this volume). Clarifying the interpretation of these metrics and their relationship to the common statistical canon would be helpful, and might facilitate wider acceptance and further development in the statistical community.

Second, competition for grant funding provides a powerful incentive for SCD researchers to embrace quantitative analysis methods, even if many of their peers are reluctant to consider them. Imagine, for example, two SCD researchers submitting good grant proposals, one with a well-justified power analysis suggesting they are likely to detect an effect of a known magnitude if it exists, and the other with no power analysis and no way to quantify an effect size in any commonly understood way. Over time, the former will have a competitive advantage over the latter.

Third, granting agencies are funding statistical researchers to develop and apply common statistics to SCDs. Eventually, the investigators on those grants are often reviewers of other grants for those same agencies. It would be surprising if those agencies and reviewers did not expect proposed SCD research to use those statistics or provide a compelling reason why not.

Finally, it is already the case that a critical mass of statistical researchers have taken up the task of developing better statistical analyses of SCDs. They will continue to do so, both in the social sciences and in medicine. After all, the problems are intellectually interesting, practically important, fundable, and timely, and the raw data are publicly available through digitization of published graphs. Why should these researchers stop?

Far from encouraging caution in adopting unfamiliar and even complex statistics, we suggest that SCD researchers enthusiastically learn them, experiment with them, and collaborate with statisticians to lend the wisdom of decades of SCD research to the development of statistics appropriate for the analysis of SCDs. Just as much, we encourage statisticians to engage with the SCD research and intervention community to learn their needs and develop accessible statistical analyses that might shed new light on the question of effective interventions. Everyone can win.

References

Beretvas, S. N., & Chung, H. (2008). An evaluation of modified R^2-change effect size indices for single-subject experimental designs. *Evidence-Based Communication Assessment and Intervention, 2,* 120–128. doi:10.1080/17489530802446328

Box, G. E. P. (1954). Some theorems on quadratic forms applied to the study of analysis of variance problems, I. Effect of inequality of variance in the one-way classroomification. *Annals of Mathematical Statistics, 25,* 290–302. doi:10.1214/aoms/1177728746

Busk, P. L., & Serlin, R. C. (2005). Meta-analysis for single-case research. In T. R. Kratochwill & J. R. Levin (Eds.), *Single-case research design and analysis: New directions for psychology and education* (pp. 187–212). Hillsdale, NJ: Lawrence Erlbaum Associates.

Gabler, N. B., Duan, N., Vohra, S., & Kravitz, R. L. (2011). N-of-1 trials in the medical literature: A systematic review. *Medical Care, 49,* 761–768. doi:10.1097/MLR.0b013e318215d90d

Hedges, L. V., Pustejovsky, J., & Shadish, W. R. (2012). A standardized mean difference effect size for single-case designs. *Research Synthesis Methods, 3,* 224–239.

Hedges, L. V., Pustejovsky, J. E., & Shadish, W. R., (2013). A standardized mean difference effect size for multiple baseline designs across individuals. *Research Synthesis Methods, 4,* 324–341.

Hedges, L. V. (1981). Distribution theory for Glass's estimator of effect size and related estimators. *Journal of Educational Statistics, 6,* 107–128. doi:10.2307/1164588

Hothorn, T., & Everitt, B. S. (2010). *A handbook of statistical analyses using R* (2nd ed.). Boca Raton, FL: Chapman & Hall/CRC.

Huitema, B. E. (2011). *The analysis of covariance and alternatives: Statistical methods for experiments, quasi-experiments, and single-case studies.* Hoboken, NJ: Wiley.

Huitema, B. E., & McKean, J. W. (2000). Design specification issues in time-series intervention models. *Educational and Psychological Measurement, 60*(1), 38–58. doi:10.1177/00131640021970358

Jenson, W. R., Clark, E., Kircher, J. C., & Kristjansson, S. D. (2007). Statistical reform: Evidence-based practice, meta-analyses, and single subject designs. *Psychology in the Schools, 44*(5), 483–493. doi:10.1002/pits.20240

Kratochwill, T. R., Hitchcock, J., Horner, R. H., Levin, J. R., Odom, S. L., Rindskopf, D. M., & Shadish, W. R. (2010). *Single-case designs technical documentation.* Retrieved from http://ies.ed.gov/ncee/wwc/pdf/wwc_scd.pdf

Kyse, E. N., Rindskopf, D. M., & Shadish, W. R. (2012). *Analyzing data from single-case designs using multilevel models: A primer.* Manuscript in preparation.

Lambert, M. C., Cartledge, G., Heward, W. L., & Lo, Y. (2006). Effects of response cards on disruptive behavior and academic responding during math lessons by fourth-grade urban students. *Journal of Positive Behavior Interventions, 8,* 88–99. doi:10.1177/10983007060080020701

Lunn, D. J., Thomas, A., Best, N., & Spiegelhalter, D. (2000). WinBUGS: A Bayesian modelling framework: Concepts, structure, and extensibility. *Statistics and Computing, 10,* 325–337. doi:10.1023/A:1008929526011

Maggin, D. M., Swaminathan, H., Rogers, H. J., O'Keefe, B. V., Sugai, G., & Horner, R. H. (2011). A generalized least squares regression approach for computing effect sizes in single-case research: Application examples. *Journal of School Psychology, 49,* 301–321. doi:10.1016/j.jsp.2011.03.004

Parker, R. I., Hagan-Burke, S., & Vannest, K. (2007). Percentage of All Non-Overlapping Data (PAND): An alternative to PND. *The Journal of Special Education, 40,* 194–204. doi:10.1177/00224669070400040101

Parker, R. I., & Vannest, K. J. (2012). Bottom up analysis of single-case research designs. *Journal of Behavioral Education, 21,* 254–265.

Parker, R. I., Vannest, K. J., & Davis, J. L. (2011). Effect size in single case research: A review of nine nonoverlap techniques. *Behavior Modification*, *35*, 303–322. doi:10.1177/0145445511399147

Parker, R. I., Vannest, K. J., Davis, J. L., & Sauber, S. B. (2011). Combining nonoverlap and trend for single-case research: Tau-U. *Behavior Therapy*, *42*, 284–299. doi:10.1016/j.beth.2010.08.006

Raudenbush, S. W., Bryk, A. S., Cheong, Y. F., Congdon, R., & du Toit, M. (2004). *HLM6: Hierarchical linear and nonlinear modeling*. Lincolnwood, IL: Scientific Software International.

Raudenbush, S. W., Yang, M.-L., & Yosef, M. (2000). Maximum likelihood for generalized linear models with nested random effects via high-order, multivariate Laplace approximation. *Journal of Computational and Graphical Statistics*, *9*, 141–157.

Shadish, W. R., Brasil, I. C. C., Illingworth, D. A., White, K., Galindo, R., Nagler, E. D., & Rindskopf, D. M. (2009). Using UnGraph to extract data from image files: Verification of reliability and validity. *Behavior Research Methods*, *41*, 177–183. doi:10.3758/BRM.41.1.177

Shadish, W. R., & Rindskopf, D. M. (2007). Methods for evidence-based practice: Quantitative synthesis of single-subject designs. In G. Julnes & D. J. Rog (Eds.), *Informing federal policies on evaluation method: Building the evidence base for method choice in government sponsored evaluation* (pp. 95–109). San Francisco, CA: Jossey-Bass. doi:10.1002/ev.217

Shadish, W. R., Rindskopf, D. M., & Hedges, L. V. (2008). The state of the science in the meta-analysis of single-case experimental designs. *Evidence-Based Communication Assessment and Intervention*, *2*, 188–196. doi:10.1080/17489530802581603

Shadish, W. R., & Sullivan, K. J. (2011). Characteristics of single-case designs used to assess intervention effects in 2008. *Behavior Research Methods*, *43*, 971–980. doi:10.3758/s13428-011-0111-y

Shamseer, L. Sampson, M., Bukutu, C., Barrowman, N., Altman, D., Moher, D., & Vohra, S. (2012). P05.50. CONSORT extension for Nof-1 trials (CENT) guidelines. *BMC Complementary and Alternative Medicine, 12* (Suppl 1): P410. (downloaded from http://www.biomedcentral.com/1472-6882/12/S1/P410)

Singer, J. D., & Willett, J. B. (2003). *Applied longitudinal data analysis: Modeling change and event occurrence*. New York, NY: Oxford University Press. doi:10.1093/acprof:oso/9780195152968.001.0001

Spiegelhalter, D., Thomas, A., Best, N., & Lunn, D. (2004). *WinBUGS user manual, Version 2.0*. Retrieved from http://mathstat.helsinki.fi/openbugs/ManualsFrames.html

Sullivan, K. J., Shadish, W. R., & Steiner, P. M. (in press). Analyzing longitudinal data with generalized additive models: Applications to single-case designs. *Psychological Methods*.

Van den Noortgate, W., & Onghena, P. (2003a). Combining single-case experimental data using hierarchical linear models. *School Psychology Quarterly*, *18*, 325–346. doi:10.1521/scpq.18.3.325.22577

Van den Noortgate, W., & Onghena, P. (2003b). Hierarchical linear models for the quantitative integration of effect sizes in single-case research. *Behavior Research Methods, Instruments & Computers*, *35*, 1–10. doi:10.3758/BF03195492

Van den Noortgate, W., & Onghena, P. (2007). The aggregation of single-case results using hierarchical linear models. *The Behavior Analyst Today*, *8*, 196–209.

Van den Noortgate, W., & Onghena, P. (2008). A multilevel meta-analysis of single-subject experimental design studies. *Evidence-Based Communication Assessment and Intervention*, *2*, 142–151. doi:10.1080/17489530802505362

Wood, S. (2010). *mgcv: GAMs with GCV/AIC/REML smoothness estimation and GAMMs by PQL*. Retrieved from http://cran.r-project.org/package=mgcv

Wood, S. N. (2006). *Generalized additive models: An introduction with R*. Boca Raton, FL: Chapman & Hall/CRC.

Zucker, D. R., Ruthazer, R., & Schmid, C. H. (2010). Case (N-of-1) trials can be combined to give population comparative treatment effect estimates: Methodologic considerations. *Journal of Clinical Epidemiology*, *63*, 1312–1323. doi:10.1016/j.jclinepi.2010.04.020

9 _____

The Role of Single-Case Designs in Supporting Rigorous Intervention Development and Evaluation at the Institute of Education Sciences

Jacquelyn A. Buckley, Deborah L. Speece, and Joan E. McLaughlin

The Institute of Education Sciences (IES), established by Congress in the Education Science Reform Act of 2002, is the primary research, evaluation, and statistics office within the U.S. Department of Education (USDOE). In this chapter, we discuss IES's support for the use of single-case designs to advance education research and the current status of these designs within IES. We begin this chapter by describing IES's legislative mission that drives its approach to evidence-based education, as well as IES's perspective on the available methodologies for advancing education research, including single-case designs. We describe single-case design as a viable experimental research methodology for projects funded by IES, and provide examples of how single-case design has been applied in funded grants within IES. Finally, we describe other IES initiatives supporting single-case design and methodology in education research.

Mission of the Institute of Education Sciences

IES's mission is to expand fundamental knowledge and understanding of education and to provide education leaders and practitioners, parents and students, researchers, and the general public with unbiased, reliable, and useful

We acknowledge our colleagues at the National Center for Special Education Research for their helpful comments and Charry Li who provided clerical assistance.

This chapter was coauthored by employees of the United States government as part of official duty and is considered to be in the public domain. Any views expressed herein do not necessarily represent the views of the United States government, and the authors' participation in the work is not meant to serve as an official endorsement.

http://dx.doi.org/10.1037/14376-010
Single-Case Intervention Research: Methodological and Statistical Advances, by T. R. Kratochwill and J. R. Levin

information. The focus of this information is on the condition and progress of education in the United States; education policies, programs, and practices that support learning and improve academic achievement and access to educational opportunities for all students; and the effectiveness of federal and other education programs (USDOE IES, 2011a).

IES comprises four centers, each charged with different functions, to help carry out this mission. The National Center for Education Research (NCER) and the National Center for Special Education Research (NCSER) support research and research training programs designed to develop our understanding of and provide solutions for the nation's most pressing education issues. The National Center for Education Evaluation and Regional Assistance (NCEE) evaluates federal education programs and sponsors the Regional Education Laboratories, the What Works Clearinghouse (WWC), and the Education Resources Information Clearinghouse (ERIC). Finally, the National Center for Education Statistics (NCES) is the primary federal entity for collecting and analyzing data related to education. The discussion in this chapter focuses on work conducted by the Centers where single-case design is addressed: the two research Centers (NCER and NCSER) and the WWC efforts in NCEE.

One aspect of the legislative mission addressed by the research Centers is to support research that will generate empirical evidence to improve the quality of education in the United States. A specific function is to provide rigorous and relevant evidence on which to ground education practice and policy. The purpose of evidence-based education research is to discover "what works" in education as well as to learn about why, when, where, for whom, and under what conditions a program works. In addition, by identifying what works, what doesn't, and why, IES aims to improve educational outcomes for all students, including those at risk of poor academic and social outcomes. One priority for IES is an emphasis on methodological rigor in the research it supports. IES adopted high standards for conducting research and evaluating research evidence and for training of researchers across the country.

IES's mission is pragmatic as well, emphasizing the importance of making education research applicable, relevant, and usable for schools. The work of IES is grounded in the principle that effective education research must address the interests and needs of education practitioners and policymakers, as well as students, parents and community members. Thus, while focused on providing evidence through rigorous research, IES is committed to building a stronger science of education that helps us understand, for example, how to improve teaching and student learning, as well as the policies and practices needed to reach these outcomes.

IES supports a variety of research methodologies, including single-case[1] designs, recognizing that answering questions of what works and for whom requires a variety of research strategies. IES's emphasis on rigor, which has been equated by some to mean a sole emphasis on randomized controlled trials, has led to an inaccurate perception that single-case designs are not acceptable methods

---

[1]Consistent with this volume's title and other chapters, IES uses "case" rather than "subject" in that the designs are appropriate for individuals as well as other clustered units, including classrooms, school-based groups, and schools.

for IES-funded research. Other chapters in this book contain detail regarding the history and current trends in single-case research so that is not repeated here. What is important to note is that IES considers single-case research methodology to be a scientifically rigorous approach for advancing evidence-based practices in education. IES supports the use of single-case designs to examine the development of new interventions through iterative testing cycles, to study the efficacy of interventions,[2] and as a complementary method to further understand the results of randomized controlled trials in efficacy studies.

Single-case methods have a strong history in the medical and psychological sciences, particularly in applied settings (e.g., Rapoff & Stark, 2007); yet, they have been used in a limited capacity in education research. Researchers who focus on students with disabilities, however, tend to embrace single-case designs in a variety of circumstances, such as when studying students with low-incidence disabilities (e.g., deafness, significant cognitive delay) when it is nearly impossible to obtain a sufficient sample size for a randomized trial without extraordinary effort and cost. As noted in the preceding, single-case designs can be also used to supplement findings from group designs to further understand, for example, differential responsiveness to an intervention regardless of the targeted disability. In addition, special education as a discipline emphasizes individual student needs and therefore single-case designs allow for a dynamic, responsive process where the development of an intervention is informed by its impact on student functioning, and allows for immediate changes to be made during the study to improve the intervention.

Three sets of activities were instrumental in placing single-case design within the larger set of research methodologies supported by IES: the narrative of the Request for Applications (RFAs) for research grants and statistics and methodology research grants, the WWC pilot Standards for single-case design, and IES's effort to build capacity in the field through hosting single-case design and analysis training institutes. These activities have informed each other as IES staff has worked toward understanding the methodology and assessing its relevance for the work that IES supports. The next section provides a discussion of the role that single-case design can play in the range of research projects funded by IES.

The Role of Single-Case Design in IES-Funded Research

IES funds a wide range of research projects as well as statistics and methodology research projects (to be discussed in a later section). Across its education and special education research programs, the range of research activities supported by IES is defined as research goals in RFAs that are published annually. There are five research goals, or types of studies, that are currently supported:

1. *Exploration (Goal 1).* These projects explore associations between education outcomes and factors that can be changed by the education system

---

[2]NCER and NCSER encourage single-case designs as a complementary method to group designs in efficacy trials; NCSER also encourages single-case designs as a primary method for determining efficacy.

(e.g., children's behaviors, teacher practices) as well as attempt to identify what variables may mediate or moderate these associations.

2. *Development and Innovation (Goal 2).* These studies are designed to
   develop and test innovative interventions (e.g., curricula, instructional
   approaches, programs, or policies) or to improve existing education
   interventions.

3. *Efficacy and Replication (Goal 3).* Projects under this goal evaluate
   whether a fully developed intervention is efficacious under limited or
   ideal conditions, gather follow-up data examining the longer term effects
   of an intervention with demonstrated efficacy, or replicate an efficacious
   intervention when varying the original conditions.

4. *Effectiveness (Goal 4).* These studies evaluate whether a fully developed
   intervention that has evidence of efficacy is effective when implemented
   under routine conditions through an independent evaluation.

5. *Measurement (Goal 5).* Projects under this goal develop and validate
   new assessments or validate existing assessments for specific purposes,
   contexts, and populations

Of these, Development and Innovation (Goal 2) and Efficacy and Replication
(Goal 3) are the goals that explicitly address single-case design in the RFAs and
are described in more detail later in this chapter. The focus of the discussion is
on projects funded by NCSER because this Center currently funds the majority of single-case design studies. Since its beginning in 2005, NCSER included
single-case research in its description of fundable designs.

DEVELOPMENT AND INNOVATION. The development of new and innovative
education interventions is critical to improving education and special education research. The purposes of these projects are to (a) develop innovative interventions, or further develop and improve existing interventions, intended to
improve student education outcomes; (b) collect data on the feasibility and
usability of the interventions in education settings; and (c) collect pilot data
to determine the promise of the intervention to improve student outcomes. To
achieve these purposes, researchers must understand limitations of current
education practice and how a new and innovative approach may improve outcomes over current practice. In addition, a critical aspect of development projects is to understand what may be feasible in authentic education delivery
settings given fiscal, logistical, and practical restraints. In typical development projects, researchers incorporate multiple methodological approaches
to determine the feasibility and usability of the intervention in the intended
setting (e.g., whether the intervention can be implemented within the context of schools) and to determine the potential impact of the intervention on
student outcomes targeted by the intervention (e.g., improved reading skills
for a literacy intervention). Understanding the intervention's usability and
feasibility often requires qualitative methods such as observations of teachers
and students using the intervention, and interviews and focus groups with
key stakeholders. In addition, development and testing of the intervention
occur through an iterative process. That is, information is used to revise the
initial intervention, through an iterative process of implementing, gathering

feedback, revising, and implementing again, to improve the ability of service delivery providers to implement the intervention, and to ensure that the intervention is reaching its intended target or targets (e.g., teacher practices or child behaviors). Development work also requires pilot testing the potential impact of the fully developed intervention on important student outcomes. The pilot study may use experimental or quasi-experimental methods to examine whether the use of the newly developed intervention leads to better student performance. The feasibility and pilot testing are critical to assess whether the intervention is worth the additional investment of testing the intervention's efficacy.

Single-case designs can be important methods for use in the iterative development process, to understand whether the intervention being developed is working as intended, and to determine what modifications may be needed to improve to potential impact of an intervention on student outcomes. In 2011, IES made more explicit the importance and usefulness of single-case design for the Development and Innovation goal (USDOE IES, 2011b). Single-case designs reside on the "continuum of rigor" that is now defined in the RFA to inform applicants of the acceptable designs for the pilot study. Single-case designs may be used as the sole design for the pilot study to test the impact on student outcomes, and they can also be combined with group designs to better understand potential impact. In addition to their usefulness in conducting the pilot study, single-case designs can be used throughout the iterative development process, such as when one component of a multicomponent intervention is being developed. Single-case designs are flexible in that a researcher can implement a series of single-case designs to understand whether the intervention is likely to achieve the outcomes anticipated and/or work out logistical or practical concerns with implementation. For example, setting or intervention characteristics can be varied across a series of single-case designs. This information can be used to further refine and develop the intervention.

EFFICACY AND REPLICATION. Development and innovation are critical to the initial development of practices to improve outcomes for students, but equally important is identifying causal effects and mechanisms. The purpose of efficacy and replication studies is to determine whether fully developed interventions (e.g., education practices, programs, and policies) produce a beneficial impact on education outcomes for students relative to a counterfactual when they are implemented under ideal conditions in authentic education delivery settings (e.g., classrooms, schools, districts). Under "ideal" conditions an applicant could propose to implement the intervention among homogeneous samples of students, teachers, schools, and/or districts. As much as possible, the question is not only whether something works but also why it works (or does not work), under what conditions it works, and for whom it works. Replication studies would then allow for testing of an intervention for which there is already evidence of a beneficial impact under conditions that differ from those of previous efficacy studies. IES has been most recognized for its support of randomized controlled experiments to evaluate the effect of interventions on student outcomes, but a variety of methodologies are allowed depending on the research question. Efficacy and replication projects are to provide causal analysis, and applicants must show how causal inferences are related to the proposed design. In addition, researchers examine the fidelity of the implementation of the intervention, as well as mediators and moderators of the effect of the intervention, all of which require a variety of research methods. Single-case design has been recognized as an appropriate design for Efficacy and Replication projects from the first RFA issued by NCSER (USDOE IES, 2005). Currently, if an applicant chooses to use single-case methodology, the proposed design must meet the WWC pilot standards described in the following sections.[3]

WWC Single-Case Design Technical Documentation

The IES's WWC reviews the research on different programs, products, and policies in education, with the goal of trying to answer the question "What works in education?" to provide educators with the information they need to make evidence-based decisions. In 2010, the WWC published guidance for single-case design studies, called *Single-Case Design Technical Documentation* (Kratochwill et al., 2010, 2013). An overview of the new standards presented in this document was incorporated into the NCSER RFA for fiscal year (FY) 2012, which stated,

> Single-case-experimental designs would be methodologically successful if, at the end of the grant period, the investigators had rigorously evaluated the impact of a clearly specified intervention on relevant student outcomes and under clearly described conditions using single-case research designs that meet (without reservation) the Institute's What Works Clearinghouse standards described in the Single-Case Design Technical Documentation (http://ies.ed.gov/ncee/wwc/pdf/wwc_scd.pdf) whether or not the intervention is found to improve student outcomes.
>
> The efficacy studies proposed must meet two sets of criteria regarding (1) the design and analysis of individual single-case studies, and (2) the set of single-case studies required to provide evidence of the efficacy of an intervention. Applicants are strongly encouraged to read the Single-Case Design Technical Documentation for a full description of the requirements for single-case research studies that will meet Institute's (WWC pilot Standards) for individual studies and for the set of studies required to establish efficacy of an intervention. (USDOE IES, 2011b, p. 52)

The RFA for FY 2013 also noted that single-case designs could be embedded within a randomized controlled trial with the following language:

> Single-Case Experimental Designs: You may propose a single-case experimental design (e.g., multiple baseline) that meets the design criteria set by the WWC. By single-case experimental designs, the Institute refers to experimental studies involving repeated, systematic measurement of a dependent variable before, during, and after the active manipulation of an independent variable (i.e., intervention) intended to demonstrate a causal

---

[3]WWC pilot Standards were not available prior to the FY 2012 funding cycle, and therefore efficacy studies funded prior to 2012 were not held to this standard.

relationship between the two variables using a small number of participants or cases. By "case," the Institute is referring to a smaller number of participants or units (e.g., classrooms, schools), and is not referring to descriptive case studies. *The Institute supports the use of single-case experimental designs as a complementary method to further understand the results of randomized controlled trials in efficacy studies (e.g., determining how manipulation of intervention components may affect outcomes for children who were nonresponsive to the intervention tested in the randomized controlled trial)* [italics added for emphasis]. If you propose a single-case experimental design as the primary means for establishing efficacy see below for Additional requirements for single-case experimental designs proposed as the primary design for efficacy. (US DOE IES, 2012b p. 54)

The WWC Single-Case Design Technical Documentation is considered a work in progress, subject to revision as the standards are put in practice with the resulting lessons learned and incorporated (see Kratochwill et al., 2013). It represents a large and public step forward in understanding how single-case design is relevant to the scientific mission of IES. For single-case studies, *design standards* and *evidence criteria* are separate considerations in the evaluation of study quality. The design standards evaluate the internal validity of the design. These standards apply to a wide range of designs, including ABAB designs, multiple-baseline designs, alternating and simultaneous treatment designs, changing criterion designs, and variations of these core designs. For example, multiple-baseline designs are required to have at least six phases (i.e., an A and a B phase for at least three staggered replicates) with a minimum of five data points per phase, to be judged as meeting design standards without reservations. For studies that meet the design standard, they are then judged against the evidence criteria. Visual analysis is conducted for each outcome variable to determine whether the study meets evidence criteria. Each *individual* single-case design study is evaluated against the design standards and evidence criteria.

To establish the efficacy of a practice or intervention using single-case design studies, WWC requires more than one single-case study to examine the impact of the same intervention, and the combination of studies is required to meet the "5-3-20" threshold. That is, results from various single-case design studies will not be combined into one report of efficacy of an intervention unless there are five research papers of single-case designs that each meet the WWC design standards and evidence criteria, conducted by at least three independent research teams at three different geographic locations, and include at least 20 cases across the studies. This threshold must be met for the WWC to evaluate the efficacy of a practice based on evidence derived from single-case design studies.

The 5-3-20 rule represents agreement among prominent single-case design researchers on how to identify effective practices evaluated within the single-case methodology. The rule and other standards in the technical document are based on work by Horner, Carr, Halle, McGee, Odom, and Wolery (2005). The proposals in the Horner et al. document were vetted by the single-case design research community (Robert Horner, personal communication, December 2011). As an example of the growing acceptance of the Standards, researchers have begun to apply them in the synthesis and evaluation of existing literature (e.g., Browder, Wakeman, Spooner, Ahlgrim-Delzell, & Algozzine, 2006; Lane, Kalberg, & Shepcaro, 2009).

Examples of IES-Funded Research Projects Incorporating Single-Case Designs

In this section we describe studies funded by IES in recent years that use single-case design as part of development and innovation as well as efficacy and replication studies. Studies are described for the development and innovation and efficacy and replication goals.

DEVELOPMENT AND INNOVATION. Linda Mason and colleagues at Pennsylvania State and George Mason Universities developed a writing strategy and fluency intervention for middle-school students with behavior disorders (Mason, Kubina, & Hoover, 2011). The base intervention, Self-Regulated Strategy Development (SRSD), is intended to improve the written expression and writing fluency performance of seventh- and eighth-grade students with behavior disorders in general education and alternative settings who are struggling with writing. During the development process, a series of multiple-probe designs across student groups were used to examine students' writing performance (expression and fluency) in both general education and alternative education settings. For example, across two multiple-baseline designs, the person who delivered the instruction was varied: a graduate research assistant or the students' special education teacher (Mason, Kubina, & Taft, 2011). Student and teacher attitudes were examined, and modifications to the intervention were made based on teacher feedback and student performance and behavior. Additional multiple-probe studies were conducted with the revised intervention and positive effects noted for all students in the primary outcome measure, quality of written responses. In addition to single-case designs, the research team conducted a quasi-experimental study with classrooms of students to understand group-administered implementation and impact on outcomes (Mastropieri et al., 2010). Students in this study mastered the components of effective persuasive essay writing, and improved from baseline to post instruction in length of fluency phases and quality of essays. Overall, this research program illustrates how single-case results can be used to refine an intervention and inform the design of a group study.

Similarly, Kathleen Lane and colleagues at Vanderbilt University (e.g., Lane et al., 2010) further developed the instructional procedures for the SRSD writing model to meet the behavioral needs of second-grade students at high risk for behavior disorders who also have poor writing skills. They also examined the feasibility and potential impact on student outcomes when implementing this program within the context of a three-tiered, school-wide positive behavior support model. Single-case methodology allowed the research team to conduct a series of quick studies to investigate learner characteristics (e.g., type of behavior problem), and setting characteristics (e.g., integration with the school-wide positive behavioral support model) to determine the most appropriate modifications that had the greatest potential to improve outcomes for students. For example, second-grade students with limited writing skills who also had either externalizing or internalizing behavior patterns were taught how to plan and write stories using the self-regulated strategy development model. Results of two multiple-probe designs, one for students with externalizing behaviors (three girls, four boys) and a second for students with internalizing behaviors (two girls, four boys), indicated that the intervention had promise for improving all students' writing skills (e.g., increases in story elements, improvements in story quality and length). Student responsiveness to the intervention did not vary consistently as a function of the type of problem behavior (e.g., internalizing, externalizing), and therefore the researchers did not need to take type of problem behavior into account in the development process. The series of single-case studies also allowed the researchers to examine various aspects of the intervention to determine which had the most promise for improving outcomes for students. For example, results showed the research team that they needed to modify the model so that self-regulation addresses writing and behavior, rather than just writing. In addition, they used features of the school-wide reinforcement system to support implementation of the secondary SRSD intervention (e.g., Sandmel et al., 2009). Again, single-case methodology allowed immediate changes to be made throughout the intervention development process to develop a responsive intervention for students, teachers, and schools.

As another example of development work, Stephanie Peterson and her colleagues, first at Idaho State University and then Western Michigan University, developed a positive behavioral intervention to be used with elementary students with disabilities who engage in severe problem behavior, such as aggression and chronic noncompliance (Peterson et al., 2009). Building on empirical work indicating that escape from task demands was the most prevalent function of problem behavior for individuals with developmental disabilities, Peterson et al. (2009) developed an intervention to decrease problem behavior in children with disabilities with escape-motivated problem behavior, and to slowly increase their participation in academic tasks without having bursts of problem behavior as task demands increased. The intervention was a choice-making intervention. When presented with demanding tasks, children were allowed to choose between completing a portion of the task, requesting a break, or engaging in problem behavior. High-quality reinforcement (longer breaks with access to highly preferred positive reinforcers) was provided for task completion. Moderate-quality reinforcement (shorter breaks with access to moderately preferred reinforcers) was provided for break requests, and low-quality reinforcement (brief breaks with no access to positive reinforcement) was provided for problem behavior. Single-case research designs (reversal designs and multiple-probe designs) were used to evaluate the effects of providing these different dimensions of reinforcement for break requests, compliance, and problem behavior and determine refinements needed to the intervention protocol. Peterson and colleagues found that different response patterns to the reinforcers emerged when the intervention was implemented across participants, but overall, participants were able to reduce problem behavior, despite problem behavior continuing to produce some level of reinforcement for the students. Several questions remained, such as individual contributions of reinforcement duration and quality (e.g., adult attention) and effects of increasing task demands over time on participant choices. However, the flexibility of the single-case methodology allowed Peterson et al. to refine the intervention throughout the development process and to explore questions of feasibility and potential impact more thoroughly perhaps than had she used a group design.

EFFICACY AND REPLICATION. As an example of an efficacy study that incorporated single-case design, Debra Kamps and her colleagues at the University of Kansas tested the efficacy of the Class-Wide Function-Based Intervention Teams intervention with elementary students with, or at risk for, serious behavior disorders in general and special education settings (Wills et al., 2009). This behavioral intervention includes class-wide intervention designed to teach appropriate behavior skills (e.g., how to appropriately gain the teacher's attention) and reinforce the use of those skills through a game format. The intervention package also includes individualized functional behavior assessment (e.g., interviews, observations) combined with function-based interventions for students who do not successfully respond to the class-wide intervention. Kamps and colleagues used a randomized controlled trial with teachers and classrooms randomly assigned to treatment or control groups to test the class-wide program. But for the students who required the individualized program, single-case reversal and multiple-baseline designs were used. The research of Kamps and her colleagues illustrates how single-case design can be used in conjunction with a group design to determine intervention effects and to acknowledge individual differences.

One limitation of group randomized trials is the masking of individual response to an intervention. That is, researchers can indicate how, on average, students respond to an intervention, but are generally unable to determine why a particular student did or did not respond positively to an intervention. Single-case design studies can be used to complement group randomized trials to better understand the impact of an intervention, and perhaps help learn ways to improve an intervention's impact on student outcomes. First Step to Success (Walker et al., 1997, 1998) is a manualized school–home intervention that has an evidence base in achieving positive outcomes for students in early elementary school who are at risk for developing aggressive or antisocial behavioral patterns. The program uses a trained behavior coach who works with each student and his or her class peers, teacher, and parents over a three-month period. First Step to Success was found to have positive effects on external behavior, emotional/internal behavior, social outcomes, and academic performance (e.g., Sumi et al., 2013; Walker et al., 2009). Research on First Step to Success has included randomized controlled trials, as well as a series of single-case design studies. One randomized controlled trial of First Step to Success funded by IES was conducted by Hill Walker and colleagues at the University of Oregon, within a large, diverse district in New Mexico where the program had not been previously implemented. The primary purpose of the study was to determine the effects and outcomes of the intervention program for English- and Spanish-speaking child populations. Results were similar to prior studies, indicating First Step to Success improved students' behavioral outcomes and academic engaged time (Walker et al., 2009). Funded as part of this larger randomized trial, Deborah Carter (Boise State University) and Robert Horner (University of Oregon) explored adding function-based behavioral support to

First Step to Success, with the goal of integrating individualized practices with a fully manualized intervention protocol. The researchers argued that manualized interventions are important because the intervention procedures can be clearly described and have written instructions that can be easily disseminated, but often schools need to tailor an intervention to a specific child and context. For example, the First Step to Success program provides participating students with access to adult (e.g., teacher) attention for engaging in appropriate behavior and removes access to adult attention for engaging in problem behavior. Although this may be appropriate for some students who exhibit problem behavior (e.g., those students who respond to adult attention), for others, their behavior is maintained through other means such as the need for peer attention. In that case, the First Step to Success program may not be as effective in changing behavior.

A single-case withdrawal design study was conducted to examine the effects of adding function-based supports and/or adaptations to the standard First Step to Success program for a kindergarten student whose behavior was maintained by high rates of peer attention, and for whom the standard First Step to Success protocol was not effective. In other words, the researchers asked whether an adaptation can be made to the First Step to Success manualized procedures that would tailor the intervention to individual student needs. In this adaptation, the class earns points for ignoring peer problem behavior, a procedure not included in the First Step to Success manual. By adding function-based supports to the standard program, the new program was able to decrease problem behavior and increase academic engagement for this student whose behavior was maintained by peer attention (Carter & Horner, 2007). A multiple-baseline study across students (Carter & Horner, 2009) was then conducted and also showed how function-based modifications can be integrated into First Step to Success to decrease problem behavior and increase academic engagement.

Additional IES Support for Single-Case Design

Earlier we noted that IES also supports methodological work relevant to education research. Through the grant program on Statistical and Research Methodology in Education, IES awards grants to advance education research methods and statistical analyses, including single-case methods (US DOE IES, 2012a). The long-term outcome of this research program will be a wide range of methodological and statistical tools that will better enable education scientists to conduct rigorous education research. Researchers intending to improve the statistical and methodological tools available to education scientists, and who are interested in single-case research are encouraged to consider this research program. Single-case experimental designs are appropriate targets for this program, as they pose several analytical challenges. For example, single-case designs violate assumptions of traditional inferential statistics (e.g., independence between observations) and small sample sizes, but they also come with the advantage of many measurements per participant (see Chapter 5, this volume). Applicants may propose research that continues exploration of various approaches (e.g., hierarchical linear modeling, nonparametric tests, measurement of effect size) for analyzing results from individual single-case studies, as well as analyzing aggregated single-case design data (US DOE IES, 2012a).

Examples of currently-funded work include William Shadish (University of California–Merced) and colleagues who are exploring the development of an effect-size statistic that is comparable to the d statistic from a between-groups experiment that would allow researchers to assess effects from both single-case and between-groups designs on comparable metrics in systematic reviews of interventions (see Chapter 8, this volume). In addition, Wim Van den Noortgate (Katholieke Universiteit Leuven) and colleagues are further developing a multi-level modeling approach for combining the results of studies that use single-case designs.

Another source of support is the Single-Case Design Training Institute. One of IES's functions is to build the capacity of the field to conduct scientifically valid research. To this end, intensive training institutes have been offered on cluster randomized trials, quasi-experimental design, and single-case designs. These training institutes are designed to build upon the skills of current researchers who wish to expand their knowledge and skill in the use of these methodologies. The Single-Case Design Training Institute covers a variety of topics including purposes and fundamental assumptions, characteristics of credible designs, relationship to group designs, visual and statistical analysis, and discussions on efforts to measure effect size. To date, 75 researchers have received the week-long training and IES plans to continue offering this opportunity.

IES also offers training opportunities for new investigators through pre-doctoral, postdoctoral, and early career development and mentoring awards (USDOE IES, 2012b). It is beyond the scope of this chapter to describe these opportunities in depth, but research institutions can apply for pre- and post-doctoral awards and can specify methodological training as one of the goals of the program. Several of the currently funded postdoctoral training programs have single-case research as an option for methodological training for fellows. The early career RFA is designed for new researchers who wish to conduct research in the field of special education. Applicants could specify learning about single-case design as an aspect of their career development plan.

Concluding Comments

Our goals for this chapter were to provide an overview of IES's mission and to describe the support for single-case design at IES within this context. We have emphasized that single-case design is viewed as a legitimate experimental approach to further the goal of IES to provide scientifically valid research that is relevant to students, teachers, parents, and other stakeholders. Although the design is primarily the province of the NCSER, it is also welcomed by the NCER for its development and innovation research goal as well as a complement to randomized controlled trials to understand factors or variables that affect the response to the intervention. In addition to recognizing single-case design within the primary research programs of the two Centers, IES also supports capacity building through a training institute and research training programs.

We also note that there is work to be done in testing the standards promulgated by the WWC. For example, design standards include interrater agreement on at least 20% of the data points in each condition (baseline, intervention) and, for multiple-baseline designs, at least six phases (i.e., an A and a B phase for three staggered replicates) are required with a minimum of five data points per phase. It will be important to test these standards as the field moves forward (e.g., to address whether 15% of the data is adequate in assessing interrater reliability, or whether 8 phases (i.e., an A and a B phase for 4 staggered replicates) with three data points is more robust than, say, the above example of six phases with five data points). These questions are in addition to the important problems of identifying effect-size metrics so that results can be pooled across studies and meaningfully used in the interpretation of effects. This is a dynamic time in the development of single-case methods and IES will continue to play an important role as the field moves forward.

References

Browder, D. M., Wakeman, S. V., Spooner, F., Ahlgrim-Delzell, L., & Algozzine, B. (2006). Research on reading instruction for individuals with significant cognitive disabilities. *Exceptional Children*, 72, 392–408.

Carter, D., & Horner, R. (2007). Adding functional behavioral assessment to First Step to Success: A case study. *Journal of Positive Behavior Interventions*, 9, 229–238. doi:10.1177/10983007070090040501

Carter, D., & Horner, R. (2009). Adding function-based behavioral support to First Step to Success: Integrating individualized and manualized practices. *Journal of Positive Behavior Interventions*, 11, 22–34. doi:10.1177/1098300708319125

Horner, R. H., Carr, E. G., Halle, J., McGee, G., Odom, S., & Wolery, M. (2005). The use of single subject research to identify evidence-based practice in special education. *Exceptional Children*, 71, 165–180.

Kratochwill, T. R., Hitchcock, J., Horner, R. H., Levin, J. R., Odom, S. L., Rindskopf, D. M., & Shadish, W. R. (2010). Single-case designs technical documentation. Retrieved from http://ies.ed.gov/ncee/wwc/pdf/wwc_scd.pdf

Kratochwill, T. R., Hitchcock, J. H., Horner, R. H., Levin, J. R., Odom, S. L., Rindskopf, D. M. & Shadish, W. R. (2013). Single-case intervention research design standards. *Remedial and Special Education*, 4, 26–38. doi:10.1177/0741932512452794

Lane, K. L., Graham, S., Harris, K. R., Little, M. A., Sandmel, K., & Brindle, M. (2010). Story writing: The effects of self-regulated strategy development for second grade students with writing and behavioral difficulties. *The Journal of Special Education*, 44, 107–128. doi:10.1177/0022466908331044

Lane, K. L., Kalberg, J. R., & Shepcaro, J. C. (2009). An examination of quality indicators of function-based interventions for students with emotional or behavioral disorders attending middle and high schools. *Exceptional Children*, 75, 321–340.

Mason, L. H., Kubina, R., & Hoover, T. (2011). Effects of quick writing instruction for high school students with emotional and behavioral disabilities. *Journal of Emotional and Behavioral Disorders*, JEBD OnlineFirst, June 7, 2011 as doi:10.1177/1063426611410429

Mason, L. H., Kubina, R., & Taft, R. (2011). Developing quick writing skills of middle school students with disabilities. *Journal of Special Education*, 44, 205–220.

Mastropieri, M. A., Scruggs, T. E., Cuenca-Sanchez, Y., Irby, N., Mills, S., Mason, L., & Kubina, R. (2010). Persuading students with emotional disabilities to write: A design study. In T. E. Scruggs & M. A. Mastropieri (Eds.), *Literacy and learning: Advances in learning and behavioral disabilities* (Vol. 23, pp. 237–268). Oxford, England: Emerald Group.

Peterson, S. M., Frieder, J. E., Smith, S. L., Quigley, S. P., & Van Norman, R. K. (2009). The effects of varying quality and duration of reinforcement on mands to work, mands for break, and problem behavior. *Education & Treatment of Children*, 32, 605–630. doi:10.1353/etc.0.0075

Rapoff, M., & Stark, L. (2007). Editorial: *Journal of Pediatric Psychology* statement of purpose: Section on single-subject studies. *Journal of Pediatric Psychology*, 33, 16–21. doi:10.1093/jpepsy/jsm101

Sandmel, K., Brindle, M., Harris, K., Lane, K., Graham, S., Nackel, J., . . . Little, A. (2009). Making it work: Differentiating tier two self-regulated strategies development in writing in tandem with school-wide positive behavioral support. *Teaching Exceptional Children, 42,* 22–33.

Sumi, W. C., Woodbridge, M. W., Javitz, H., Thornton, S. P., Wagner, M., Rouspil, K., & Severson, H. (2013). Are short-term results the first step to long-term behavioral improvements? *Journal of Emotional and Behavioral Disorders.* Advance online publication. doi:10.1177/1063426611429571

U.S. Department of Education, Institute of Education Sciences. (2005). *Request for applications special education research grants 2006* (84.324A). Washington, DC. Author.

U.S. Department of Education, Institute of Education Sciences. (2011a). *Building partnerships that produce relevant, useful research: Director's biennial report to Congress.* Washington, DC: Author.

U.S. Department of Education, Institute of Education Sciences. (2011b). *Request for applications special education research grants 2012* (84.324A). Washington, DC: Author.

U.S. Department of Education, Institute of Education Sciences. (2012a). *Request for application number: IES-NCER-2013-01.* Retrieved from http://ies.ed.gov/funding/pdf/2013_84305D.pdf

U.S. Department of Education, Institute of Education Sciences. (2012b). *Request for application number: IES-NCSER-2013-02.* Retrieved from http://ies.ed.gov/funding/pdf/2013_84324B.pdf

Walker, H. M., Kavanagh, K., Stiller, B., Golly, A., Severson, H. H., & Feil, E. G. (1997). *First step to success: An early intervention program for antisocial kindergartners.* Longmont, CO: Sopris West.

Walker, H. M., Kavanagh, K., Stiller, B., Golly, A., Severson, H. H., & Feil, E. G. (1998). First step to success: An early intervention approach for preventing school antisocial behavior. *Journal of Emotional and Behavioral Disorders, 6,* 66–80.

Walker, H. M., Seeley, J. R., Small, J., Severson, H. H., Graham, B. A., & Feil, E. G., . . . Forness, S. R. (2009). A randomized control trial of the First Step to Success early intervention: Demonstration of program efficacy outcomes within a diverse, urban school district. *Journal of Emotional and Behavioral Disorders, 17,* 197–212. doi:10.1177/1063426609341645

Wills, H. P., Kamps, D., Hansen, B. D., Conklin, C., Bellinger, S., Neaderhiser, J., & Nsubuga, B. (2009). The Class-Wide Function-Based Intervention Team (CW-FIT) program. *Preventing School Failure, 54,* 164–171. doi:10.1080/10459880903496230

Part II

Reactions From Leaders in the Field

10

Single-Case Designs and Large-*N* Studies: The Best of Both Worlds

Susan M. Sheridan

Intervention research is difficult. Although basic questions among applied intervention researchers on the surface may seem simple and straightforward, they become immediately complex once human, contextual, and interpersonal variables emerge. The challenge is compounded when demands for understanding variability in the human condition require us to ask "for whom" or "under what conditions" an intervention works, or when investigating theories of change. The following pages embark on a discussion of the use of single-case designs (SCDs) in a line of intervention research on parent–teacher (conjoint) consultation and explore the many contributions of SCD frameworks for answering critical research questions. A description of the evolution of this work will illustrate issues encountered that led us to adopt at times alternative methodologies. Finally, the need for mixed (single-case and large-*N*) designs for the next generation of intervention science is explored.

For more than 20 years I have been conducting research on consultation, behavioral interventions, and parent–teacher relationships. A generally clear and predictable process has been evident as this research has moved along a rather systematic trajectory of developing, testing, refining, and validating the consultation intervention. The general process is outlined in Exhibit 10.1. SCDs have provided the foundation for this work. They have proved essential in the early stages of intervention development, feasibility, and efficacy testing, and they continue to inform larger investigations of intervention effects. Our questions have expanded from determining the effects of carefully delineated intervention protocols for specified samples in select settings, to identifying general outcomes using large-*N* designs with an eye toward generalization and

The development of this chapter was supported in part by Institute of Education Sciences, U.S. Department of Education Grants R324A100115 and R305C090022 to the University of Nebraska–Lincoln. The opinions expressed are those of the author and do not represent views of the Institute of Education Sciences or the U.S. Department of Education.

http://dx.doi.org/10.1037/14376-011
Single-Case Intervention Research: Methodological and Statistical Advances, by T. R. Kratochwill and J. R. Levin

Exhibit 10.1.   Ten Steps Along the Intervention Research Trajectory

---

Step 1: Identify an issue or problem
Step 2: Create strategies
Step 3: Pilot/assess feasibility
Step 4: Evaluate with intensity/precision; small sample
Step 5: Replicate and extend with new sample, problem, context
Step 6: Develop theory
Step 7: Test on larger scale
Step 8: Assess mechanisms of change (theory)
Step 9: Investigate influential contextual/situational variables
Step 10: Test effectiveness on large scale

---

large scale impact. Along this journey, we have found ways to capitalize on the strengths of both SCDs and randomized controlled trials as complementary methodologies toward the advancement of intervention science.

Most field researchers begin exploring topics of interest based on an issue or problem that they have encountered or that needs attention. For example, I began with a series of studies investigating the effects of interventions on the children whose behaviors they were targeted to change. An interest in interventions that connect families and schools became pronounced when I was working as a school-based practitioner. I observed repeatedly a divide between schools (including special programs, general classrooms, and administrative structures) and the families they were commissioned to serve. Too often, this divide created disconnected experiences and significant challenges in children's adaptation. As a response, my colleagues and I modified previously proven teacher-focused consultation strategies (Kratochwill & Bergan, 1990) to include parents in joint and collaborative problem solving. Soon thereafter, I began researching conjoint behavioral consultation (CBC), an indirect process for addressing children's learning and behavioral problems by bringing together parents and teachers and implementing structured problem-solving methods in a joint, cross-system process (Sheridan & Kratochwill, 1992; Sheridan, Kratochwill, & Elliott, 1990). Strategies to adapt traditional approaches to behavioral consultation, bringing together parents and teachers and identifying cross-system targets, influences, and strategies, were developed and piloted.

Like many intervention scientists, the basic research question we posed early on in most CBC outcome studies was "Is Intervention A (CBC) effective at producing a desired change in Behavior B for Child?" This efficacy question, investigated through careful specification and manipulation of independent variables, is the hallmark of SCDs, which are extremely well positioned to answer questions with intricate detail on specific individuals, classrooms, or in some cases, larger units (e.g., White & Bailey, 1990). In the case of CBC, the significance of family–school connections in treating selective mutism was field-tested in a single-case format, with very promising results from both implementation (acceptability, social validity) and efficacy perspectives (Sheridan, Kratochwill, & Ramirez, 1995). Experimental examination of CBC ensued through a series of graduated studies. Through the careful specification and manipulation of independent variables, documentation and assessment of intervention implementation, repeated measurement of outcome variables, and analysis of behavior change in terms of level, trend, and other meaningful metrics, much was learned about the efficacy of well-defined and carefully implemented CBC strategies under tightly controlled conditions. The first experimental study utilized multiple-baseline designs to investigate the effects of CBC (and teacher-only consultation) on peer interaction behaviors for socially withdrawn children (Sheridan et al., 1990). We found positive effects for interventions implemented in the context of parent–teacher consultation, with generalized effects across home and school settings. However, under conditions of teacher-only consultation, effects were localized to the school setting only. Furthermore, maintenance of effects appeared stronger under conditions in which both parents and teachers contributed to consultation and implemented interventions in both of their respective settings.

Simple adaptations to replicate and extend our questions and findings with new problems, samples, and contexts followed. Through a series of SCDs, our findings were replicated across unique target behaviors such as academic performance (Galloway & Sheridan, 1994), different samples (Weiner, Sheridan, & Jenson, 1998), and distinctive disability groups (Colton & Sheridan, 1998). With the use of experimental methodologies (predominantly multiple-baseline designs), experimental control was achievable, and great confidence was placed in our findings.

The intensive nature of SCD research allowed for iterative hypotheses to be formed regarding the nature of variations in treatment effects. For example, whereas initial investigations explored structural features of intervention delivery across home and school settings as the operative feature of CBC, response variations under unique intervention conditions suggested that other mechanisms may be at work. Galloway and Sheridan (1994) found that structural elements such as implementation of behavioral intervention components across settings were effective, but the processes inherent in the CBC context produced results superior to those in a noncollaborative context. Specifically, children whose parents participated in both conditions demonstrated increases in homework completion and accuracy, which is not surprising given all we know about the benefits of parental involvement at bolstering specific academic outcomes (Christenson & Reschly, 2010; Fan & Chen, 2001). The patterns of student performance were stable and consistent under CBC conditions that brought parents and teachers together in joint, collaborative communication and problem solving. However, when parents' involvement was confined to one-way (school to home) communication as indicated in a home-note manual, gains were relatively less pronounced and short-lived. This finding added credibility to our developing theory that *relationships between parents and teachers*—and not simply parents' involvement in intervention implementation—contributed to the effects of CBC. That is, more than simply imposing structural features of problem solving and cross-setting intervention implementation, we began to theorize that the conjoint and collaborative meetings wherein parent and teachers are brought together to exchange ideas, share responsibility, and expect accountability seems to contribute to positive intervention effects.

How Does the Intervention Work?

A theory can serve as a guiding framework that helps to organize assumptions, explain relationships, interpret phenomena, and make meaning out of observations. Theories are necessary within intervention sciences to understand the causes for and nature of human responses. Theories link hypotheses together logically into a coherent explanation; advances are made when this connected set of hypotheses receive empirical support. Thus, educational/psychological intervention scientists are increasingly concerned with creating and validating theories for *how* a particular approach acts. Understanding the mechanisms at work when an intervention is implemented (i.e., discerning the manner in which the independent variable influences the dependent variables of interest) is increasingly important in educational, social, and behavioral sciences. Such careful and systematic scrutiny of the functional nature of an intervention's effects allows for clarity and precision not only in the specificity of theory of change, but also—importantly—for design and implementation efforts. Furthermore, by uncovering the processes by which an intervention is exerting influence on behavior, we become increasingly able to address the underlying question of *how or why* the intervention works.

To test theories of change in a way that unveils the pathways by which our interventions operate, it is first necessary to hypothesize the central components that operate to produce change. Indeed, SCDs can play a role in the systematic identification of operative components ("active ingredients") via components analyses using dismantling strategies, or they may help articulate proposed pathways by which our interventions work through the identification of the strength and contributions of intervention components or elements. In this tradition, we can operationalize and test the active ingredients of interventions and examine, using experimental SCD methods, their promise for producing desired effects.

Throughout the early studies assessing efficacy of CBC, we began recognizing the benefits of parent involvement in consultation for purposes beyond generalization. Information gleaned from participants in focus groups and anecdotal conversations led us to believe that partnerships between parents and teachers, and not simply the involvement or presence of parents, were contributing to our effects. Repeatedly a diverse array of participants described high levels of satisfaction and preferences for collaborative work (Sheridan, Eagle, & Doll, 2006). Thus, the importance of mutual, bi-directional communication and positive relationships between families and schools became a central variable in our intervention model, and a primary feature as we began to theorize about the nature of our effects.

Interest in exploring the parent–teacher relationship as a salient variable influencing (and being influenced by) CBC led us to introduce self-report measures (i.e., parent- and teacher-report forms of the Parent–Teacher Relationship Scale—II [PTRS–II]; Vickers & Minke, 1995) into our research. The systematic use of the PTRS–II in the context of many SCDs enabled us to explore the construct in a deliberate way. Aggregating across 48 cases of children aged 6 and younger derived from separate small-N designs and SCDs, we found statistically significant improvements in parents' ratings of communication and their overall relationship with teachers following CBC (Sheridan, Clarke, Knoche, & Edwards, 2006).

This evidence pointing to the effects of CBC on the parent–teacher relationship in the early childhood context led us to investigate the operative role of the relationship variable systematically. Along the sequence of intervention development and evaluation (see Exhibit 10.1), studies testing relationships between independent (predictor), mediating, and dependent (outcome) variables became necessary. Testing the role of parent–teacher relationships within our theory of change became increasingly relevant as a salient research question. However, because controlling human relationship quality is difficult within SCDs, we set forth on studies utilizing complementary designs that allowed us to explore hypotheses about the mediating role of parent–teacher relationships on the effects of CBC. Research with large numbers of participants was increasingly necessary to ensure sufficient statistical power to test such relations, and this theory was explored in a study using multilevel models and mediation analyses.

In a large-scale randomized controlled trial involving 207 students with or at risk for behavioral disorders, their parents, and 82 teachers in 21 schools, we (Sheridan, Bovaird, et al., 2012) found CBC to produce significantly greater gains in teacher-reported adaptive behaviors and parent and teacher reported social skills. Furthermore, significantly greater improvements in the parent–teacher relationship were found for CBC participants relative to controls. Particularly relevant in support of our theory, changes in parent–teacher relationships mediated the effects of CBC on student outcomes. In fact, in the absence of CBC, relationships between parents and teachers of students with behavioral problems deteriorated over time.

Interventions for Whom or in What Context?

The question of impact is not a static or unidimensional one. Responsive and responsible intervention scientists now must address a plethora of questions that extend well beyond basic outcomes to explore the utility of intervention effects for the well-being of its constituents, with a concern for the public at large. The impact of an intervention tested through SCDs is determined not only by virtue of its ability to uphold effects over replicated trials, but also through nuanced investigations that allow us to refine interventions for multiple contexts, participants, and conditions. Such information, uncovered empirically, may influence decisions of practitioners and policymakers when determining a target audience or setting in which an intervention can or should be recommended.

Research testing the effects of interventions is always conducted in a particular context (Shadish, Cook, & Campbell, 2002). In applied settings (e.g., schools, homes, neighborhoods), extra-intervention variables present potent and sometimes significant influences on an intervention such that its effects are uniquely transformed in their presence. The interaction of an intervention and relevant contextual variables is real. SCDs contribute to context analyses by clearly defining setting characteristics (Horner et al., 2005), thereby allowing for understandings of how interventions affect outcomes of interest under certain conditions. Treatment effects of interventions in specific contexts such as residential treatment settings (Didden, Korzilius, van Oorsouw, Sturmey, & Bodfish,

2006), households functioning at poverty threshold (Taverne & Sheridan, 1995), or within rural schools (Owens, Murphy, Richerson, Girio, & Himawan, 2008) have been investigated with SCDs.

The meaning, preference, and utility of interventions are often unveiled through designs that allow us to determine empirically the conditions under which an intervention addresses a particular issue. Educational and psychological intervention scientists are increasingly concerned with understanding whether treatments can be expected to function in certain contexts or under various conditions. This line of inquiry requires researchers to hypothesize and test conditions under which interventions can be expected to work. SCDs do this through the investigation of treatment effects in unique practice contexts by clearly defining the setting parameters within which the intervention is being tested, and relevant individual characteristics defining the sample. Sometimes even in the presence of significant effects, relationships between intervention elements and measured outcomes cannot be fully elucidated without understanding individuals, groups, problems, settings, or other conditions for whom or within which observed response patterns exist.

SCDs are particularly useful for allowing intensive scrutiny of individual cases, exploring variation in response to the treatment in question, and observing idiosyncratic phenomena that contribute to case outcomes (Barlow, Nock, & Hersen, 2009). Detailed analysis of nonresponders is equally informative and beneficial to the identification of outcomes among treatment responders (Horner et al., 2005). This is a unique strength of SCDs relative to traditional group designs that consider "nonresponders" as outliers. Also, variations can be introduced and assessed to discern important and practical information on certain processes illustrating change (i.e., patterns under various conditions; operative features). In our CBC work, we (Sheridan, Eagle, Cowan, & Mickelson, 2001) explored questions of context in a study that built on years of SCD studies. In particular, aggregating more than 52 SCDs of students with a variety of presenting concerns and disorders, a model fitting age and symptom severity was found to predict school effects relatively well, such that older students (age 11 and older) with less severe symptoms and younger students (age 5–7) with more severe problems prior to CBC experienced greater improvement.

Idiosyncrasies or interactions between interventions and settings are more challenging to test in traditional SCD frameworks. For example, variables such as teacher (e.g., credentials, training, expectancies), student (e.g., degree of cumulative risk factors), or environmental characteristics (e.g., distance from urban center, size of school) and other contextual features may create implicit or explicit conditions that influence the uptake and efficacy of interventions. Characteristics of the treatment agent (e.g., training level of teachers, mental health status or educational background of parents) may interact with intervention components such that differential effects are observed, depending on various personal characteristics. Determining whether these variables function reliably to influence an intervention requires systematic analyses that test whether these characteristics moderate a treatment's effects.

Our earlier findings led us to explore variables that may moderate (either amplify or depress) the effects of CBC in a more systematic manner. Using data from our randomized trial, we explored the role of age, severity, disability, and family risk as moderators of CBC's effects. With this sample of students with behavioral concerns, age and severity did not moderate CBC's effects as expected. Cumulative risk, however, amplified its effects such that as levels of family risk increased, behavioral problems (noncompliance, teasing, tantrums) decreased (Sheridan, Ryoo, Garbacz, Kunz, & Chumney, 2013).

Ease and fidelity of implementation are yet other aspects of an intervention that may modify their influence on chosen dependent variables. Interventions in the real world tend to be multifaceted and complex. Rarely are all facets of interventions implemented as designed and intended. Analytic frameworks for use in SCDs are being developed to objectively interpret or model the effects of dosage, adherence, quality of implementation, and other typical variations of treatment fidelity on consultation effects (Sanetti & Kratochwill, 2010). Given the specificity with which implementation features can be assessed in studies utilizing small samples, SCDs are uniquely equipped to explore the effects of treatment variations in practice. Meaningful interpretative frameworks remain to be demonstrated.

How Do We Know the Intervention Worked?

In an era characterized by pronounced scrutiny and accountability, consumers (such as the general public), users (including policymakers), and funders of research (e.g., the National Institutes of Health and Institute of Education Sciences) are concerned with *impact*. The question of impact requires attention to methods or metrics for instilling confidence in findings from SCDs to diverse audiences. Thus, researchers need not only design elements but statistical tools to respond to the question "How do we know that Intervention A causes change in Behavior B?" With a consumer base that extends well beyond researchers, scholars, and academics and includes practitioners, politicians, and laypersons, research findings must be easily digestible and interpretable. Developments in the standardization of SCD features required for determination of evidence-based interventions are providing the context for this to occur (Kratochwill et al., 2010). However, uncertainty remains about the most appropriate and reasonable method for determining meaningful and reliable effect sizes in the context of SCDs. Metrics such as effect sizes that can be readily translated into meaningful terms are sorely needed to provide convincing and ready documentation of the importance of researched interventions. In particular, methods for SCD researchers to determine effect sizes under typical applied conditions (e.g., when the collection of extensive data is unreasonable or randomization impractical) are gravely needed to allow SCD researchers to communicate the impact of their interventions. The inability to readily and reliably quantify intervention outcomes from most applied SCD studies remains one of the most significant challenges lurking in the field, hindering the communication and dissemination of findings in a convincing way to broad and relevant constituencies.

It is exciting indeed that highly esteemed basic and applied statisticians and research methodologists are now aggressively dealing with these germane issues (see various chapters in this volume).

The Best of Both Worlds

It is increasingly apparent that the issues we try to tackle in educational and behavioral intervention research (those same issues that got us started in this line of work to begin with) are complex and multidimensional. Applied researchers are concerned with multiple aims that collectively advance a line of scientific work. The establishment of functional relations, which has been the primary strength of SCDs since their inception, is the first important step in understanding intervention utility and impact in applied settings. Indeed, it is among the most prevalent design options for applied researchers in the early stages of developing and field-testing interventions. Intensive graphic presentation and visual inspection, including the use of systematic and rigorous interpretive guidelines (e.g., Gast, 2010; Chapter 3, this volume), will likely always be the cornerstone of SCDs. They allow field researchers to test hypothesized relations between independent (intervention) and dependent (outcome) variables, and provide important efficacy information in a manner that is more time and cost effective than randomized trials (Horner et al., 2005). Importantly, exciting developments are quickly infiltrating the field. Advances in SCD methodologies such as the use of randomization (Edgington, 1975; Chapter 2, this volume) are transforming the field by creating opportunities for the conduct of randomized experiments using small samples, which is a distinctive characteristic in some applied situations. Similarly, Chapters 5 and 6 (this volume), and others herein, propose additional SCD and analytical approaches that can tease apart interaction questions and mimic group crossover designs, for example.

Given the inherent evolution of research trajectories (Exhibit 10.1), field-based researchers may need to look to SCD methodologists to begin identifying means to link large- and small-N designs to create a new field of mixed methods approaches. Some efforts and suggestions have been made using hierarchical linear modeling (e.g., Nugent, 1996). Specification of processes, procedures, and parameters for studies that integrate the strengths of multiple methods (SCDs plus traditional large-N designs) may represent the next generation of methodological advances in the educational and social-behavioral sciences. Within traditional large-N designs, for example, SCDs can be useful for investigating nuances to intervention effects. Group designs that combine individual case data into an aggregate pool mask individual variations and patterns. Needed are mixed method designs to discern treatment effects at scale, and also explore variations within conditions at an individual case level. Exploration of effects for students who are high or low performers, whose parents and teachers have unique relationship histories, or who report other variations associated with theory-relevant characteristics are examples. We are attempting to explore such an approach (quantitative mixed methods) in a current large-scale randomized controlled trial wherein multilevel modeling will allow us to test intervention effects over time as evidenced in rural classrooms randomly assigned to treatment or control conditions. Juxtaposed on these main effects will be repeated measures of individual students with behavioral concerns collected in home and school settings that may reveal patterns indicative of unique response variations. Design features to increase both the experimental and ecological validity of this approach are sorely needed.

References

Barlow, D. H., Nock, M. K., & Hersen, M. (2009). *Single case experimental designs: Strategies for studying behavior change* (3rd ed.). Boston, MA: Allyn & Bacon.

Christenson, S. L., & Reschly, A. (Eds.). (2010). *Handbook of family-school partnerships.* New York, NY: Routledge.

Colton, D., & Sheridan, S. M. (1998). Conjoint behavioral consultation and social skills training: Enhancing the play behavior of boys with attention deficit-hyperactivity disorder. *Journal of Educational & Psychological Consultation*, *9*, 3–28. doi:10.1207/s1532768xjepc0901_1

Didden, R., Korzilius, H., van Oorsouw, W., Sturmey, P., & Bodfish, J. (2006). Behavioral treatment of challenging behaviors in individuals with mild mental retardation: Meta-analysis of single-subject research. *American Journal on Mental Retardation*, *111*, 290–298. doi:10.1352/0895-8017(2006)111[290:BTOCBI]2.0.CO;2

Edgington, E. S. (1975). Randomization tests for one-subject operant experiments. *Journal of Psychology: Interdisciplinary and Applied*, *90*, 57–68. doi:10.1080/00223980.1975.9923926

Fan, X., & Chen, M. (2001). Parental involvement and students' academic achievement: A meta-analysis. *Educational Psychology Review*, *13*, 1–22. doi:10.1023/A:1009048817385

Galloway, J., & Sheridan, S. M. (1994). Implementing scientific practices through case studies: Examples using home-school interventions and consultation. *Journal of School Psychology*, *32*, 385–413. doi:10.1016/0022-4405(94)90035-3

Gast, D. L. (2010). *Single subject research methodology in behavioral sciences.* New York, NY: Routledge.

Horner, R. H., Carr, E. G., Halle, J. W., McGee, G., Odom, S. L., & Wolery, M. (2005). The use of single-subject research to identify evidence-based practice in special education. *Exceptional Children*, *71*, 165–179.

Kratochwill, T. R., & Bergan, J. R. (1990). *Behavioral consultation in applied settings: An individual guide.* New York, NY: Plenum Press. doi:10.1007/978-1-4757-9395-6

Kratochwill, T. R., Hitchcock, J., Horner, R. H., Levin, J. R., Odom, S. L., Rindskopf, D. M., & Shadish, W. R. (2010). *Single-case designs technical documentation.* Retrieved from http://ies.ed.gov/ncee/wwc/pdf/wwc_scd.pdf

Nugent, W. R. (1996). Integrating single-case and group-comparison designs for evaluation research. *Journal of Applied Behavioral Science*, *32*, 209–226. doi:10.1177/0021886396322007

Owens, J. S., Murphy, C. E., Richerson, L., Girio, E. L., & Himawan, L. K. (2008). Science to practice in underserved communities: The effectiveness of school mental health programming. *Journal of Clinical Child and Adolescent Psychology*, *37*, 434–447. doi:10.1080/15374410801955912

Sanetti, L., & Kratochwill, T. R. (2010). Project PRIME: Planning Realistic Intervention Implementation and Maintenance by Educators (Research grant funded by the Institute of Education Sciences CDFA# 84.324A–Teacher Quality–Goal Two).

Shadish, W. R., Cook, T. D., & Campbell, D. T. (2002). *Experimental and quasi-experimental designs for generalized causal inference.* Boston, MA: Houghton-Mifflin.

Sheridan, S. M., Bovaird, J. A., Glover, T. A., Garbacz, S. A., Witte, A., & Kwon, K. (2012). A randomized trial examining the effects of conjoint behavioral consultation and the mediating role of the parent–teacher relationship. *School Psychology Review*, *41*, 23–46.

Sheridan, S. M., Clarke, B. L., Knoche, L. L., & Edwards, C. P. (2006). The effects of conjoint behavioral consultation in early childhood settings. *Early Education and Development*, *17*, 593–617. doi:10.1207/s15566935eed1704_5

Sheridan, S. M., Eagle, J. W., Cowan, R. J., & Mickelson, W. (2001). The effects of conjoint behavioral consultation: Results of a four-year investigation. *Journal of School Psychology*, *39*, 361–385. doi:10.1016/S0022-4405(01)00079-6

Sheridan, S. M., Eagle, J. W., & Doll, B. (2006). An examination of the efficacy of conjoint behavioral consultation with diverse clients. *School Psychology Quarterly*, *21*, 396–417. doi:10.1037/h0084130

Sheridan, S. M., & Kratochwill, T. R. (1992). Behavioral parent–teacher consultation: Conceptual and research considerations. *Journal of School Psychology*, *30*, 117–139. doi:10.1016/0022-4405(92)90025-Z

Sheridan, S. M., Kratochwill, T. R., & Elliott, S. N. (1990). Behavioral consultation with parents and teachers: Delivering treatment for socially withdrawn children at home and school. *School Psychology Review*, *19*, 33–52.

Sheridan, S. M., Kratochwill, T. R., & Ramirez, S. (1995). Diagnosis and treatment of elective mutism: Recommendations and a case study. *Special Services in the Schools*, *10*, 55–77. doi:10.1300/J008v10n01_04

Sheridan, S. M., Ryoo, J. H., Garbacz, S. A., Kunz, G., & Chumney, F. L. (2013). The efficacy of conjoint behavioral consultation on parents and children in the home setting: Results of a randomized controlled trial. *Journal of School Psychology, 51,* 717–733.

Taverne, A., & Sheridan, S. M. (1995). Parent training in interactive book reading: An investigation of its effects with families at-risk. *School Psychology Quarterly*, *10*, 41–64. doi:10.1037/h0088298

Vickers, H. S., & Minke, K. M. (1995). Exploring parent–teacher relationships: Joining and communication to others. *School Psychology Quarterly*, *10*, 133–150. doi:10.1037/h0088300

Weiner, R., Sheridan, S. M., & Jenson, W. R. (1998). Effects of conjoint behavioral consultation and a structured homework program on math completion and accuracy in junior high students. *School Psychology Quarterly*, *13*, 281–309. doi:10.1037/h0088986

White, A. G., & Bailey, J. S. (1990). Reducing disruptive behaviors of elementary physical education students with Sit and Watch. *Journal of Applied Behavior Analysis*, *23*, 353–359. doi:10.1901/jaba.1990.23-353

11

Using Single-Case Research Designs in Programs of Research

Ann P. Kaiser

Single-case designs (SCDs) can serve many purposes in a comprehensive program of intervention research. Those purposes include (a) an initial demonstration of a functional relationship between an independent variable and dependent variable, (b) replication of the effects of a previously studied independent variable with a new population or in a new setting, (c) examination of the dosage or duration of treatment required to change a dependent variable, (d) examination of the effects of an independent variable on multiple measures of a behavior, (e) comparison of the relative efficiency of two treatments for changing a dependent variable, (f) development of sequential interventions to impact a single dependent variable, and (g) examination of generalization and maintenance of the effects of the intervention. As methodologists work to develop metrics of intervention effects for aggregating data to assess the effects of interventions implemented in SCDs, it is important to consider the range of purposes for which an SCD study might have been selected (see Chapter 1, this volume).

The purpose of this chapter is to discuss the use of SCDs in a comprehensive program of research. To accomplish this goal, I first describe a program of research that has incorporated both single-case and conventional group designs to develop an effective early communication intervention. I discuss some of the advantages and limitations of using SCDs in this area of research. Then, I suggest some ways in which SCDs might be used to inform the design of subsequent larger scale randomized clinical trials. Finally, I discuss some considerations when designing SCD studies with the intention of aggregating data to demonstrate the magnitude of effects.

Early Communication Intervention Research Program: Enhanced Milieu Teaching

Early intervention to promote the development of communication skills is an important area of applied research. It is estimated that between 10% and 15% of children under the age of 5 are significantly delayed in the development of

http://dx.doi.org/10.1037/14376-012
Single-Case Intervention Research: Methodological and Statistical Advances, by T. R. Kratochwill and J. R. Levin

spoken language (Law, Boyle, Harris, Harkness, & Nye, 2000). Language delays may be primary (i.e., not resulting from another identified developmental condition) or secondary (i.e., resulting from a primary developmental disability such as autism, Down syndrome, or traumatic brain injury). Early language delays are frequently persistent (Preston et al., 2010) and associated with later difficulties in learning to read (Snowling, Bishop, & Stothard, 2000), in academic skills (Prior, Bavin, & Ong, 2011), and in social relationships (Hart, Fujiki, Brinton, & Hart, 2004). For many children with language impairments, early language intervention may be essential to their long-term functioning and inclusive participation in education and social settings (Kaiser, Hester, & McDuffie, 2001).

Enhanced Milieu Teaching (EMT) is a naturalistic language intervention that promotes functional use of new language forms in the context of everyday interactions with caregivers and teachers (Kaiser, 1993). EMT uses environmental arrangement, responsive interaction, language modeling, and systematic prompting procedures to teach functional spoken language. More than 30 studies have examined the effects of variations of EMT with a range of children, including children with autism, children with intellectual disabilities, and children at risk because of poverty (Kaiser & Trent, 2007).

The EMT model used in many studies conducted by our research group is *Caregiver-Implemented EMT* (Roberts & Kaiser, 2012). In this model, the therapist works directly with the child and trains the caregiver to use the EMT procedures. Training typically occurs across clinic and home or classroom. Both workshops and individualized caregiver training sessions are provided; the number of individualized sessions varies based on the child-participant population's need for support in learning to communicate. Over the course of more than a dozen studies, we have developed manualized protocols for implementing and monitoring the fidelity of (a) the EMT strategies used by the therapist with child; (b) the specific teaching and coaching strategies the therapist uses to teach and support the caregiver to implement the EMT intervention in the clinic, in the classroom, and/or at home; and (c) caregiver use of the EMT strategies during training across settings and activities.

EMT research has some unique features that pose challenges for SCD research. First, the basic intervention model is triadic (therapist–caregiver–child) and relies on a cascading model of effects (therapists teach caregivers the EMT intervention; caregivers implement the EMT intervention to teach children, children learn and use new language skills as a result of caregiver use of EMT strategies). To demonstrate the effects of the EMT intervention, change must be demonstrated in the caregiver (use of EMT strategies) and the child (use of target communication skills). Fidelity must be measured on both the therapist teaching the caregiver and the caregiver teaching the child. Demonstrating change in caregiver skills is relatively straightforward because caregivers quickly learn EMT strategies when taught by therapists using established instructional methods. We have used multiple-baseline designs across EMT components, replicated across caregivers to evaluate the effects of teaching use of EMT strategies (e.g., Hancock, Kaiser, & Delaney, 2002; Kaiser, Hancock, & Nietfeld, 2000).

Demonstrating the effects of caregiver use of EMT strategies on child communication in an SCD is somewhat challenging. The effects of training caregivers to use EMT on children's behavior are cumulative. A multiple-baseline design across caregiver behaviors is an appropriate SCD for demonstrating the effects of teaching caregivers because four EMT strategies are taught sequentially. However, a multiple-baseline approach across caregiver behaviors results in sequentially teaching the components of EMT over 20 or more intervention sessions. Caregiver behavior change across the full set of EMT behaviors is gradual, rather than abrupt; and the dosage of caregiver teaching increases over time as caregivers learn the EMT strategies and use them at criterion levels. The effects of the sequential teaching of the four EMT components to parents is a gradual increase in the dosage of EMT provided to the child; the full package of procedures may not be learned and used until 20 sessions of intervention have occurred. The increase in dosage and precision of EMT use is gradual and reflected in gradual changes in child communication.

Second, in addition to the gradual increase in caregiver dosage and precision using the EMT strategies, the demonstration of effects of this training in SCD is more difficult because socially important measures of child communication (such as spontaneous, communicative use of new words) are slow to change. The most important changes in child communication may occur near the end of teaching caregivers the EMT components. In a recent study enrolling toddlers with receptive and expressive language delays and typical cognition, we were able to show a functional relationship between training caregivers and changes in child use of language targets (Roberts, Kaiser, Wolfe, Bryant, & Spidalieri, 2012). Most caregivers learned the EMT strategies quickly, and the target children, who had typical cognitive skills, responded quickly to the change in their caregivers' use of individual language support strategies. Demonstrating the relationship between changes in specific EMT strategies and child social communicative utterances in an SCD with children who have autism or significant cognitive impairments is more difficult because changing their spontaneous functional use of language requires intensive, longer-term intervention (see Kaiser et al., 2000). Choosing a more global dependent measure of child communication (such as total prompted and unprompted communication) results in a clearer demonstration of a functional relationship between caregiver use of EMT and child behavior because the rate of child total communication can be changed immediately by prompting. Total prompted and unprompted communication is a less valid indicator of developmentally important, functional changes in children's communication skills.

Although there are several possible SCDs that could be used in the EMT research, many of them are not appropriate given the populations, the focus on functional communication outcomes, or the triadic, cascading intervention model. For example, SCD choices for investigating the effects of early language intervention are limited by desired nonreversibility of these most social valid and developmentally important dependent behaviors (spontaneous functional social communication).

In spite of these limitations, we have used SCDs to demonstrate the effects of teaching caregivers and of the EMT language strategies when implemented by therapists, teachers, caregivers, and siblings (Kaiser & Trent, 2007). We have used the direct observational methods typically associated with SCDs to carefully describe generalization across persons and settings and maintenance over time (Hancock & Kaiser, 2002; Kaiser et al., 1996; Kaiser & Roberts,

2013). By observing children and their caregivers at home, across routines, and over time, we have established that EMT intervention dependably results in generalization across settings and maintenance over time. These studies have also indicated that variations in child generalization and maintenance are associated with caregiver responsiveness and language modeling in those settings, but a functional relationship between caregiver and child behavior in generalization settings is demonstrated conclusively in the SCD. The continuous monitoring of generalization during the course of the primary intervention provides some indication of the magnitude of treatment effects that are needed to produce dependable across-setting generalization in both caregivers and children.

In choosing SCDs, we evaluate the relative strengths and weaknesses of the design considering the extent to which it controls for threats to internal and external validity. No single design is perfect. It is important to understand the specific threats to validity in the application of any given design and to address these threats as pragmatically as possible by making appropriate adjustments to the design. For example, we use multiple probes, rather than continuous observation, to limit the number of baseline observations while maintaining the requirements for concurrent multiple-baselines across participants. We structured the design to measure maintenance and generalization across everyday settings and activities to increase the external validity of the study. Similarly, in our research we have identified a number of potential internal validity threats associated with SCDs (and for some designs more than others) in language intervention research. Present space limitations do not permit an accounting of the specific internal-validity threats here, but discussion of issues that are relevant to our field of research may be found elsewhere (e.g., Warren, Brady, & Fey, 2008).

Using SCDs as a Foundation for Group Experimental Research

SCD studies can provide empirical information for designing group experimental studies and as the foundation for larger-scale treatment evaluation (see Chapter 10, this volume). First, using SCDs, variability in response to the intervention within and across participants and over time can be observed directly in time-series observational data. Both the consistency of effects and the variability across participants (caregivers and children) provide information about how much instruction and training are needed. For example, across studies caregivers have varied in the amount of training that is needed for them to change their use of specific language support strategies. Most caregivers change their responsiveness and matched communication turns within one to four sessions of training, whereas five or more sessions of training are required to reach criterion levels for rate and accuracy of milieu teaching prompts. For children with very low rates of communication in baseline (fewer than five spontaneous utterances per 10-minute sample), changes in rate of spontaneous communication will not be evident until their caregivers have learned at least three language support strategies (responsiveness, matched communication, model and expand communication targets) and between 12 and 15 sessions of caregiver training have been completed. Changes in the rate of spontaneous communication during caregiver implementation occur more quickly when children have moderate rates of spontaneous communication during baseline. Thus, more sessions of caregiver training and supported caregiver implementation are needed (36 vs. 24 sessions) in dyads with preschool children who have intellectual disabilities than in dyads with toddlers who have typical cognition and delayed language. For children with autism spectrum disorders (ASDs) generalization across partners, settings, and materials is limited unless intervention occurs across these contexts; thus, interventions for children with ASD must continue for more sessions and involve more partners and settings to achieve generalized effects than interventions for toddlers with language delays only.

Our research team has typically included pre–post and follow-up measures from standardized assessments (Hemmeter & Kaiser, 1994). Although changes on standardized measures in SCD studies must be interpreted with caution, we include them as an estimate of distal or generalized changes resulting in language from the EMT intervention. Examining the amount (magnitude) and the consistency (how many participating children) of change on standardized measures allows us to estimate dosage effects and to begin to estimate the statistical power needed to detect effects in a group study. In a recent analysis, we examined the change in number of different words (NDWs) during intervention sessions to estimate the amount of within-intervention change needed to gain a single point on a standardized measure of language (Kaiser, Camarata, Roberts, & Goldstein, 2011). On average, children needed to gain between 1.46 and 2.33 spontaneous NDWs in intervention to show a 1.0 point gain on the Early Vocabulary Test (EVT; Williams, 2007) at the end of intervention (NDW:EVT). However, these gain ratios differed by population and by intervention agent. Children needed to demonstrate a larger number of spontaneous different words during caregiver-implemented intervention than they needed to demonstrate during therapist-implemented intervention to gain one standard score point on the EVT in testing. The NDW:EVT ratios in the final EVT assessment are shown for different populations and intervention partners in Table 11.1. This correlational analysis suggested that changes in spontaneous use of different words during intervention sessions could indicate child progress detected on a standardized measure. Such information could be used to specify treatment duration at the beginning of a study or to make principled changes during the treatment (e.g., increase duration or intensity of intervention) to produce desired outcomes at the end of treatment using an adaptive treatment design (Murphy, 2005).

Table 11.1. Ratio of Number of Different Words Observed in Intervention to 1 Point Gained on the Early Vocabulary Test for Different Child Populations and Enhanced Milieu Teaching Interventionists

Test administrator	Intellectual disabilities	Down syndrome	Autism	Language impairment
Therapist	1.52	9.00	1.46	1.74
Caregiver	2.33	50.00	1.23	2.03

In the course of several SCD studies, we have developed and validated the criteria for fidelity of implementation by observing how changes in child communication were associated with higher levels of caregiver EMT fidelity and how specific procedures for teaching caregivers influenced caregiver use of the EMT procedures with their children. The precise measurement of caregiver training as an independent variable across studies has advanced our development of manualized treatments for group-design studies and resulted in a unique and evidence-based approach to caregiver training (Roberts et al., 2012). The consistently high levels of treatment fidelity reported in group-design studies is directly related to the precise quantification of caregiver training and caregiver implementation that were developed in SCD studies.

Strengths and Limitations of SCDs in Comprehensive Programs of Research

The strengths of SCDs in comprehensive programs of research are several. First, such designs are ideal during the development of interventions. In particular, the immediate effectiveness of the intervention can be ascertained and the timing of effects can be used to determine the dosage of intervention needed to achieve proximal or immediate effects. The demonstration of a functional relationship between the introduction of the intervention and a socially valid dependent variable provides the first level of evidence of treatment effects. Second, time-series data can demonstrate cumulative effects of increased dosage or duration of the intervention. Certain designs, such as multielement designs or alternating treatment designs (Gast, 2010), can be used to determine the relative effectiveness of adding components to a basic intervention package (see also Chapter 1, this volume). For example, the addition of e-mail feedback to the basic teach, coach, model, and review instructional package for teaching caregivers might be investigated as it affects caregiver acquisition and generalization of the EMT teaching strategies. Third, repeated observational measures across settings and conversational partners can be used to provide a comprehensive assessment of generalization during intervention and of maintenance after the intervention.

The general strengths and limitations of SCDs associated with threats to internal validity are well established (Horner et al., 2005). There are other limitations that are specific to SCD characteristics, just as there are limitations within the design characteristics of group experimental design. First, SCDs are most effective when the dependent variable is performance of a discrete, observable behavior, such as number of initiations or responses during an interaction. SCDs are less useful for demonstrating a functional relationship between an intervention and a general outcome, such as social competence or language development. Second, the nature of the intervention is limited by the design. Long-term, multicomponent, sequential, and cumulative interventions where treatment components are introduced gradually do not produce immediate shifts in level, trend, or variability, as are required to establish a functional relationship between independent and dependent variables. Third, comparison of treatments is possible in several SCDs (e.g., alternating treatments, withdrawal or reversal designs, parallel treatment designs; Gast, 2010), but each design has strict requirements for the independent measures (target behavior) and comparability of the stimuli. In general, these comparisons of treatment designs are limited to single independent variables (e.g., prompting procedures, type of feedback for correct responses) rather than complex interventions. Fourth, although the individual is the unit of analysis and serves as his or her own control, the contribution of the individual to the outcome cannot be analyzed specifically. This limitation is because the EMT model is dyadic; both caregiver and child contribute to the outcomes. For example, the four children in the Roberts et al. (2012) study were very similar in baseline responding and assessed language and cognitive abilities; however, one child demonstrated a distinctly different pattern of response to the EMT intervention than the other three children. Implementation by parents varied slightly, but not in a manner that was systematically related to the differences in child outcomes. The differences in child language performance were presumably related to child and/ or parent characteristics, but we could not determine this empirically. Finally, both types of intervention (operationally defined, observable, deliverable with high fidelity) and the measures of effectiveness of the intervention (discrete, observable measures that can be measured as number, percentage or rate) are influenced by the requirements for time-series measurements with high levels of interobserver agreement. Thus, early language interventions studied with SCDs are more likely to have a relatively small set of observable components rather than a general curricular approach provided across the day and over many months. The outcomes studied are specific behaviors rather than changes in developmental level or general language skills. Table 11.2 provides a summary of these strengths and weaknesses.

The framework of SCD enhances the procedural fidelity of the treatment. The treatments typically are delivered to individuals or a small number of groups

Table 11.2.   Strengths and Limitations of Single-Case Research Design (SCD) Studies

Strengths	Limitations
<ul><li>Developing interventions</li><li>Developing fidelity standards for interventions</li><li>Measurement of immediate outcomes; showing a clear functional relationship</li><li>Examination of generalization; maintenance</li><li>Indications of dosage; intensity of treatment needed to reach criterion levels</li><li>Flexible design allows adaptations to insure response to treatment</li></ul>	<ul><li>Focus is on learning targets or well-defined behavior rather than general outcomes</li><li>The nature of the intervention is influenced by the design itself; interventions delivered in SCDs may be more precise due to continuous monitoring of treatment effects and fidelity; treatment targets may be more limited in order to be measured through direct observation</li><li>Comparing treatments is possible, but can be complex and limited in application</li><li>Although the individual is the unit of analysis, it is not easy to understand the contribution of the individual to the outcome</li></ul>

of individuals (e.g., dyads, classrooms, groups of students). The time-series design framework requires continuous monitoring of both the outcome (the dependent variable) and the delivery of the treatment (the independent variable). Frequent assessment of the reliability of measurement and fidelity of implementation (as much as 30% of the experimental sessions) virtually insures that treatment fidelity and the reliability of the measurement of outcomes will be high. As result, interventions that are delivered in SCD studies may be more precisely implemented and accurately measured than treatments delivered in group designs or in practice. It is possible that interventions delivered in SCDs may yield more robust outcomes than those from interventions delivered in group designs in which fidelity may be monitored less frequently and less precisely. Many interventions delivered in SCDs continue until individuals demonstrate criterion performance levels for the outcome variable. This type of individualization of treatment dosage is rarely possible in group designs where treatment is a standard length or dosage for all participants. Further, researchers using SCDs may systematically adapt treatments based on the response or progress of an individual participant to reach criterion levels of performance and document their adaptations with changes in experimental conditions. These adaptations result in consistent positive outcomes, but varied dosage and treatment combinations and neither the individualization of the package nor the exact replication of the dosage and treatment combination may be possible in group designs. In sum, the features that make SCD useful for developing and studying behavioral treatments also lead to assessing the effects of treatment under the particular circumstance of high levels of fidelity and individualized dosage. Any conclusions about the effectiveness of a treatment must take into account that the findings are achieved in the context of the highly specified, precisely delivered treatment that was continuously monitored to determine its effects on targeted, observable behaviors. Table 11.3 suggests some ways in which common SCDs influence the specific outcomes and some ways in which the design must be considered when using the outcomes of these studies to judge treatment effects across studies or as a basis for developing larger scale studies.

Should Researchers Adapt SCDs to Promote the Aggregation of Data for Estimating Effect Sizes?

The answer to this question is not simple. Although systematically characterizing the effects of an intervention from time-series data has distinct benefits, the designs of many SCD studies do not lend themselves to aggregation of effects without loss of critical information. Designing SCD studies for the primary purpose of contributing data to such aggregated analysis may limit the utility and benefits of such designs, particularly in programmatic research. Extended baselines have the advantage of yielding more stable estimates of base rates but may be unacceptable in studies in which the need for changing the behavior is pressing (e.g., in functional communication training to replace a challenging behavior) or when the extended baseline requires parents and their children to participate in many home visits over a long period of time (e.g., 10 weeks to collect 10 data points). Further, differences in the scope of measurement of the

Table 11.3. Information About Treatment Effects in Four Common Single-Case Designs (SCDs)

SCD type	Design logic	How the design constrains information about treatment effects	Information that can be useful in subsequent group experimental design studies	Considerations in reporting outcome data
Withdrawal of treatment (ABA) and replication of treatment (ABAB)	Reversibility of behavior and replication	Limited to behaviors that can be reversed (e.g., performance other than learning; no ethical considerations associated with withdrawal of treatment; maintenance is not a concern).	Limited to behaviors that are performed but not expected to be learned; reversibility suggests that behavior may decrease if treatment is not being implemented continuously.	Conditions may be relatively brief, especially returns to baseline. Change observed in brief conditions may not represent maximum values or typical variability that occurs over a longer intervention period.
Multiple-baseline across behaviors	Replication	Behaviors generally considered to be independent (not interrelated); responsive to the identical intervention; relatively quick to change.	Design increases time required to demonstrate effect of intervention across behaviors that may function or typically be learned together; may not clearly indicate time required for intervention with multiple targets at once (e.g., to teach sight reading of 20 common words).	Data are summarized and reported at the behavior level rather than for the individual participant.

(continued on next page)

Table 11.3. Information About Treatment Effects in Four Common Single-Case Designs (SCDs) (*Continued*)

SCD type	Design logic	How the design constrains information about treatment effects	Information that can be useful in subsequent group experimental design studies	Considerations in reporting outcome data
Multiple-baseline across participants	Replication	Results should be consistent across participants (immediate effect, magnitude of effect, amount of intervention required). Variability ideally is explained by baseline behavior or by other measured behavioral characteristics. Can be used to evaluate generalization and maintenance.	Variability in participant response can be a useful indicator of the range of responses likely in a group design and helpful in estimating magnitude of effects and dosage.	Variability across individuals in timing (e.g., sessions to criterion) and magnitude of change in response to treatment must be considered, ideally with attention to individual baselines.
Alternating treatment and adapted alternating treatment	Comparison of treatments	Comparison of treatments focuses on relative efficiency as well as effectiveness of the treatments. Comparable but independent sets of skills or target behaviors are needed for each treatment.	May be very useful for selection of the most effective treatment from two or three instructional interventions that are known and demonstrated to be effective. Must have consistent effects across participants to inform group-design choices. Typically a very small number of target behaviors or skills are taught in each intervention; thus, results may be limited to targeted skill sets.	Both treatments may be effective. Reporting must capture both effectiveness (clear change from baseline) and relative efficiency (comparison between treatments in time to criterion). Number of skills taught in each condition should be evaluated as a further indication of effectiveness/efficiency.

dependent variable may constrain the meaningful interpretation of aggregated outcome data. For example, it seems problematic to combine effect sizes from measures that address the same general construct (such as language production) but measure the construct at distinctly different levels of difficulty or generality. For example, one study might measure a small number discrete variables (e.g., correct production of two specific labels in each leg of a three tier multiple-baseline design across sets of words) compared with another study that employs a broad productive measure of language use (total number of different words used spontaneously and communicatively across three settings in a three-tier multiple-baseline study). In the first study, unknown words (with near-zero baselines) might be learned to criterion in a short period of time, yielding a large effect size, few overlapping data points, and indicating efficient acquisition. In the second study, the criterion of spontaneous, productive use in natural context might result in slower acquisition (indicating less efficiency), overlapping data, and a relatively small effect size. Concern with comparable constructs and units of measurement is not limited to aggregating data from SCDs; the same concern applies to aggregated data in group designs. When there are a sufficiently large number of studies in either group experimental designs or SCDs, the impact of the unit of measurement could be investigated through moderator analyses. When there are few studies investigating a general construct such as productive language, care must be taken to informally examine the impact of unit of measurement on effect sizes and to note any constraints in combining effect sizes across studies.

In general, the design of SCD studies should not be compromised to facilitate aggregation of results. The choice of socially important measures and utilizing SCDs to answer specific questions in a program of research may not yield data that are easily aggregated across studies. The choice of measures should be driven by the purpose of the study, not primarily by the need to demonstrate large and immediate effects (see Chapter 1, this volume). The measure should be an appropriate behavioral indicator of the desired treatment outcome, operationally defined, observed reliably and responsive to change in the independent variable. Measures do not always meet all these criteria equally well. Socially valid measures of important behavior changes may be slower to change. Designing studies with aggregation of effects as a goal might lead researchers to choose the easily changed measure over the more important but harder to change measure and this would be unfortunate. Within a program of research, there is ideally progress toward demonstrating effects on the most important outcomes of interest. Thus, later studies might contribute less evidence of effectiveness when they have been designed to impact more challenging behavioral outcomes (e.g., conversational language episodes rather than use of individual words or target utterances).

Studies are designed to answer specific questions beyond the demonstration of a primary effect of the intervention. The logic of SCDs depends on evaluation of data for evidence of shifts in level, trend, and variability associated with the introduction of the treatment or change in the independent variable *across multiple conditions*. Although statistical methods can account for each of these indicators of change between any two adjacent conditions, it is difficult for a statistical analysis to characterize the pattern of data across the set of conditions that comprise the study (but see Chapter 7, this volume). The sequence of conditions and the pattern of resulting data vary depending on the purpose or the study, as potentially does the stage of development of the intervention within a research program. For example, early in a research program, simple demonstrations of an effect of the intervention across participants are important (e.g., Kaiser & Hester, 1994). Later, comparisons of treatment variations may be used to advance the understanding of the contribution of components of the intervention. In a recent study, we compared EMT with moderately high rates of Milieu Teaching prompts to EMT without prompting in an adapted alternating treatments design enrolling four toddlers with ASD (Kaiser et al., 2012). The purpose of this study was to determine whether EMT prompting (once per minute) reduced spontaneous child utterances compared to EMT without prompting.

Replication is a foundational criterion for SCDs and at least one demonstration and (with the exception of ABAB designs) two replications are the minimal standard for evidence of a functional relationship between the independent and dependent variable in most SCDs (Kratochwill et al., 2013; Odom et al., 2005; see also Chapter 1, this volume). Again, how replication is achieved depends on the primary questions addressed by the study. In programs of research, studies may be designed to answer questions that go beyond the demonstration of effects of the intervention; the most important findings may not be those associated with a primary demonstration of the effects of the treatment. For example, in some EMT studies, demonstrating generalization of the treatment across settings and maintenance over time is a primary purpose of the study (e.g., Kaiser et al., 2000). Aggregating data from studies designed to answer different or later stage questions about treatment variations may yield an unrepresentative estimate of the effects of the intervention. Alternatively, by focusing on aggregation of effects across studies, we may potentially discourage researchers from conducting studies that are useful in developing an intervention program.

Two examples illustrate this point. First, some studies are designed to compare two treatment conditions. In studies using alternating or parallel treatment designs, treatment variations are implemented concurrently or alternatively and the relative effectiveness of the treatments (e.g., trials to criterion, number of items learned) is the primary focus. Studies using these designs may not include a baseline condition because established treatment variations are being studied and the baseline is not essential to the design (Gast, 2010). Second, some multielement designs compare conditions in sequences to provide specific information about variations in the treatment package (e.g., in a study including a sequence of conditions ABABB'BB' where B' is the addition of a tangible reinforcer for student responses in a large-group letter-naming intervention, the B' condition is compared with the combination of teaching procedures [B] that does not include the cue). The pattern of data between the contrasting conditions and across the overall sequence of conditions is of greater interest than the demonstration of the effects of the intervention compared to baseline. Such studies are not appropriate candidates for aggregating data for evidence of a primary effect of the intervention, but they are important studies in developing and refining interventions.

Promoting generalization and maintenance of effects remains one of the most important goals of intervention research, particularly educational intervention research. More than three decades after the seminal paper by Stokes and Baer (1977) about the importance of programming for generalization, it is still the case that many interventions demonstrate primary effects without consistently affecting behavior outside the intervention context or over time. Aggregated data describing primary effects of the intervention may provide information about the immediate impact of the intervention but does not indicate whether the treatment effects maintained. Aggregating data about generalized and maintained effects of interventions, in addition to data on the primary effect of interventions, is a logical solution; however, the design challenges are considerable. Often generalization data are collected via intermittent probes across contexts, people, or response opportunities concurrent with baseline and intervention conditions. Experimental control of generalization and maintenance data using SCD logic may not be clearly demonstrated, and this is a fundamental limitation in both interpreting and aggregating the data. Maintenance data, by definition, are collected at the end of an intervention phase (not during baseline or during the primary intervention). There are few guidelines for evaluation of the extent to which these data are controlled by the parameters of the SCD or for estimating the magnitude of effects of the intervention during a maintenance condition.

Attention to social validity in the design of experiments using SCD must not be lost at the expense of studies that yield appropriate data for estimating the magnitude of effects across studies. Social validity is reflected in the design of nearly every feature of SCD studies in (a) the importance of the problem being studied, (b) the selection of measures that represent the most meaningful measure of the behavior to be changed, (c) the choice of designs that promote analysis of the behavioral phenomenon while adhering to the ethical standards for treatment, (d) the intent to produce changes in behavior that is sufficient to benefit the participants, (e) attending to the generalized and maintained effects of treatment, and (f) evaluating the acceptability of the treatment and the relative importance of the reported change in behavior to the participants and significant others. Aggregating effects across studies does not, in principle, threaten the foundational validity of SCD studies. However, studies designed exclusively to yield data for aggregated analyses that do not adhere to principles of social validity should not be considered as good examples of SCD evidence. It is possible to separate principles of applied behavior analysis that guide the construction of socially valid studies from SCD, but it is not wise to do so (Baer, Wolf, & Risley, 1968; Wolf, 1978). Those principles include examining behaviors that are socially important, using intervention procedures that are social acceptable, and confirming that the social importance of the effects, based on feedback from consumers familiar with the problem and the treatment (Wolf, 1978, p. 207).

Conclusion

Advancing knowledge of the effects of interventions is an important goal for applied researchers. Programs of research that utilize both SCD studies and group experimental methods are increasingly common because of the mandate for experimental studies of educational interventions (Shavelson & Towne, 2002).

Some of the potential contributions of SCDs in comprehensive intervention research programs that include group experimental designs are (a) developing interventions, (b) analyzing the effects of treatment variations, (c) focusing on individual responses to treatment, (d) expanding an intervention to meet the needs of a new population, (e) developing procedures to teach indigenous intervention agents to deliver the intervention, and (f) investigating strategies to promote generalization and maintenance. The information gained in a systematic series of SCDs exceeds the information on effects gained by repeated demonstrations of the primary effects of an intervention. Advances in scientific understanding of important treatments are more likely to be achieved through analysis within the logical framework of SCD studies in combination with group experimental designs than by reducing the principled features of SCD studies to generate data that are optimal for analysis using statistical methods. In this chapter, I have provided an example of a research program that has yielded important information about how naturalistic language intervention can improve children's communication. What we have learned in this program of research across studies using varied methodologies is more than we could have hoped to learn using either exclusively SCDs or exclusively group experimental methods.

References

Baer, D. M., Wolf, M. M., & Risley, T. R. (1968). Some current dimensions of applied behavior analysis. *Journal of Applied Behavior Analysis, 1*, 91–97. doi:10.1901/jaba.1968.1-91

Gast, D. L. (2010). *Single subject research methodology in behavioral sciences.* New York, NY: Routledge.

Hancock, T. B., & Kaiser, A. P. (2002). The effects of trainer-implemented enhanced milieu teaching on the social communication of children who have autism. *Topics in Early Childhood Special Education, 22*, 39–54. doi:10.1177/027112140202200104

Hancock, T. B., Kaiser, A. P., & Delaney, E. M. (2002). Teaching caregivers of preschoolers at high-risk: Strategies to support language and positive behavior. *Topics in Early Childhood Special Education, 22*, 191–212. doi:10.1177/027112140202200402

Hart, K. I., Fujiki, M., Brinton, B., & Hart, C. H. (2004). The relationship between social behavior and severity of language impairment. *Journal of Speech, Language, and Hearing Research, 47*, 647–662. doi:10.1044/1092-4388(2004/050)

Hemmeter, M. L., & Kaiser, A. P. (1994). Enhanced milieu teaching: Effects of caregiver-implemented language intervention. *Journal of Early Intervention, 18*, 269–289. doi:10.1177/105381519401800303

Horner, R. H., Carr, E. G., Halle, J., McGee, G., Odom, S., & Wolery, M. (2005). The use of single subject research to identify evidence-based practice in special education. *Exceptional Children, 71*, 165–179.

Kaiser, A. P. (1993). Caregiver-implemented language intervention: An environmental system perspective. In A. P. Kaiser & D. B. Gray (Eds.), *Enhancing children's communication: Research foundations for intervention* (Vol. 2, pp. 63–84). Baltimore, MD: Paul H. Brookes.

Kaiser, A. P., Camarata, S., Roberts, M., & Goldstein, H. (2011, November). In A. P. Kaiser (Chair), *Measuring early communication outcomes.* Symposium conducted at the American Speech-Language-Hearing Association Convention, San Diego, CA.

Kaiser, A. P., Hancock, T. B., & Nietfeld, J. P. (2000). The effects of caregiver-implemented enhanced milieu teaching on the social communication of children who have autism. *Early Education and Development, 11*(, 423–446. doi:10.1207/s15566935eed1104_4

Kaiser, A. P., Hemmeter, M. L., Ostrosky, M. M., Fischer, R., Yoder, P., & Keefer, M. (1996). The effects of teaching caregivers to use responsive interaction strategies. *Topics in Early Childhood Special Education, 16*, 375–406. doi:10.1177/027112149601600307

Kaiser, A. P., & Hester, P. P. (1994). Generalized effects of enhanced milieu teaching. *Journal of Speech & Hearing Research*, *37*, 1320–1340.

Kaiser, A. P., Hester, P. P., & McDuffie, A. S. (2001). Supporting communication in young children with developmental disabilities. *Mental Retardation and Developmental Disabilities Research Reviews, 7, 7*, 143–150.

Kaiser, A. P., James, M., Smith, M., Baucom, A., Warrington, T., Roberts, M., & Nietfeld, J. (2012). *The effects of Milieu prompting on spontaneous communication in children with autism.* Unpublished manuscript, Vanderbilt University, Nashville, TN.

Kaiser, A. P., & Roberts, M. Y. (2013). Parent-implemented enhanced milieu teaching with preschool children with intellectual disabilities. *Journal of Speech, Language, and Hearing Research*, *56*, 295–309. doi:10.1044/1092-4388(2012/11-0231)

Kaiser, A. P., & Trent, J. A. (2007). Communication intervention for young children with disabilities: Naturalistic approaches to promoting development. In S. Odom, R. Horner, M. Snell, & J. Blacher (Eds.), *Handbook of developmental disabilities* (pp. 224–245). New York, NY: Guilford Press.

Kratochwill, T. R., Hitchcock, J., Horner, R. H., Levin, J. R., Odom, S. L., Rindskopf, D. M., & Shadish, W. R. (2013). Single-case intervention research design standards. *Remedial and Special Education*, *34*, 26–38. doi:10.1177/0741932512452794

Law, J., Boyle, J., Harris, F., Harkness, A., & Nye, C. (2000). Prevalence and natural history of primary speech and language delay: Findings from a systematic review of the literature. *International Journal of Language & Communication Disorders*, *35*, 165–188. doi:10.1080/136828200247133

Murphy, S. A. (2005). An experimental design for the development of adaptive treatment strategies. *Statistics in Medicine*, *24*, 1455–1481. doi:10.1002/sim.2022

Odom, S. L., Brantlinger, E., Gersten, R., Horner, R. H., Thompson, B., & Harris, K. (2005). Research in special education: Scientific methods and evidence-based practices. *Exceptional Children*, *71*, 137–148.

Preston, J. L, Frost, S., Mencl, W., Fulbright, R., Landi, N., Grigrenko, E., . . . Pugh, K. (2010). Early and late talkers: School-age language, literacy and neurolinguistic differences. *Brain: A Journal of Neurology*, *133*, 2185–2195. doi:10.1093/brain/awq163

Prior, M., Bavin, E., & Ong, B. (2011). Predictors of school readiness in five- to six-year-old children from an Australian longitudinal community sample. *Educational Psychology*, *31*, 3–16. doi:10.1080/01443410.2010.541048

Roberts, M., Kaiser, A., Wolfe, C., Bryant, J., & Spidalieri, A. (2012) *The effects of systematic teaching on caregiver use of language support strategies.* Manuscript submitted for publication.

Roberts, M. Y., & Kaiser, A. P. (2012). Assessing the effects of a parent-implemented language intervention for children with language impairments using empirical benchmarks: A pilot study. *Journal of Speech, Language, and Hearing Research*, *55*, 1655–1670. doi:10.1044/1092-4388(2012/11-0236)

Shavelson, R. J., & Towne, L. (Eds.). (2002). *Scientific research in education.* Washington, DC: National Research Council, National Academies Press.

Snowling, M., Bishop, D., & Stothard, S. (2000). Is preschool language impairment a risk factor for dyslexia in adolescence? *Journal of Child Psychology and Psychiatry, 41*, 587–600. doi:10.1111/1469-7610.00651

Stokes, T. F., & Baer, D. M. (1977). An implicit technology of generalization. *Journal of Applied Behavior Analysis*, *10*, 349–367. doi:10.1901/jaba.1977.10-349

Warren, S. F., Brady, N. C., & Fey, M. E. (2008). Communication and language: Research design and measurement issues. In E. Emerson, C. Hatton, T. Thompson, & T. R. Parmenter (Eds.), *The international handbook of applied research in intellectual disabilities* (pp. 385–405). Chichester, England: Wiley. doi:10.1002/9780470713198.ch19

Williams, K. T. (2007). *Expressive Vocabulary Test* (2nd ed.). San Antonio, TX: Pearson Education.

Wolf, M. M. (1978). Social validity: The case for subjective measurement or how applied behavior analysis is finding its heart. *Journal of Applied Behavior Analysis*, *11*, 203–214. doi:10.1901/jaba.1978.11-203

12

Reactions From Journal Editors:
Journal of School Psychology

Randy G. Floyd

In this chapter, I (a) share my reflections on single-case design (SCD) research in general and information presented in this book more specifically and (b) describe some of the effects of the research described in this book on the *Journal of School Psychology*'s operations and some emerging trends I have observed across manuscripts submitted to the journal since I became its editor-in-chief.

Reflections

In contrast to group-based research designs that may necessitate lots of person power (e.g., recruitment agents and test examiners) to conduct because of the large number of participants required, some of the most basic SCD studies are more readily conducted in schools and other applied settings (see, however, Kratochwill & Williams, 1988). A friend of mine frequently says that SCDs were developed by scientist-practitioners primarily for applied uses and with little intent of generalizing the results beyond the targeted cases. Although I understand the benefit of these methods for determining what is true or illusory for individuals in practice, I am additionally excited about recent innovations described in this book that allow analysts to draw evidence-based conclusions from bodies of SCD research. For instance, the Reichow, Barton, Sewell, Good, and Wolery (2010) study described in Chapter 3 employed SCDs to examine the effects of weighted vests on the engagement, stereotypy, and disruptive behaviors of children with developmental disabilities. Across my years of teaching an undergraduate course addressing abnormal child psychology, I have been astounded by students' awareness of largely untested, probably ineffective, and mostly pseudoscientific interventions for childhood mental disorders (which Reichow et al., 2010, concluded about the efficacy of weighted vests). In surveying many of the innovations described throughout the earlier chapters, I realized

http://dx.doi.org/10.1037/14376-013
Single-Case Intervention Research: Methodological and Statistical Advances, by T. R. Kratochwill and J. R. Levin

that numerous small-scale, well-designed studies using SCDs—conducted by scientists and scientist-practitioners—could go a long way in addressing the claims made by purveyors of alternative therapies about "what works" in treating such children. However, it seemed to me that we do a very poor job of training undergraduate psychology students in using these methods.

When I have taught psychology research methods courses at the undergraduate level, I have frequently omitted the textbook chapters focusing on SCDs or focused on only a few basic design types during lectures. Furthermore, when I have required students to complete independent research projects as part of these courses, I have never encouraged them to consider an SCD study. I, like my colleagues in my department, frequently encourage (a) survey or observations studies that produce descriptive statistics or correlations and (b) ex post facto studies contrasting participants' responses based on prior group classifications. SCD studies that are well designed and well controlled would seem to promote a better understanding of causal effects and scientific thinking, allow students to address practical issues, and prepare them to use these methods in the practice of psychology. But in discussing SCDs with the approximately 10 other instructors of research methods courses in my department, I learned that very few of them provided coverage of SCDs during their courses. Personally, I recall no coverage of SCDs during my own undergraduate training in psychology—and there was also minimal coverage in my doctoral training in a school psychology program accredited by the American Psychological Association. What little I know (and have been able to teach students) about SCDs came largely from my own self-study—from books focusing on them (e.g., Kazdin, 2010) as well as books focusing on applied behavior analysis (e.g., Cooper, Heron, & Heward, 2008)—occurring after I earned my doctoral degree. There are school psychology doctoral programs that provide extensive training in using SCDs during applied practice and research, but I wonder how many other school psychologists had similar inadequate training in SCDs to mine.

Journal Management

Before beginning the editorship of the *Journal of School Psychology*, I processed the review of two manuscripts employing SCDs that were submitted to the journal. It was unsettling to me that, in both cases, reviewers were strikingly inconsistent in their judgments about the quality of the designs and data collection decisions described in these manuscripts. In one case, an editorial board reviewer was so adamant about lack of experimental control when introducing new phases across participants in a multiple-baseline design (due to lack of stability of intervention effects, based on visual analysis) that it was deemed a fatal flaw in the study. When I reviewed the literature at that time, I saw no definitive rules addressing this issue, and when I asked another editorial board reviewer to consider and comment on this specific issue, this reviewer asserted that the prior criticisms were inaccurate and that some (but not all) aspects of the study indicated experimental control. Based on this experience, I pondered for a few weeks the plight of those applied intervention researchers employing SCD who submit their manuscripts for peer review. I suspect that they face many frustrations when they encounter such inconsistencies across reviewers' comments and recommendations.

Although the goals of peer review are to screen out weak contributions to the professional literature and refine manuscripts so that they present the most meaningful results, this drastic variability across reviewers evaluating SCD research has surprised me on multiple occasions. I do not recall such drastic differences in opinion in evaluation of non-SCD research designs and data collection across more than 100 other manuscripts I have processed as action editor. During the past few years, several useful resources have been published to guide researchers and peer reviewers: Kazdin (2010), the What Works Clearinghouse (WWC) single-case design standards (Kratochwill et al., 2010, 2013), and a chapter on evaluating SCDs (Egel & Barthold, 2010) in *The Reviewer's Guide to Quantitative Methods in the Social Sciences* (Hancock & Mueller, 2010). I could have benefited from these resources in the instances I have described.

The *Journal of School Psychology* is unique among school psychology journals in that a portion of its editorial board is composed of statistical and methodological advisors; furthermore, at least one associate editor also serves in this role. A few years ago, I reviewed statistical and methodological advisors' self-reported areas of expertise, and I was surprised to see that none of these brilliant scholars, who have been superbly trained in quantitative methods and who are highly research productive, indicated expertise with single-case research. Almost everyone reported correlational research, experimental research, multilevel modeling, multivariate designs, factor analysis, and structural equation modeling as areas of expertise, and even qualitative research was marked more often than single-case research.

Although biased sampling and errors in memory may have skewed my conclusions, I suspect that these problem are due (a) to lack of thorough undergraduate and graduate training in using SCDs (as I noted previously) and (b) to the relatively low frequency of studies using SCDs submitted to journals like the *Journal of School Psychology*. I believe now that fewer than 5% of articles submitted to the *Journal of School Psychology* address SCDs in some way. Judging by results from a recent study (Shadish & Sullivan, 2011) indicating that SCDs appeared in 21 psychology and education journals in 2008, my experience with the *Journal of School Psychology* is probably not incongruent with that of many other editors. Only 126 of 1,098 (11.48%) articles William Shadish and his team reviewed included SCD studies, and more than 67% of those studies were published in only five journals—mainly journals focusing on applied behavior analysis and developmental disabilities, such as autism spectrum disorder. Results also revealed that the core school psychology journals published three or fewer articles describing the results of SCDs in 2008. Despite the *Journal of School Psychology*'s publishing three articles including SCD studies in 2008 (10%; Shadish & Sullivan, 2011), the *Journal of School Psychology* published only one such article in 2010 (4%), one in 2011 (3%), and zero in 2012. Assuming that the percentage of published articles of any type roughly reflects the percentage of submitted manuscripts of that type, it seems that for many journals at present, manuscripts describing the results of SCDs are rare.

Innovations and Trends at *Journal of School Psychology*

As I shared in my inaugural editorial (Floyd, 2012), I would like for *Journal of School Psychology* to be the journal outlet for the best scientific research, scientific thinking, and scientific theory development in school psychology. In selecting individuals to serve on *Journal of School Psychology*'s editorial board, my goal was to recruit some of the strongest content area experts and strongest statistical and methodological advisors in school psychology and related fields. In particular, I sought to increase the number of associate editors with extensive experience with SCDs and to recruit others with expertise in this area to serve in various capacities. I feel fortunate to be able to share these positive results. For example, Tasha Beretvas, a strong contributor to methodology in this area, agreed to serve as an associate editor for the journal. John Ferron, another strong contributor to methodology in this area, agreed to serve as a statistical and methodological advisor. Dr. Ferron reviews all manuscripts submitted to *Journal of School Psychology* that describe studies using SCDs to promote publication of the most high-quality research stemming from these methods. Finally, Tom Kratochwill and Joel Levin, editors of this volume and strong contributors to research and training in this area for more than 30 years, agreed to serve the *Journal of School Psychology* as senior science and editorial consultants to guide me and the associate editors in meeting our goals. Dr. Kratochwill commented on a commissioned article focusing on science and pseudoscience in school psychology authored by Lilienfeld, Ammirati, and David (2012). In his commentary (Kratochwill, 2012), he very clearly addressed how SCD research can be used to test pseudoscientific claims and how it is particularly useful in addressing issues associated with negative effects research.

One initiative of the former editor of the *Journal of School Psychology*, Ed Daly III, was to publish articles focusing on advances in statistical analyses to improve the quality of research articles published in school psychology journals. In fact, in a themed issue of *Journal of School Psychology* published in early 2010, articles focused on applying state-of-the-art analysis to group-level data. For example, the articles addressed estimating missing data (Baraldi & Enders, 2010), conducting moderation and mediation analyses (Fairchild & McQuinlin, 2010), and completing multilevel modeling (Peugh, 2010). One trend in manuscripts submitted to and articles appearing in the *Journal of School Psychology* that is consistent with Daly's initiatives—and with the content of this book—is a focus on SCD methodology and analysis. For example, in 2011, the *Journal of School Psychology* published both an article by Levin, Lall, and Kratochwill (2011), which presented results from Monte Carlo simulations examining a comparative effectiveness randomization test used during SCD studies, and one by Maggin, Swaminathan, et al. (2011), which presented a method using generalized least squares regression to produce effect size estimates for SCDs that control for autocorrelation. In 2012, the *Journal of School Psychology* published both an article by Mercer and Sterling (2012), which addressed decision making during visual inspection of SCD data, and one by Levin, Ferron, and Kratochwill (2012), which presented results from Monte Carlo simulations evaluating nonparametric randomization and permutation statistical tests applied to SCDs (with the latter article selected by our editorial board to receive the *Journal's* 2012 "Article of the Year" award). I am pleased to report that SCD methodology and analysis appear to represent a niche topic for the *Journal of School Psychology.*

The *Journal of School Psychology* has also seen the application of recent work to interpret the collective results of SCD research to inform evidence-based practice. One research team, led by Daniel Maggin (Maggin, Chafouleas, Goddard, & Johnson, 2011; Maggin, Johnson, Chafouleas, Ruberto, & Berggren, 2012), has published two systematic reviews of the single-case research literature using the criteria from the WWC single-case design and evidence criteria (Kratochwill et al., 2010, 2013). In Maggin, Chafouleas, et al. (2011), the authors evaluated the research focusing on token economy systems, and in Maggin et al. (2012), the authors evaluated the research focusing on group contingency interventions. These studies provide superb models of the application of the WWC single-case design and evidence standards.

References

Baraldi, A. N., & Enders, C. K. (2010). An introduction to modern missing data analyses. *Journal of School Psychology, 48*, 5–37. doi:10.1016/j.jsp.2009.10.001

Cooper, J. O., Heron, T. E., & Heward, W. L. (2008). *Applied behavior analysis* (2nd ed.). Upper Saddle River, NJ: Pearson.

Egel, A. I., & Barthold, C. H. (2010). Single subject design and analysis. In G. R. Hancock & R. O. Mueller (Eds.), *The reviewer's guide to quantitative methods in the social sciences* (pp. 356–370). New York, NY: Routledge.

Fairchild, A. J., & McQuinlin, S. D. (2010). Evaluating mediation and moderation effects in school psychology: A presentation of methods and review of current practice. *Journal of School Psychology, 48*, 53–84. doi:10.1016/j.jsp.2009.09.001

Floyd, R. G. (2012). A golden anniversary: Celebrating successes and establishing a vision for the future of the *Journal of School Psychology. Journal of School Psychology, 50*, 1–6. doi:10.1016/j.jsp.2011.12.001

Hancock, G. R., & Mueller, R. O. (Eds.). (2010). *The reviewer's guide to quantitative methods in the social sciences.* New York, NY: Routledge.

Kazdin, A. (2010). *Single-case research designs: Methods for clinical and applied settings* (2nd ed.). New York, NY: Oxford University Press.

Kratochwill, T. R. (2012). Comments on "Distinguishing Science From Pseudoscience in School Psychology": Evidence-based interventions for grandiose bragging. *Journal of School Psychology, 50*, 37–42. doi:10.1016/j.jsp.2011.11.003

Kratochwill, T. R., Hitchcock, J., Horner, R. H., Levin, J. R., Odom, S. L., Rindskopf, D. M., & Shadish, W. R. (2010). *Single-case designs technical documentation.* Retrieved from http://ies.ed.gov/ncee/wwc/pdf/wwc_scd.pdf

Kratochwill, T. R., Hitchcock, J. H., Horner, R. H., Levin, J. R., Odom, S. L., Rindskopf, D. M., & Shadish, W. R. (2013). Single-case intervention research design standards. *Remedial and Special Education, 34*, 26–38. doi:10.1177/0741932512452794

Kratochwill, T. R., & Williams, B. L. (1988). Personal perspectives on pitfalls and hassles in the conduct of single subject research. *Journal of the Association for Persons with Severe Handicaps, 13*, 147–154.

Levin, J. R., Ferron, J. M., & Kratochwill, T. R. (2012). Nonparametric statistical tests for single-case systematic and randomized ABAB . . . AB and alternating treatment intervention designs: New developments, new directions. *Journal of School Psychology, 50.* doi:10.1016/j.jsp.2012.05.001

Levin, J. R., Lall, V. F., & Kratochwill, T. R. (2011). Extensions of a versatile randomization test for assessing single-case intervention effects. *Journal of School Psychology, 49*, 55–79. doi:10.1016/j.jsp.2010.09.002

Lilienfeld, S. O., Ammirati, R., & David, M. (2012). Distinguishing science from pseudoscience in school psychology: Science and scientific thinking as safeguard against human error. *Journal of School Psychology, 50,* 7–36. doi:10.1016/j.jsp.2011.09.006

Maggin, D. M., Chafouleas, S. M., Goddard, K. M., & Johnson, A. H. (2011). A systematic evaluation of token economies as a classroom management tool for students with challenging behavior. *Journal of School Psychology, 49,* 529–554. doi:10.1016/j.jsp.2011.05.001

Maggin, D. M., Johnson, A. H., Chafouleas, S. M., Ruberto, L. M., & Berggren, M. (2012). A systematic evidence review of school-based group-contingency interventions for students with challenging behavior. *Journal of School Psychology, 50.* doi:10.1016/j.jsp.2012.06.001

Maggin, D. M., Swaminathan, H., Rogers, H. J., O'Keeffe, B. V., Sugai, G., & Horner, R. H. (2011). A generalized least squares regression approach for computing effect sizes in single-case research: Application examples. *Journal of School Psychology, 49,* 301–321. doi:10.1016/j.jsp.2011.03.004

Mercer, S. H., & Sterling, H. E. (2012). The impact of baseline trend control on visual analysis of single-case data. *Journal of School Psychology, 50,* 403–419. doi:10.1016/j.jsp.2011.11.004

Peugh, J. L. (2010). A practical guide to multilevel modeling. *Journal of School Psychology, 48,* 85–112. doi:10.1016/j.jsp.2009.09.002

Reichow, B., Barton, E. E., Sewell, J. N., Good, L., & Wolery, M. (2010). Effects of weighted vests on the engagement of children with developmental delays and autism. *Focus on Autism and Other Developmental Disabilities, 25,* 3–11. doi:10.1177/1088357609353751

Shadish, W. R., & Sullivan, K. J. (2011). Characteristics of single-case designs used to assess intervention effects in 2008. *Behavior Research Methods, 43,* 971–980.

Reactions From Journal Editors: *School Psychology Quarterly*

Randy W. Kamphaus

Single-case research is not any different than other designs and methodologies in that the competition to get published in the most prestigious scientific journals is fierce. The odds are against the authors. As of this writing, the rejection rate for the journal that I edit, *School Psychology Quarterly* (*SPQ*), is a daunting 86%. On the other hand, single-case design submissions are not as plentiful as I had imagined when I became a journal editor 5 years ago. In the last 18 months of my tenure, I processed a total of 96 new submissions (inclusive of all of the year 2011 and half of 2012), only one of which was a single-case design. I did, however, receive numerous submissions from scholars who are well known for their single-case research expertise, many of which ultimately were published in *SPQ*.

An article by Tyler David Ferguson, Amy Briesch, Robert Volpe, and Brian Daniels (2012) in the December issue entitled "The Influence of Observation Length on the Dependability of Data" serves as one example of a study that is highly relevant to single-case researchers: the effects of classroom observation length on reliability. They found that considerably longer observations than have been conducted in some past studies are likely necessary to improve reliability. An article by Lisa Sanetti and Thomas Kratochwill (2009) entitled "Treatment Integrity Assessment in the Schools: An Evaluation of the Treatment Integrity Planning Protocol" serves as another example of well-known single-case researchers who have published in *SPQ*.

Intervention studies continue to be submitted and published in *SPQ*, some of which have been authored by well-known single-case researchers. These researchers, however, typically adopted randomized controlled trials or quasi-experimental designs. For example, Shawna Peterson-Brown and Matthew Burns (2011) published a study entitled "Adding a Vocabulary Component to Incremental Rehearsal to Enhance Retention and Generalization" where 61 elementary grade students were randomly assigned to one of two conditions.

http://dx.doi.org/10.1037/14376-014
Single-Case Intervention Research: Methodological and Statistical Advances, by T. R. Kratochwill and J. R. Levin

In that same issue, Keith Herman, Lindsay Borden, Wendy Reinke, and Carolyn Webster-Stratton (2011) published a study entitled "The Impact of the Incredible Years Parent, Child, and Teacher Training Programs on Children's Co-Occurring Internalizing Symptoms." In this study, 159 families and children were randomly assigned to one of five experimental conditions or one control condition. The *SPQ* publication record suggests that while single-case design submissions to *SPQ* have been minimal, some well-known single-case researchers conducting intervention studies continued to have a strong publication record in our journal.

I will leave conjecture about the causes of the lack of single-case journal submissions to others (see Chapters 12 and 14, this volume). Instead, I focus the remainder of this chapter on a few ways in which authors of single-case research design studies can proactively respond to common reasons for manuscript rejection. I also recommend lengthier treatises on writing works for scientific journal article submissions. Articles by Maxwell and Cole (1995) and Sternberg (1993) are particularly informative.

There are unique methodological considerations associated with any design or methodology that have been raised by editorial review board members during my tenure as editor. In the words of Wilkinson (1999), "Occasionally, proponents of some research methods disparage others. In fact, each form of research has its own strengths, weaknesses, and standards of practice" (p. 595). Narrative researchers, for example, have to take special steps to mitigate interpretive bias, item response theory methodologists seeking to calibrate test items have to be concerned about Type 1 errors, and most behavioral scientists have to adopt careful sampling strategies. I think it wise for single-case researchers to proactively address these known shortcomings in their journal article submissions.

Methodological researchers seek to improve the effectiveness of a research paradigm. Then these improvements in methodology have to also be reflected in works seeking to be published in competitive outlets. By way of example, a relatively recent methodological study by Wolery, Busick, Reichow, and Barton (2010) demonstrated the lack of accuracy of four methods for aggregating results across single-case designs. As this finding becomes known it will be important for authors of new submissions to cite this methodological limitation when aggregating findings across cases, or as support for the decision not to aggregate. The current volume will serve single-case researchers well in that regard (see also Chapter 8, this volume). It will serve as an important compilation of methodological considerations that single-case researchers can check and address as they conduct their studies, as well as highlight methodological improvements in their journal article submissions.

In the interest of avoiding overlap with other chapters in this volume, I will use the remainder of this work to point out three design considerations for single-case researchers. These three considerations are based on my editorial experience with manuscript reviewers. There are about 50 journals like *SPQ* that are tracked by the American Psychological Association (APA) as "educational psychology" publications, broadly defined. It could very well be that these considerations will generalize to similar publication outlets.

Sampling, Culture, and Generalization of Findings

Problems with the applicability of research findings to population subgroups have led to a concern among manuscript reviewers about the generalizability of research findings. An article by Huang et al. (2005) serves as an exemplar of the concern within psychology about culturally competent practice. Similarly, Hovey's (2000) study provides a compelling example of research producing evidence in support of the importance of cultural context. This study yielded credible evidence suggesting that minority status is, in and of itself, related to poorer mental health outcomes.

In addition to research studies, the incorporation of cultural variables into the behavioral science research enterprise has been hastened by numerous sets of guidelines and position papers on the topic. The influential APA, for example, promulgated the strong *Guidelines on Multicultural Education, Training, Research, Practice, and Organization Change for Psychologists* in 2002 (http://www.apa.org/pi/oema/resources/policy/multicultural-guidelines.aspx). Relevant to this chapter, Guideline #4 reads, "Culturally sensitive psychological researchers are encouraged to recognize the importance of conducting culture-centered and ethical psychological research among persons from ethnic, linguistic, and racial minority backgrounds" (p. 11). Furthermore, the history of culturally homogenous sampling and, therefore, flawed inferences, was cited as a central reason for the promulgation of these guidelines, as indicated in this quote:

> A number of scholars have voiced concerns about the cultural limitations of psychological research in the United States.... Second, although scholars began to heed the call for culturally diverse samples in research, many research samples continue to be predominantly White and middle class with People of Color underrepresented in these samples. When the samples are racially diverse, they are much more likely to be samples of convenience, which may not be representative of the target group, such as samples of college students representing all Asian Americans. This affects the external validity of a study, or to whom the findings may be generalized (Fuertes, Bartolomeo, & Nichols, 2001; Sue, 1999). Sue (1999) suggests that psychological science has ignored external validity problems, and that we have erred in the direction of inaccurately generalizing from findings based on small subsets of people to the population at large. (p. 11)

Based on this seemingly ubiquitous concern about incorporation of culture and language into behavioral science research, I recommend that single-case researchers attend to issues of culturally sensitive sampling. Researchers must do so to support the argument that their findings hold the potential to be widely applicable and replicable. Specifically, I suggest that single-case design studies in child psychological and educational research add children of various cultural and linguistic subgroups, including urban children (given that this is the setting where most children are reared and educated in the United States), children from various ethnic groups, and immigrant children, to name just a few important population subgroups. Expanded and inclusive sampling is now expected in child psychological and educational research to support generalizability of findings, whether the study includes one or 1,000 participants.

Making the Methodological Case

The availability of modern statistical analysis software has lead to a rapid expansion of statistical methodology with a corresponding increase in the ease of use of these same programs. The expansion of statistical methodology remains rapid and journal article reviewers, especially the early career ones, are steeped in this training. It has been my experience that this generation of manuscript reviewers fully expects statistical sophistication in each manuscript that they review.

I offer, as an example of the statistical sophistication of early career manuscript reviewers, the methodology coursework offered in the Institute of Education Sciences–sponsored predoctoral educational research program at Johns Hopkins University (see http://krieger.jhu.edu/ies). Excerpts from topics of study in course syllabi shown on the website include

> logic models and program theory, threats to validity, experimental and quasi-experimental designs, qualitative and mixed methods designs, ethics, and cost-benefit analysis . . . drawing cause-effect inferences, including completely randomized assignments; known unconfounded assignments, covariates, and the role of Fisher's, Neyman's and Bayesian methods; ignorable assignments, propensity scores and sensitivity analysis; nonignorable assignments arising from deviations to protocol, treatment-noncompliance, direct and indirect effects, methods of instrumental variables, loss to follow-up and methods of latent ignorability, and encouragement designs. . . . [L]ogic of inference and research design issues, fixed effects models, instrumental variables, propensity scores, regression discontinuity, multilevel models and the analysis of longitudinal data. . . . [P]rinciples of psychometrics (including reliability and validity), the statistical basis for latent variable analysis (including exploratory and confirmatory factor analysis and latent class analysis), and item response theory.

And the list goes on. A manuscript reviewer trained in this manner may, nevertheless, have little exposure to principles of single-case research designs, visual analysis, and any single-case research specific statistics used.

Faced with such statistical and design sophistication yet incomplete knowledge on the part of reviewers, I suggest that single-case researchers make the case for their methodology much in the same way that one prepares a research grant proposal for a methodologically diverse review panel. In other words, all of the methodological and statistical choices made, as well as those not made, should be explicit and supported by citations. And authors should assume that assumptions regarding single-case methods, their strengths and weaknesses, and the lack of need for statistical methods may not be obvious or preferred by talented early- and midcareer scientific reviewers, and senior reviewers who are methodologically current. Sternberg (1993) astutely noted the need to write for a methodologically diverse audience in his article on 21 tips for winning acceptance letters. His suggestion #14 reads as follows:

> Write for a somewhat broader and technically less skilled audience than you expect to read the article. Writers tend to overestimate the knowledge

and technical sophistication of their readers, as well as the extent to which readers share their exact interests. You should therefore write for a slightly broader and less knowledgeable audience than you expect will read the article, keeping in mind that you want to avoid insulting your audience. Somewhere between "Visualize Maculation Decamp," and "See Spot Run," lies both your audience and the Land of Acceptance Letters. (p. 13)

Adherence to the *Test Standards*

The *Standards for Educational and Psychological Testing (Test Standards)* have taken on a more prominent role in the training of psychologists and educational researchers with each edition since 1974, the most recent one being published in 1999 (American Educational Research Association, APA, & National Council on Measurement in Education, 1999). Two reasons these standards have become more influential is that they have become better developed with each iteration, taking increasingly strong stances with regard to the definition of the concepts of reliability and validity, and expanding their scope by covering issues of fairness, and test use and misuse in greater detail. Part of the reason for the influence of the *Test Standards* can also be credited to the deliberate way in which they are developed and the esteem of the measurement scientists charged with their development. Their influence is far reaching, such as changing the language we use to speak about validity, such as the shift from referring to the "validity of tests" to the "validity of test score inferences." According to the *Test Standards*, tests are not in and of themselves either valid or invalid. Validity is now only a property of test score inferences. So now researchers do not refer to valid measures per se but to "valid inferences" based on the test scores yielded.

Training in the latest *Test Standards* therefore may lead manuscript reviewers to pose questions about the reliability and validity evidence associated with measures used in single-case research investigations and, indeed, the fairness of such measures. The *Test Standards* require that reliability and validity evidence be specifically documented for any measure utilized, whether it is a formal test, collection of permanent products or records, observations, or other measures. Thus, the study cited earlier by Ferguson et al. (2012) regarding the amount of observation time needed to create a dependable (i.e., reliable) measure would be most appropriate for supporting a single-case researcher's choice of observation length. I think that citation of methodological studies such as this one would strengthen a manuscript submission in the eyes of reviewers seeking to adhere to the *Test Standards*.

Given that one third of the chapters in the *Test Standards* are devoted to this topic, the problems associated with Office Discipline Reports, or ODRs, serve as an example of the lack of fairness associated with a measure sometimes used in single-case research in schools. The influential work by Bradshaw, Mitchell, O'Brennan, and Leaf (2010) matched children on teacher rated classroom behavior, teacher ethnicity, and other key variables. Based on a detailed and thorough analysis of the use of ODRs in 381 classrooms, the authors concluded that "as such, ODRs may not be truly objective indicators of student behavior problems, but rather an indicator of the teachers' use of removal from the classroom as a disciplinary strategy" (p. 517). Leading to concerns about fairness, this investigation replicated similar studies that found ODRs to produce significant disproportionality between ethnic groups (e.g., Skiba et al., 2008). African American students had 24% to 80% greater odds of receiving an ODR compared with White students.

The increasing adherence to the *Test Standards*, and their incorporation into the training of the current and next generation of editorial reviewers, require all researchers to offer reliability and validity evidence in support of the measures chosen, whether they be formal "tests," classroom or clinic observations, or disciplinary records kept by schools. At a minimum, author inclusion of reliability, validity, and fairness evidence holds the potential to mitigate choice of measure or variable questions on the part of the manuscript reviewer, which, even if eventually effectively answered by the author, will nevertheless delay the editorial decision on a manuscript.

Conclusion

Credible advice for preparing manuscripts for publication is available in many sources (e.g., Levin, 1992; Maxwell & Cole, 1995; Sternberg, 1993; Wepner & Gambrell, 2006). The three publication pointers provided herein differ somewhat from those provided by these earlier authors because of the currency of educational and psychological research methodological issues at the time of this writing. Today, cultural and linguistic sampling issues, the availability and prevalence of advanced methodological and statistical training in doctoral education research programs, and measurement sophistication and concerns about measurement fairness are among the central issues to be addressed in manuscript submissions to scientific journals.

References

American Educational Research Association, American Psychological Association, & National Council on Measurement in Education. (1999). *Standards for educational and psychological testing.* Washington, DC: American Psychological Association.

Bradshaw, C. P., Mitchell, M. M., O'Brennan, L. M., & Leaf, P. J. (2010). Multilevel exploration of factors contributing to the overrepresentation of Black students in office disciplinary referrals. *Journal of Educational Psychology, 102,* 508–520. doi:10.1037/a0018450

Ferguson, T. D., Briesch, A., Volpe, R., & Daniels B. (2012). The influence of observation length on the dependability of data. *School Psychology Quarterly, 27,* 187–197.

Herman, K., Borden, L., Reinke, W., & Webster-Stratton, C. (2011). The impact of the Incredible Years parent, child, and teacher training programs on children's co-occurring internalizing symptoms. *School Psychology Quarterly, 26,* 189–201.

Hovey, J. D. (2000). Acculturative stress, depression, and suicidal ideation in Mexican immigrants. *Cultural Diversity and Ethnic Minority Psychology, 6*(2), 134–151. doi:10.1037/1099-9809.6.2.134

Huang, L., Stroul, B., Friedman, R., Mrazek, P., Friesen, B., Pires, S., & Mayberg, S. (2005). Transforming mental health care for children and their families. *American Psychologist, 60,* 615–627. doi:10.1037/0003-066X.60.6.615

Levin, J. R. (1992). Tips for publishing and professional writing. *Mid-Western Educational Researcher, 5,* 12–14.

Maxwell, S. E., & Cole, D. A. (1995). Tips for writing (and reading) methodological articles. *Psychological Bulletin, 118,* 193–198. doi:10.1037/0033-2909.118.2.193

Peterson-Brown, S., & Burns, M. (2011). Adding a vocabulary component to incremental rehearsal to enhance retention and generalization. *School Psychology Quarterly, 26,* 245–255.

Sanetti, L., & Kratochwill, T. (2009). Treatment integrity assessment in the schools: An evaluation of the treatment integrity planning protocol. *School Psychology Quarterly, 24,* 24–35.

Skiba, R., Horner, R., Chung, C. G., Rausch, M. K., May, S. L., & Tobin, T. (2008, March). *Race is not neutral: A national investigation of African American and Latino disproportionality in school discipline.* Paper presented at the annual meeting of the American Educational Research Association, New York, NY.

Sternberg, R. J. (1993). How to win acceptances by psychology journals: 21 tips for better writing. *APS Observer, 5,* 12–13, 18.

Wepner, S. B., & Gambrell, L. (2006). Epilogue. Beating the odds: Getting published in the field of literacy (pp. 167–170). In S. B. Wepner & L. Gambrell (Eds.), *Writing for literacy publications: Top ten guidelines.* Newark, DE: International Reading Association.

Wilkinson, L. (1999). Statistical methods in psychology journals: Guidelines and explanations. *American Psychologist, 54,* 594–604. doi:10.1037/0003-066X.54.8.594

Wolery, M., Busick, M., Reichow, B., & Barton, E. E. (2010). Comparison of overlap methods for quantitatively synthesizing single-subject data. *Journal of Special Education, 44,* 18–28. doi:10.1177/0022466908328009

Reactions From Journal Editors:
School Psychology Review

Matthew K. Burns

In this chapter, I address three difficult issues arising from the chapters in this book, including the role of randomization, statistical analyses within single-case design (SCD), and computing effect sizes—all essential aspects of SCD methodology that are currently the topic of much debate. I discuss my reflections on these issues; their potential implications for research and training; and implications for the journal of which I am editor, *School Psychology Review* (*SPR*), as well as publishing SCD research more generally.

Three Issues That Affect SCD Methodology

Randomization, statistical analyses, and the reporting of effect sizes are all essential components of large-group designs but are points of debate within SCD research. I briefly comment on these three debates in the following paragraphs.

Randomization

SCD has its roots in clinical practice and has long operated from the idea of responding to the data (Kennedy, 2005). Although responding to the data has great clinical appeal, randomizing certain elements of the design could likely lead to more internally valid decisions. Kratochwill and Levin (2010) discussed the role of randomization within SCD, and I encourage readers to review that article for more information. Practitioners have a lower threshold for internal validity than do applied researchers and including randomization in SCDs would likely strengthen researchers' causal claims and could increase the likelihood of the study being published in a research journal.

http://dx.doi.org/10.1037/14376-015
Single-Case Intervention Research: Methodological and Statistical Advances, by T. R. Kratochwill and J. R. Levin

Statistical Analysis of SCD Data

Several chapters in this book have discussed using statistical analyses of SCD data to control Type I error rates. Although controlling error rates is clearly beneficial, statistically analyzing time-series data using conventional parametric methods is potentially problematic because of the lack of independence of the data. Manuscript authors would have to provide a convincing rationale to include conventional analyses and should probably include an estimate of autocorrelation. However, nonparametric approaches to analyzing SCD data do not seem to increase Type I error rates (Levin, Ferron, & Kratochwill, 2012) and are an intriguing option. In the approach outlined in Ferron and Jones (2006), a visual analyst who is "blind" to the study examines multiple-baseline data and specifies the correct order in which the participants received the intervention. In a four-case study, for example, if the visual analyst chooses the correct sequence, then the Type I error probability is less than .05 ($\frac{1}{4} \times \frac{1}{3} \times \frac{1}{2} \times \frac{1}{1} = \frac{1}{24} = .0417$). Moreover, analyzing the data with a "blind" visual analyst allows for the interventionist to employ response-guided techniques while at the same time providing statistical analyses of the data. Although the role of analyses in SCD research is still up for debate, I argue that nonparametric options such as the one outlined by Ferron and Jones could increase confidence in conclusions from SCD data and would likely be welcomed additions to manuscripts that report SCD studies (see also Chapter 5, this volume).

Effect Sizes

One final topic that is of particular note regards reporting effect sizes for SCD data. Researchers are more frequently reporting effect sizes for group data and meta-analyzing data, but meta-analyses of SCD studies are much less common than those of group designs, at least partly due to the lack of an accepted effect size. Parker and colleagues have recently provided multiple interesting options for effect sizes, such as percentage of all non-overlapping data (PAND; Parker, Hagan-Burke, & Vannest, 2007) and non-overlap of all pairs (NAP; Parker & Vannest, 2009; see also Chapter 4, this volume). Continuing research in this area is needed. A recent issue of the *Journal of Behavioral Education* (Burns, 2012) was dedicated to meta-analyzing SCD studies. Reporting effect sizes for SCD data may be of limited value because capturing the effect with one number cannot provide the type of rich information obtained from visual analysis, but SCD researchers should continue to consider meta-analytic approaches in order to more fully join the evidence-based practice movement (Shadish, Rindskopf, & Hedges, 2008; see also Chapter 8, this volume).

Science With Practical Applications

Richard Feynman was a Nobel-Prize winning physicist who has had a notable impact on the current state of science and scientific inquiry. One of his most famous ideas was the concept of "cargo-cult science" (Feynman, 1985, p. 340).

Feynman explained that during World War II remote islands in the South Seas were used as airbases for the United States' war effort. The inhabitants of the islands were greeted by their visitors with gifts from their cargo. After the war ended and the visitors left the islands, the inhabitants attempted to get them to return by building replicas of the equipment used by the visitors and to emulate their actions. In other words, they built mock airplanes and airports out of wood in hopes that the real airplanes would return and bring their cargo with them.

Feynman cautioned that cargo-cult scientists engage in methods that resemble the scientific method but do not sufficiently utilize scientific practices to result in valid conclusions, much like the island natives who built wooden airplanes and airports. He explicitly listed educational and psychological research as particularly susceptible to cargo-cult science methods, and he recommended that heightened skepticism and unabashed honesty in reporting results were both necessary to prevent the less than scientific approach.

SCD research can be a tool that works against cargo-cult science. What would make the observations of a physicist "scientific," considering that there is no random assignment in physics? Arguably, three things enhance the scientific merit of observations: (a) skeptical interpretations of data, (b) control of potentially confounding variables, and (c) replication. Controlling variables within the research design is a fundamental aspect of experimental control, and systematic or direct replication of the effect are essential components of SCD research (Kratochwill et al., 2013; Levin & Kratochwill, 2013; Sidman, 1960). In fact, positive exemplars of good science provided by Feynman (1985) were highly consistent with rigorously constructed SCDs.

In addition to providing data with strong internal validity, SCD is a highly feasible method of conducting applied research because there frequently is no control group–condition or possibility of collecting data from large groups of participants. Moreover, it is often difficult to convince school principals to allow for a control group of students who are intentionally denied an intervention. SCD is also highly flexible and can provide a range of options that can make it likely to find an appropriate design for each given question (Riley-Tillman & Burns, 2009).

Because SCD research can be used in highly applied to settings to reach internally valid decisions, school-based practitioners should be well trained in these methods. SCD research has frequently been described as critical to the evidence-based practice movement in pre-K–12 schools (Burns, 2012; Horner & Kratochwill, 2012; Odom et al., 2005). It is not always necessary to implement an experimental design that meets current SCD standards (Kratochwill et al., 2013), because the decision being made may not warrant such an effort or the behavior may not allow for reversing or withdrawing the intervention (e.g., self-injurious behavior; see Riley-Tillman & Burns, 2009). Thus, well-constructed AB designs (including those that are replicated across participants) may still play an important role in practice-based evidence (Kratochwill et al., 2012). SCD methodology is an important skill for scientifically-based practice and should be part of the training program of any preservice school psychologist, special education teacher, or school-based professional who engages in data-based decision making.

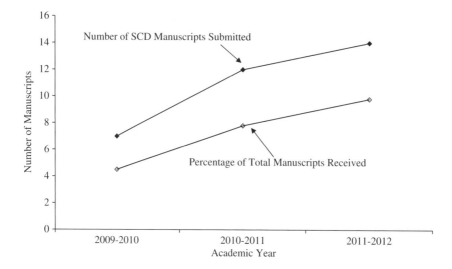

Figure 14.1. Number of single-case design (SCD) manuscripts submitted to *School Psychology Review* and the percentage of all manuscript submissions that were SCD, by academic year.

Implications for *School Psychology Review*

SCD can facilitate data-based decisions in schools, and school psychologists are experts in data-based decision making (Ysseldyke et al., 2006). Thus, SCD should be a central component of preservice training for school psychologists, but the role of SCD within school psychological research is less clear. *SPR* welcomes SCD studies as submissions. However, the journal receives relatively few SCD manuscripts. As shown in Figure 14.1, the number of SCD papers that were submitted to *SPR* in 2009–2010 was in the single digits and represented less than 5% of all submissions. That number has continued to increase, but SCD studies still represent just less than 10% of all manuscript submissions to *SPR*.

As editor of *SPR*, I have taken substantial steps to attempt to demonstrate that *SPR* will publish SCD studies. First, I appointed an associate editor with considerable expertise in SCD methodology. Second, SCD was explicitly added to author guidelines as a methodology that is suitable for *SPR*. Finally, I appointed several board members with varying content expertise, but with strong SCD research skills.

Although *SPR* welcomes SCD submissions, many SCD studies are unfortunately not relevant to *SPR*'s focus and mission. Ellis (2005) suggested that in order for educational innovations to truly influence practice, there should be convincing research regarding its theoretical basis, its effectiveness in highly controlled settings, and the consistency of results when applied in natural settings. School psychological research continues to provide outstanding research regarding intervention effectiveness and consistency of implementation (e.g., Bolt, Ysseldyke, & Patterson, 2010; Sanetti & Kratochwill, 2009), both of which are necessary lines of inquiry. However, school psychology research has yet to adequately address theoretical implications and doing so will move our science to a more mature presence (Burns, 2011). SCD research is often focused on intervention effectiveness (Odom et al., 2005) and only rarely suggests theoretical implications. In order to be published in a national research journal like *SPR*, a manuscript should include potential implications for advancing theory. With the exception of papers published in the journal's *Research Into Practice* section, reports of intervention effectiveness without implications for theory are not appropriate for *SPR*.

Importance of Theory

In addition to providing information that is useful for understanding innovations, theory helps us better contextualize research data. Consider the free health screenings that many communities use to promote early identification of potential health difficulties. Although everyone could intuitively note the importance of early identification in treating health problems, the president of the Minnesota Academy of Family Practice argued against these health screenings because they did not examine the entire body, did not consider risk factors and family history, and were essentially a "blind search for disease" (Yee, 2009). Medical diagnosticians cannot understand risk data without fully considering the context in which they were collected, which is analogous to the role of theory within research in that the data cannot be adequately interpreted unless they are contextualized within theory (Burns, 2011).

Tharinger (2000) recommended that practitioners should avoid interventions without a solid theoretical foundation because theoretical and conceptual frameworks provide the structure to guide practices and solve problems. Practitioners could certainly note the value of an intervention with a strong empirical base, but the lack of a conceptual framework for their practice or for the intervention research would make it difficult to understand the potential utility of the intervention and to judge the potential effectiveness of a new intervention for which the research base is still being developed. Moreover, theory is the best way to advance intervention research (Hughes, 2000) because research without a guiding theory results in disjointed incrementalism with a focus on problems to be solved rather than positive goals to be sought; fragmented and disparate findings; and "a sequence of trials, errors, and revised trials" (Lindblom, 1979, p. 517). Finally, identifying the theoretical underpinnings of an intervention allows us to better adapt it to specific settings without sacrificing efficacy, and to consider potential broader implications.

SCD and Theory

SCD is ideally suited to study the effectiveness of various interventions, but if SCD researchers also identify the necessary, desirable, and sufficient conditions for interventions to be successful, then practitioners can recognize which aspect of the intervention is unalterable and that which can be changed to accommodate different environments (Sheridan & Gutkin, 2000). Researching the most important aspect of an intervention could identify the underlying causal mechanisms, which would have direct implications for theory.

A causal mechanism is the often unobservable processes that actually bring about the desired outcome (Mahoney, 2002). SCDs can isolate the effect that individual variables have on the dependent variable and can systematically compare them (Kratochwill et al., 2013). Thus, SCD researchers could use established theory to hypothesize about variables that most directly lead to the desired effect and compare them. For example, incremental rehearsal (IR; Tucker, 1988) is an academic intervention for which there is a considerable research base (Burns, Zaslofsky, Kanive, & Parker, 2012) but for which the causal mechanism is not clear. We engaged in a line of inquiry that used various theories to derive potential causal mechanisms and used SCD to test them. From a behavioral perspective we hypothesized that the increased long-term retention associated with IR could be directly linked to providing a high ratio of known items within the learning task but also could be due to providing high opportunities to respond (OTR; Greenwood, Delquadri, & Hall, 1984). The hypothesized causal mechanisms were then studied by keeping the ratio of known items the same, but varying the level of OTR across two conditions (high and moderate OTR) using an alternating treatment design, which resulted in a strong effect for high OTR over moderate OTR (Burns, 2007). Subsequent research could keep OTR the same and vary the ratio of known items across phases, or could use four phases that examine the interaction of the two variables.

In addition to directly comparing independent variables that could be most directly linked to the intervention effectiveness, SCD could examine potential mediating variables. Mediating variables are those that underlie the relationship between an independent and dependent variable (Baron & Kenny, 1986). SCD designs could carefully control the presence of potential mediating variables, which could in turn better explain the effects, derive new hypotheses about the effects, and integrate existing knowledge (Mahoney, 2002). Although identifying mediators is most often conceptualized as a series of statistical analyses, as outlined by Baron and Kenny (1986), Wu and Zumbo (2008) proposed a "manipulationist view in which a cause is manipulated to show if the occurrence of the effect pattern is consistent with an experimenter's hypothesis" (p. 371). Thus, mediating variables can be identified by manipulating the hypothesized causal mechanism as an independent variable to determine its effect on the dependent variable. Certainly, although the utility of SCD in determining mediating variables and causal mechanisms is a matter of debate, it is a conversation worth having so that SCD methodologies can continue to influence the evidence-based practice movement, can advance intervention research, and can continue to publish in top research journals.

Conclusion

SCD research is important to applied research and data-based decision making in applied settings, but there are still significant issues to address. Many of the important issues discussed in this chapter are already being studied by methodological researchers. The role of SCD research in developing and advancing theory is an additional topic that SCD researchers should consider in order to advance our understanding of various phenomena and to continue to publish SCD research in top research journals.

References

Baron, R. M., & Kenny, D. A. (1986). The moderator–mediator variable distinction in social psychological research: Conceptual, strategic, and statistical considerations. *Journal of Personality and Social Psychology, 51*, 1173–1182. doi:10.1037/0022-3514.51.6.1173

Bolt, D. M., Ysseldyke, J., & Patterson, M. J. (2010). Students, teachers, and schools as sources of variability, integrity, and sustainability in implementing progress monitoring. *School Psychology Review, 39*, 612–630.

Burns, M. K. (2007). Comparison of drill ratio and opportunities to respond when rehearsing sight words with a child with mental retardation. *School Psychology Quarterly, 22*, 250–263. doi:10.1037/1045-3830.22.2.250

Burns, M. K. (2011). School psychology research: Combining ecological theory and prevention science. *School Psychology Review, 40*, 132–139.

Burns, M. K. (2012). Meta-analysis of single-case design research: Introduction to the special series. *Journal of Behavioral Education, 21*, 175–184. doi:10.1007/s10864-012-9158-9

Burns, M. K., Zaslofsky, A. F., Kanive, R., & Parker, D. C. (2012). Meta-analysis of incremental rehearsal: Using phi coefficients to compare single-case and group designs. *Journal of Behavioral Education, 21*, 185–202. doi:10.1007/s10864-012-9160-2

Ellis, A. K. (2005). *Research on educational innovations* (4th ed.). Larchmont, NY: Eye on Education.

Ferron, J., & Jones, P. K. (2006). Tests for the visual analysis of response-guided multiple-baseline data. *Journal of Experimental Education, 75*, 66–81. doi:10.3200/JEXE.75.1.66-81

Feynman, R. P. (1985). *Surely you're joking, Mr. Feynman! Adventures of a curious character.* New York, NY: Norton. doi:10.1119/1.14087

Greenwood, C. R., Delquadri, J. C., & Hall, R. V. (1984). Opportunity to respond and student academic achievement. In W. L. Heward, T. E. Heron, D. S. Hill, & J. Trap-Porter (Eds.), *Focus on behavior analysis in education* (pp. 58–88). Columbus, OH: Meril.

Horner, R. H., & Kratochwill, T. R. (2012). Synthesizing single-case research to identify evidence-based practices: Some brief reflections. *Journal of Behavioral Education, 21*, 266–272. doi:10.1007/s10864-012-9152-2

Hughes, J. N. (2000). The essential role of theory in the science of treating children: Beyond empirically supported treatments. *Journal of School Psychology, 38*, 301–330. doi:10.1016/S0022-4405(00)00042-X

Kennedy, C. (2005). *Single-case designs for educational research.* Boston, MA: Allyn & Bacon.

Kratochwill, T. R., Hitchcock, J. H., Horner, R. H., Levin, J. R., Odom, S. L., Rindskopf, D. M., & Shadish, W. R. (2013). Single-case intervention research design standards. *Remedial and Special Education, 34*, 26–38.

Kratochwill, T. R., Hoagwood, K. E., Kazak, A. E., Weisz, J. R., Hood, K., Vargas, L. A., & Banez, G. A. (2012). Practice-based evidence for children and adolescents: Advancing the research agenda in schools. *School Psychology Review, 41*, 215–220.

Kratochwill, T. R., & Levin, J. R. (2010). Enhancing the scientific credibility of single-case intervention research: Randomization to the rescue. *Psychological Methods, 15*, 124–144. doi:10.1037/a0017736

Levin, J. R., Ferron, J. M., & Kratochwill, T. R. (2012). Nonparametric statistical tests for single-case systematic and randomized ABAB, AB, and alternating treatment intervention designs: New developments, new directions. *Journal of School Psychology, 50*, 599–624.

Levin, J. R., & Kratochwill, T. R. (2013). Educational/psychological intervention research circa 2012. In I. B. Weiner (Series Ed.) & W. M. Reynolds & G. E. Miller (Volume Eds.), *Handbook of psychology: Vol. 7. Educational psychology* (2nd ed., pp. 465–492). New York, NY: Wiley.

Lindblom, C. E. (1979). Still muddling, not yet through. *Public Administration Review, 39*, 517–526.

Mahoney, J. (2002, August) *Causal mechanisms, correlations, and a power theory of society.* Paper presented at the annual meeting of the American Political Science Association, Boston, MA. Retrieved from http://www.allacademic.com/meta/p66368_index.html

Odom, S. L., Brantlinger, E., Gersten, R., Horner, R., Thompson, B., & Harris, K. (2005). Research in special education: Scientific methods and evidence-based practices. *Exceptional Children, 71,* 137–148.

Parker, R. I., Hagan-Burke, S., & Vannest, K. (2007). Percentage of all non-overlapping data (PAND): An alternative to PND. *The Journal of Special Education, 40,* 194–204. doi:10.1177/00224669070400040101

Parker, R. I., & Vannest, K. (2009). An improved effect size for single-case research: Nonoverlap of all pairs. *Behavior Therapy, 40,* 357–367. doi:10.1016/j.beth.2008.10.006

Riley-Tillman, T. C., & Burns, M. K. (2009). *Evaluating educational interventions: Single-case design for measuring response to intervention.* New York, NY: Guilford Press.

Sanetti, L. M. H., & Kratochwill, T. R. (2009). Toward developing a science of treatment integrity: Introduction to the special series. *School Psychology Review, 38,* 445–459.

Shadish, W. R., Rindskopf, D. M., & Hedges, L. V. (2008). The state of the science in the meta-analysis of single-case experimental designs. *Evidence-Based Communication Assessment and Intervention, 2,* 188–196. doi:10.1080/17489530802581603

Sheridan, S. M., & Gutkin, T. B. (2000). The ecology of school psychology: Examining and changing our paradigm for the 21st century. *School Psychology Review, 29,* 485–501.

Sidman, M. (1960). *Tactics of scientific research: Evaluating experimental data in psychology.* New York, NY: Basic Books.

Tharinger, D. (2000). The complexity of development and change: The need for the integration of the theory and research findings in psychological practice with children. *Journal of School Psychology, 38,* 383–388. doi:10.1016/S0022-4405(00)00035-2

Tucker, J. A. (1988). *Basic flashcard technique when vocabulary is the goal.* Unpublished teaching materials, University of Tennessee at Chattanooga.

Wu, A. D., & Zumbo, B. D. (2008). Understanding and using mediators and moderators. *Social Indicators Research, 87,* 367–392. doi:10.1007/s11205-007-9143-1

Yee, C. M. (2009, February 8). Medical tests at churches aren't what docs ordered: Screenings by for-profit companies are popular, but experts say the exams waste money and can create anxiety. *Minneapolis Star Tribune.* Retrieved from http://www.startribune.com/lifestyle/39266627.html?page=1&c=y

Ysseldyke, J., Burns, M., Dawson, P., Kelley, B., Morrison, D., Ortiz, S., . . . Telzrow, C. (2006). *School psychology: A blueprint for training and practice III.* Bethesda, MD: National Association of School Psychologists.

Index

About the Editors

Thomas R. Kratochwill, PhD, is Sears Roebuck Foundation–Bascom Professor at the University of Wisconsin–Madison, director of the School Psychology Program, and a licensed psychologist in Wisconsin. He is the author of more than 200 journal articles and book chapters. He has written or edited more than 30 books and has made more than 300 professional presentations. In 1977 he received the Lightner Witmer Award from Division 16 (School Psychology) of the American Psychological Association (APA).

In 1981 he received the Outstanding Research Contributions Award from the Arizona State Psychological Association and in 1995 received an award for Outstanding Contributions to the Advancement of Scientific Knowledge in Psychology from the Wisconsin Psychological Association. Also in 1995, he was the recipient of the Senior Scientist Award from APA Division 16, the Wisconsin Psychological Association selected his research for its Margaret Bernauer Psychology Research Award. In 1995, 2001, and 2002 the APA Division 16 journal *School Psychology Quarterly* selected one of his articles as the best of the year. In 2005 he received the Jack I. Bardon Distinguished Achievement Award from APA Division 16. He was selected as the founding editor of *School Psychology Quarterly* in 1984 and served as editor of the journal until 1992. In 2011 Dr. Kratochwill received the Lifetime Achievement Award from the National Register of Health Service Providers in Psychology and the Nadine Murphy Lambert Lifetime Achievement Award from APA Division 16.

Dr. Kratochwill is a fellow of APA Divisions 15 (Educational Psychology), 16, and 53 (Clinical Child Psychology). He is past president of the Society for the Study of School Psychology and was cochair of the Task Force on Evidence-Based Interventions in School Psychology. He was also a member of the APA Task Force on Evidence-Based Practice for Children and Adolescents and the recipient of the 2007 APA Distinguished Career Contributions to Education and Training of Psychologists. He is the recipient of the University of Wisconsin–Madison Van Hise Outreach Teaching Award and a member of the University's teaching academy. Most recently he has chaired the What Works Clearinghouse Panel for the development of *Standards for Single-Case Research Design* for review of evidence-based interventions.

Joel R. Levin, PhD, is Professor Emeritus of Educational Psychology, University of Wisconsin–Madison and University of Arizona. He is internationally renowned for his research and writing on educational research methodology and statistical analysis as well as for his career-long program of research on students' learning strategies and study skills, with more than 400 scholarly publications in those domains. Within the American Psychological Association (APA), he is a Fellow of Division 5 (Evaluation, Measurement, and Statistics) and Division 15 (Educational Psychology).

From 1986 to 1988 Dr. Levin was head of the Learning and Instruction division of the American Educational Research Association (AERA), from 1991 to 1996 he was editor of APA's *Journal of Educational Psychology,* and from 2001 to 2003 he was coeditor of the journal *Issues in Education: Contributions From Educational Psychology.* During 1994–1995 he served as chair of APA's Council of Editors, and from 1993 to 1995 he was an ex-officio representative on APA's Publications and Communications Board. Dr. Levin chaired an editors' committee that revised the statistical-reporting guidelines sections for the fourth (1994) edition of the *American Psychological Association Publication Manual,* and he served on a similar committee that revised the fifth (2001) and sixth (2010) editions of the manual. From 2003 to 2008 he was APA's chief editorial advisor, a position in which he was responsible for mediating editor–author conflicts, managing ethical violations, and making recommendations bearing on all aspects of the scholarly research and publication process.

Dr. Levin has received two article-of-the-year awards from AERA (1972, with Leonard Marascuilo; 1973, with William Rohwer and Anne Cleary) as well as awards from the University of Wisconsin–Madison for both his teaching and his research (1971 and 1980). In 1992 he was presented with a University of Wisconsin–Madison award for his combined research, teaching, and professional service contributions, followed in 1996 by a prestigious University of Wisconsin–Madison named professorship (Julian C. Stanley Chair). In 1997 the University of Wisconsin–Madison's School of Education honored Dr. Levin with a distinguished career award, and in 2002 he was accorded APA Division 15's highest research recognition, the E. L. Thorndike Award, for his professional achievements. In 2010 AERA's Educational Statisticians Special Interest Group presented him with an award for exceptional contributions to the field of educational statistics, and most recently, in 2013 the editorial board of the *Journal of School Psychology* selected his 2012 publication (with John Ferron and Thomas Kratochwill) as the *Journal's* outstanding article of the year.